Eye of the Storm

Eye of the Storm

Twenty-Five Years in Action with the SAS

PETER RATCLIFFE, DCM

with Noel Botham and Brian Hitchen

LEWIS
INTERNATIONAL, INC.

First published in the United States in 2000 by
Lewis International, Inc.
2201 NW 102nd Place #1
Miami FL33172
USA

Tel.: 305-436-7984/800-259-5962
Fax: 305-436-7985/800-664-5095

This edition published by arrangement with
Michael O'Mara Books Limited, London, UK

ISBN 1-930983-01-8

1 3 5 7 9 10 8 6 4 2

Designed and typeset by Martin Bristow
Printed and bound in England by Clays Ltd, St Ives plc

Contents

Chapter

To Susanna,
and
to Kirsty and Katie

Illustrations

The author and fellow candidates after passing SAS Selection
On Operation Storm: the mortar pit on Diana One, Dhofar, 1973
The author and Taff cleaning their SLRs on Diana One
Sangar on Diana One, Dhofar, 1973
Deploying to a new location by helicopter, Dhofar, 1975
Second tour, 1974: the author at Tawi Atair
A mortar pit at the Simba position, Dhofar, 1975
Green Five, the sangar at Simba shared by the author
The author with part of a Katyusha rocket that killed an SAS trooper at
    Simba
Captured adoo coastal location near the Yemeni border, 1975
SAS members logging captured adoo ammunition and equipment, 1975
Mountain Troop members and a crashed Wessex on the Fortuna
    Glacier, South Georgia (*Trustees of the Imperial War Museum: neg. no.*
    FKD 53)
HMS *Antrim*'s Wessex with the stranded SAS men from the Fortuna
    Glacier aboard (*Lieutenant K. White, RN*)
The captured Argentinian submarine *Santa Fe* moored at Grytviken,
    South Georgia (*Lieutenant K. White, RN*)
First-day cover franked by SAS members during their raid on the
    Grytviken post office
Another view of the *Santa Fe*, showing damage caused by Royal Navy
    helicopters (*Lieutenant K. White, RN*)
The author's Mention in Despatches, awarded for leading a patrol on
    West Falkland
A wrecked Argentinian Pucara at Pebble Island after the SAS's raid,
    May 1982 (*Trustees of the Imperial War Museum: neg. no. FKD 654*)
D Squadron members checking Land Rover 110s prior to deployment,
    January 1991
SAS trooper and off-road motorcyle beneath the tailplane of a C-130
RAF Special Forces Chinook flying low over the desert during the Gulf
    campaign (*David McMullon*)

Acknowledgements

I am grateful to a number of people for their help and encouragement in the preparation of this book, among them:

My good friends Mike McMahon, Hugh Leman and Duncan Bullivant, for their loyalty, friendship and support over the years.

Brian Hitchen and Noel Botham, for all their research and endeavour in the writing of this book.

Michael O'Mara, my publisher, for giving me the opportunity to tell my story, and also my editor, Toby Buchan, for his professionalism and attention to detail during the editing of the book.

A special word of thanks to Laurie Milner of the Imperial War Museum, for writing and narrating the voice-over for the CD of the firefight during the Dhofar campaign.

David Rowlands for permission to reproduce his painting of the Sergeants' Mess meeting in the Wadi Tubal, Western Iraq, which I commissioned from him after the Gulf campaign, and which later hung in the Sergeants' Mess at Stirling Lines, Hereford. David was the only professional artist who was in the theatre of war in the Gulf at the invitation of the British Army, and was attached to the crew of a Warrior infantry fighting vehicle of 4 Armoured Brigade.

In particular, to my good friend JAK – the cartoonist Raymond Jackson – who sadly died in 1997 and so didn't have the chance to read the book. I am grateful, too, to his wife, Claudie, for permission to reproduce JAK's version of the Sergeants' Mess meeting in Iraq, and to their son Patrick for his photograph of me on the jacket. My thanks, too, to Doug London for supplying the negative of JAK's cartoon.

To my godson, George, and his brother Charles, for all the enjoyment we have playing football together.

Lastly, to all those other ex-members of the Regiment who are my friends, but whom I cannot name.

We are the Pilgrims, master; we shall go
Always a little further: it may be
Beyond that last blue mountain barred with snow,
Beyond that angry or that glimmering sea.

from *The Golden Journey to Samarkand* by James Elroy Flecker

(These lines are engraved on the memorial clock tower at the
headquarters of 22 Special Air Service Regiment in Hereford.
Also engraved on the tower are the names of all members
of the Regiment killed in training or in action.)

Prologue

THE half-moon that had lit our way to the target dipped over the horizon. A little later came the dawn – thin streaks of light that gradually unrolled the darkness across the valley to reveal a scene of raw beauty and unexpected tranquillity. We continued to keep watch on the target – a *bait* (native hut) on a rocky hillside – from our concealed ambush positions, every man keyed up for a sight or sound that would let us know the adoo were approaching, unaware of our presence.

The patrol commander gestured for Jimmy and me to move forward to a dry-stone wall, which formed one side of an open pen where the goats were kept, though it was now empty. I was carrying a 7.62mm GPMG, a belt-fed weapon, some 4 feet long and weighing just over 24 pounds, and with a nominal rate of fire of 1,000 rounds a minute. It's a ferocious weapon with a killing range of up to a mile in the right circumstances.

I flicked down the bipod beneath the barrel and rested its feet on top of the wall, keeping my head down as I sighted along the weapon, even though any adoo in the hut couldn't have seen me in my new position. Then I heard a low murmur to my right, 'They're in the back of the bait. Stand by.' Now I could really feel the adrenalin pumping.

Just then a man in a green shirt came out of a side entrance in the bait. He was very dark-skinned and was carrying a rifle.

'Is that an adoo?' I whispered to Jimmy, not wanting it to turn out that the first person I ever shot was a civilian. But before he could answer the man had gone back inside and another, even darker-skinned Arab came out, wearing only a sarong.

'No, he's a jebali,' muttered Jimmy.

'No. Not him, the other one,' I hissed.

'What other one?' Our whispered conversation was starting to sound like a comedy turn.

Almost immediately another man appeared from the back of the hut. He was lighter-skinned than the other two, and was carrying what looked like an AK-47 light automatic rifle – the famous Soviet-designed weapon which is capable of firing off a twenty-round magazine in less than two seconds. He walked right round to our side of the hut before he spotted us. By now he was perhaps thirty feet away and I could see him clearly.

I watched his eyes narrow as he recognized his predicament. He started to go into a crouch as he swung the rifle in his right hand forwards and upwards, at the same time grabbing the barrel in the palm of his left hand as he tried to bring the weapon up to a firing position. It was then that I squeezed the GPMG's trigger.

The adoo never had a chance. My first two-second burst – more than thirty rounds – took him right in the body. I could see fragments of flesh being torn out of his back by the exiting bullets, and he was slammed backwards against the bait wall by the sheer weight of the fire hitting him. I fired again, and one of my rounds must have struck the magazine on his rifle, for it suddenly blew up. The upper part of his body was simply torn to shreds.

Just as this gruesome sight was registering with me, I heard Jimmy shout, 'There are two more getting away at the back.' I couldn't see them from my position, so I yanked the machine-gun off the top of the wall and, holding it up to my shoulder like a rifle, crabbed along sideways until I could see the adoo backing down the hill, all the time firing short bursts towards them. Above my head and somewhere off to my left I heard the zing-like crack of high-velocity rounds going past as the men behind me opened up.

I opened fire again, sending the rest of the rounds in the ammunition belt streaming towards the two men in one long burst. There were others firing alongside me so I'm not sure who killed the second man, but he suddenly spun round and dropped his weapon. Great gouts of blood spurted from multiple wounds in his chest as he went down.

Less than five minutes after it had started the shooting was all over. Silence once more returned to the hillside. Cautiously we moved forward, and three members of Mountain Troop went in and cleared the hut, which Jimmy and I skirted as we headed down the hill. One of the two men who had fled from the back of the hut was dead, although it was impossible to know if I had had a hand in his killing. He had been hit by at least half a dozen rounds. His companion appeared to have got away, though he may have been wounded. The fourth man had been shot dead on the far side of the building by other members of the patrol. I hadn't even seen him until we came across his body.

I was feeling strangely high – the kind of high you get after a few drinks, but before actually becoming drunk – although I knew that this reaction was caused by the adrenalin still chasing about inside my system. I had come through my first contact with an enemy. My first firefight. And I had killed a man for the first time.

It was a strange feeling. Later, as we made our way back to White City, I thought, 'This is really good. I've just seen my first action, and I've done all right.' I had no regrets at all. A little sadness for the man I'd killed, perhaps, that he might have had a wife and a family as some of our guys had wives and families. Yet in the end he had courted his own fate by becoming a terrorist.

Jimmy was pleased with the way I'd performed, but cautioned restraint. Patting me on the back, he told me, 'It's easy to dish it out, but it's a different story when you've got to take it. So don't go thinking you're a vet. You're still just a young pup.' In truth, I didn't feel very different, and certainly not like a hero. But what I did know was that I felt genuinely proud to have done my job, and to have taken down an enemy who, given a few more seconds, might well have finished me off instead.

I had been with D Squadron of the SAS for about three months when, in January 1973, my squadron was first posted to the Sultanate of Oman. Strategically placed at the southern end of the Arabian Gulf, this tiny independent state controlled the right of free passage over the richest oil tanker sea lanes in the world. In the wrong hands, Oman could pose a huge threat to the West – and that was where we came in. The SAS were discreetly there on loan to the Sultan, to stop communist-backed terrorists, known locally as *adoo* (Arabic: enemy), from seizing power and turning the country into a Marxist state – with catastrophic results for the flow of Gulf oil to the West.

Whatever their ideology, the adoo were brutal, cold-blooded and uncompromising killers, and on most days I and my fellow SAS soldiers found ourselves on the receiving end of rifle and machine-gun fire, under grenade and mortar attack, or targets for Soviet-built high-explosive rockets.

And I was loving every moment of it. At the age of twenty-two I had reached a position which I would not willingly have exchanged with any other living soul. I was a highly trained professional in the uniform of the world's toughest and most admired regiment, doing what we did best. I felt complete. A contented man.

A far cry indeed from the snotty-nosed kid who had grown up in abject poverty in the northern slums of Lancashire with a more than even chance of ending up in jail.

*   *   *

In June 1991, eighteen years after I had been blooded in Oman and four months after my return from the Gulf War, I found myself aboard an RAF VC10, flying to the United States with the adjutant for a meeting with the US Rangers. After a couple of hours my companion looked at his watch, checked that it was past midnight in the UK, and hoisted his briefcase on to his knees. Having fished around inside it for a while he suddenly gave a satisfied cluck and took out an envelope, which he handed to me with the words, 'I have been asked to give you this.' It was addressed to me, but when I opened the envelope and read the letter it contained I could hardly believe what it said – in fact, I had to read it twice before its content sank in. Signed by the CO of 22 Special Air Service Regiment, it told me that I had been awarded the Distinguished Conduct Medal for my services during the Gulf War.

To me, there was something slightly unreal about the situation as the two of us clinked glasses of gin and tonic at 30,000 feet over the North Atlantic. The adjutant simply said, 'Well done. Cheers!' going on to explain that the reason he had not given me the letter earlier was because the Honours List was strictly embargoed until one minute past midnight in Britain.

So it came about that, one beautiful late-summer's day a few weeks later, I went to Buckingham Palace with the other members of the Regiment who were to be decorated for their actions during the Gulf campaign. There was nothing in the newspapers about the investiture, since it was held in secret to protect the identities of soldiers serving in the SAS, but it was reported afterwards with the usual mixture of half fact and whole fantasy. What really happened was this:

On the day of the investiture I travelled to Duke of York's HQ in the King's Road, Chelsea, the headquarters of UK Special Forces, and there changed into my very best uniform. Then, with the rest of the guys from the Regiment who were being honoured that day, I climbed into a coach that was waiting well away from where anyone could get a picture of us. We travelled the short distance to the Palace with the curtains deliberately drawn, so that no one could photograph our arrival or our departure – it would not do for our pictures to get into the files of hostile individuals or organizations.

In the Throne Room, when my turn came I marched up and stood to attention before the Queen. She smiled slightly, and said that the Gulf War must have been very frightening. So I told her how I had felt during those weeks on patrol, at which she looked at me a bit oddly. 'Oh!' she said. And that was it – end of conversation. She presented me with the Distinguished Conduct Medal and simply walked away. End, also, of audience with Queen Elizabeth II of Great Britain.

When she had said the war must have been very frightening, perhaps I shouldn't have replied as I did.

'Actually, Your Majesty, I quite enjoyed it.'

Thirty years ago, no one would have figured me for a soldier. At the time, I was a scarcely educated, often dishonest, streetwise kid from a poverty-stricken slum home – in the end, a broken home – in the depressed industrial north-west of England. Almost without prospects, I joined the army for all the wrong reasons: to get away from a miserable, dead-end existence as a manual labourer, and because I had been thwarted in my efforts to emigrate to Australia. I owe to my regiments – first the Parachute Regiment, then, for twenty-five years, the Special Air Service Regiment – the fact that I am not still a manual labourer in a dead-end job or, even worse, in prison. I owe a great deal more than that, however, most of which I could not put into words, and all of it priceless.

Someone told me once of a remark of Dr Johnson's, that 'Every man thinks meanly of himself for not having been a soldier, or not having been at sea.' I don't know whether that's true or not – I rather doubt it, in fact, especially nowadays, as we move further and further away from a general experience of war – but what I do know is that I gained from the SAS a sense of self-worth and confidence while soldiering with the best in any army, anywhere in the world.

This book, then, is for 22 Special Air Service Regiment and the men who made and continue to make it, with not always uncritical affection, but always with gratitude.

PETER RATCLIFFE, DCM
August 2000

Chapter One

O n the night I was born – in a council flat in Salford, Lancashire, nearly fifty years ago – blizzards raged across the north-west of England for six hours. My mother remembered that the stark outlines of Salford's dockland slums, clustered at the end of the Manchester Ship Canal, lay softened under a blanket of white that morning. It was the only time in donkey's years that the city had looked clean, she said.

L.S. Lowry, the matchstick-man artist who spent a lifetime painting Salford's crumbling, soot-streaked houses and soul-destroying cotton mills, seems to have missed the opportunity of capturing the moment. Not of recording the birth of a matchstick child – baby production being the major industry there at that time, since there was little work – but of showing Salford looking pretty. But then, Lowry went for accuracy, preferring his slums to look miserable, rather than as if they were covered in icing sugar.

When I was a few years older, I found out that virgin snow in Salford was usually defiled before daybreak by yellow trails of spattered cats' piss, long before kids like me could mould it into frozen missiles, and even longer before it melted to grey slush and oily puddles that seemed to reflect the grim lives of the people who lived there.

My mother was a staunch Roman Catholic, something reflected in the number of children she had. My brother, David, had been born two and a half years before me, and three other children – Jean, Stephen and Susan – were to follow. My father was a bread-delivery man who had flirted with Catholicism, although he never converted. His interest in the faith was not religious, however, but arose because he wanted somewhere to park his car, an old Wolseley Four Forty-Four largely held together by thick layers of black paint. The parish priest had offered to let him park it for free in the church grounds if, in return, my father became a Roman Catholic, but in the event the only time he ever went near the church was to collect or park his car. For my dad there was always a means to an end.

He worked hard, to be fair, getting up at 4.30 each weekday morning to go to the bakery to pick up the van and begin his rounds. I never knew him have a day off sick in his life. On Saturday mornings we kids would help him on the bread van and then, in the afternoons, we'd go to Old Trafford to watch Manchester United play. I became an ardent fan, and by the time I was eight years old I was regularly going to the ground by myself. My problem, however, was lack of cash, so to pay my way through the turnstiles I used to steal money from my father's pockets.

He must have suspected that I had been nicking his change, because I'll never forget what happened the day he caught me at it. He said very little, just made me pack my things in a suitcase and then took me down to the local police station. There, behind the wooden counter in the front hall, was the largest police sergeant I had ever seen. What was worse, he was obviously waiting for me. 'Come with me,' he said in a deep, official-sounding voice, and marched me off down a grey-painted corridor and into a room where another stern-faced copper took my fingerprints, handing me a piece of tissue paper with which to wipe the sticky black ink off my fingers. Then, gripping my arm with fingers that felt like pliers, the sergeant put me in a cell, slamming the steel door – also painted grey, like all the metal in the place – shut with a bang that sounded like the end of the world. I was scared to death, tears of sheer fright pouring down my cheeks.

If I'd hoped the police would be moved by my plight, however, I was disappointed. They left me alone in that cell for about half an hour, though it seemed like forever. Then the sergeant unlocked the door and gave me a hell of a bollocking. He told me that if I didn't stop thieving, I would wind up spending most of the remaining years of my life in a cell like the one I'd just left. Looking back, I could see that my father must have arranged the whole charade with the police. Nevertheless, I was so terrified by the experience that it stopped me from stealing – well, for a time, anyway.

During the Second World War, my father had served in the Royal Navy as a signals operator in destroyers. I remember him giving me a Morse key for my birthday one year. He never tried to teach me the code, however – not that I wanted to learn it. He just wanted to practise his own Morse at home.

He had received all sorts of medals for his war service. He was not in the least militarily minded and never took any great care of his decorations, simply leaving them lying around in the bottom of a drawer. Given to foraging anywhere in the house where I thought there might be something – especially cash – that I could use, I soon came upon them.

As these things go, they were nothing very special, just campaign medals of the kind awarded to someone just for having been there, like the Atlantic Star. It was not until much later that I realized what being on the Atlantic convoys must have been like, and how courageous my father, and all the sailors who did that job for up to five years, when life expectancy for any of them was often measured in weeks, had been. By then, however, it was too late to undo the damage.

I had found a pawnbroker who bought medals. Well, not exactly found, for I had actually been looking for one like him for some time, but once I had located him I became, for a time, one of his most regular customers. I used to take the medals, one at a time, down to the pawn shop, where the owner would give me a half-crown (12½ pence) for each of them. I never redeemed them, and no doubt they were sold on to some collector when the time limit for their redemption expired. I spent the money watching Manchester United play, telling myself that the medals were being used in a good cause.

My father never knew where his medals had gone. Probably he thought they had been lost during one of our dozen or so house moves, for my mother, who had something of the gypsy in her character, was always swapping council houses and flats with other people. She'd answer adverts from similar-minded people and we'd just exchange houses. It was always within a radius of about ten miles, but we moved so often that I sometimes forgot where we lived.

By 1958 we were halfway through this housey-housey cycle and living in Wythenshaw, a rough, sprawling council estate on the southern outskirts of Manchester. Outsiders reckoned that council-house tenants in Wythenshaw were so savage that the weak were killed and eaten. It wasn't that bad – but it was pretty bad.

In those days, even in rough areas, many working-class households kept a 'best' room set aside like a shrine in their houses. We were no exception, maintaining what we called 'the parlour' even though desperately short of space. There we were, a family of seven crammed into a three-bedroom terraced house. I had to sleep in a bed with my brother, my two sisters slept in another room, and my younger brother, who was at a school for the deaf and only came home at the weekends, also slept in our bed. An extra room would have made an enormous difference, yet we only went into our parlour, the ground-floor room at the front of the house, at Christmas, Easter or Whitsun. It was pristine – so spotlessly clean that you could have performed brain surgery on the floor. Meanwhile, when we weren't asleep in bed my mother and father and the rest of us all lived in the back room like the Old Woman Who Lived in a Shoe. It was complete bedlam.

The back room also contained the kitchen and a large scullery sink. My mother had a washing machine with a mangle on top, into which she hand-fed the clean wet clothes. The mangle rollers would squeeze out most of the water, which whooshed into the sink. Mum would then take the damp, flattened washing and hang it to dry from a wooden airer fixed to the ceiling, which could be raised and lowered by a rope that ran over pulleys. She spread newspapers on the carpet to catch the drips. On washing days we'd all sit watching television, peering round hanging clothes. Everything was dripping wet, and, coupled with the heat from the coal fire, the effect was like being in the jungle.

We had a tiny back yard, half of which had been laid with crazy paving, while the other half consistied of a tiny patch of balding grass that backed on to the boundary fence and, beyond that, the playing fields of the primary school I attended. On that scrap of garden – you couldn't dignify it with the word 'lawn' – my brothers and I built a den, which we used as the headquarters for a gang we recruited from among other kids in the street. Sometimes we broke into the school tuck shop and nicked packets of crisps, at others we went shoplifting biscuits from the corner store. It was not really badness. We just dared each other, as children will.

We were bored a good deal of the time, too, and some of the traditional boys' pastimes were closed to us. None of us was in the Boy Scouts. The scoutmaster was far too well aware of our collective reputation as tearaways to let us in; besides, we couldn't have afforded the uniform. When the Scouts held a 'Bob-a-Job' week to raise funds, however, we went round the houses pretending that we were members of the local pack. We'd do the jobs all right, but we'd keep the money for ourselves.

We got away with most of our light-fingered or dishonest activities through a combination of luck and guile. I came thoroughly unglued, however, when I was found to have been stealing from the collection box at the local Catholic church, where I was a trainee altar boy. Perhaps bothered by conscience, I took only a very small sum, but I made the mistake of buying sweets with it in one of the local shops.

A particularly nosy neighbour of ours – curiously, I still remember her name, Kath Sykes – who lived about four doors away from us, was in the shop at the time. Next day she told my mother, 'If you'd told me you had wanted something from the shop I would have got it for you.'

When my mother replied that she hadn't needed anything, the eternally inquisitive Kath said that she'd seen me in there buying something at the counter. My mother knew that I had no money, and that therefore I didn't have any reason to be in a shop unless she'd sent me to get something.

Retribution wasn't long in coming. When I got home Mum called me to her and asked me, 'Peter, what were you doing in the shop?' There was a note of sternness I didn't much care for. I looked away and said, 'Nothing.'

Perhaps it was the result of a Catholic upbringing, but whenever I lied I used to go bright red. Now I felt my face and neck flushing. My mother took one look and said, 'You're lying to me. Now, what were you doing in that shop?' So I told her that I'd bought sweets with money I'd found in the street on my way back from the church. Without a moment's pause back came the answer, 'You've stolen the collection money.'

My denials were hopeless, for the more I protested the more obvious it became that I was lying. When she finally got me to own up she dragged me off to the priest. He gave me a terrible telling off, full of sin and damnation, and sacked me as a trainee altar boy. This had been a fairly good number because I could earn about ten shillings (50 pence) for helping him at weddings, of which there seemed to be quite a number. So I lost a good job for stealing threepence.

I can still hear that priest telling me that I was guilty of stealing money from the Church, and that this was a mortal sin. What he meant was that I was stealing money from him. He was well known as a drinker, and between the booze and the bookies he spent a bundle of money that wasn't his, as priests are supposed to be poor. I had often seen him at Manchester United matches, too. Even as young as I was, I didn't see that he had any great right to lecture me about sin.

With all our moves from place to place, I ended up attending several different schools, which I don't suppose did much for my education. I did at least go to school – my parents saw to that – but no one would have called me academically brilliant. I was always very good at mathematics, however, and especially at mental arithmetic, which I found a piece of cake. But I had a terrible stammer, which made speaking in class a torment, even when I was confident I knew the answer. Nor could it be said that the teachers at my primary school in Walkden did anything to help it. Once we were putting on a school play, *The Pied Piper of Hamelin*. I had been given a speaking part, but on the last night of rehearsals the whole show had to be cancelled because I couldn't get my words out. On the following day one of the teachers brought in a tape recorder to record our voices. 'That's how you sound,' he said, playing back the tape after I had stuttered and stammered into the microphone. I slowly grew out of my stammer, mainly as a result of joining the army, I think, but to this day I hate hearing my voice on tape.

When I was nicking my father's medals, we were living in a three-bedroom council house in a terrace in Little Hulton, a giant housing estate that had been built to house people who, like us, had been moved from the Salford dockland slums, which were due to be demolished. We were poor, although we didn't know how poor because everybody around us was in the same state. Some of our neighbours were so close to the breadline that they drank out of jam jars and scavenged coal that the railway trucks had dropped on the line. We were a good deal better off than that, but still a long way below anything that might have been called comfortable. We got watered-down milk every day, for example. My mother would buy pasteurized milk in a bottle with a crown cap on it, similar to those still used on beer bottles. She'd take two empty bottles just like it, and put a third of the milk in each, then top them all up with cold tap water and snap the tops on again. That way we got three pints of milk out of one, enough to last us a day.

With only my father's meagre wages from the bakery to live on, by Thursday of each week we had always run out of money for food, so on those days we ate toast and dripping. My brother and I also came home from school at lunchtime on Thursdays because we hadn't enough money for school dinners. Friday, when my father was paid, was the big day in our house – that's when we had chips.

Yet although the family never had any money to spare, as a kid I was never short myself, largely because I had so many scams going. After school I used to chop wood for an old gypsy who lived near by. We wired it into bundles, and he would then go round on his cart selling the firewood from house to house. He'd always give me a few shillings for helping him, and loose change he left around the place would also find its way into my trouser pockets. If he noticed, he never said anything. Probably he expected me to steal. Besides, he had his own scams running, and he could see that I was only a snotty-nosed kid who was no threat to any bigger bits of villainy he might have been into.

Worse, and despite the warning from the police sergeant, ripping off the firewood seller wasn't the only stealing I did. I take no pride in it now, but as a boy I seem to have spent a good deal of time and energy on being dishonest. My mother had a tick card running at the local corner shop, where they would mark down what she had taken and she would pay later. (In Harrods this is called a 'customer account'. In a corner shop it's called 'tick'.) I would go to the shop and tell the woman behind the counter, 'My Mum wants a siphon of soda.' She would often give me a funny look, since people around there rarely bought soda water because they couldn't afford any whisky to go with it – except at Christmas, perhaps.

Anyway, the shop would put the siphon on my mother's tick account and I would take it and go round the corner and squirt the soda down a drain. Then I'd take the empty siphon – in those days they were substantial glass bottles wrapped in fine wire mesh like chicken coop wire – to another shop and get the deposit of five shillings (25 pence) 'buck' for turning it in. When my mother went to pay her bill at the corner shop, she'd have a row over why they were charging her for a soda siphon she'd never had. She never tumbled to the fact that it was me, however.

She never discovered another of my scams, either. Tesco had just opened a supermarket in Walkden, about two miles away from our home in Little Hulton, and my brother and I used to be sent there to buy the family meat for the week. Mum always gave me enough money to buy a cow's heart. I would get that from the meat counter first and hide it in the bottom of the shopping bag – they didn't have wire baskets in those days – and then buy something really cheap which I would pay for at the checkout with the money I had been given, without mentioning, of course, that I had a cow's heart concealed in my bag. Back at home I'd give my mother the correct change for the heart, as though I'd actually paid for it, and surreptitiously pocket the difference between the price of the meat and the small item I'd actually bought. I always felt that I had only stolen from Tesco, and not from my mother – although in fact I was stealing from both of them.

Several of my schoolfriends had newspaper-delivery rounds, but I didn't think the job was worth it. Getting up at five or six in the morning to deliver papers and then doing it again in the afternoons after school, and all for seven shillings and sixpence (37½ pence) a week, seemed like a mug's game to me. In the mid-1960s, however, during the summer holidays in Little Hulton when for two weeks most of the town's factories and works shut down, I manned a newspaper stand for a firm called Tillotson's, which owned the *Bolton Evening News*, among other titles.

By six o'clock each morning I'd already be at work, selling the national dailies under a covered newspaper stand alongside a bus stop in the centre of town. In the afternoons, I sold the *Bolton Evening News* and the *Manchester Evening News* to people as they made their way home. When the boss came round to check the figures at the end of the day, I would tell him that I had been short on deliveries of one of the nationals. He would note the shortfall, which he would then be able to reclaim from the newspaper distributor who supplied the stand, and I would pocket the money I had made from selling the papers that had supposedly not been delivered. Apart from what I trousered in ill-gotten gains, I was paid about £10 a week for running the stand. In those days, that was about what a lot of grown men were earning – and I was only fourteen years old.

During the rest of the summer months I worked in Tillotson's newspaper shop in the town, running a machine which printed the 'Stop Press' items on to the back of each edition of the *Bolton Evening News*. When I had run off several dozen, I would take them down to the bingo hall, where I would hold a copy up and shout, 'Night racing . . . Last winners.' Since almost everyone had a bet at one time or the other, I'd usually sell the lot. It always seemed to be pissing down with rain, but on an average evening I'd make about fifteen shillings (75 pence), and on a really good Friday night double that amount. In the days when people were paid at the end of each week, you could be sure of them having enough money for a flutter on Fridays.

Even though I was only fourteen, I used to have to buy all my own clothes from money I'd earned. Luckily I still wore short trousers for much of the time, which didn't cost me as much as full-length ones. I was also still being sent to church every Sunday by my mother, which did mean wearing long trousers. I'd go to early Mass, and by the time I got back my father would already have made the breakfast. It was always porridge, which he used to cook the night before and warm up in the morning. It was really horrible stuff, so thick and lumpy that you might have eaten it with a pick and shovel, and I hated it.

One Sunday morning after Mass we were sitting round the kitchen table when my father, noticing my distaste for the glutinous grey mass in front of me, ordered, 'Eat your porridge.' He knew that I didn't like it, so he stood behind my chair and repeated, 'Eat your porridge. If you don't, I'll empty the bowl over your stupid little head.' By then I had done everything I could to improve or disguise that porridge. I'd stirred in cold milk and put sugar on top of it, and poked it around the bowl with my spoon. But I still couldn't bring myself to eat it. Twice more my father ordered me to eat it, and twice I refused.

I had just bought my first long-trouser suit, which I had put on for Mass that morning. It made no difference to my father. I just sat there while he took hold of the bowl and poured the porridge all over my head. The whole lumpy, sticky mess, milk and all, ran down my face and collar all over my new suit and down my legs.

Just then my mother came in, and saw straight away what had happened. Turning to Dad, she snarled at him, 'You swine!' Then she grabbed the HP Sauce bottle off the kitchen table and belted him across the head with it, almost knocking him cold. It opened a gash in his head that looked like an axe wound, and blood went everywhere, adding to the porridgey mess on the floor. I never had to eat my father's porridge again; but then, their marriage didn't last much longer, either.

I was not very big for my age during my schooldays, although I could hold my own in a fight. I had joined the Salford Police junior boxing club, partly to learn to defend myself, and partly because I was beginning to take an interest in girls, and hoped my fighting skills would attract them; I had never paid them much attention until then. Nor did they pay me much attention, and even as a boxer none of them looked at me twice. The whole business was fraught with traps for the unwary or inexperienced teenager, in any case. We used to call the girls we knew by their surnames, because if you used a girl's first name she would think you fancied her. I would have used everyone's Christian names if I could have got away with it, but all my mates would have taken the mickey.

For one reason or another I didn't have much luck with the opposite sex during my early teens, or for some time afterwards, for that matter. Until one night, a couple of years later, when I was working on a building site in Preston, my Irish mates on the shovel took me into a pub. They started joshing a good-looking, large-breasted girl, and asked her which of us she fancied. She pointed to me. So began my first real affair, although it only lasted for three months before she ditched me. She said I was a boring bastard. I probably was. God knows how it lasted even as long as it did, because I hadn't the slightest idea how to treat a girl properly. I knew about sex, in a pretty basic sort of way, but she didn't seem to be as keen on that as I was. But then, being more experienced, no doubt she expected a more virtuoso performance. Whatever the reason, though, I was dumped.

It was not a new experience for me, as it happened, for my parents had conditioned me to it some years earlier. Perhaps they had one fight too many, or perhaps the incident with the HP Sauce bottle still rankled, but they decided to split up – or at least, my mother did. She found herself another man and went off with him to live in Morecambe, a run-down resort town on the Lancashire coast. When she left in a furniture van, I went with her. I was nearly fifteen years old and didn't have much choice, although my father didn't see it that way. To him, my departure was as great a betrayal as my mother's behaviour.

It was not many weeks before they got fed up with Morecambe – which was not at all surprising, given the nature of the place then – and my mother's new man took a job in Preston, a city about thirty miles away.

So he and my mother took off. There may have been room for me in the house in Preston where they were going to live, but I was caught in a bind. I'd just got a job and didn't want to risk giving it up and being out of work. I simply couldn't afford to leave and start the whole business of trying to find work again, which, for an unqualified fifteen-year-old in the 1960s, was almost impossible anyway. It was better for me to stay behind and live in a crummy boarding house in Morecambe.

It was ironic, really. I hadn't wanted to leave home. Instead, home had left me.

Chapter Two

S EAGULL'S NEST was a red-brick house whose dreary frontage was not improved by a front door that somebody had painted in a shade of bilious green. It stood five streets back from Morecambe's sea front, a yellowing cardboard 'Vacancies' sign permanently hanging from a string in its bay window. It seemed the sort of place that would always have vacancies.

The only other 'guest' in the boarding house was a middle-aged man with one leg. Every night he clumped about in his room like Long John Silver, needing only a talkative parrot to complete this picture. He was what we then called a queer, and even at an age not usually remarkable for its tenderness towards others, I sometimes felt a bit sorry for him. Having only one leg was surely tough enough without being gay as well (this was before homosexuality was decriminalized), and the chances of his finding a partner in Morecambe must have been all but non-existent.

I loathed Morecambe. But I stayed on my own there for six months because the wage I received as an apprentice plasterer on a building site – £5 a week – meant that I couldn't afford to move from Seagull's Nest. The boarding-house rent left me with just 10 shillings (50 pence) for the week, although my rent also included meals. Every working day, without fail, the landlady gave me a packed lunch of grated-cheese sandwiches. I loathed cheese sandwiches, as well.

I decided that I wasn't cut out to be a plasterer, so I left Morecambe and moved to Preston, where I got a job as an apprentice joiner. I started work on the British Home Stores on Fishergate. The one good thing about Preston was that I was playing a lot of football whilst I was there. Two guys on the local team I played for worked at the Labour Exchange, and not long afterwards I went to share a house with them in Ribbleton, a suburb of Preston. I was now earning a few bob and life became a bit easier. Not much, it was true, but a bit.

Always football crazy, I set off to hitchhike to London one Friday night in September 1968 to watch Manchester United play against West Ham. I got my first lift around midnight at the Preston junction of the M6 and arrived in London at about midday. Once at the

Hammers' ground at Upton Park I found that the gates had been smashed down by the mob and I got in for free. And to make matters even better, United won 3-1.

Thereafter, however, things began to go wrong. At the match I met a friend who had also hitched down, so we decided to thumb lifts back north together. We waited for ages until, eventually, we got a lift in a van as far as the Northampton turn-off on the M1. By now it was three o'clock in the morning and pouring with rain. There was a telephone box at the junction where we'd been dropped, so we crammed into it and tried to get some sleep.

But two guys crouching on the floor of a telephone box is not exactly comfortable – although I've since slept in places that made that phone-box floor seem like the Ritz. We shivered and dozed fitfully for an hour or so until, some time after four o'clock in the morning, a man banged on the door and asked if he could use the phone. We struggled out into the rain and, soaked through, walked into Northampton, still wearing our Manchester United scarves and hats. Plodding wetly through the dark town, we finally reached the station, only to find that the ticket inspector, thinking we were troublemakers, would not let us into the station. It was here that we decided to separate.

Wearily, I went on, heading out of Northampton and thumbing each vehicle that passed me. Eventually, the driver of a big, brand-new, completely empty motor coach stopped and took me as far as the Derby junction of the M1. It was now ten o'clock in the morning. From the junction I walked twenty miles to Matlock with not even a sniff of a lift. I was absolutely knackered. On arrival at the station there was a train about to leave for Manchester. I raced to the ticket window, hoping to give my name and address in exchange for a ticket. The man on duty there said he didn't have time to sell me a ticket, and to get on the train immediately as it was about to leave. I hadn't even opened my mouth. I should have had the sense to ask him how much the fare was.

At Manchester, I left the train and made my way to the barrier. When I was asked to show my ticket, I simply said that I'd lost it. The ticket collector didn't say another word. He just blew his whistle, at which two policemen arrived, who immediately led me off to an office, where they asked how far I had come. Foolishly, I said Matlock, and that I didn't remember how much I'd paid.

They'd heard lies like that before, and were no more inclined to believe mine than anyone else's. Telling me that I would be charged with an offence, they took my name and address before escorting me to a bus and paying my fare to Preston. By now, I was completely exhausted. I slumped on the back seat and fell asleep. I awoke as the bus was driven into a large garage. When I asked the bus driver where we were, he informed me: 'Blackpool'. I couldn't believe my bad luck, for I was now faced with another hitchhiking expedition back to Preston. I eventually made it home in the early hours of Monday morning.

The police were not going to forget me, and it was obvious that I was going to be in deep trouble. I had no idea what the penalty was for attempting to defraud the railway, or whatever offence it was I'd committed, but I wound myself up into believing that it might be very severe. Then I had a brainwave: I went down to the army recruiting office in Preston and told the recruiting sergeant that I wanted to join up. A large man with a brick-red face, he scowled at me and, clearly used to youths arriving one jump ahead of their day in court, asked whether I had a criminal record.

'Not yet, but I will have', I told him. 'I got booked last night for riding free on the railway.'

The sergeant took this in his stride, remarking, to my relief, 'We'll soon get that sorted out.' He sat me at a table, took down my details, and had me complete all sorts of IQ and aptitude tests before sending me on my way, telling me that I would be contacted in due course. I went back to work, still bluffing my way as an apprentice joiner. I didn't have much skill or interest in carpentry and couldn't see myself doing this for the rest of my life.

True to his word, the recruiting sergeant contacted me three days later. He had fixed an appointment for me to have a medical and said that he had talked the police into dropping the charges, since, if I had a criminal record, I couldn't go into the army. He told the police that I would send the price of the ticket I'd dodged, plus 10 shillings for the bus fare home, and they had accepted the deal. I was in the clear.

I packed in my job as an apprentice and signed on at the Labour Exchange, where I was sent off to numerous jobs by my mates who worked there. The jobs ranged from labouring on building sites to working in a dairy, hooking crates of milk from a conveyor belt on to milk trucks. The job wasn't particularly interesting but it paid well, and there was plenty of milk to drink.

There I was, four months short of my eighteenth birthday, and fed up with Preston, fed up with my work, fed up with the way I lived. And now that I was off the police hook, I was damned if I was going to go into the army. Even I knew, however, that escaping the military once they had their hooks into you was no easy matter. I therefore decided to emigrate to Australia, on a £10 assisted passage which the government there was advertising in order to attract people to the life Down Under. The recruiting sergeant was very nice about it, all things considered, when I telephoned to tell him the good news. No doubt he thought the army had had a lucky escape.

A few days later I presented myself at Australia House in Manchester, where I filled in a load of forms, one of which asked whether I was willing to serve in Vietnam if I was called up by the Australian Army. I signed it; indeed, I'd have signed anything to get out of Preston. The city's slogan in those days was 'Proud, Pretty Preston'. 'Pissing-down Preston' would have been more like it. I kept thinking about all that Australian sunshine, and about Bondi Beach, and then I ran out of things to think about because I knew little about Australia, except that it had kangaroos and aborigines and was a hell of a long way away.

I must have been acceptable to the Australian immigration authorities – or at least the forms I'd filled in must have been – for in due course Australia House telephoned to say that I was to stand by to fly out on the following Friday. I had elected to fly out because I couldn't afford to go by ship. In fact, the £10 emigrants' fare was the same for either mode of travel, but by sea you had on-board expenses for several weeks as you sailed to the other side of the world. Then the blow fell. They phoned again to say that as I was under twenty-one years of age I needed written parental approval.

Getting my mother to sign the papers proved easy enough, but I still needed my father's signature. I hadn't seen him in years, but I knew that he was still living in the same house and I remembered the phone number. So I called him.

'Who's that?' he asked.

'Peter.'

'Peter who?'

'Peter, your son.'

There was a long pause. Then he said, 'What do you want?' Clearly things had not changed much.

I explained that I needed to talk to him, and he grudgingly invited me to his house on the following Saturday. He was pleasant enough when I turned up, especially as we hadn't seen each other for about four years. We went to watch the speedway at Belle Vue in Manchester and afterwards had a few drinks. It was then that I told him that I was emigrating to Australia. He thought it was a good idea until I mentioned that he'd have to sign a paper giving his consent. Then he stopped thinking it was a good idea. In fact, it became a very bad idea. If I got into debt, he said he'd be held legally responsible for the money owed. So he wasn't going to sign, and that, as far as he was concerned, was that.

I wasn't done yet, however. Back in Preston I forged his signature on the document and took it to Australia House. Luckily, before I could pull the papers out of my pocket a woman clerk told me that my father had telephoned to say that he refused to sign the paper, and had made it clear that he was not prepared to argue the toss about it.

As I stood there, feeling shattered, with all my dreams about Australia going down the drain, the woman patiently explained once again that without both my father's and mother's consent I would have to wait until I was twenty-one. My father had well and truly queered my pitch. Cunning as ever, he had been at least one jump ahead of me, for he must have guessed that I would forge his signature after he'd refused to endorse my application.

Now I was really depressed. Although I had the job in the dairy, I knew that my life was going nowhere. As I sat slumped miserably on the top deck of a bus one morning, with another exciting day of hooking crates of milk to look forward to, I saw a massive billboard bearing a famous British Army recruiting poster of the time: 'Join the Professionals and become a Soldier of the Seventies.' I jumped off at the next stop.

In my desperation, I simply thought I'd give the recruiting office another try, hoping they didn't remember me – the guy whom they had got off a police charge, and who'd then more or less told them to get stuffed. Clad in the sort of reefer jacket made popular by the Beatles and a hat not unlike a Russian admiral's, I shoved open the door. With my long hair hanging scruffily well over my collar, I must have been a recruiting sergeant's vision of hell.

As it happened, they didn't remember me. So I filled in all the papers again and completed all the tests. I sat, hands in pockets, on a hard chair and heard one sergeant say to another, 'Come and have a look at this.' I guessed that he was talking about me, and immediately assumed that they were going to kick me out.

But it was the test papers they were interested in. Apparently I was the only would-be recruit they had ever seen who had answered all the questions correctly. They gave me that 'What do you want here?' look, but were obviously keen to get me to sign on. They told me what a wonderful life it was in the army, then tried to talk me into joining one of the army's technical corps. 'With these results you could become a technician, maybe join the Royal Corps of Signals,' one of them said. To me, however, it was the Parachute Regiment or nothing. So I sat there, periodically repeating, 'No, I want to join the Paras.'

I was aiming for the top, I knew that. But I didn't want to waste my time in some unglamorous, technically minded, mostly non-combatant corps like the Engineers, the Signals or the REME. Eventually they gave up arguing because by then they knew that if I didn't get a shot at the Paras, I'd walk straight out of the door. Although I had not the slightest idea what I would have done then . . .

They sent me for a medical, which in due course I attended. I must have passed, for in November 1969 I received notice telling me that I was going into the army the following week. I was determined to spend Christmas with my mates, however, and therefore asked them to postpone the date I was due to join. The recruiting office agreed and I was ordered to report back there on 5 January 1970. That Monday morning I borrowed 2 shillings (10 pence) off the Labour Exchange guys I was sharing the house with and, with my kit stuffed into a supermarket plastic bag, made my way to the recruiting office. This time I'd left my Russian admiral's outfit back at the house and was wearing a sports jacket and grey trousers, so I looked a bit more respectable, or at least conventional.

I was taken upstairs to a room where a middle-aged officer who looked like a relic from the Second World War sat me down and lectured me about how boring it would be for me in the Paras, rushing about the place doing forward and backward rolls. As it quickly became obvious that he didn't know what he was talking about, the conversation sort of tailed off after a bit. Eventually he stopped talking about the Paras and swore me in on the Bible. After that brief ceremony he gave me a day's pay – about 23 shillings (£1.15), which was a fortune in those days for me to have as spending money – and an army clerk then issued me with a rail-travel warrant to Aldershot. The money even paid for breakfast in the first-class dining car on the train.

At about four o'clock that afternoon I arrived in Aldershot, the sprawling garrison town which is the traditional home of the British Army. Outside the railway station I asked someone how to get to Browning Barracks, the Parachute Regiment's depot, and he pointed to a double-decker bus. I climbed aboard and the bus eventually got going, only to meander all around Aldershot. There seemed to be soldiers everywhere – marching, running with packs on their backs, trotting in track suits, hanging out of the backs of canvas-topped trucks that were painted a dull olive green, drilling on barrack squares, stamping up and down on guard duty. I'd never seen so many soldiers in my life.

But it was when I began seeing my first Paras that my heart started racing. I was getting really excited about becoming one of these guys in their red berets and parachute smocks when the bus driver shouted 'Browning Barracks.'

The place differed dramatically from the yellow-brick barrack blocks that the bus had passed, clusters of buildings with names like Badajos commemorating ancient victories. For a start, Browning Barracks had an old Douglas C-47 transport aircraft – the famous Dakota, which had ferried so many Paras to battle during the Second World War – parked on the lawn outside the gates. The building blocks that flanked the two large parade grounds were modern, with lots of glass, making them light and airy, and the whole barracks immediately had a good feel to it.

Having left the bus and gone through the gates, I realized I had no idea where to report. I spotted an office and was looking for the door when a woman came to the window and asked if I was lost. 'No,' I replied, 'I've joined the army.' I gave her my name and, after she had looked it up on a list attached to a clipboard, she told me that I was expected and asked where my kit was. Wordlessly I held up my plastic bag. She must have felt sorry for me, because she invited me in and gave me a cup of tea. Then she pointed me in the direction of another building, which she said was the Transit Block.

By now it was about 4.45 and the last grey light of a winter's afternoon was fading fast. I made my way over to the building and was directed to a small room where I found two other recruits, both Welsh, and both later to join the SAS. Apart from them, there were four grey-painted metal beds with steel springs and no mattresses, blankets or pillows; there was precious little other furniture either. We sat there and waited for somebody to come. But nobody did, so at about seven o'clock we set off to find something to eat, shambling around the barracks in our civvy clothes and non-military haircuts.

We finally located the NAAFI, where we each bought a meat pie and a cup of tea. Then we made our way back to the Transit Block, resignedly concluding that we were expected to sleep that night on the bare metal springs, without mattresses or blankets. Yet, even though it was cold and uncomfortable on that metal bed, I was dog tired and went

out like a light. When we woke in the morning and took off our shirts
to have a wash, our backs were covered with diamond-shaped indents
from the metal springs. We looked as though we'd been lashed with a
cat-o'-nine-tails.

At around nine o'clock the door opened and a soldier in uniform
entered. He told us his name was Corporal Palmer and asked when we
had arrived. I said, 'About a quarter to five, sir. Last night.'

'Don't call me "sir",' he snapped, furious that nobody had told him
that we three had been due to arrive. Then he asked where we had slept.
He looked mildly incredulous when we pointed to the metal springs,
remarking, 'What, there? That's a good start. Come with me and get
the mattress and bedding you should have collected last night.'

As it happened, we had missed the intake for the Parachute
Regiment, which was held every month. More recruits began arriving
that morning but, like us, were all too late. We would therefore have to
wait until the following month's intake to be formally drafted into the
regiment, although we were to remain at the barracks for the time
being. Having drawn bedding and a certain amount of army clothing,
though not proper uniform, we were given tests and interviews and put
through an assault course, before undergoing an assessment and
meeting the officer who would be in charge of us, who spoke briefly
about the Paras and what would be expected of us.

One of the tests involved being taken to a trinasium, which is where
the directing staff (DS) work out whether you have the confidence to
make a parachute jump. The test itself required us to walk along a
length of scaffolding tubing fixed about thirty feet in the air. Having
shuffled along this to the middle, we had to stop, bend over and touch
our toes, before making our way to the far end.

I was terrified – literally shaking – because I can't stand heights.
Nevertheless, when my turn came I obediently climbed up and inched
my way through the routine. Having succeeded once I dreaded doing
the test again, but I had to. Several times. Somehow I managed not to
fall off, and, either by luck or good acting, the instructors didn't notice
that I was scared to death.

After four days of tests, trips to the assault course and other more or
less mindless activities, Friday came and with it pay parade. When I
reached the head of the line I was given a paybook to sign, after which
the Pay Corps corporal handed me about £29 and a few shillings. The
supervising officer then said, to my considerable surprise, 'Off you go.
You've got three weeks' leave.' Bloody hell, I thought, on leave already

and I've only just arrived. What was more, I hadn't had so much money in my pocket since, aged fourteen, I had run that newspaper stand. We got ready to go, though first we had to hand in the gear they'd given us to wear while we were in the barracks. Suddenly we were back in civvies.

I reported back to Browning Barracks on the first Monday in February. With my fellow recruits we were finally kitted out with uniform, boots, and all the other paraphernalia of the newly joined recruit, then put into our sections, each under a section corporal, and assigned to another four-man room in the Transit Block. I'd had my collar-length hair cut in January, but it still wasn't short enough for the British Army. Now they gave me a haircut that left me looking like a convict just beginning his sentence.

In a sense, that is exactly what we were doing – beginning a sentence. There must have been some one hundred and ten hopefuls on that first day, but after six weeks there was barely a handful of us left. The reason was simple – the NCOs and instructors very quickly and very ruthlessly weeded us out. One screw-up and you were out, told that there was no place for you in the Parachute Regiment, invited to try again with another unit, and sent on your way.

In those first days we were shown how to put on our new kit and how to wind on our puttees – long khaki bandages that were wound round the legs from boot-top to knee. It didn't take long to learn the shortcuts, however. If you were going to pass the course you had to learn fast, which was what survival in the Paras was all about. Slower-thinking recruits had no chance, and a steady drip of departures began almost from day one.

Every day there was a barrack-room inspection. Apart from everything else – 'everything' meaning having all your kit immaculate and neatly squared away in the prescribed manner – this meant 'boxing' your bedding, creating from unruly bedclothes a pack like a square biscuit, with every edge razor sharp and perfectly aligned. The order was first a blanket, then a sheet, then another blanket and then another sheet. Then a final blanket went over everything to form an outer cover. All the edges had to be even, and you then laid this 'biscuit' of wool and cotton at the proper place on top of the mattress each morning. Without fail you had to strip your bed and put two pillows and two folded pillow cases next to your boxed bedgear.

After three days, I learned the trick of laying out my biscuit of folded bedclothes for inspection and then, after the inspection, very carefully stowing it away on top of my locker. It stayed there, unused, for six months, except for the few minutes every day when it was laid out on my bed. I slept between the mattress and the mattress cover, thereby saving myself half an hour of effort in the mornings. I also had a brand-new, spotlessly clean washing and shaving kit which was never used apart from laying out for inspection – I actually used a second set which I kept well concealed. All our kit, and the room itself, had to be perfect or trouble followed, which meant, among much else, that we had to polish our boots until we could see our reflections in the toecaps, and shine the floor till it gleamed like a plate-glass window.

Our platoon officer was Lieutenant Rupert Smith, now Lieutenant-General Sir Rupert Smith. He was a very fair man, as were his two sergeants. In this I was lucky, although I didn't know that for some time. If I had joined a month earlier – the first date given to me by the recruiting office in Preston – life would have been hell. That intake, it turned out, had been supervised by a group of NCOs who were little short of monsters. These regularly tossed their recruits' blankets and other gear out of the barrack-room windows, leaving the bewildered young soldiers to scramble frantically around outside, often in rain and snow, trying to gather it up and put it all back together again for yet another inspection by the bullies who had roughed up their gear in the first place.

The truth is that there are a lot of NCOs of that type in the British Army. They are very tough on their subordinates, but crawl to everybody above them – or to anyone bigger and stronger who holds the same rank as they do. Give them some poor ignorant squaddie who can't answer back, however, and they are in their element. I have never had time for men like that, and I was fortunate that, in Lieutenant Smith and his NCOs, I had decent superiors.

I underwent six months' basic training, which was mainly made up of drill, running and hard slogs on route marches. Bit by bit we turned into soldiers. When a man joins the Parachute Regiment he is issued with a series of coloured shoulder tags to mark his progression through the training course. The first badge is green (it doesn't take a genius to work out why); then, after six weeks, you move on to wearing a blue tag. By that time, so many of your intake have been kicked out as unsuitable for the Parachute Regiment that you feel like an old hand when you see that month's new recruits arrive.

The NCOs never stopped reminding us that selection for the Paras was a very greasy pole. Because of the pace and the brutality of the training course, the rate of attrition is enormous, and fewer than one in five of those who start out are allowed to finish the course. Some men simply decide to quit, because they know they will never make it. The training is undoubtedly effective, however, for what comes out at the end of it puts the fear of God into other countries' armies.

After six weeks, although we recruits – those of us still left, that is – had got as far as the blue-patch stage, we were still a long way short of winning the right to wear that maroon beret with its chromium-plated badge of a winged parachute. There were endless drills and classes, and miles of tracks to be run and tons of logs to be carried on bleeding shoulders through mud and slime, until we felt that our arms were being pulled from their sockets, that our legs were turning to jelly, and that our hearts would burst.

Log-running is the nearest thing the British Army has to a medieval torture rack. But it is all part of the very deliberate hardening process, like plunging white-hot steel into cold water to temper the metal – except that, instead of steel, it was muscle and willpower the DS were toughening and testing. They were constantly pushing us further than we thought we could go, until we were covering distances that only weeks earlier would have had us on our backs in the nearest emergency ward.

The emphasis was always on aggression. So whenever we looked like slackening, we were ordered into the gymnasium for a 'milling' bout. Milling is peculiar to the Parachute Regiment, and consists of two men, often mates, standing toe-to-toe on a mat and beating hell out of each other. And if they don't go at it hammer and tongs, there is always a pug-nosed physical training instructor ready to take the place of the guy getting a soft ride. The PTI will then belt the chap who had been pulling his punches, knocking him all over the place.

Training NCOs encouraged their squads to attack other passing squaddies. They wanted to see men knock each other out of the way as they ran, disputing the other side's right of way on the pavements beneath the horse-chestnut trees that flank Aldershot's barrack roadways. After brief but frequently bloody skirmishes, the NCOs would call off their squads, for all the world like whippers-in at a hunt bringing their hounds back into line.

Several times I saw training corporals grab the helmet chinstraps of fast-fading recruits and run them across the assault-course finishing line. Then, when the exhausted man collapsed in a heap, the NCO would plant a well-aimed boot up his backside. Other slowcoaches often spent their NAAFI breaks doing a hundred press-ups, while their mates slurped mugs of thick, sweet, rather gritty tea and bit into rock buns baked by cooks who would never be in any danger of being prosecuted for misrepresentation under the Trade Descriptions Act.

So the laggards and the weak were thinned from our ranks. Dispirited and demoralized, they often simply bought themselves out of the army for £20 before the inevitable axe could fall. Indeed, I got myself into trouble with the brass for encouraging several of the fading recruits to buy themselves out long before they had been warned that they would not make the grade. There is little point in watching a man punish himself when you – and he – know there is going to be no reward for him at the end. It seemed ludicrous to me, even though all of us considered quitting at some time or another during those hardening months. So I tried to convince a number of our intake to leave while they were still ahead, something which the authorities soon came to hear of. As a result, one day I was summoned before an officer, who told me that I was a troublemaker and asked why I had encouraged other recruits to buy themselves out of the army but had not done so myself.

'Because I never had twenty quid, sir,' I answered, although it wasn't the truth. I never for a moment doubted that I would not get through – not that I dared tell him that. The outcome was that he told me he was watching my performance, the clear implication being that the slightest failure or transgression would see me kicked out. It was scarcely news, however, for we were watched from dawn to dusk – and even beyond that during night exercises.

There was another cloud on my horizon, however, for while I enjoyed my basic training in the Parachute Regiment, I dreaded the thought of actually parachuting. In fact, the closer we got to going to RAF Abingdon in Oxfordshire for jump training, the more scared I became. Nor could I understand the guys who were looking forward to it, who struck me as being quite mad.

The Royal Air Force does not waste money sending trainee paratroopers up in an aircraft until the instructors know that the recruits can do the business. As a result, on our arrival at Abingdon, and after the usual lectures and practices and a certain amount of jump training in a vast hangar, we were first of all winched up in a cage suspended beneath a helium-filled balloon. The large silver-grey blimp is tethered by a steel cable, three-quarters of an inch thick, which winds around the drum of a large winch mounted on the back of a truck. The winchmen and their gear are protected from the vicious lash-back of a broken cable by a lattice canopy of heavy-gauge steel mesh. Trainee paratroopers stand in the cage while the balloon to which it is attached is allowed to rise on its cable to 800 feet. Then the jumping begins.

Old hands at Abingdon took a sadistic pleasure in telling us of one trainee who had 'Roman candled' – that is, his parachute had failed to open – and how he'd fallen 800 feet to smash through the winch cage like pickled red cabbage. I thought I was going to be sick, but kept an expressionless face. The instructors are watching for reaction, and I was not going to let anyone know how scared I really was.

In the back of the 4-ton truck that took us to the DZ – dropping zone – that first morning, some of the more gung-ho trainees were singing a famous song about a parachutist whose canopy had not opened. Set to the tune of the Battle Hymn of the Republic, one of the verses ran, 'Oh, they scraped him off the tarmac like a pound of strawberry jam.' I just sat there by the tailboard, saying nothing, but fervently wishing they'd shut up.

When our time came, we shuffled into the balloon cage and stood there anxiously with our instructor as the winch cable paid out until we were at 800 feet. There was very little wind – which was a pity, for if there had been more than a strong breeze the jump would have been cancelled. And I would have been allowed to live for one more day . . .

The first men jumped, and presumably landed safely – I didn't look. Then my name was called and I stepped forward to stand at the door of the cage. The instructor advised the NCOs on the ground, 'One to come.' I stepped towards the edge and crossed my arms, as we'd been taught in the hangars hundreds of feet below. Only this wasn't a hangar. It was a cage under a balloon, swaying about high above the green drop zone. Beyond were fields of ripening wheat edging to the horizon and a pale blue sky dotted with cottonwool clouds.

We had been told not to look down but to look up and concentrate on the fringe of the balloon. I did so, until the instructor shouted, 'Red on. Green on. Go.' Oh fucking hell! I thought as I jumped off the edge. It was terrifying.

Suddenly I felt the parachute open. It tugged at my harness and I looked up and saw the canopy floating above me like a silken airborne jellyfish. And I knew that I wasn't going to die – or not then, anyway.

The canopy opened, and then it shut again, and then reopened. We had been warned about that, however, so I managed not to panic. Moments later I heard shouts from the ground, the parachute-jump instructors yelling at me to pull down on my left or right lift web or steering cord, to hold on and get my feet and knees together. I was totally confused. I had shut my eyes again and only opened them moments before I hit the ground, landing, as I was always to do after that, like a sack of spuds. I was never to get a parachute landing quite right.

The second balloon jump should have been easier but because I now knew what was happening, it wasn't. What made it worse, however, was the fact that the man before me refused to jump. Three times the instructor went through the routine. But the soldier would not step off the platform. No matter how much he was screamed at, he just kept shouting 'No, no, no!' The balloon was hauled down and he was taken away. We never saw him again.

While this may seem harsh, the fact that a man gets no second chance makes sense. A man suddenly refusing to jump when the Paras are going into battle might be the guy carrying spare ammunition or the radio. His refusal would immediately jeopardize the lives of the rest of the team, as well as their mission. Seen in that context, it becomes clear why the Parachute Regiment cannot take the chance of a man losing his nerve at a crucial moment in an operation.

A few weeks after those first jumps and I'd made it: I had successfully completed the Parachute Regiment entry course. With flying colours, as it turned out. At the passing-out parade on the barracks square in Aldershot, I received my red beret from a general, who then also presented me with a plaque for being Champion Recruit of my intake.

It was a beautiful July day. The regimental band played and, puffed up with pride, I felt ten feet tall as I marched across crunchy gravel and snapped to attention in front of the general.

Almost everyone else had their families and girlfriends there to watch them parade, but I had deliberately not invited my mother, because before the event I had thought that it was all a bit naff. So, instead of my family, I had invited my two former housemates from the Preston Labour Exchange to come and watch the parade. They loyally turned up, and I was glad they did, but suddenly, when it came to my turn to march out and collect the red beret and those blue, embroidered wings, I knew it wasn't naff and it wasn't showing off. Above all, I realized, albeit too late, that I should have had my mother there. Even so, I felt so proud of that red beret that for days afterwards I wore it day and night. It affected all of us like that – my friend Taff, the chap in our intake who won the big award for Champion Shot, was every bit as pleased and proud as I was.

After the passing-out parade I went on leave to Brighton with my two mates from Preston. We had a tremendous time, except that my Para wings didn't seem to impress any girls in the seaside town. Maybe the spots on my face outweighed the wings on my sleeve, for I certainly never got lucky. Then at the end of my leave I was posted back home to spend a week in the Preston recruiting office as a sort of living advertisement for what a great life it is in 'the Professionals'. After that I returned to Aldershot, posted to the 1st Battalion the Parachute Regiment. I was no longer a recruit, but a soldier.

I was no longer a potential emigrant to Australia, either, nor a bored apprentice joiner, nor any of the other things I'd been or might have been. I had changed a lot in those six months. I had more respect for other people and more respect for myself. I was more disciplined, fitter and better trained than I had ever been in my life. I had a job and a possible career.

I had even acquired a nickname, because in the Paras everyone has to have a nickname. I have, though, spent years trying to work out how the platoon corporal chose mine. ''Ere,' he said, 'where are you from?' When I told him Salford, he said, 'That's it then. You're a Salford Billy.' I'd never heard of any Salford Billies, but from then on I was no longer Peter. My nickname was 'Billy', and that's what I answered to.

Then, on 20 September 1970, along with the rest of the 1st Battalion, I was posted to Northern Ireland. Life was never to be the same again.

Chapter Three

RAIN. A thin, persistent, miserable drizzle, the kind that finds its way down your neck, seeming to soak your clothes far worse than any proper downpour, was what welcomed us to Northern Ireland.

I had never been abroad before, and although Northern Ireland was not really 'abroad', it had that curious feeling of foreignness about it. Partly that was the language. When I first arrived in Belfast, it took me weeks to understand a word some of the locals were saying – and they were supposed to be speaking English. Though I'm damned if it sounded like any English I'd come across before. To my ears, it was more like strangulation than speech. Mind you, to be fair, I doubt whether an Ulsterman finds pure Salford speech that comprehensible.

Camouflaged trucks took us to our barracks in Belfast. On the drive in we passed row upon row of nearly identical, soot-streaked, red-brick houses. The rows stood back to back, as if lacking the dignity to stand alone. I tried to imagine George Best, my Manchester United hero, kicking a football in the street outside the Belfast house where he grew up. Graffiti – mostly political slogans – fought for space on walls and fences. As the cheapest form of advertising the IRA could find, it was everywhere, Republican mottoes sometimes standing alone, sometimes overscored with equally inflammatory Loyalist phrases.

Yet when we stopped at traffic lights, people smiled at us as they passed by. One old woman switched her walking stick to her left hand and with her right made a sign of the cross. 'God bless you, boys,' she called, and even I had no problem understanding her.

We were to need that old women's blessing many times over before we were pulled back to the mainland two years later. By then, the cups of tea once so kindly offered to British soldiers by some of the Catholic population stood a fifty-fifty chance of being laced with rat poison. This was 1970, and 'the Troubles' – this latest round of them, that is – were not much more than a year old. People still had hope, and in those days many Catholics saw the British Army as their deliverer from Protestant excesses; the same, albeit in reverse, was true of many Protestants. No one then foresaw that the problem would escalate enormously, and would last another thirty years – and perhaps longer. How could they have done? It is not generally in human nature to predict the worst.

As for me, I found that one of the great things about being with a proper working unit, after spending months in training, was the end to hours of meaningless bullshit. Though the Paras were turned out as smartly as any Guards regiment, the days of mindlessly boxing our bedding were over. We were still expected to sweep and polish the barrack-room floors, but instead of boxing the bedclothes each day, we simply made the bed neat and tidy and went to work.

Apart from boots, puttees and battledress trousers, we wore Dennison smocks and our red berets. Wearing a steel helmet might seem to have made more sense, but the red berets were much more effective. Their distinctive colour allowed the terrorists to see who they were dealing with while we were still a mile away. Once they knew they were confronting the Parachute Regiment, the IRA recognized that they were dealing with the toughest and most effective troops in the British Army. Most times, they'd pull out and leave us alone.

In fact, because our don't-mess-with-us reputation had gone ahead of us, we tended to have less trouble from the IRA than other regiments. The terrorists frequently backed off at the sight of the red beret and waited until another battalion with a less fearsome reputation took over the tour of duty. Then they would direct their activities against our successors.

I remember a Yorkshire battalion, the Green Howards, starting a tour in Belfast and taking a number of casualties, losing five or six men killed by the IRA. Their morale slumped so low that we were sent in to relieve them. We were barracked in the Flax Street mill in the city's Ardoyne area, right in the heart of IRA territory, yet we didn't have a single incident. The reason was simply because the IRA took the view that if the Paras are here, leave it alone until they have gone away again.

We were both feared and respected, depending upon who was expressing a view, and which side they were on. People knew we were a tough force and that, when challenged, we didn't pull our punches. Even so, the fear factor was always with us in Northern Ireland. You never knew when a sniper had you in the cross hairs of his telescope sight, or when an explosive charge might detonate – until it was too late.

The trick was to keep moving. Running from corner to corner, moving all the time so that nobody could draw a bead on you. We covered each other, and every action was quick, quick, quick. If you kept moving, you kept breathing – or at least, you had a hell of a sight better chance of staying alive.

Life in Northern Ireland was horrible. We never got any leave, and we always seemed to be on standby for something. We were constantly called out to deal with riots, and the locals would chuck bricks and petrol bombs at us. Yet we never suffered anything too life-threatening, partly because of the regiment's reputation, and partly because of the directions we received when it came to handling trouble. The CO was not given to allowing his men to be humiliated by a bunch of hotheads. If they hit you, he said, make sure you are in the right, and then grab them with as much force as you reckon it takes, though no more.

In Belfast in the early 1970s, Friday and Saturday nights meant rioting, since those rioters who had jobs could lie in the following day. The mayhem had to be seen to be believed, although it could generally be contained before it got too out of hand. Even so, there were dangers for soldiers beyond the obvious ones of being attacked. One Friday night we were called out to deal with the usual missile-throwing, petrol-bombing mob. Wearing flak jackets, we had rushed into the crowd to grab a few ringleaders and sling them into the back of trucks to be carted off to the police cells. The violence went on until three o'clock in the morning, and we were pretty exhausted by the time we trailed wearily back to barracks.

I was still sleeping when a warrant officer walked into the barrack room on the Saturday morning and, grabbing my shoulder, shook me awake. He then shoved an army Intelligence Corps flashcard – a photograph mounted on card used to identify suspected terrorists – under my nose. For a few moments, I didn't know where I was, let alone who the guy on the flashcard was supposed to be. Slowly the cobwebs cleared, however, and I heard the sergeant-major telling me that I was to attend court when the man I had arrested on Friday night was arraigned. The man in the photo on the card.

When tear-gas rounds are popping and police sirens are wailing and yobs are chucking bricks and petrol bombs at you, and there are milling groups of people and smoke and confusion everywhere, no one has time to take a good look at the rioters they are grabbing. If someone gave us grief, we went in hard, cracking his knees with our weapons or banging the rifle butt into his shoulders where it hurt. That tended to take a rioter's mind off lighting any petrol bombs.

We seized them by whatever bits of their clothing we could lay a free hand on and, dragging them out of the crowd, threw them over the tailboard of the nearest truck. From then on they were the responsibility of the police, who took them away, checked their records and questioned them to see if they were on any wanted lists, and banged them up in cells pending a court hearing to establish their guilt or innocence in the matter of charges ranging from causing an affray or incitement to riot, to grievous bodily harm, or worse. While on the subject of the RUC, I have often read of them being accused of bias, tending to favour Protestants. I never saw any bias, however. They were tough men, true, but they upheld the law in a place and in circumstances where that was all too often a very difficult thing to do.

It was not often that a terrorist 'hard man' got caught in the net, however. Their leaders were too smart to let them get close to a confrontation in which there was nothing to be gained but aggravation. Besides, the local aggrieved citizenry gave the RUC and the army plenty of trouble without any of the IRA having to get involved beyond offering a bit of encouragement.

But I went to court and gave evidence that I had arrested the defendant in question. He denied it vehemently, while his barrister claimed that he had never been in trouble with the police before. 'Only because he's never been caught before,' I said, at which the ruffled defence brief called me a smart alec. The judge believed me, however, and found the still-protesting prisoner guilty of whichever offence he'd been charged with.

As serious and potentially dangerous as these riots could be, there were also funny incidents too. Soon after we arrived in Belfast we were called out to quell a riot of angry Roman Catholics. Basically, the ordinary people of Northern Ireland are warm-hearted, decent souls. Being a Roman Catholic myself, I often felt sorry for the Catholics who did most of the rioting, because there is no doubt that they had had a rough time at the hands of the Protestant majority. Besides, rioting probably brightened up their otherwise dull lives.

As riots go, this one was not much to write home about. We were held in reserve in a parallel street while soldiers from another battalion tried to dodge the half-bricks and the jars of piss that were being hurled at them. Gradually the situation began to get out of hand, and we were warned to be ready to go in and do our bit. When it was finally decided to deploy us, we unfurled a big banner and held it up for all to see. In large letters, it told the mob to disperse and go home immediately.

Unfortunately, none of the local demonstrators could read Arabic – which was what the words on the banner were written in. Our masterpiece of peaceful riot control, it turned out, had last been used in Aden during the 1960s, and had been brought out to Northern Ireland without anybody checking to see what it said – or in which language it said it.

It proved singularly effective, however. When we unfurled the banner, the shouting and jeering stopped. For a moment there was dead silence. Then the crowd began to laugh. Standing behind the banner, none of us could see what they were laughing about, so an officer sent a man round to the front to find out what was so amusing.

He came back, also laughing, and reported that the warning to disperse was in Arabic, at which the officer said, 'I'm getting awfully bored by all this. Now tell them – in English, please – to pack in this nonsense and go home. Pronto.' And they did, still laughing and pointing to that idiotic banner as they walked away.

By the early 1970s the IRA operated under its own terms, many of them quite far removed from the fight for a united, republican Ireland. In South Armagh, for instance, they seemed able to recruit a special brand of psychopath to 'the Cause'. But there was no 'Cause' any more. Much of the IRA's leadership was little more than a bunch of gangsters, controlling armed robbery, protection rackets, smuggling, and a great many other illegal activities.

When someone had their kneecaps blown off as a punishment, as often as not the real reason that the IRA had crippled him was because he'd been muscling-in on their territory, or had in some way failed to follow their line. The bullets through the legs were a warning. If he was mad enough to dabble again, the next bullet would have been in his head.

All these 'punishment beatings' were ostensibly carried out in the name of cleaning up the community. But the truth is that most of Ulster's Catholic population, who had at first welcomed the protection of the IRA as a buffer against marauding Protestant terrorists, came to live in abject fear of their 'protectors'. They came to wish, above all, for peace with their Protestant neighbours, and for the gunmen to disappear from their communities for ever, so that they could all get on with their lives.

We called South Armagh 'bandit country' because there were few places British soldiers could walk or army vehicles drive without the very real danger of being taken out, particularly around Crossmaglen, which sits only yards from the border with the Republic.

The landscape is a sinister mix of rocky outcrops and hilly fields bordered by high hedgerows and deep ditches. Culverts, carrying streams and run-off water from the fields on either side, run beneath the roads and lanes. It was possible for terrorists to plant remote-controlled bombs in any one of these, detonating the device by radio signal from the safety of their hilltop hideouts. They could be away and over the border into the Irish Republic before the ambulances, coming to pick up the pieces, had even started their engines.

Some British Army units patrolled those lanes – and did so to their cost. Not the Paras, however. We never walked the lanes. Instead, we went into the fields behind the ditches and hedges, planning our own routes over fences and streams as we went. Anywhere but along those potential death-traps of roads with their hedges and ditches which, apart from culvert bombs, were perfectly suited to terrorist ambushes.

We rarely followed the same route twice, and worked out our every move. Furthermore, we tried to second-guess our enemy. On patrol in Northern Ireland we often parked ourselves somewhere near a police station or other likely IRA target. Then, when the terrorists attacked, we could rapidly move in and grab them.

The emphasis was on grabbing them. There has been a great deal of rubbish written about the British government instituting a shoot-to-kill policy in Northern Ireland. The truth is self-evident, however. Had there been such a policy, allowing British soldiers or the RUC to kill known terrorists on sight, the IRA would not have lasted more than a few months. The truth is that, although they had some exceptionally good snipers, as well as skilful bomb-makers, the terrorists were up against superior fighting men – better trained, better disciplined, better armed and equipped, better supported, and often much more experienced. Like any fairly small, clandestine terrorist organization, the IRA does not like to get involved in a real firefight. Instead, its operatives seek to kill or injure as many people as they can with the bomb or the bullet and then get out as fast as possible. Many of those IRA 'heroes' who, without a second's thought, would kill and maim innocent people, including women and children, would not hang around for a shoot-out with real soldiers.

As for us, every soldier knew just how far he could go in retaliation. In his pocket, he carried with him at all times the famous 'yellow card' spelling out the Rules of Engagement (ROE). Although these ran to several paragraphs, what they said, in a nutshell, was that if you felt that your life or the lives of other security forces or civilians were in immediate danger, or that government property was in danger of being destroyed, you could open fire. It was all there in the rules, and everyone knew that failing to abide by them would bring severe consequences.

When a civilian, even a known terrorist, was killed by the military, the Royal Ulster Constabulary would immediately launch an investigation. That is an understatement, in fact – 'crawl all over the soldier or soldiers who did the shooting' would be a more accurate description.

If a soldier had shot a civilian, however, as a result of what he had perceived to be a threat, and stuck to the truth as he knew it, simply telling his RUC questioners, 'I thought the man was armed and that my life was endangered, so I shot him,' then he would be in the clear. Even if it turned out that what the dead man had brandished or appeared to be carrying was not a gun, it was quite rightly reckoned that to have fired under those circumstances was not the soldier's fault. That, though, is a very far cry from there having been an official shoot-to-kill policy. It was straight IRA propaganda, and they are very good at that.

They were even better at it after Bloody Sunday. On 30 January 1972, the British army, and the Paras in particular, handed the terrorists material for the kind of propaganda coup they could only ever have dreamed of. Their dreams became our nightmares, however, all wrapped up in one terrible tragedy. When the firing stopped, twenty-six civil-rights marchers – not terrorists – had been shot. Thirteen of them were dead, and a woman would later die of her wounds in hospital.

Even before these events, however, I had already decided to leave the Parachute Regiment, and to apply for selection by the SAS. True, I was proud of my regiment, and proud of what I had achieved in it, yet for all that I had become disillusioned with the red beret. There was too much bullshit for my liking. I wanted to join the SAS, where bullshit took a back seat to actual soldiering. The selection course is notoriously hard, but I intended to give it my very best shot. Beyond that, however, I had already decided that if the SAS wouldn't have me, then I would quit the British Army.

Because of the killings in Londonderry on that Sunday, some Paras were soon afterwards ordered home. As we left our barracks for the drive to the airport and the flight to the mainland, the cookhouse radio was playing Roy Orbison's song 'It's Over'. But for the Paras – indeed, for all those involved – it was not over, and never will be. Bloody Sunday will always be there, haunting a great British regiment. For ever.

Chapter Four

IT was not the warmest welcoming speech that I had ever heard. But when the Selection Officer of 22 Special Air Service Regiment had finished speaking, none of us was in any doubt about where we stood.

It was a sunny Monday morning in August 1972, and I was one of 120 servicemen who had signed up for Selection – the chance of winning a place in the SAS. We had all been waiting expectantly in the Blue Briefing Room at the Regiment's headquarters, Bradbury Lines in Hereford,* when a giant of a man with thick red hair had suddenly swept into the room and bounded up on to the small stage that stood at one end. The Captain had arrived.

'Welcome to Hereford', he said. He spoke with an educated Highland accent. 'It's good to see that you've all arrived here.' He paused, then added, 'Take a good look at one another. Because, in most cases, it will be the last you ever see of each other.

'I can assure you that, even though there are a hundred and twenty of you now, at the end of this Selection there will be no more than a handful left. And for those of you who are left, the Regiment takes you in, chews you up and spits you out.'

Another pause for effect, before he added, 'And we don't give a fuck.' Then he just walked off the stage and out of the room.

Around the briefing room, half-baked grins disappeared from several faces, and candidates slyly looked at each other, trying to weigh their own and each other's chances of surviving the world's toughest military testing ground.

I had left the Parachute Regiment depot in Aldershot the previous week with the farewell words of the company sergeant-major still rattling around in my head. He was a man who had seen too many trained paratroopers leave for SAS Selection. He didn't like Selection, and he didn't like the SAS because they took his men. Above all, he didn't like me, because I had applied to win a place in the Regiment.

* Now Stirling Lines, having been renamed in honour of the Regiment's founder, the late Lieutenant-Colonel Sir David Stirling.

'If you mess up, don't bother coming back here,' he had shouted at me as I left for Hereford. Thanks a lot, I'd thought. As it happened, I had no intention of going back to the Parachute Regiment because, no matter what they threw at me, I was determined that I was going to pass Selection. So far as I was concerned, the CSM could go and screw himself.

After the Selection Officer's precipitate departure, his place on the Blue Room stage was taken, in rapid succession, by the various instructors from the Regiment's Training Wing. They made it abundantly clear that they were going to be watching our performance like ravening wolves circling a potential victim, maintaining a never-ending lookout for the slightest sign of weakness.

On our arrival at Bradbury Lines, we had been accommodated in four wooden huts, and had spent an anxious night wondering what the next day would bring. We found out soon enough. Immediately after those Monday morning briefings, we were all split into different groups. Our weapon-handling capabilities were assessed. Regardless of a candidate's soldiering experience or his weapons skills, the instructors ran their own rule over them to assess their usefulness according to the dictates of the SAS – not those of any other regiment.

What this meant in practice is that they were a good deal more critical than instructors in other units. None the less, if they felt that a man could be trained, then he would get the finest possible tuition in weaponry, navigation and map reading, sabotage and demolition, intelligence-gathering, and learning how to work in four-man patrols deep behind enemy lines. Above all, he would be taught to survive against enormous odds.

After that first morning, we were put into squads for the Selection process. The candidates were mainly from the Paras or the infantry. As with any such group, there were all sorts of guys trying to pass for all sorts of reasons, but the common denominator was that we all ended up with 55-pound bergens on our backs while the instructors tried to break us.

Because, between application and final Selection, there is a long slog ahead, most of it uphill, literally as well as metaphorically. By the end, you feel as though you have walked every inch wearing chains. After two weeks of a gruelling regime, which begins with a standard battle-fitness test and ends with seemingly endless ascents and descents of rugged Welsh mountains in all sorts of weather, we had lost half the hopefuls – and we were not even halfway through the course.

Any man aged between twenty-one and thirty-two and serving in the British armed forces or one of the two Territorial Army units of the SAS, is eligible to apply to the Regiment for Selection. If he meets those criteria, the sole remaining proviso is that he must have at least thirty-six months still to serve. Once accepted, all he has to do then is pass the course, although that is a great deal easier said than done. Even so, there has been a great deal of rubbish written about Selection, much of it by people who passed and want to make themselves out, wrongly, to be supermen. For although it is the toughest human proving ground in the world, Selection is not just about muscle and brawn, or even sheer endurance. It is a battle for a man's mind, and a test of his will to win.

On one occasion during Exercise Sickener – so called because it is designed to make candidates sick – we had spent the day going up and down those Welsh hills like yo-yos. Having arrived at the top of one, we were then ordered to go down again carrying a five-gallon jerry can, which we were to fill with water from a river at the foot of the hill. I had a tin mug hooked on my webbing belt, and I used this to fill the jerry can, since it's impossible to fill one in the shallow, fast-flowing Welsh streams by immersing it. It's a slow and laborious process. When full, the can weighs around 50 pounds. I lugged it back up the hill, still carrying my weapon – a self-loading rifle (SLR), the standard British Army infantry weapon of the day – and with the weight of the bergen on my back. At the top of the hill the instructors were waiting. 'Now empty it out and go back and do it again,' they said. I watched guys hand in their jerry cans after the first run, saying they'd had enough. We never saw them again. They were immediately 'RTU-ed' (returned to unit), catching the next train out from the now famous Platform 2 at Hereford station.

When we started Selection there were twenty men in each squad. The instructors make bets with each other as to how many men they can get rid of in three days. They stick with you, trying to rattle you, telling you that you have no chance of passing the course. Why not pack it in now, they say, because they are going to see to it that you fail.

Once they have cracked a man and he's quit trying and shuffled off to the truck, the first stage of his ignominious departure back to his unit, they move on to their next target and start work on him. One of them told me, 'Right, Ratcliffe, you're next to fail.' To some candidates, however, the instructors don't even have to say a word. These just quit of their own accord. Whatever they may have thought Selection was going to be like, it has turned out to be immeasurably worse. They don't want to know any more, with the result that they come to view the initials 'RTU' with something approaching relief.

So the thinning-out process continued relentlessly. On one occasion our instructors deliberately deprived us of sleep for three days and nights. They had us pitch our bivouac tents at the base of the great concrete spillways of a huge dam in the remote Elan Valley in mid-Wales, some 45 miles north-west of Hereford. Water thundered incessantly down the channels, and it was nearly impossible to sleep because of the constant roar of the torrent. As exhausted and battered as we were from all the frigging around during the day, we eventually dozed off, only to be awakened in the middle of the night. Over the roar of the dam run-off, the instructors shouted, 'OK! Get your kit on. Let's go, let's go!' And we were off on a fast march over the hill and back again, returning wearily to our bivouac area. Then, when they decided that we'd settled down, they woke us again and sent us out on a march like the one we'd just finished.

By first light we were up again and marching over more hills. The SAS does not run, except when there is good reason to hurry – we march. And we march fast. So, to see if we had it in us, if we had the stamina and the willpower needed to make it through Selection, we marched and marched and marched, over or through any obstacle. We slithered through mud and stumbled over ankle-breaking rocks, climbed treacherous stone walls and risked tetanus, or worse, on rusty barbed wire. We waded, chest deep, through icy water. In the Brecon Beacons, where much of the course takes place, even August suns rarely last long enough to take the chill from the lakes and reservoirs. The water always seemed to be freezing to me. But I was damned if I was going to give in.

Sometimes we'd finish a march and find the trucks waiting for us. They looked incredibly inviting, with their big canvas canopies to keep out the wind and the almost constantly pouring rain. We would be told to get in and everybody would breathe a secret sigh of relief. The torture was over. We were getting a ride, back to camp, with luck – to warmth and light and hot food and, best of all, sleep.

But sometimes, too, an instructor would blow away our hopes. Once, just after we'd settled gratefully in the truck, one of the DS bellowed, 'Right, everybody. Get back off the trucks. We're going to march across the mountain for another twenty clicks [kilometres].'

Without a murmur, because you dared not let them see that they were getting to you, we shouldered our bergens. Then, grabbing our weapons, we climbed off the tailgate and back out into the pouring rain. We had only marched about two hundred yards when one of the guys said, 'Shit to this. I've had enough.' There and then he packed it in. Leaving him behind, we marched another couple of hundred yards. Then the instructor shouted, 'OK, lads. Stop. You've finished. You can get back on to the trucks.'

We had been conned. The guy who had quit had only needed to walk for another two hundred yards and he'd have been OK. He didn't know that, however, and had paid the price – instantly RTU-ed. As for the rest of us, we had shown that we had been willing to go on for 20 kilometres. The instructors' had told them what they wanted to know: that the man who gave up was not the sort of soldier the Regiment wanted. What they were looking for was someone who could hack an arduous situation. So that if you were humping ammunition up steep hills or through thick jungle, and even though you were utterly exhausted or just thoroughly fed up, you could still handle it mentally as well as physically. They were not looking for supermen – just people whose minds could triumph over their flagging bodies, however tough the conditions.

I would be willing to bet, however, that instructors were meaner in my day than is the case now. They would, for instance, sometimes wake us at two o'clock in the morning, load us into trucks and dump us out on the Welsh mountains while they tried to break us. Relentlessly, they would march us for miles up and down hills. They would wait for us to climb back up some hill, then send us down again. 'Do it again. Do it again,' was all they said. That was all we heard, until we thought we'd go crazy. Which is precisely the idea. The instructors want you to quit. And they know from experience that if they ride men hard enough, most of them will say, 'Stuff this for a game of soldiers. I'm chucking it in.' These, of course, are not the men the SAS is looking for.

Furthermore, under the Selection rules anyone can quit, at any time. There is no stain on a man's military record for his having failed. A candidate has only to say that he has had enough and there is always a truck near by, waiting to take him back to Hereford, from where he will make his way back to his unit to resume service where he left off. He will not be seen again by his fellow candidates when, eventually, they arrive themselves back at the barracks, for by then he will either be waiting for a train on Platform 2 at Hereford station, or already long gone.

As they marched us in the pouring rain, I kept thanking God that it was August and not January, when the Welsh hills would have been covered in snow. Not that the kinder weather hampered the instructors, for they delighted in breaking men individually. One corporal told me, 'You're going. You're not going to pass.' I pulled myself up from the mud and told him, 'No I'm not. I'm staying.' So it went on, as they tried again and again to grind us down.

Although, deep down, the instructors know whether or not they have a good squad, they still take bets on how many they will fail. Some guys on my Selection course had no chance, but, as arrogant as it may seem to say so, I knew my chances were better than even. I put my heart and soul into it. No bastard was going to grind me down. For me, failure was never an option, and I had a slight advantage in some respects – I had already been through Para training.

It is not surprising that the SAS draws 60 per cent of its men from the Parachute Regiment, for there is no doubt that being a Para gives a man a bit of an edge. Their own training has well fitted paratroopers to being pushed harder and harder, and as often as not when other men drop out, the Paras are still there, rock solid and reliable. Five other Paras came with me from Aldershot – and we all passed Selection.

When it came to the final part of Selection, Test Week – every SAS candidate's greatest trial – we had six marches to complete, each of them with a heavy bergen on our backs as well as our weapons and belt kit. The bergen started at 35 pounds, and its weight was increased each day until, for the final endurance march, it was up to 60 pounds. The packs were weighed at the start of the march and weighed again at the end; sometimes, to surprise us, the instructors would weigh our packs in the middle of a march. And if a man's bergen didn't weigh as much as when he had started out – because he'd junked some of the make-weight rocks and bricks along the way – he was off Selection. Binned immediately.

I never used my water bottles. When I came to a stream, I found it easier to use the tin mug hanging on my belt to scoop up a cup or two of water. If I needed a piss, I would always do so away from the stream where I was, so as to be certain not to contaminate the water. I never ever suffered from drinking stream water, and certainly it was better than carrying all the extra weight of water bottles on my belt kit for miles and miles.

Selection rules were tough, as I've said, and never more so than during Test Week. No one cuts you any slack. You were, for instance, meant to complete each march within a set time. Being late, even by a few seconds, at the finish of any two of the marches meant automatic failure. What made this even more difficult was that no one told you how long each march was supposed to take. A few hours later, those candidates who had dropped out or been binned would be RTU-ed and left waiting for a train and a lonely return to their units. In their private den, the instructors would smile and run a red marker pen across the mugshot of the failed candidate pinned up on the office wall. Slip up on Selection and you were history – or rather, less than history, since nobody would even remember your name twelve hours later.

The worst marches both involved Pen-y-fan, a fearsome hill, rising to 2,908 feet and dominating the Brecon Beacons, the Welsh mountains where the SAS does much of its training, and which lie some thirty miles south-west of Hereford. The first march – deceptively christened the 'Point-to-Point' by gloating instructors – involved making three separate ascents from the base to the peak of Pen-y-fan, all this counting as one march. It was common knowledge that we were expected to complete the Point-to-Point in less than six hours.

The finale of the body-breaking six days that made up Test Week was a gut-twisting, 46-mile endurance march covering most of the ground we had become familiar with in the previous foot-slogging tests. Again, we knew that the time limit was twenty hours, which meant that on downhill stretches we had to maintain a sort of semi-trot in order to beat the deadline. And with 60-pound bergens on our backs, pain and exhaustion soon dominated our days.

Indeed, pain was a constant companion during Selection, reaching new peaks during Test Week, so that if some part of your body stopped hurting, you wondered if it had dropped off. Each day the aches grew worse and the pain was no longer something that came in waves, but a continuous agony. Webbing cut deep grooves into the skin, and the canvas strap at the base of my bergen chafed until my back became one great joined-up bruise with patches of flesh rubbed raw and bleeding. Salty sweat ran down from my shoulder blades and into the wounds, leaving me feeling as though fire ants were stripping my flesh.

At night, we painted gentian violet on to our wounds, although that was not much more than a damage-limitation exercise. The sores and cuts never really had time to scab over properly before, next day, the crusts would be broken open and the suppurating flesh would begin to weep again. What was more, most of the wounds turned septic. But although the damage was painful, in your heart you knew that it wouldn't kill you. So you forced yourself onward. Like the sound of a railway carriage crossing a set of points, one phrase tapped out a continuous rhythm in my head: 'Never-give-up . . . never-give-up . . .

never-give-up', until I doubt whether I would have been able to stop before the finish even if I had been ordered to do so.

I got through. I survived Test Week, which meant that there was a fair chance that I would succeed in passing Selection. But though my determination was stronger than ever, I knew that I would only have to fall foul of an instructor who needed to win a bet to be slung out on my ear. The failure rate in Test Week had been 90 per cent. Of the original 120 candidates, there was only a handful of us left. Those of us who had made it were given forty-eight hours' leave and told to report back to Hereford for first parade on the Monday morning, when we would start fourteen weeks' Continuation training. The Regiment was not ready to take us in yet. Not by a long chalk.

While it is easy for an instructor to see when a guy can't hack it during Test Week and the gruelling run-up to it, during Continuation they really have to watch everyone even more closely. For the next fourteen weeks, they have to work out whether a man can really think under pressure, whether he can fit in effectively in a four-man team (the four-man patrol is the basic unit around which the SAS is structured, unlike the rest of the army), or whether he's a loner who might – indeed, almost certainly will – become a hazard to the rest of his team. Perhaps most important, they have to decide whether that smile on his face is real, or whether there lurks beneath it a chronically miserable misfit. The reason is simple: a sense of humour can be a priceless asset when the odds are stacked against you.

Continuation winds up with training in survival techniques and in undergoing interrogation. For Survival, soldiers are not even allowed so much as a penknife, and before the start we were strip-searched in the Blue Room. The instructors were determined that we would not have anything with us that might increase our chances of surviving undetected in the wilds. During these exercises, half a battalion of infantry and fifty off-duty policemen, some with dogs, are searching for you – and if they don't find you, the helicopters will. The odds are heavily stacked against evading capture for more than an hour or two, but sometimes all you need to stay free that bit longer than the rest is the sense to rely on human nature and on people not spotting the obvious.

I remember, while on Selection, being put into a fenced area near Hereford that was no more than a mile square. We were told that we were on the run, and that though we had to stay within the fences we were to evade capture for twenty-four hours. Four of us found a man-made hide that had been used by an SAS team for training purposes prior to being sent into no man's land in Eastern Europe to spy on Russian troop movements. The hide was about eight feet square by six feet deep, and had, concealed in its roof, a viewing point into which, if you had one, you could insert a long periscope, allowing you to look out without being seen by anyone outside.

The four of us went inside the hole and closed the camouflaged hatch in the roof. In time, however, the searchers located it, and a soldier with a torch dropped through the hatch and landed on the earth floor. He shone the light in our faces and counted us out loud. 'One, two, three, four. Out!' he ordered. Outside, an Alsatian dog was barking madly as the three men I was with climbed out of the hole, followed by the soldier who'd found us.

But in one wall of the hide there was a small recess, used as a lavatory by soldiers hiding there, the resultant waste then being collected in a polythene bag for disposal later. So, instead of climbing out with the others, I took a chance and slipped into the recess. Above me, I could hear the hunters arguing about how many men had been in the hole. The dog was still barking, and one of the men said, 'But where's the other chap? I'm sure there were four.' He climbed back into the hole and shone his torch around the walls, but in the deep shadows thrown by the torchlight he failed to spot the recess, and so couldn't see me. Climbing back out, he closed the hatch and I heard him say, 'God, that's funny. I could have sworn there were four of them.' He was right, of course. The fourth was still there, and I stayed in that hide for the rest of the twenty-four hours without anyone finding me again. I learned a valuable lesson, too: given nerve and luck, you really can get away with anything.

On the whole, though, those instructors on Survival didn't miss a trick. Every scrap of our clothing was searched for anything we might use to help us – money, matches, even knives. They peered into our ears and our hair, and even looked up our backsides – which is, I suppose, one of the penalties of being an instructor. Satisfied that we had nothing going for us, they issued us with heavy old Second World War battledress for the exercise. Our footwear was carefully scrutinized because, in the past, people had been known to hide money in recesses they had cut in the soles or heels of their boots. And, since there were shops in the area of Wales where they were going to dump us, if we'd had money we could have bought materials to help us evade capture – like food, for instance.

We left Hereford on a Sunday afternoon in a 3-ton truck. They dropped us off in four-man patrols in different areas and we were given a place at which we were to rendezvous – if we managed to escape detection and capture. The instructor gave me a dead squirrel, a few potatoes and an empty bean can with a length of string for a handle, in which we were supposed to boil any food. Which was, of course, nonsense, since we had no matches and, as usual, it was pouring with rain. Furthermore, even if I had managed to light a fire in that countryside, the smoke would have been seen from miles away. I would have been found before I'd had time to get thoroughly wet.

The hunters are looking for you right from the moment you get off the truck. But whether you stay undetected for as long as you are meant to, or get spotted and picked up earlier, you know you are going to face the Interrogation phase of the exercise.

As a prisoner of war, the only pieces of information you are permitted to give your captors are the 'Big Four': your name, rank, army number and date of birth. We were taught never to say 'Yes' to anything, and never to say 'No', so that, in answer to the question 'Is this your name?', for instance, we would answer 'That is my name' or 'That is not my name'. The reason for this is because an enemy can use your one-word affirmatives and negatives from a recorded interrogation in a remastered tape or video to make it appear that you are confessing to them.

When it came to the Interrogation exercise, each of us was dragged into a room, stripped naked and blindfolded. Then the interrogating crew began to make remarks about the size of a man's prick or the shape of his balls, or demanded to know whether he masturbated, the aim being to humiliate the prisoner. I found it curiously easy to ignore their gibes, simply by sticking to the Big Four in answer to any direct questions.

After some time I was taken outside and made to lean against a wall at an angle of 45 degrees with my fingers spread wide against the bricks and my legs apart. Extra loud 'white noise' – electronically generated sounds resembling continuous hissing and humming – was then played through speakers at a very high volume, and a rubber pouch containing rancid, horribly stinking, tinned army-issue cheese was hung under my nose. I reckon I spent three hours at a time like that. From time to time they poured buckets of water over my head so that I was soaked and cold. If a man smoked, as I did at the time, they blew cigarette smoke in his face, in an attempt to weaken his resolve.

Whatever the discomfort, however, the reality is that, unlike a genuine enemy, they can only hold you for twenty-four hours; more tellingly, they are only allowed to interrogate you for a total of eight hours out of the twenty-four. As would not be the case if you were captured by a real enemy, you know how long you will have to endure before it will all stop. Apart from that knowledge, the fear factor is the other main element missing from the Interrogation exercise, for the simple reason that you know that your 'captors' are not going to torture you as a genuine enemy might – and, in the case of several SAS soldiers captured during the Gulf War, did. You only have to remain calm and use your mind to shut out the insults and to overcome the cramp and the cold and the discomfort. In short, you can fool the interrogators. Besides, after all a man has been through during the rest of Selection, Interrogation is like a walk in the park.

Throughout the exercise, you can't help noticing a number of people wandering about wearing white armbands. These are genuine umpires, and you know that they are not out to trick you into giving away information; they will also give straight answers to direct questions. This useful piece of information was to stand me in good stead towards the end of Interrogation. I was being taken down from the wall at the finish when I noticed an officer with a white armband walking around drinking a cup of something steaming. So I asked him the time, and he told me, 'Five to three – in the morning.' I was then taken back to the interrogation room where I found waiting for me the Selection Officer – he of the disheartening speech of welcome – and a colonel from the Joint Services Intelligence Wing (JSIW). At their direction I sat on a hard chair, waiting to see what would happen. As it turned out, the first question the colonel asked me was what time I thought it was.

'Five to three, sir!' I shouted.

He looked at the Selection Officer for a moment, and then said in wonderment, 'Did you hear that? Bloody marvellous. Bloody marvellous. Well done.' He must have thought that during the hours I'd spent leaning against that wall I had been counting off the seconds. Sadly, he didn't think it was so bloody marvellous when I explained that I'd just asked the same question of one of the umpires.

Later, during a debriefing before we were taken away and given something to eat, they asked us what we had thought of the ordeal. I gave a diplomatic answer, but in fact I was perfectly well aware that Interrogation is not a tough test. If I had really been captured and interrogated by a genuine enemy, I would not have known what was coming next, and would almost certainly have been subjected to far more brutal physical abuse, possibly over a period of weeks. In an exercise, however, you know that the experts grilling you are not allowed to shoot you, or pull out your fingernails, or beat you up, or inject you with drugs, or any of the thousands of other hideous tortures of which so many regimes are capable. Indeed, sleep deprivation is probably the harshest thing you have to face during Interrogation.

Yet you need to be subjected to that for far longer than they can manage before your mind starts slipping the clutch and you begin to hallucinate. Above all, as I have said, the fear factor, and especially the fear of the unknown, was missing – and it still is on the Selection exercises they do today.

However necessary it may be to train soldiers to withstand an enemy's attempts to extract information, I believe that the whole interrogation exercise is both antiquated and deeply flawed. We were trained using film shot during the Korean War, which had ended nearly twenty years earlier. Whatever the effectiveness of the mainly Chinese interrogators in their often brutal treatment of Allied PoWs during that war, the fact is that there are drugs available today that will make a prisoner tell his captors whatever they want to know a sight faster than if they were to gouge out his eyes. As a result, training men in ways of limiting the information they give an enemy while under the influence of drugs should be of paramount importance. It may be, of course, that for medical or scientific reasons this is not possible. Nevertheless, it should certainly be considered.

All in all, I have to say that I regard the Interrogation part of Selection as little more than a farce. While it is moderately useful in preparing a soldier for some of the indignities he might suffer as a PoW, and in giving him some practice in answering direct questions with the Big Four, the fact that he knows he has only to hang on for, at most, twenty-four hours, and that the DS cannot subject him to the kind of physical torture an enemy might apply, severely limits its value.

Interrogation ends Selection. Mine finished in the early hours of Sunday. Monday morning saw the survivors – those who had passed – assembled in one room of the Training Wing building. We didn't need to use the Blue Briefing Room. There were not enough of us left to have filled one corner.

Once assembled, we were told we had passed and that the commanding officer of 22 SAS, the then Colonel Peter de la Billière, known throughout the Regiment as 'DLB', would be arriving shortly to present us with our berets. He walked into the room and we all stood. He then went to each of us, handing us our sand-coloured berets and shaking our hands with a brief 'Well done'. He was not much of an orator. Only later would we learn that he was a great soldier, and a brilliant tactician with a superb military brain.

One hundred and twenty men had started out on Selection back in August. Eleven of us had got through. And I was one of them. I was in the SAS. Although I was careful not to let anyone see it, it was the proudest moment of my life. It remains so to this day.

There was an amusing sequel to my transfer from the Paras to the SAS. In June 1972, while still with 1 Para, I was stationed at Bruneval Barracks in Aldershot, and was spending a lot of my time training for SAS Selection, which I was due to attend in just two months. A Para instructor who was also going on Selection and who was based just down the road in Browning Barracks, told me that he had a spare Fablon-covered map of the Brecon Beacons, and offered to lend it to me. This was good news, since getting hold of a decent map in those days was extremely difficult, so I walked down to Browning Barracks during my NAAFI break to pick up the map.

The Para battalions identify themselves from each other with different-coloured lanyards, which are wrapped around the left shoulder and have a knife attached to the free end, which is tucked into the tunic or shirt pocket. The colours are red, blue and green, representing 1, 2 and 3 Para respectively, while members of Depot Para wear a lanyard made up of all three colours. Having collected the map, I was just leaving Browning Barracks when a great booming voice roared at me, 'Hey, you! Hey! YOU!'

'Fuck!' was my immediate thought, for this was the voice of the RSM, Nobby Arnold, a legend in the Paras, and a man to be feared and avoided at all costs. I turned round at once, marched smartly up to him and halted, bringing my right leg up to my waist and driving it immediately into the ground.

'Sir!' I said, looking rigidly ahead of me.

Nobby was about six foot three with a build to match. A former heavyweight boxer with the Paras, his nose had taken some punishment over the years so that when he spoke there was a nasal tone in his voice.

'What are you doing in my camp?' he demanded, identifying me as being from 1 Para by my red lanyard (he, being Depot, wore the tri-coloured lanyard).

'I've come for a map of the Brecon Beacons, sir.'

'Why do you need a map of the Brecon Beacons?' he replied. 'Are you going on your junior NCO course?'

'No, sir, I'm going on SAS Selection.'

'You're fucking well *what*? You're leaving the finest regiment in the world to go and join that shower?' His tone of disbelief and contempt sounded even more threatening because of the nasal whine in his voice.

'Yes, sir.'

'Well, listen to me, son, the next time you come into my camp you knock on my door and say, "Excuse me, sir, can I come into your camp?" and I will say, "Yes." Do you understand?'

'Yes, sir.'

'Now march away.'

I turned to my right, once again banging my right foot hard to the ground, and walked away. At once there came another scream from the RSM.

'I said MARCH! What you need is more drill. Now get on that square.'

I put down my map and marched out on to the barrack square, with Nobby hard on my heels. For an hour he drilled me in quick time – 'Left, right, left, right, left, right, mark time, left, right, left, right, about turn!' – on and on it went until the sweat was pouring off me. Eventually the relentless stream of orders and the tireless nasal voice stopped, and he let me go. Thankfully, I picked up my map and marched, my arms swinging, in the direction of my barracks – or at least until I was out of the RSM's sight.

When I returned, the platoon sergeant demanded to know where I'd been.

'I've been doing drill with the RSM of Depot,' I replied.

'Don't get funny with me,' he said. 'Where have you been?'

'I've just told you. I've been doing drill with the RSM.'

He still didn't believe me. 'All right ' he said, 'I'm going to check your story and if you're lying, I'm going to have you.' And with that he went to the Company Office and rang the RSM.

'Oh, good morning, sir. My name is Sergeant Hutchinson, platoon sergeant of Machine-Gun Platoon, 1 Para. Have you been drilling one of my soldiers, sir?'

'Yes, I fucking well 'ave, Sergeant,' Nobby bellowed down the phone, 'and while you're at it, you can get your arse down 'ere at lunchtime, because you're not doing your job properly.'

The conversation was overheard by the company clerk, who

immediately informed the platoon. This was too good to miss, so at lunchtime we went down to Depot, found a strategic location from which we could see without being seen ourselves, and watched our platoon sergeant being drilled by RSM Nobby Arnold. He didn't say a word when he got back, but we all knew where he'd been.

Six months later, having passed Selection and left the Paras, I was back in Aldershot to attend the funeral of the second-in-command of the SAS, who had sadly been killed in France. After the ceremony we went to the Para Depot for lunch, and later congregated around the coach that was to take us back to Hereford. Standing there in my best uniform (Number 2 dress) and SAS beret, I suddenly saw out of the corner of my eye the large, immaculately turned-out figure of RSM Nobby Arnold. Noticing that the RSM was staring at me, this rough, tough SAS soldier immediately sought refuge behind the coach. Nobby must have spotted the move and gone the other way, for he ambushed me as I crept along. I didn't know what to expect, but he put his arm round my shoulder and said, 'Do you remember me, son?'

'Yes, sir,' I replied.

'Glad to see you made it,' he said, and gave me an approving punch on the arm before walking away.

Chapter Five

As almost all the world knows nowadays, there are four squadrons in 22 Special Air Service Regiment, and four troops in each squadron: Air, Boat, Mountain and Mobility Troops. Their titles are pretty much self-explanatory, but there are refinements within their areas of specialization that ought to be mentioned.

Air Troop are the free-fall parachuting experts. They specialize in high-altitude, low-opening (HALO) descents, an effective means of arriving in their designated area of operations without the enemy on the ground being alerted by the presence of a low-flying aircraft. At night, they will leave the aircraft at 25,000 feet and breathe oxygen from cylinders on their chest packs, only opening their parachutes when they are 4,000 feet above the ground. During a daylight jump from the same altitude they will shave another 1,000 feet off the height at which they open their chutes, bringing them in from around 3,000 feet. From that height they are down and in position before an enemy, even assuming he has seen them, has had time to blink. When all four troops of a squadron are jumping at night, Air Troop jump at lower altitude, say around 13,000 feet. They will then mark out the landing strip for the squadron while the pilot circles. All badged members of the SAS are trained parachutists, but the Air Troops are the experts. Soldiers are, however, expected to learn all the disciplines, so that no one will find himself at a loss working with a troop that specializes in something other than his own area of expertise.

Boat Troop's role is mainly that of getting a squadron of men ashore from surface ships, using Gemini rubber inflatables powered by outboard motors. They are all expert scuba divers and go sub-surface for reconnaissance work. Among them are a number of highly skilled underwater demolition men; they have to be extremely skilful, because explosions underwater are the most dangerous of all.

Mobility Troop use specially adapted long-wheelbase Land Rovers which fairly bristle with weaponry. These are supplemented by a number of motorcycles, which are used for reconnaissance, communication between vehicles on the move, and to scout suitable routes for the troop or squadron. Every member of the troop has to be able to ride a motorcycle as well as drive a Land Rover, and all have some training as mechanics. But among the men of Mobility Troop are skilled mechanics who have completed special training enabling them to strip and repair the Land Rovers and bikes in the most appalling situations. No matter where, no matter what the problem, these guys can fix it, by feel and in pitch dark, if necessary. Beyond that, everyone is trained in driving or riding, for long periods if needed, in terrain and conditions that would defeat a mule, and also in driving at night using passive night goggles (PNGs), since an SAS patrol on a clandestine mission cannot use lights.

One of the main roles of Mountain Troop is to get an entire squadron up a cliff or other obstacle by means of a fixed climb. They go first, free climbing the cliff or rockface and fixing clamps and rope-anchor points into the surface so that the squadron can follow. Training on Mount Everest and other peaks in the Himalayas, in the high Andes of South America and the Swiss and French Alps, they are all expert mountaineers and skiers. They are taught to operate in the very worst of weather conditions, and during whiteouts will burrow into deep snow holes for survival until the blizzard has passed. Some of them took part in the 1976 British expedition to Everest, and again in the expedition of 1984, during which one member of the Regiment was killed in an avalanche. As will be seen, in the liberation of South Georgia in 1982 D Squadron's Mountain Troop was to be tested to the limit.

Once he has been assigned to a troop, an SAS man tends to stay there. Under certain circumstances, however, a man will cross-train between disciplines, making him double- or even multi-skilled, and thus even more valuable to the Regiment. It should be said, though, that it sometimes doesn't work out that way – as it certainly didn't with me and freefalling.

I was a staff sergeant when I tried it. After two or three hours' ground training, we climbed aboard an RAF C-130, the famous transport aircraft generally known as the Hercules, and one squadron of which is permanently assigned to special operations, mainly by the SAS. At 13,000 feet the tailgate opened and I launched myself up the loading ramp. The RAF instructor who would jump with me was enormously experienced. One minute he was looking into my eyes and giving me the thumbs up, and the next we were both falling through the sky. Then he was suddenly close behind me as we hurtled down, adjusting my leg straps.

I have already confessed that I don't like heights, and I now discovered that I was the worst freefaller ever to take to the sky. I was flipped on to my back so many times I began to feel like a pancake. Whenever I managed to correct my position, I'd start spinning and then be flipped the other way.

Any movement you make with your hands or legs while freefalling at 120 miles an hour causes a reaction. To show you what I mean, if you put your hand out of the sunroof of a car travelling at 80 miles an hour, the wind pressure will slam it backwards against the rear edge of the aperture. Now imagine doing 120 miles an hour – 176 feet per second – with your entire body feeling the force. The slightest movement unbalances you. Though others get the hang of freefalling soon enough – and many of them come to love it – I was never able to sort myself out, with the result that I was completely useless at it.

I did eight jumps in about four days, after which the instructor told me that I was not only a danger to myself, I was a danger to other people in the sky as well. To be honest, his words were music to my ears, because it meant there was not much chance of them ever using me for freefall.

Three years later, during exercises in Jordan, I used to amuse myself by joshing Air Troop about their having to be crazy to like jumping out of aircraft. In return, they poked fun at my almost legendary lack of freefall prowess. It was all good-natured stuff – except that, one day, they suddenly asked me if I was going to jump with them the next morning. They had reckoned that I would say, 'Fuck that for a game of soldiers' and simply walk away. Only I didn't. To their surprise – and mine – I said 'Yes.' I immediately regretted it, but having put my pride on the line, I had no option but to go through with it.

There was worse to come. John, the parachute-jump instructor and himself an expert freefaller, told me that I'd be using a square-shaped parachute for the jump; 'It's all we've got with us,' he said. I had only jumped before using the standard large round chutes. With them you always got a canopy. You might get twists, and they didn't steer very well, but they'd always get you down. The square parachutes were highly steerable, and thus far more useful to men trying to land in a precise location, but if you got twists in the cords you had to cut the chute away by pulling two clips on your shoulders, then go back into freefall and pull your reserve.

Having had all this explained to me by John, I was definitely having second thoughts. Seeing this, he simply said, 'OK. I'll pin you.' What he meant was that, when the time came for me to jump, he would stand on the tailgate of the aircraft with his back to the exit. I would stand facing and holding on to him. Then he would step off and I would fall forward and go into the freefall position. He would therefore be able to keep me stable while I was doing whatever I had to do to try to maintain my position. Then, when we got to 3,500 feet, he would let me go as I pulled the chute, and that would ensure a full canopy.

Once again pride overtook me, however. Grateful as I was for his help, I heard myself saying, 'Tell you what John, why don't I just jump on my own? Otherwise they'll all take the piss out of me. Then you come and pin me straight away and get me stable.' Not really being aware of my utter ineptitude, he agreed, so we went and did a bit of training on the ground for an hour because I hadn't done any freefall for three years.

The next morning, I strapped on my parachute and all the other paraphernalia, wondering, not for the first time, what I'd let myself in for. Air Troop had twelve men jumping that day from 13,000 feet. I was to go first, followed by John and the rest of the guys. After a nervous eternity, the tailgate opened. The red light came on, then green, and I launched myself forward, twisting in the air to get into the right freefall position. But I immediately became unstable. Flipped over and over by the airstream, I tossed every which way as I tried to get stable.

Where the hell was John? He was supposed to be coming to get me. I couldn't see him or anyone else. The ground and the sky whirled upside-down or right-way-up, and I was hurtling towards the earth like a rag doll slung from the roof of a tower block. Terrified? That's a polite understatement for the way I felt. I had an altimeter on my wrist and the bloody thing was clocking off the decreasing height as the earth rushed towards me. Where the hell was John?

Seconds into the jump and I was all over the sky, desperately trying to get stable. It was hopeless, completely beyond my abilities. One second I was dropping head first, the next I was on my back looking towards Heaven. And, at that moment, metaphorically speaking, Heaven seemed far, far too close.

At 4,000 feet I pulled the handle. Bang! The chute opened, the harness slamming into me with a breath-stopping jerk. I'd got a canopy, thank God. I could survive this, I thought, if I didn't try to do anything clever. I told myself just to leave everything alone. Not to touch a thing. To do nothing. Just land.

And I did.

At the debriefing afterwards, the guys said that as soon as I left the tailgate I went so badly unstable that they couldn't get near me. Apparently the whole troop had tried to catch me, but I was dropping like a stone, faster than anyone could manage in controlled freefall. Eventually, however, they did manage to close up, and though I saw no one, one of the troop, Stan, who could 'fly' in freefall like a bird, actually zoomed in and managed to grab me. I didn't see him or feel anything, but it was he who stabilized me. It was then that I pulled the handle, felt the shock as the chute opened and saw the canopy above me. By then Stan had whirled away, and I thought it was just good fortune that had ensured that my parachute had deployed safely. Hearing the others at the debriefing, and reflecting on what might have been, confirmed me in my view that I can do without freefalling. It is a view that I hold to this day.

Soon after being badged, a candidate knows which squadron he is going to, because those are the ones with vacancies. In the case of my intake, five of us had been assigned to D Squadron, which had two vacancies in Mobility Troop and three in Boat Troop. We had been told to sort out among ourselves which troop we wanted to go to. All of us wanted to go into Mobility Troop. Partly we fancied ourselves at the wheel of a heavily armed vehicle, belting across country, but mainly none of us liked the idea of working for most of the time in cold water.

On arrival at D Squadron, we were called, in alphabetical order, into the office of the then squadron commander, Major Bruce Niven. Since my surname begins with R, I was fourth down the list. And naturally, the first two in to see the Boss had expressed a preference for Mobility Troop. Looking up from his paperwork, the OC said, 'Right, Ratcliffe. You're going to Boat Troop.' I'd known this was what he would say, but I thought I'd have a stab at getting him to change his mind. Standing doggedly in front of his desk, I told him somewhat nervously that I'd rather go to Mobility Troop.

'You'll go where there is a vacancy, and the vacancy is in Boat Troop,' was the predictable reply. I didn't move. 'No, sir,' I said, 'I can't stand water.' Major Niven looked at me quizzically and asked if I was scared of water. 'I'm not *scared* of water, sir. It's just that I'm not very confident in it.'

For some reason this must have struck a chord with the OC, with the result that Denis, one of the guys who had been in his office before me, was switched from Mobility and sent to Boat Troop instead of me. So that was how I came to be assigned to Mobility Troop, riding on the Land Rovers while Denis did the swimming. It was a useful lesson in the fact that in the SAS you make your own luck. But although I'd got my way, I'd stitched Denis up, and he never forgave me for it.

When a man is badged into the Regiment, he finds himself in a different career structure. For the first year he will keep the rank he came in with, and is paid accordingly by his previous regiment or unit. After that year, he reverts and becomes a trooper although, as an incentive to stay, he will be paid the same as a corporal in an ordinary unit; as a corporal, he will be paid the same as a sergeant. Thereafter, he cannot attain the rank of sergeant until he has served with the Regiment for a minimum of seven years. Once such men are promoted to sergeant, however, we think of them as the engine room of the SAS, important cogs in the machinery that drives the Regiment forward. But there is a long way to go before they reach that stage of their careers.

At any time in his first four years with the SAS, a man will either be returned to his original unit or fully accepted into the Regiment. This means, in effect, that he has four years in which to prove himself. His assessment papers are signed by his squadron commander and passed to Regimental Headquarters (RHQ), where they are countersigned by the Regimental Sergeant-Major, who adds a pen portrait of the man being assessed. From there, they go to the adjutant, 2IC, and finally to the CO. If they all agree and sign the papers without reservations, then the soldier under assessment will continue in the SAS.

Flaws in a man are usually first spotted by his squadron commander or squadron sergeant-major, mainly because they see him every day of the week. If the flaws are serious – or serious in the Regiment's eyes, at least – he will be called in and told that he is not being recommended for a career in the SAS. Eventually, he will be summoned to the CO's office and informed that he is not up to the standard required and that he is to be returned to his original unit.

When someone is RTU-ed, he is never sent back with a bad report, nor is his unit told why he has been sent back. His record merely shows that his service skills are no longer required by the SAS. The fact is that anyone who undertakes and succeeds in passing Selection is a different breed of man. And he will go back to his regiment not only a far better soldier than the majority of men in it, but one with something to offer that regiment. In other words, because he is not considered suitable for the SAS in no way means that he is not a good soldier. Indeed, if he hadn't been pretty special in the first place, he would never have got as far as he did.

Four years is a long time to be under scrutiny, yet quite often a man's inadequacies don't come to light for many months. His fitness level may drop, for instance, or he may turn into a barrack-room lawyer, although we didn't get many of those. When I joined the Regiment, I was told by one old hand, 'Opinions are like arseholes. We all have one.' Bear in mind, members of the Regiment are universally outspoken and like to voice their opinions, because they all have a tendency to think they are budding generals. (If this seems ludicrous, it's worth noting the number of very senior generals of the British Army in recent years who are ex-SAS.) They are also fond of the sound of their own voices.

Some men are sent back to their units because they simply can't fit in, others because their intellects are not always up to the level necessary for the jobs they are called upon to do. This last sometimes doesn't show up until a man has attended a series of demanding training courses dealing with, say, medical matters, or signalling, or demolition, where the complexity of the subject and the technical expertise demanded can defeat all but the best.

On the subject of the SAS and casualties, when a man is injured, particularly in the field, he has to have the best immediate medical attention available until he can be delivered into the hands of skilled surgeons. The SAS sends men for medical-attachment training to several hospitals around the country that are sympathetic to our medical needs, so allowing us to gain hands-on experience.

Together with a mate called Jock, I was sent on medical attachment to an NHS hospital on the south coast. Arriving on a Monday morning, we reported to the casualty department, where the first person we bumped into was Richard Villars, a former SAS medical officer, later to write a book of his experiences entitled *Knife Edge: Life as a Special Forces Surgeon*. After leaving the service Ricky had become an orthopaedic consultant, and this was also his first day at the hospital. He invited us to his clinic. Donning white coats like real doctors, we sat behind him as he settled at his desk.

After a while there was a knock at the door and an old woman in her eighties shuffled in. Ricky smiled at her and said breezily, 'Come in, old thing, and sit down.' When she was comfortable, he asked, 'So what's wrong with you, old thing?' She immediately launched into a rambling complaint, the gist of which was that her shoulder hurt so much that she could not sleep. Ricky disagreed; it wasn't her shoulder that was hurting, he said, but her neck, whereupon the two of them argued for several minutes about the source of her pain.

He sent her to the X-ray department and an hour later she returned, clutching the plates. Ricky looked at them and remarked, 'Call that a neck, old thing? It's a load of old rubbish.' In order to ease her pain, he said, he was going to have her put in traction. The old woman wasn't giving up yet, however. 'But what about my shoulder?' she demanded. Again he told her it was her neck that was the problem, and yet again to her complete disbelief, as well as her annoyance. As the poor old thing walked out, she shouted, 'Well, you want to try sleeping with my shoulder, then.'

The door banged to behind her. We looked at the newly arrived orthopaedic consultant. He was grinning. 'You bastard!' I said. To which, still grinning, he replied, 'You've got to treat them firmly.'

Such moments aside, I found the medical course fascinating. Most of my time was spent in Casualty, but I watched operations in the theatre, carried out post-mortems – simple pathology – and spent some time on the wards. All the time my knowledge was increasing, and most of it has stayed with me, so that I even know how to amputate a leg. I have to say, though, that I wouldn't let any SAS mate chop my leg off. I'd rather take my chances with gangrene . . .

When, in the summer of 1977, I went with another SAS member for a refresher course at another hospital, this time in the north-west, the consultant in charge wouldn't let us wear white coats, telling us we had to wear green coats instead – like the hospital porters. Being somewhat pissed off with this, we rang the head of the Medical Wing in Hereford and moaned about the ruling. However, he told us not to rock the boat and to go along with the consultant's decision because, apparently, it was difficult to get our men accepted for training at this particular hospital. The result was that although the nursing staff all knew who we were and what we were doing there, a lot of people called us porters, which used to amuse the nurses enormously.

One warm afternoon – the weather here seemed a good deal better than I remembered it from earlier times I had spent in the city – a man who'd fallen and cut his knee arrived in Casualty. With a large wink, the staff nurse told us that it was our turn to deal with the patient. The guy was lying on the bed in a curtained-off cubicle when we walked in wearing our green porter's outfits. The staff nurse turned to my partner and asked, 'Have you done much suturing, Colin?'

Colin, who had a Lancashire accent so broad you could spin cotton from it, shook his head and admitted, 'Well, only on bits of rubber and oranges.' At this the guy with the gashed knee reared up from the bed and screamed, 'I'm not an orange! You're not touching me!'

Two days later, a joiner turned up in Casualty, having put a wood chisel through the palm of his hand. It was my turn to play doctor, so I went into his cubicle with a student nurse called Anne, a stunning blonde. We were doing a no-touch routine. So after scrubbing our hands, we put the equipment pack on its side and opened it with plastic forceps, and from then on didn't touch anything with our bare hands.

I examined the man's wound, feeling along his arm with my gloved hands, at which he said, 'All right, Doc?' I mumbled, 'Er, yep, fine thanks.' In fact, I was so nervous my hands were shaking. Selecting a suture with which to stitch the cut, I left it too short and pulled the thread straight through. In all, I did that five times. When the patient asked how many stitches I'd given him so far, I answered 'None.'

'That's funny,' he said. 'I felt it go through several times all ready.' Eventually, after a dozen attempts, I managed to get three stitches into the guy's palm, which seemed to do the trick. Anne, however, was standing behind him and laughing herself silly at my efforts. Nevertheless, I managed to give him an anti-tetanus injection, bandaged him up and sent him on his way.

The following Saturday night, Colin and I knocked off work at the hospital at about nine o'clock in order to go nightclubbing. We walked into a place called the Minstrel. We were pretty certain we wouldn't know a soul there, and we were right – until suddenly, somebody shouted from the bar, 'All right, Doc?'

It was the joiner from Casualty. He was standing there, waving his bandaged hand at me. He bought me a pint and told all the girls who were with him how I'd stitched his wound and bandaged his hand. Somewhat embarrassed, and slightly anxious that my appreciative ex-patient might discover that I was a long way from being a doctor, or even a qualified paramedic, I muttered something about doing so many, I'd forgotten. Laughing, he said that when he'd told his sister, a local nurse, how his hand had been stitched by a doctor in a green coat, she'd said, 'Don't be daft. Only porters wear green coats.' He thought her comment was hilarious, so if he reads this, he'll know his sister was pretty nearly right all along.

If the courses we were sent on had their funny moments, so too did life in Bradbury Lines. In Mobility Troop, as in the other troops, all the men who didn't have homes in Hereford lived in communal rooms in the long wooden huts that were a feature of the camp, and which predated the Regiment's arrival. The only privacy was afforded by lockers separating the beds.

One night I and a friend of mine, invariably known as 'Jimmy' after a famous disc jockey, were asleep in our beds when the door opened and in tiptoed Taff, another friend who had passed Selection with me. Despite his attempts at silence he woke us, partly because it was obvious he was not alone. He'd smuggled a woman into the camp and, once safely in, had brought her into our hut. In the semi-darkness, and because of the lockers, she couldn't see that we were sleeping in the same room.

They lay on his bed and he asked her what turned her on. Keeping very quiet, Jimmy and I listened in fascination as she told him, and within minutes they were hard at it. The pair of them were well away and pretty oblivious to their surroundings, but when we heard Taff tell her not to speak with her mouth full, we two listeners couldn't help but let out a couple of suppressed giggles.

At once she stopped whatever she was doing, anxiously whispering, 'What's that noise?' Taff told her that there was a budgie in the corner, and asked her to get on with what she'd been doing when she left off. They were at it most of the night, which just goes to show that all that bloody marching doesn't necessarily leave a man incapable of further physical effort . . .

Even ignoring such incidents, our daily routine was pretty informal, and a far cry from the drill and bull of the Paras. Each morning the troop sergeants appeared and we would all assemble in the Interest Room. We'd have a squadron meeting, which we called 'prayers', and then, if nothing was happening – that is, there were no courses, exercises or operations in which we were involved or which we were planning – then the rest of the day was ours.

In those days, soon after I first joined the SAS, we might finish work by ten in the morning, which left us with periods we called 'prime time'. Those who lived away from the camp could go home, and any of us could go out and enjoy ourselves, although we were not permitted to take ourselves out of reach of the camp.

I remember returning on a Monday evening in June from my first tour on Operation Storm in Dhofar. We had been away for five months. As the coach brought us down Callow Hill on the road from Ross-on-Wye, we suddenly saw the cathedral and the city of Hereford spread out below us. It was a beautiful sight, and a delight to eyes that had seen nothing but heat haze, dust devils, sand and barren rock for six months. It meant we were coming home, home to the place we had missed so much, and had looked forward so greatly to seeing again.

It would be wrong, however, to give the impression that service in the SAS of the early 1970s consisted mainly of loafing around between operations. In those days, when we weren't enjoying 'prime time', our lives were all 'Go, go, go!' No sooner had we arrived in the camp from Dhofar and dumped our kit, than we streamed down into the town for a night's drinking. Yet by 4 am next morning, hangovers or not, we were on a coach heading for South Cerney, near Cirencester, where we were parachuting. Two days after that, we flew off on exercise to Greece. Our lives settled into a kind of varied round of exercises, courses, Regimental business, operations and 'prime time', and most of us never really knew from week to week what we'd be doing next.

Although I had met the troop commander, Adam, I hadn't actually soldiered with him because we had been in a split location in Dhofar. He proved to be an exceptionally nice guy. As I talked with him at South Cerney, he told me that I was going to be in his patrol during the exercise in Greece, so that he could have a good look at me and see what I was like. I didn't know it then, but the truth was that without his glasses he probably couldn't have seen me at all.

We parachuted in to Greece, and began the exercise in blistering heat. All day we lay up in concealed positions, moving only at night. Before our first night move Adam came to me and said, 'Billy, I want you to be lead scout and take a bearing to the railway line. We'll cross the line, which runs due north, and then I want you to go north-west to the road. Once there, we'll take another bearing.'

I said, 'OK, Boss,' and went off to ready my kit. In the patrol was a big Southern Irishman we called 'The Ditch', on account of the way he kept running Land Rovers into ditches. He could drink thirty bottles of Guinness a night without falling down, and still carry on the next day as if nothing unusual had happened. He must have had the constitution of an ox, although he was not the fittest man I'd ever met. All he seemed to do was drink and smoke. Three years later, however, he suddenly took up running and became a fantastic marathon runner. We couldn't believe that he'd ever stop smoking. He was a good soldier and a decent bloke, but if driving Land Rovers wasn't his long suit, neither was navigation, as we were shortly to learn.

The order of march was myself, Adam, The Ditch, two Greek soldiers who were attached to us, and finally Lance, a character to rival The Ditch, though in a completely different way, and who had saved our lives in Dhofar. Once night fell, we prepared to move. Using the North Star, I took a rough bearing on a landscape feature in the distance and led off. It took about forty minutes to get to the railway line, and once we had crossed it I readjusted north-west and moved off again.

We'd been going for about an hour when Adam made a clicking noise to indicate that we would take five minutes' rest by a big tree up ahead. I stopped there and Adam came up to the tree, then there was a long gap before the two Greeks arrived, followed by Lance. In the distance we could hear The Ditch grunting.

I sat down. Eventually, groaning and wheezing The Ditch came up – and immediately called me a cunt. When I asked him what was wrong, he almost exploded. 'What's wrong? What's *wrong*? This isn't a fucking Grand Prix. Slow down and use your compass.' So I told him that I was navigating by the North Star, at which he went barmy. 'Using the North Star? You daft cunt. It moves.'

At this point Adam said, 'Oh, Ditch. The North Star doesn't move. I use it myself.' But The Ditch wasn't having any of it. 'Listen here, Boss,' he said, 'I'm astronav-trained, and I'm telling you the North Star moves.' We couldn't convince him, and the argument ended when we moved out a few minutes later. It is a fact, however, that although the earth rotates, the North Star does not move – which is why it's so useful for navigation.

The Ditch was only one of the somewhat larger-than-life characters in D Squadron's Mobility Troop, but such people could be found throughout the SAS. In G Squadron, for instance, there was a sergeant-major from Southern Ireland called Mick whose ways were famous throughout the Regiment. One day, as he sat at his desk, a young signaller came in and asked if he could have a word. The squadron was about to depart for an exercise in Norway and Mick was up to his tonsils in paperwork. 'What do you want?' he asked, his shortness not much mitigated by his rich Irish brogue. Whereupon the signaller nervously told him that he couldn't go to Norway because his wife had left him.

Mick simply stared at the poor man, and then said, 'Listen. I've got sixty guys in that room who would give their right arm to be in your position. Now fuck off and consider yourself lucky.'

Before the squadron left for Norway, Mick went ahead of them, as a sergeant-major does, to get things ready and running smoothly for the main body on arrival. A few days later the C-130 transporting the rest of G Squadron landed at Bergen on the Norwegian coast and the lads all got off and climbed into the coach that was to take them to the exercise location. As they settled down, Mick climbed aboard and addressed the men. 'Listen up, youse spunkbags' – he always called everybody spunkbags, though he didn't mean any harm by it – 'the drive will take us three hours and we are going to stop halfway for a cup of coffee and a piss. Any questions?' At which the young – and very naive – signaller whose wife had left him put up his hand.

'What do you want now?' growled Mick.

'I haven't got any Norwegian money, sir.'

'Well,' said Mick, 'you'll just have a piss then.' The rest of the squadron dissolved into laughter.

Warrant officers and NCOs were not immune themselves from becoming the butt of others' humour, however, sometimes as a result of their own ineptitude. In the 1970s, my former troop sergeant, also called Taff, was doing FAC training. FAC stands for forward air control, and requires the deployment of men on the ground to guide in by radio the fighter-bomber pilots and direct them on to any target the ground force wants destroyed. On this occasion, Taff was required to bring in an RAF Hawker Hunter and guide it on to the simulated target. So he got on the radio and said, 'Hello, Hunter. This is Delta One Zero. I have you on visual and I can also see you. Over.'

It was clear that the pilot almost wet himself laughing, for we could see the aircraft wandering all over the sky as he rocked with mirth.

It has to be said that Taff had a gift for making people laugh. Once, during a refresher course in astro-navigation, I remember Arthur, our very enthusiastic and long-suffering instructor, rubbing his hands in anticipation of all the wonderful problems we were going to solve that day.

'OK lads,' he said 'let's get ourselves thinking. Taff: how many degrees are there in a circle?'

Taff thought hard for a moment, before replying, 'You can't catch me out on that one. It depends on the size of the circle.' The classroom walls reverberated with our laughter.

Given The Ditch's eccentric belief in a wandering North Star, and Taff's notion of measurement, it is not, perhaps, any wonder that members of the SAS – myself included – sometimes get lost. But then, so does the rest of the army.

So much has been published about the SAS in the last quarter-century, and particularly since the Princes Gate hostage rescue in 1980, that public interest seems at times to amount almost to an obsession. And of the various aspects of the Regiment that have come to notice, nothing seems to fascinate people more than weaponry. Over the years, I have read a great deal about the weapons the SAS are supposed to have. How men get saddlers to make fast-draw holsters for their automatics, have private armourers tailor their weapons to their own needs, and send off to gunsmiths for silencers. These and countless other similar claims are all nonsense, however, part of the body of myths that has grown up around the SAS.

One of these myths concerns the so-called 'fighting knife'. In actual fact, there is no such weapon issued in the British Army, despite what other accounts may say, although individuals within the SAS may choose to carry a knife they have acquired themselves. Nor is there much use for them: wielding a knife in combat, rather than a firearm, is likely to get you killed sooner rather than later, and for clandestine operations, or those requiring a high degree of stealth, members of the Regiment are issued with silenced weapons. Where a knife could be useful, though, is in situations in which a soldier is forced to live by his wits in a hostile environment, and without the usual support in the way of weapons, rations, transport, and so on.

Make no mistake, though, the Special Air Service is the best-equipped regiment in the British Army. No other unit has better kit than we have. The system is brilliant; in effect, the Regiment has carte blanche on weapons purchase, and on all sorts of other equipment besides. Thus whatever the SAS wants, the SAS gets. If they want to try out a new weapon, the Ministry of Defence (MoD) makes sure that they have the opportunity. And if they like it, then it is purchased for them.

But there is absolutely no need for anyone ever to have a personalized weapon. In fact, it would be a hindrance in battle because we have to have standardized ammunition that everyone can use. A soldier using a 7.62mm-calibre rifle when his comrades are all using weapons of 5.56mm calibre will be left with a useless piece of junk when he runs out of ammunition, quite apart from the problems of resupplying ammunition in several different calibres.

Each weapon used by a man in the field is issued by the Quartermaster. Its serial number is logged, and no weapon or ammunition is ever issued without the man signing for it. It is true that there was a time when men were allowed to keep personal weapons in the camp armoury, because there was then an SAS pistol club and people liked to do combat shooting as a sport. That has long gone, however. Today there is simply not the remotest likelihood that any member would be allowed to use his own weapons in the field. A man gets to use the same weapon from the armoury, until such time as another is issued to him for whatever reason.

The weapons bought by the SAS are mainly American, British or German. There are some weapons from manufacturers in other foreign countries, notably the Belgian-built Minimi 5.56mm machine-gun and the Swiss-built Sig Sauer automatic pistols, but nobody uses Beretta automatics, as numbers of secret agents do in movies, because these and similar weapons are regarded as 'ladies' pistols' with little stopping power.

Our main weapons remain the American-built 5.56mm M16 rifle, the standard-issue US service rifle, and the Browning High Power 9mm pistol, built by the giant Belgian FN concern, which owns Browning. The German company Heckler & Koch also produce good weapons which include the 9mm MP5 range of submachine-guns. The handguns used by the SAS are always automatics because revolvers, although far less likely to jam, are both less powerful and less accurate. The police use .38 Special revolvers, but the magazine capacity of such a weapon is simply not great enough, the most telling point against their use by the SAS. An automatic pistol can take magazines loaded with twelve or twenty rounds, compared with six for most revolvers, and the rate of fire is higher, factors which make automatics* far more useful in a firefight.

The selection of weapons on offer to the SAS is vast, and it has been said that each man in the Regiment has eight weapons. Naturally he doesn't carry them all with him at any one time, but they are available to him according to circumstances. Generally, though, he will have his M16, or otherwise a machine-gun, and a pistol, and there is then a whole range of other weaponry on which he can draw. Even in an anti-terrorist operation, however, it is the patrol commander, not the individual soldier, who chooses what weapons will be needed for a given situation, and these will then be issued according to his directions.

You simply do not have people saying, 'Right, I'm going to be using so and so weapon.' The patrol commander weighs up the task, and will then tell his men, 'You carry an M203 and take x amount of ammunition, you take an M16, you take the Minimi or the GPMG. I'll take an M16 and a pistol. OK?' (An M203 is a 40mm grenade launcher fixed beneath the barrel of an M16, thus making two very effective weapons in one; the GPMG – general-purpose machine-gun – is the standard-issue 7.62mm machine-gun of the British Army – a relatively light, powerful and accurate belt-fed weapon capable of being used in a sustained-fire role.) Each man then draws his weapons according to the patrol commander's orders – a call for a 2-inch mortar, for instance, means each man taking two rounds apiece for it as well as his own

---

* In fact, semi-automatics, to be strictly accurate, in that they fire a single shot each time the trigger is pressed, rather than firing continuously as true automatic weapons – machine-guns, for instance – do.

weapons and kit – no more and no less. Reports that men are invited to 'pick your weapon', like so much else that is written about the SAS, belong to the realms of myth, not reality.

If there are many myths about the Regiment's weapons and equipment, as well as about which operations it has or has not taken part in, there seem to be even more about who has actually served in the SAS. If you were to add together everyone who claims to have been badged, the total would come to far more than the strength of the entire Royal Artillery, the largest regiment in the British Army, and way, way above the very modest establishment of the SAS. The reasons for this slightly sad habit of making false claims are not difficult to work out, but it does seem to be very widespread. Indeed, in his book *Ghost Force*, Ken Connor, one of the Regiment's longest-serving members, estimates that the number of people who claim to have been on the balcony of the Iranian Embassy in Princes Gate in May 1980 comes to about 15,000 – and rising.

I have only been twice to the Special Forces Club in London, and I have to say that I will never go again. For obvious reasons, the club has a CCTV camera over the door and an entryphone system for letting members and their guests in, once identified. It doesn't identify fakes, though. More genuine heroes and heroines have walked through that door than you can shake a stick at – and, sadly, some Walter Mittys, too. The latter hang around the bar, telling tall tales about their exploits and generally bullshitting each other. Meanwhile the real people who have been there and have the scars to prove it listen and don't say a word. These people are known to each other and don't need to lie. They also know perfectly well when what they are hearing is a tissue of lies, boasts and half-truths.

There are even a number of elderly women who are members of the club, though sadly fewer each year. These are the courageous female SOE agents who were parachuted into Occupied Europe during the Second World War, and for them I have enormous respect. As for the Walter Mittys, however, they get right up my nose. I was in the Special Forces Club on Burns Night in 1993, and had enjoyed a good evening with a bunch of friends. After dinner I was standing at the bar with the Regimental Sergeant-Major of 21 SAS, one of the Regiment's two Territorial units, when a guy came over and introduced himself. I shook his hand and told him that my name was Billy Ratcliffe.

He looked at me a moment, and then, to my astonishment, said, 'You're not Billy Ratcliffe.' I assured him I was, whereupon he emphatically repeated that I wasn't. For a moment he almost convinced me that I was not who I thought I was. He went on to say that he had been talking, only the previous week, to 'Billy Ratcliffe of the SAS'. By this time I was getting pretty angry. 'He's over there, in that picture,' he said, pointing to a print of the painting, which I had commissioned, of the Sergeants' Mess meeting we had held behind enemy lines in the desert during the Gulf War, when I had been RSM of 22 SAS.

'That's me in the picture,' I said. 'No, it isn't,' he replied. Clearly I was not going to convince him, so I left him talking to the RSM and walked out into the night before my anger got the better of me, musing on the strange feeling of knowing there's somebody out there claiming to be you. In my view, the club's committee needs to take much greater care in approving applicants for membership.

I sometimes meet people in Civvy Street who know of my background. Often they will say that they know somebody else who was in the SAS. I tell them to go back and ask their friend which squadron he served in and the name of his squadron commander. And the odd thing is, they always come back and say that their friend has told them that he can't give out that kind of information.

There are hundreds, perhaps even thousands, of SAS phoneys around. Between them, they spin enough yarns about the Regiment to knit every badged member – former or still serving – a good-sized sweater apiece. And that is probably the only thing about these people that *is* true.

Chapter Six

IF our politicians had to go out and keep their own promises, honouring our often dubious treaties of friendship in parts of the world that will never feature in the holiday brochures, we would have a House of Commons full of pacifist isolationists.

Unfortunately for the common soldier, however, we are still a long way from such a happy turn of events, which is why, in 1973, I found myself, by way of a very tortuous and clandestine route, bound for Oman, the independent sultanate on the Arabian Gulf. Or to be exact, for Dhofar, a province in the south of Oman which 90 per cent of British schoolchildren couldn't point to on an atlas.

Oman then was a country with very little to recommend it, at least to our eyes. Its borders were, and are still, largely undefined, its people were among the most poverty-stricken in the world. There were a great many poisonous snakes, scorpions and spiders, while the ubiquitous mites, lice and flies carried diseases such as dysentery and scrub typhus. Temperatures ranged from over 120 degrees Fahrenheit on the low ground during the day to below freezing at night on the plateaux. Dehydration and sunstroke could be fatal, while sunburn was just extremely painful. You needed to drink at least a gallon of water a day simply to feel more or less normal.

A five-month tour in these conditions would have finished off most of our politicians, and that was before I come to the real danger, and the reason for our being there: the continuous war being waged against the Marxist-backed rebels, or People's Front for the Liberation of the Occupied Arabian Gulf, to give them their full name. Locally these brutal, cold-blooded, uncompromising killers were known as the *adoo*, which, predictably, means 'enemy' in Arabic. They were also, to a man, convinced atheists.

Until 1970, Oman had been ruled by a despotic and cruel Sultan whose almost medieval tyranny had made him deeply unpopular among the people. It was then that his Sandhurst-trained son, Qaboos, took over in a bloodless palace coup inspired, if not actively backed, by the British.

71

Bloodless, that is, except for the old Sultan himself, who decided not to go gently. Not being quite the trusting father Qaboos imagined him to be, he had an automatic pistol concealed in his robes. On being told that he must abdicate, he drew this and fired off the whole magazine, managing to kill one servant, wound a senior courtier and shoot himself in the stomach and foot. That evening, after abdicating, he was flown to London in an RAF Viscount. Once recovered from his self-inflicted injuries, he spent the last two years of his life there in glorious exile.

Within hours of taking over, Qaboos's first act, under Oman's treaty with Britain of 1789, was formally to request British assistance in putting down the Marxist-inspired insurgency. He asked specifically that the SAS be sent to support the Sultan's forces in crushing the adoo. The first of our guys were on the ground there by the following day.

Not that the British public became fully aware of this piece of latter-day gunboat diplomacy until a considerable time later. But Britain, in the shape of the Foreign Office and the Conservative government of the then Prime Minister, Edward Heath, had as compelling reasons for supporting Qaboos as she had for encouraging the coup in the first place.

Oman is one of the southernmost nations in the Middle East. In the south-east it is bordered by the Arabian Sea, and its north-western border faces Saudi Arabia and the United Arab Emirates. Its western border, however, marches with Yemen, a Marxist state that had recently incorporated the former British protectorate of Aden, where British troops, badly supported if not actually betrayed by Whitehall, had been kicked out in an inglorious and politically bungled fiasco. The Yemeni government was now supplying Russian-sponsored weapons, ammunition and equipment to the adoo, as well as providing them with training and a safe haven once they crossed back into Yemen from Oman.

Victory for the adoo in Oman would leave the communists controlling the Gulf of Oman, which forms the country's northern border, the entrance to the busiest and richest sea lane for the world's oil tankers – the waters of the Persian Gulf. To this would be added the not inconsiderable oil reserves of Oman itself, which had been operating with increasing efficiency and output since 1964. These were rich prizes, and their loss to the communists would be a severe blow to the West in general, and Britain in particular.

The young Sultan was not so naive as to imagine that he would not have to pay for all this assistance. So for the next six years, mainly in secret and personally supported by Heath and, after 1974, by the Labour government of Harold Wilson, the SAS maintained a presence in Oman under the codename 'Operation Storm'. It was they, who, in the end, were principally responsible for putting down the insurrection on the jebel – and for most of that time men of the Regiment never went for more than forty-eight hours without coming under serious enemy fire. Having done three tours on Operation Storm, I have to say that no matter how many bushels of riyals, bars of gold or barrels of oil the Sultan was paying, or the goodwill that accrued to Britain in this strategically vital part of the world, it wasn't enough.

By the time I arrived for my first tour in Oman in January 1973 the 'hearts-and-minds' campaign implemented by the former CO of 22 SAS, Lieutenant-Colonel Johnny Watts, was already paying dividends, beginning to win over the locals in favour of the young Sultan. Coming as it did after the Regiment's stunning successes in Malaya and Borneo during the 1950s and 1960s, this campaign would confirm the SAS as the most successful counter-insurgency unit in the world.

Its basic idea was to supply medical and veterinary care for the half-million or so people in the arid and mountainous province of Dhofar – where the adoo were at their most active and dangerous – and their animals, and to drill for new sources of water. The veterinary aid was particularly inspired, as the Dhofari's main concern after himself was his livestock – his family and his tribe came much further down his list of priorities. We also set up a local radio station broadcasting propaganda for the Sultan and his government, to counteract the communists' Radio Aden, and organized the printing of thousands of leaflets explaining the new Sultan's policies and attacking communist methods and ideology. The leaflets were dropped from the air in selected areas of Dhofar.

Most telling of all, perhaps, was our offer to arm and train any of the Muslim tribesmen who wanted to protect themselves and their property against the increasingly vicious and ruthless adoo. Certainly the insurgents had some very strange ideas about how to win friends and influence people. If any of the people they liberated refused to deny the existence of God, and these were most frequently the elderly, they were tortured, often to death. In this respect, and although operating on reversed principles, the adoo would have given the Inquisition an extremely good run for its money.

Children were snatched from parents and sent for reschooling in Yemen, and the young of both sexes were shipped off to training camps in China and Russia, to return thoroughly indoctrinated in Marxist theory and dogma. Among the ordinary Dhofaris, anyone suspected of supporting Qaboos, or anyone denounced by a fellow tribesman for holding similar sympathies, would be tried and executed on the spot, usually by beheading.

All in all, the province was a kind of 'lost world', a hellhole with a lunar landscape and an unforgiving climate. But then, we were hardly being sent there for a holiday, or for the good of our health. We were there because, in their wisdom, the Foreign Office and the government of the day had decreed that that is where we should be.

I left for my first tour in Oman in January 1973, by which time the SAS had been involved there for nearly three years. D Squadron were flown out from RAF Lyneham in Wiltshire to Cyprus, and from there by way of a couple of other destinations before finally landing at Salalah in Dhofar, the province's principle town. It was a small place with a population of about ten thousand, and apart from the airport, which by then was being used mainly as a military base by the Sultan's forces, seemed to our eyes to have very little going for it. The men there may have been on the side of the angels when it came to loyalty to the Sultan and his government, but they all looked pretty villainous to me, while the women had all their assets completely hidden from view. They may have had hour-glass figures to rival Monroe and faces to match, but if so we never got to see them. The Muslim majority were always muffled up in voluminous hanging garments and yashmaks. Nevertheless, the local young men must have found ways of penetrating all those outer wrappers, for the birthrate in Oman was nearly twice the world average, and 41 per cent of the country's population were under the age of fifteen. At the time, I reckoned that if screwing were to be made an Olympic sport, then the Omani team would have won every medal in every category. It was obviously their main national pastime.

The second seemed to be shooting at the SAS.

From the airport at Salalah we were transported directly to our temporary camp at Um al-Gwarif, known to us as UAG, which was about four miles away. The idea was for us to stay there for three or four days in order to acclimatize ourselves, sort out our equipment and receive our final briefings, before being helicoptered to the *jebel*, the mountain area of the province, where much of the trouble was to be found. In the event, however, a small group of six of us, including myself and Jimmy, one of my friends from Mobility Troop, were sent to the coastal town of Mirbat, about fifty miles to the east, and the scene of a famous battle between the SAS and rebels in 1972. Our role there was to keep a presence on the ground, deliver medical aid to the local people, and to carry out patrols and gather information. It was a beautiful place, like a remote holiday destination with its ancient fort and sea and miles of sand, but we found life there extremely boring. After three weeks, however, we were summoned back to UAG and told that we would be deploying to the jebel in a few days' time.

Our exact location was to be one of a pair of positions the Regiment had established and which we intended to fortify. About three miles apart, 'Diana One' and 'Diana Two' were in the range of foothills over-looking a wadi from where the adoo would launch their frequent attacks on Salalah. Some of their rockets had hit civilian repairmen working on the jets and helicopters for the military, and they had even destroyed aircraft on the ground. Without protection the men had threatened to go on strike, something that would have brought the war on the Omani side to a halt in that region, since it was from Salalah's airport that the Sultan's air force operated against the adoo in Dhofar.

Before we deployed to Diana One, Jimmy decided that it would be a great wheeze if he and I were to hitch a ride in a military plane or helicopter and visit some of the members of Mountain Troop, who were in a base known as 'White City'. This lay to the east on the edge of the Darbat Plateau, and overlooked the coastal strip between Salalah and Rakhyut, on the border with Yemen. Since the adoo were primarily based in Yemen, it was an important position, for groups of insurgents were constantly crossing the border in both directions. Jimmy had managed to con us a ride in a Skyvan, a small, twin-piston-engined transport aircraft that looked like a bumblebee in flight and sounded worse, but which would, we hoped, carry us in one piece up to White City. The squadron OC had no objections to our going when we approached him, but warned, 'Get back here in forty-eight hours.' We needed no second bidding and, grabbing our bergens and rifles, we were away.

From the air the Dhofari landscape looked every bit as alien and hostile as it did close to, rather like the pictures from Armstrong's moon walk – mysterious, uninviting and threatening.

The guys in Mountain Troop seemed happy enough to see Jimmy and we spent most of the time drinking strong tea and chatting. Left to myself, however, I think I would have preferred to have stayed put in the bar at UAG, looking at the pictures of girls printed on the Tennant's lager cans. Since the Skyvan made the run most days, we expected to be riding out on the next one within twenty-four hours, so I'd be back in the bar before too long.

That was until intelligence came in that an adoo patrol was using a nearby *bait*, or native hut, as a breakfast stop-off point each morning, and Mountain Troop were immediately tasked with laying an ambush for them. At Jimmy's suggestion, the White City troop commander agreed to take us along, Jimmy promising me, 'I'll get you blooded.' This did not seem at all unlikely, as we were both assigned to the main killing group, which consisted of six men; the remainder were placed in two cut-off groups whose task was to prevent any enemy escaping.

I had long anticipated the moment when I would come under fire for the first time, and perhaps be forced to shoot to kill in retaliation. I hadn't quite imagined, however, that it would be in circumstances such as these, or that it would be sprung on me so suddenly. I could feel the sudden tension that had invaded my body, and experienced a rush of adrenalin.

'Right,' I replied. There wasn't much else I could have said.

The plan was simple. We would leave our base at 2200 hours that night in order to ensure that we would be established in a good ambush position when the adoo arrived in the morning – if they did arrive. Our back-up was a *firqat*, Arabic for 'company', made up of former rebel *jebalis* (Dhofaris from the jebel region) who had switched sides, and a troop of *geysh*, mercenary soldiers from the province of Baluchistan in Pakistan who were employed by the Sultan's armed forces, and some of whom I quickly discovered were little better than useless. The firqats were a different matter, however. Organized, trained and paid by the SAS with money provided by the Sultan, they were a merciless, bloodthirsty lot who, when a firefight started, would hitch up their sarongs and rush like wild dervishes into battle. Good fighters, I learned to appreciate having them on our side.

It took us about two hours to reach the target and another half-hour for us all to get into position around the bait, which had been built on a rocky hillside. After that there was nothing for it but to wait, and wait we did. It began to look as though the intelligence about the adoo patrol was wrong – a common enough occurrence throughout the campaign – and the patrol commander said he would give it a further half-hour and then we would leave.

The half-moon that had lit our way to the target dipped over the horizon and a little later came the dawn, thin streaks of light that gradually unrolled the darkness across the valley to reveal a scene of raw beauty and unexpected tranquillity. We continued to keep watch from our concealed positions, every man keyed up for a sight or sound that would let us know the adoo were approaching, unaware of our presence.

This time the wait was a short one. Well before the deadline we spotted four figures making their way in single file up a long slope towards the hut. I estimated that at their speed it would probably take them thirty minutes to reach it.

The patrol commander gestured for Jimmy and me to move forward to a dry-stone wall, which formed one side of an open pen where the goats were kept, though it was now empty. I was carrying a 7.62mm GPMG, a belt-fed weapon, about 30 inches long and weighing just over 24 pounds, and with a nominal rate of fire approaching 1,000 rounds a minute. It's a ferocious weapon with a killing range of up to a mile in the right circumstances.

I flicked down the bipod beneath the barrel and rested its feet on top of the wall, keeping my head down as I sighted along the weapon, even though the adoo couldn't see me in my new position. Then I heard a low murmur to my right, 'They're in the back of the bait. Stand by.' Now I could really feel the adrenalin pumping.

Just then a man in a green shirt came out of a side entrance in the bait. He was very dark-skinned and was carrying a rifle.

'Is that an adoo?' I whispered to Jimmy, not wanting it to turn out that the first person I ever shot was a civilian. But before he could answer the man had gone back inside and another, even darker-skinned Arab came out, wearing only a sarong.

'No, he's a jebali,' muttered Jimmy.

'No. Not him, the other one,' I hissed.

'What other one?' Jimmy queried. Our whispered conversation was starting to sound like a comedy turn.

Almost immediately another man appeared from the back of the hut. He was lighter-skinned than the other two, and was carrying what looked like an AK-47 light automatic rifle – the famous Russian-designed weapon which can fire off a twenty-round magazine in less than two seconds. He walked right round to our side of the hut before he spotted us. By now he was perhaps thirty feet away and I could see him clearly.

I saw his eyes narrow as he recognized his predicament. He started to go into a crouch as he swung the rifle, which he was carrying in his right hand, forwards and upwards, at the same time grabbing the barrel with his left hand as he tried to bring the weapon up to a firing position. It was then that I squeezed the GPMG's trigger.

The adoo never had a chance. My first two-second burst – more than thirty rounds – took him right in the body. I could see fragments of flesh being torn out of his back by the exiting bullets, and he was slammed backwards against the bait wall by the sheer weight of the fire hitting him. I fired again, and one of my rounds must then have struck the magazine on his rifle, for it suddenly blew up. The upper part of his body was simply torn to shreds.

Just as this gruesome sight was registering with me, however, I heard Jimmy shout, 'There are two more getting away at the back.' I couldn't see them from my position, so I yanked the machine-gun off the top of the wall and, holding it up to my shoulder like a rifle, crabbed along sideways until I could see the adoo backing down the hill, all the time firing short bursts towards them. Above my head and somewhere off to my left I heard the zing-like crack of high-velocity rounds going past as the men behind me opened up.

I opened fire again and sent the rest of the rounds in the ammunition belt streaming towards the two men in one long burst. There were others firing alongside me so I'm not sure who killed the second man, but he suddenly spun round and dropped his weapon. Great gouts of blood spurted from multiple wounds in his chest as he went down.

Less than five minutes after it had started the shooting was all over. Silence once more returned to the hillside. Cautiously we moved forward, and three members of Mountain Troop went in and cleared the hut. The firqat and the geysh were still in their original positions, and didn't appear to have taken any part in the ambush.

One of the two men who had fled from the back of the hut was dead, although it was impossible to know if I had had a hand in his killing. He had been hit by at least half a dozen rounds. His companion appeared to have got away, though he may have been wounded. The fourth man had been shot dead on the far side of the building by other members of the patrol. I hadn't even seen him until we came across his body.

I was feeling strangely high – the kind of high you get after a few drinks, but before actually becoming drunk. I knew, however, that this reaction was caused by the adrenalin still chasing about inside my system. I had come through my first contact with an enemy. My first firefight. And I had killed a man for the first time, too.

It was a strange feeling. Later, as we made our way back to White City, I thought, 'This is really good. I've just seen my first action, and I've done all right.' I had no regrets at all. A little sadness for the man I'd killed, perhaps, that he might have had a wife and a family as some of us had wives and families. Yet in the end he had courted his own fate by becoming a terrorist.

Jimmy was pleased with the way I'd performed, but cautioned restraint. Patting me on the back, he told me, 'It's easy to dish it out, but it's a different story when you've got to take it. So don't go thinking you're a vet. You're still just a young pup.' In truth, I didn't feel very different, and certainly not like a hero. But what I did know was that I felt genuinely proud to have done my job, and to have taken down an enemy who, given a few more seconds, might well have finished me off instead.

We spent the rest of that day in the White City base, and on the following morning hitched a ride back to Salalah in the Skyvan. Next day, Jimmy and I were deployed to the spot in the foothills known as Diana One. Though God alone knows what had inspired some deranged officer to name such a bleak and unfriendly position, with no attractive or in any other way redeeming features whatsoever, after a Roman goddess. Furthermore, as though sensing our disapproval, the gods decided to give us another enemy contact within our very first hour there.

Diana One's main position was a man-made sangar, a roofless observation post (OP) consisting of a pit dug out of the ground surrounded by a stone enclosing wall reinforced with sandbags. On the hillside scattered behind it were three other smaller dugouts, the centre one of which was the mortar pit. Most days the adoo would send out snipers whose job was simply to hamper our activities by forcing us to keep our heads down. In the sangars themselves you were reasonably safe, but leaving the position even at night was always a nervous outing. It's very hard to crouch and try to wipe your backside, and then struggle back into your trousers and bury the results, while there's an unseen sniper with a night sight out there somewhere, trying to part your hair.

They were at it the day we arrived to begin our four months of occupancy. We soon learned that it was pointless trying to spot their positions, for the terrain was a sniper's paradise, with limitless cover provided by a never-ending range of gullies and hillocks and occasional loose boulders. Daytime attacks, we learned, usually came at about 1100 hours, when the sun was in our eyes. This was the softening-up period, however. The more serious stuff happened just before last light, although in semi-darkness the muzzle flashes at least gave us something to aim at. On that first day we seemed to be catching it from three different positions.

There was one Spargan machine-gun nest on the side of the hill which sprayed us with 12.7mm armour-piercing rounds, and a couple of other pockets from where the adoo were firing AK-47s, good communist weapons supplied through the Yemenis.

Our standard rifle at that time was the 7.62mm L1A1, invariably known as the SLR (self-loading rifle), which was adapted to fire single shots only, unlike the FN rifle from which it was derived, which was fully, rather than semi-automatic. But we also had the single-shot M79 grenade launcher, which could chuck a 40mm high-explosive grenade up to 400 metres. On top of that, we were capable of delivering a whole assortment of bombs from the 81mm mortar – high-explosive, white phosphorus and parachute-suspended illumination rounds. After detonation, anything the phosphorus touched started burning, including metal and flesh.

Most of these firefights with the adoo lasted about twenty minutes. For us they were incredibly frustrating. When we returned fire we never knew if we had scored a hit, as the distances were too great even to hear the scream of a wounded man. Furthermore, we knew that any adoo we did kill or wound would be carried away by their comrades, leaving nothing for a patrol to find except, if we were very lucky, a pool of dried blood or blood splashes on a rock.

As far as we could work it out, the enemy would send an attacking unit of between ten and twenty men, but it was very difficult to tell just how many. The only way to estimate their numbers was to try to judge by the number of rounds coming in or, at night, by counting the muzzle flashes. We did go out on foot patrols in attempts to locate the snipers, but it was actually worse than looking for a needle in a haystack. The terrain of those foothills was a rocky nightmare of broken ground and jumbled boulders.

The only thing of which we could be certain was that if they didn't attack us at last light, then they were off attacking Diana Two, three miles away. With only sixty men in-country at any one time, the SAS were spread rather thin on the ground. In each main position there would be some half a dozen of us, a firqat of ex-rebel Dhofaris and a unit of geysh, though the latter were little better than cannon fodder.

The firqat were different, however. They had come into being between 1970 and 1971 when 200 of the rebels, alienated by the Marxists' anti-religious fervour and bully-boy tactics, surrendered to the government after the young Sultan offered a general amnesty. They were formed into firqat units by the SAS under the man appointed as their leader, Salim Mubarak. He was a tough fighter and passionate nationalist, and before his conversion had been second-in-command of the rebels' eastern section. After his surrender under the amnesty he had been invited by Major Tony Jeapes of 22 SAS to take command of the adoo he had brought in with him and turn them into an elite fighting group, called the Firqat Salahadin, after the famous twelfth-century Arab leader who had defeated the Crusaders.

Backed by the SAS, they won two major victories against the rebels, and this started a general speeding up in the defection rate. Under Sultan Qaboos's decree, any adoo who gave himself up and agreed to serve the Sultan received an automatic pardon and a well-paid job with the firqats. In addition, his family were looked after and given free medical treatment, again organized by the SAS. Those who were captured and refused to accept the terms of the amnesty, however, were thrown in gaol, and having visited one of these foul places during my first tour in Oman I can vouch for the fact that the lifestyle enjoyed – if that's the word – by prisoners was very far from comfortable. The cells were little more than holes in the ground, the stench was overpowering, and the conditions indescribable.

Living in a very confined space, as we did on the Diana positions, created two major problems. The first was boredom, and this was exacerbated by the second: the fact that the smallest thing anyone did that was even slightly out of the ordinary could get on your nerves to the point where you wanted to yell at the 'culprit' to stop. It might be someone slurping his tea, or always making a crunching noise when he ate hardtack biscuits, or perhaps the way a man blew his nose or cleared his throat – or even snored.

Other factors added yet further to our mental and physical discomfort. On Diana One, we were there to hold a position. Not to take ground or track down the enemy to their lair and wipe them out, but to stay. Our orders were just to sit there and take whatever they threw at us, retaliating when we could. It was a strain on us all, and although we tried to defuse confrontations that arose between us, and above all to keep our sense of humour alive, there were times when you just wanted to scream with the boredom and frustration and monotony of it all.

Then there was the heat. It cooled slightly when the sun went down, and most nights were cold enough to need a sleeping bag. But the days were stiflingly hot and with very little wind, and by the time the sun was at its hottest the temperature in a sangar would be well over 100 degrees

Fahrenheit. Our water was invariably tepid to hot, and as it came in oil drums that hadn't been washed out properly, it tasted foul.

The best relief from all this was to try to gain a little space for yourself, and the only way of achieving this was to go and visit one of the other locations on the hill, where a change of face – or at least a change in unbearable personal mannerisms – could bring a little relief.

There were certainly plenty of characters among the Mobility Troop members on Diana One, and in a normal environment, such as Hereford, we would have revelled in one another's company. But Dhofar was far from being 'normal', and there everything, including people's personalities, came over differently. But although some of these guys could easily get on your nerves when things were normal, when we were under fire they were the greatest men to have alongside you in the world.

On Diana One we would occasionally carve out a new sangar, something that had to be done using explosives because the ground was so hard. And it had to be done at night, and above all quickly, because until we had sunk a decent-sized hole we were sitting targets for the adoo snipers.

On one particular occasion, I had been working all night alongside Nick, an amusing character and a good mate (sadly he was later killed in a car accident). You could only work for so long at a stretch before you needed a rest, and just before dawn Nick and I decided to call it a night and slipped into our sleeping bags. It was very cold. I welcomed snuggling into the warmth of my 'green maggot' and was asleep within minutes. I was awoken by an urgent shout of 'Stand to!' to find tracer rounds and lead streaming through the air above and around us. The enemy had launched a pre-dawn raid, and we were the target of the moment.

All hell had broken loose, with tracers zipping by only inches above our heads as we lay in the shallow sangar. It's hard to get out of a sleeping bag without sitting up, and to have done so would have meant almost certain death from an adoo bullet. So I yelled to Nick, 'Roll along the ground your way and we can get a bit more cover where the hole is deeper.'

Even rolling isn't the easiest thing to do when you're wrapped inside a sleeping bag, but somehow we managed. Once behind a few inches of cover we tried to peep over and see where the shots were coming from, but we were up against the usual problem: we couldn't properly identify where the adoo were hiding. It was pointless exposing ourselves more than we had to, just to fire off a few ineffective rounds.

'What would be *preferable* is for us to fire *effective* rounds,' Nick suddenly remarked in an accentuated, affected officer's accent, and we both suddenly convulsed with laughter. It's often the way, for when tension is high laughter seems to come more easily. If our enemy could have seen us, hugging our sides and crying with laughter, they would have been convinced we were stark raving mad. Perhaps for those few minutes we were indeed a little mad, but it helped us get through until the adoo ceased firing and the bullets stopped singing by just above our heads. Silence descended once more. We sat with our sleeping bags wrapped round us, keeping warm while we waited for first light. After a reasonable period of quiet I said to Nick, 'I'm going to try and get a little more sleep.' But I think he must have already dozed off, for there was no answer.

What seemed like only seconds later I was stunned by the most godawful bang close by. Now the adoo were mortaring us. We worked out the general direction from where we thought their fire was coming and retaliated with our own mortars, but I doubt we got close enough even to scratch them. Eventually they tired of trying to land a direct hit on our new site, and Nick and I shrugged off our sleeping bags and got on with the excavation work. I wouldn't say that we learned to be blasé, exactly, about the attacks, but when they came virtually every day, and sometimes twice a day, they somehow became less intimidating.

One morning, not long after this rather one-sided firefight, an SEP (surrendered enemy personnel) arrived at the approaches to the main base on Diana One and gave himself up. It was still the Sultan's rule that any surrendering rebel was to be given the chance of signing on with the firqat. If he agreed, he would be given an automatic pardon, and would then be debriefed and sent on to join the local forces.

The man who handled his surrender was a staff sergeant named Jerry, on loan from Mountain Troop. And according to Jerry, when he gathered us round, the young adoo had an interesting tale to tell. He knew of a cave in a wadi quite close by that was used as a store by the rebels, and was full of ammunition and weapons. If we could seize these arms it would be a tremendous bonus to our friends in the firqat attached to us, because they received a bounty on all weapons and ammunition they captured from the enemy.

'If this little SEP is right,' Jerry continued, 'it should be a worthwhile outing. We'll leave here at twenty-one hundred – the firqat, the geysh and ourselves. The surrendered adoo will act as guide. Carry whatever weapons you want. Any questions?'

'What time is the brief, Jerry?' I asked.

'Don't you listen to anything?' he shot back. 'That *was* the brief. Those were your orders. All right?'

And that was me well and truly put in my place. In fairness, I ought to point out that in those days notes for a full briefing were frequently written on half a cigarette packet.

The cave was about ten kilometres away, and most of the route was along mountain-hugging tracks, with a thousand-foot drop on one side. Just the thing to keep you alert on a dark night, stumbling along the edge of a precipice. After what seemed like hours of slow and careful walking we finally came to a wadi running along the foot of a cliff, which had several deep caves gouged out of its walls. The young adoo who had surrendered – he was not a day over seventeen – stopped in front of one and told Jerry that this was the place where the weapons were.

By this time, every one of us was wondering if we were being led into some kind of death trap. At least, I certainly was – and so too, thank God, was Lance, who just happened to be an expert demolitionist. In the light of what we discovered, he can be forgiven the eccentricities of his character. Because while the rest of us were shuffling around wondering what the hell to do next he was down on his hands and knees with a torch, minutely examining the floor and sides of the cave by its dim light.

Almost at once he discovered that the place really was booby-trapped. Had we gone blundering in, the whole lot of us would have been blown to Kingdom Come and beyond. Within minutes, however, Lance had defused the device and we were able to enter the cave. Inside there were arms and ammunition a-plenty, a major find whose loss would be a severe blow to the adoo. The geysh and the firqat staggered away laden down, although since I didn't stand to make anything out of it, I decided that they could do their own carrying. Walking back along that precipice in the dark was going to be bad enough just carrying my own rifle. If they wanted the bounty, then they could carry the booty.

Eventually we staggered into Diana One at first light, absolutely exhausted. Tired as I was, something nagged at my mind, for I still wasn't sure if our SEP was a genuine deserter or had deliberately tried to walk us into a trap. Neither, admitted Jerry, was he. 'I'll hand him over to the firqat and let them work out the answer,' he said. 'If we still see him hanging around here tomorrow then I guess we'll know he was genuine.' With that he wandered off to grab a well-earned kip.

By this time we had turned our new sangar into a real home from home. Since the mortar attack we had added dozens more sandbags and boulders to the walls, and had also erected a roof of corrugated iron supported by several large steel pickets. This was covered with stones to weight it down in high winds, and then the whole lot was spread with branches of trees and bushes and other foliage. From a distance it looked like a clump of undergrowth that had been there for years.

It was finally finished the day after the capture of the arms in the cave, and we decided to celebrate by inviting an old friend round for tea. Taff and I had signed on together in the Paras, and had later suffered, and passed, Selection together. The three of us occupying the sangar had put down a 'floor' of flattened empty ration boxes to stop the sharp rock chips digging into our knees when we knelt down to fire the machine-gun through its slit. Given our cardboard carpet and the well-built roof, the whole place was really quite cosy and snug. For a seat we used a lump of rock which we had dug out of the earth, and we were all sitting on this, congratulating ourselves on being nicely hidden away from the enemy, when there was an almighty great crash just outside. It was a mortar round exploding, and within seconds there was enemy fire coming in on all sides, small-arms rounds as well as mortar bombs.

Gradually I was able to pick out a pattern. You could hear the 'plop' as the distant mortar was fired, and would then start counting. Thirty seconds later you would hear the explosion as the bomb completed its journey.

Then the unthinkable happened. Suddenly there was a flash above our heads and something smashed through the roof. Smoke and dust filled the sangar, and for a stunned moment or two we could hardly see anything. Initially I thought the blast had been safely absorbed when the round had burst through our roof, its main effort expended in breaking through the layers of branches and stones and corrugated iron. Then I looked down to the cardboard mat at my feet and saw a pool of blood forming there. I shouted at the others to look as well, and suddenly we all began feeling ourselves to see if we had been hit.

Then someone yelled, 'Ahhrrrr!' – and I immediately thought, 'Thank fuck. They got him and not me.' Afterwards, Nick and I were able to laugh together over the fact that he had had the identical reaction, and had silently expressed our relief in exactly the same words.

It turned out Taff had been hit in the back and was bleeding quite badly. We ripped aside his uniform top and fastened a thick padded field dressing over the wound, then gave him a shot of morphine from the vial which, like the rest of us, he carried around his neck. But until the mortar bombardment and small-arms fire stopped there was little else we could do, except hope that another round didn't find its way into the sangar.

After fifteen minutes or so the enemy fire slackened and finally stopped. At once we got on the radio and requested RHQ to send in a helicopter for a casevac. Meanwhile we dragged Taff outside and put a replacement dressing on the wound.

A proper examination of the inside of the sangar then showed what had happened. A 12.7mm armour-piercing round from a Russian-built Spargan heavy machine-gun had smashed through the roof and broken a steel picket support, and had then flown around inside the sangar, bouncing off the walls. At one point it must have ricocheted off Taff's back with such force that it stunned any pain he would otherwise have felt immediately. The round had then buried itself under the cardboard on the floor, where I found it. There wasn't a mark on it. It was only after I had spotted the blood and we started checking ourselves out that the feeling had returned to Taff's back, and with it had come the pain. We had all been pretty lucky, however. If that round had come in straight, then any one among the three of us might have been badly wounded, or even killed. As it was, Taff was back from the hospital inside a week, none the worse for his close encounter with an AP round.

Had there been any deaths or serious casualties among us it might have been different, but during that four-month tour my section of D Squadron seemed to possess charmed lives. There were a few wounded in other sections operating elsewhere, but no one seriously. Not that I lost any of my respect for the adoo, however – far from it. These rebels had been trained originally by the Chinese and now by the Russians, who were at the time an established presence in Yemen as 'advisers'. In addition, the adoo were masters of moving about the harsh landscape of the jebel, and of launching sudden stand-off attacks, after which they would melt back to their hideouts or over the border. They had been supplied with modern weapons and plenty of ammunition, all brought in to them, with other supplies, mainly by camel over the Yemeni border. The combination of these factors made them a formidable enemy, as well as a difficult one to stop.

As curious as it may seem, and as dangerous, tedious or uncomfort-able as it had often been, I enjoyed my time in Oman. True, I was not exactly sorry when our tour of duty there came to an end in May 1973, though I was not likely to forget about it in a hurry either. I had come of age – as a soldier, I mean – and in doing so had learned some valuable lessons. I had found out what it was like to be shot at, and how easy it was to take another's life. My future as a soldier no longer held any terrors for me. I had discovered what I was able to withstand, and to hand out. I don't know whether I was a better man as a result of what I had gone through, but I was certainly a good deal more confident.

Halfway through my stint on Diana One I was given three days' rest and recuperation, otherwise known as R&R. The time was spent in UAG drinking beer and generally chatting and exchanging war stories with other members of D Squadron, who were also on R&R. One day I visited the NAAFI in Salalah and bought a cassette recorder, which would now be a rather antiquated piece of equipment. On my return to Diana One, I placed the machine on the sangar wall with a view to recording a contact when the adoo next attacked. I didn't have to wait long and as soon as I heard the sound of an incoming mortar I pressed the record button. I was astonished, years later, to learn from a leading military historian that the resulting six-minute tape - which features heavy automatic and machine-gun fire from the adoo, as well as me returning fire with a GPMG – is one of only a very small number of recordings made during an actual firefight. The tape is now lodged with the Imperial War Museum in London.

Returning to Oman and Dhofar a year later was not something I had particularly looked forward to, but it didn't cause me any sleepless nights either. My companions were most of the same guys from D Squadron with whom I had shared the last tour. Only the location was different. In 1974 I was assigned to Tawi Atair. *Tawi* is Arabic for a well, but I was never to find out what *atair* stood for, although if it means 'where one is never dry' I should not be even slightly surprised.

It was the monsoon season when we arrived, which meant that it drizzled heavily every day. It was always humid, with an endless covering of low cloud, swarms of mosquitoes and other biting bugs, a sea of mud under foot and a landscape that had suddenly become very green. Most of the time it was pointless going out because you could hardly see a thing through the haze of wetness. There was no fresh food, only tinned stuff, because everything went mouldy so quickly. Mould grew on the inside of the tents, on your equipment, and even on your clothes.

We were in that location for four months, and I never once felt properly dry. We lived in tents, which made a change from sangars, the disadvantage being that they were not as effective in keeping out incoming fire. That was something which certainly hadn't changed, for our old friends the adoo still paid regular visits, shooting up the camp two or three times a week.

The base at Tawi Atair was fairly large and, besides an airfield, even boasted a field hospital and a permanent doctor, since it was not always possible to fly aircraft in or out during the monsoon if anyone needed emergency treatment. Our supplies came in on a purely haphazard basis, and our mail and newspapers were always a few weeks old.

The troop staff sergeant, also called Taff, was second-in-command of our particular group and, as an antidote to our just sitting there and getting shot at – which seemed to be standard procedure in Dhofar – he would lead us on occasional sorties against the enemy. Sometimes we would be accompanied by the troop commander, Tim, and sometimes Taff alone would lead us, for Tim had absolute, and justified, faith in his troop staff sergeant.

Short, stocky and as hard as nails, if Taff said it was Monday then it was Monday, regardless of what day of the week it actually was. He was not someone you would ever want to mess with. He was, however, a genuine original, and he could be extremely funny. On occasion he would put on a strangled, affected, upper-class-officer's accent and treat us to the most hilarious briefings – even though what he was actually saying was deadly serious.

'We are going out on patrol,' he would announce in his strained, funnel-throated voice (it came out as 'Weah gaying ite on p'troal'). 'Now remember, there are two types of fire. There is effective fire, and there is ineffective fire.

'Ineffective fire is when it goes over your head or hits the ground in front of you. That's when we keep going. You understand that, chaps? We keep going.

'Effective fire is when it's knocking your belt kit off. Then it is right and proper to go to ground. OK? Let's go, then.'

Our first sortie with Taff came a few days after we had settled in, and on this occasion Tim also came along. Our task was to recce some baits about six or seven kilometres west of our location, which intelligence reports stated were being used by the adoo as places from which to replenish their food and water. Our party consisted of half a dozen of us from the Regiment, one firqat unit and a company of geysh. Because of low cloud and constant drizzle we would have to move to within 300 metres of the suspected enemy's location if we were to be able to make out anything at all.

That seemed fine in theory, until, having arrived at the enemy position, we were spotted by the adoo, who opened fire. It was only then, as we moved to take cover, that we discovered that our company of geysh had stayed put while we leapfrogged forward – right past the enemy position – and that as a result we had the rebels bottled up between us. We at once began to return their fire, whereupon the adoo took cover in a bait and behind rocks, not yet realizing they were trapped. It was at this point that Taff was seized by an idea.

'Listen in, lads,' he said. 'Billy, you have the machine-gun. Put down covering fire and keep their tiny heads down while Tommy Palmer and I go right flanking.' Tim seemed happy with the plans, and I set up the GPMG and began to fire short bursts at the adoo position to make sure they didn't try to break out. Taff, meanwhile, summoned over our Arabic interpreter.

'Tell the firqat that we are going right flanking,' he said. 'Down there to the right. Now.' The interpreter repeated in Arabic what he had said, whereupon the firqat, almost to a man, replied with some vehemence, 'Mushtaman, mushtaman,' which means 'bad,' but clearly also meant, 'no way'.

The firqat's reaction didn't seem to faze Taff, however. 'Right,' he said, 'we'll do this a different way. Tell them Palmer and I will do this alone. Billy, when we get down there I'm going to wave my white handkerchief, which is the signal that I want you to check firing, because it means that we'll be right on top of the nearest enemy position and we don't want you bastards shooting us.

'I'll judge just how close when I get down there. But I'll take it to the limit. So don't carry on firing after I wave my handkerchief. All right?' I nodded, acknowledging that I had understood him.

'Now come with me, Tommy,' Taff ordered, and headed off downhill, the pair of them keeping low as they darted between whatever bits of cover they could find.

By now the firqat had realized Taff was being serious, whereupon the ten of them decided to follow him down, darting between boulders and bushes as they set out for the enemy position. As for me, I just concentrated on pouring 7.62mm rounds into the enemy's main position. I was lying down, using a bipod, and had a stack of 200-round belts next to me.

Taff crept to within about five metres of the adoo before waving his handkerchief – at which point the troop commander shouted, 'Check firing! Check firing! They are surrendering.'

'No they're not, it's Taff,' I yelled back at him. By then, however, Taff
and Tommy had opened fire on the adoo with their automatic weapons.
The heavy fire at almost point-blank range caught the rebels by surprise
– several were just mowed down where they stood.

It was all over after that. Those of the adoo who hadn't been killed or
badly wounded ran for it, simply vanishing into the misty drizzle.

Taff should have been decorated for what he did that day. As it was,
he got nothing save a pat on the back from Tim and another from the
squadron commander. That was always the way in Dhofar, not least
because the presence of the SAS there was still more or less deniable. In
May 1980 Tommy Palmer would be one of the stars of the Regiment's
brilliant operation to release the hostages held in the Iranian Embassy
in Princes Gate, London, an operation which, more than any other,
brought the SAS to wide public notice, and initiated the media's
obsessive interest in the Regiment. Tragically, he was later killed in a car
accident.

We took one prisoner, who had been shot in the leg, and carried him
on a stretcher back to Tawi Atair. He was only a teenager, and very
scared. The adoo used to kill their prisoners, usually by beheading, and
this boy must have thought that he was about to suffer the same fate at
our hands. His wound was a nasty one, but we got him safely back to
base where the regimental doctor, a legendary character renowned for
his ability to enjoy himself when off duty, managed to save his leg.
When he was well enough and the weather had cleared slightly he was
airlifted out and put in prison. Had he surrendered, of course, he would
have received the Sultan's pardon. But this young rebel was too
committed to the Marxist cause – or too frightened of reprisals by the
adoo.

As if the adoo were not enough, there were also plenty of venomous
snakes where we were, although if you kept your hands away from
crevices in the sandy walls they tended not to bother you. Nevertheless,
it was always a good idea to check inside your sleeping bag before
climbing in, and to shake your boots out in the morning before sliding
your feet in, in case a scorpion or two had taken a liking to your
footwear.

Playing games was one of our chief ways of combating boredom, and
we played a lot of scrabble and chess and ludo. Nick and I made a ludo
board out of cornflake packets, and we derived more enjoyment from
playing that than anything else. Taff, though, was a scrabble enthusiast.
It has to be said, however, that he wasn't a very good player, and he had

some peculiar rules which were all his own. Still, playing with our troop staff sergeant was never dull.

During a game one day he put down 'head', so when it came to my turn I added 'round', forming the word 'roundhead'.

'What the hell is that?' said Taff.

'"Roundhead," of course,' I said.

'What does it mean?'

'They were soldiers in the Civil War,' I told him.

'*Roundhead*,' he roared. 'You'll be putting down blackhead, square-head and bloody Birkenhead next . . . Never heard of it,' he added. 'Get it off!' And off it had to go.

On another occasion I put down the word 'heaven', whereupon Taff asked, without any irony, 'What the hell is that?'

'Heaven. You know, like up in the sky.'

This was clearly more than he could stand, for he looked at us and asked, 'Have you been there? Have you been there?' Then he got out his map and demanded, 'Show me where this heaven is,' before yelling, 'Get it off!'

With the end of the monsoon came the real heat. There was no shade and no wind, and our drinking water, which was supplied in 45-gallon metal drums brought in by helicopter, actually bubbled in the sun. The water was warm and, as I have said, tasted of the oil the drums had once contained. Drinking our obligatory eight pints a day was sheer purgatory.

With that heat, combined with an endless diet of tinned food, tainted water and myriad flies, we frequently got the runs. But at least in Tawi Atair we had a makeshift toilet, whereas on other locations, like Diana One the previous year, we'd had to crap on the jebel and bury the results.

Tawi Atair was almost civilized in this respect, however. We had dug a deep hole and then cannibalized wooden boxes to build a frame and a regular thunderbox over the pit. Down below there were hordes of shit beetles, a rather unnerving sight if you happened to glance beneath you. They were massive, beginning life about a quarter of an inch long but rapidly growing to the size of crabs.

Even more frightening was finding yourself still enthroned on the thunderbox, and effectively helpless, when we came under adoo attack. Torn between the risk of catching an enemy bullet, or otherwise of falling into that heaving pit, alive with shit beetles, in an attempt to dodge the fire, all of us would have opted for the former as being much the lesser of two evils. I have to admit, however, that not all the fire came from the adoo. The officer commanding the geysh was an Australian captain, a nice chap and a good soldier – he needed to be the latter, given the quality of the geysh as troops – but inclined to be rather over-fastidious, perhaps a hangover from his former civilian occupation as a shirt-seller. One night he was using the thunderbox in, as he thought, splendid isolation, when the darkness was split by bursts of tracer over his head, punctuated by single shots. He dived for cover, thoroughly entangled in his trousers and desperate to avoid the dreadful fate of fetching up in the horrible, beetle-ridden pit; as he did so, the air all but turned blue with his choicest Aussie obscenities. He was not altogether amused later when he discovered that the firing had come, not from the rebels, but from me and three or four others, blazing away over his head with a GPMG and our SLRs. It was, looking back, rather a disgraceful thing to do – I can only plead the sheer tedium of much of our time at Tawi Atair.

Such diversions did at least serve to take our minds off the enemy and our discomforts, but the greatest distraction of that tour was a scandal involving one of our own. Fred was a corporal, and a ringer for the kind of crooked, secondhand-car-and-anything-else-going salesman often portrayed by George Cole. By nature and preference a small-time villain and con man, Fred treated his posting to Dhofar as a personal challenge to his criminal ingenuity. It was a challenge to which he effortlessly rose, albeit with a scam which eventually backfired.

Fred had noticed that when our 4-ton trucks showed signs of wearing out, they were usually handed on to one of the firqat or to the geysh units, having first been put back into more or less good order by a REME unit attached to us. It was almost child's play for our smooth-talking hero to persuade a naive young REME mechanic that it was virtually his duty to 'liberate' a couple of the trucks and point them in the direction of the Dhofari jebalis, who were in desperate need of transport. Especially when Fred offered to slip the mechanic £200 of the £1,000 he was making by selling the trucks to a Dhofari he had chatted up in the local village.

All went well, and in due course two trucks trundled out of the repair depot with Dhofaris driving them. And all would have remained well if one of the trucks hadn't broken down, even before it reached the buyer's farm. Unfortunately for Fred, the angry jebali then decided to lodge an official complaint with British Army Headquarters, and duly towed in the broken-down truck behind the other 4-tonner. When he started to demand his money back, a bored officer struggling through another dreary day pricked up his ears and decided to investigate – just to liven things up.

In no time at all Fred and his young pal from REME were arrested, charged and sent back to the UK. After a court martial, Fred was sentenced to six months in the 'Glasshouse' – the army gaol at Colchester – and thrown out of the Regiment, though we never found out what happened to the mechanic. But we were all very grateful to Fred, for whatever the trouble he had brought upon himself, the gossip and speculation arising from the scandal did at least help to pass the time.

On the whole, and despite the conditions at Tawi Atair, I found my tour of Oman in 1974 no worse than that in 1973. Furthermore, no one in D Squadron was killed, and there were, on balance, probably a great many more laughs than tears.

It was to be a very different story in 1975, however, when D Squadron was deployed to Oman for the final time. That tour brought tragedy, and for me it would bring about a final metamorphosis. I would leave Dhofar a fully seasoned veteran, having been exposed to the kind of horrors which only modern warfare is capable of dreaming up – and delivering.

Thereafter there would be nothing, ever, that war could throw at me that I would be unable to handle.

Chapter Seven

My final posting to Dhofar came late in the summer of 1975, and from the moment we stepped off the aircraft at Salalah I knew we were in for a scorcher. We were greeted by a cloud of flies and dust, and from the look of the billowing dark clouds to the south, the certain prospect of a monsoon downpour before nightfall. To add to our discomfort, dusk would also bring out the mosquitoes in their thousands.

Home sweet home it was not, but at least we were to be spared another soul-destroying stint at Diana One, or in the only slightly less monotonous but still wearisome Tawi Atair. This time the Sultan wanted us to shut off, once and for all, the main rebel supply route from Yemen into Dhofar. This in turn meant that we would be carrying the battle to the enemy, rather than sitting impotently in a holding location, providing daily target practice for the adoo.

One of the first things I noticed was that the quality of our air-transfer service had improved. Instead of the weirdly shaped Skyvan transport aircraft, which required some sort of landing strip in order to get in or out of a location, we were more and more using the US-built Huey helicopter, famous for the part it played in the Vietnam War; there had only been a few Hueys in-country on my first tour, and we had hardly ever gone in them.

The rugged, dramatic and, in its way, starkly beautiful terrain was unchanged, however. Our destination was a major border position called Simba, on the western edge of Dhofar's great southern plateau, from where we could look down on the Yemeni coastal town of Hauf. I say 'Yemeni', but in fact the Sultan, having studied various hundred-year-old maps of the area, had decided Hauf was part of Oman's Dhofar province, and was intent on reclaiming it. What further strengthened his determination was the fact that Hauf was the city from which the camel trains set out on the rebel supply route into Dhofar.

Our main job, apart from helping with the taking of Hauf, was to block this supply route. The Sultan meant to mount his major ground offensive at the end of the monsoon season, deploying his Baluchistani mercenary army and the firqats to seize Hauf. Meanwhile he was all in

favour of a little softening up of the city by air and artillery bombard-
ments, as a taste of things to come. We had a grandstand view of the
first big attack, which came in October and started when a squadron of
Hawker Hunters, ground-attack aircraft of the Sultan of Oman's Air
Force operating from their base at Midway in central Oman, came out
of the rising sun to blast Hauf from the sea.

It was hardly a textbook operation, however. The pilots had either
been dragged from their beds too early and were still half asleep, or they
were nervous of getting in too close to the anti-aircraft guns ringing the
city, because the end result was only of real concern to the fish cruising
innocently below the surface of the Arabian Sea – which is where all the
first wave of bombs and rockets ended up.

We had watched this débâcle from a distance, and found it
frustrating. 'Wouldn't it be a good idea,' suggested one of our troop, 'if
we patched in to their wavelength and talked the pilots in from here?'
From high on the plateau, two miles to the north, we were in a perfect
position to act as forward air control. The Boss gave his OK, with the
result that for the Hunters' second run we had a direct radio link
through to the pilots in their cockpits.

Bingo. It was a case of every one a winner. Not a single bomb or
rocket of the second batch fell short of its target. Furthermore, that was
only the start. As soon as the Hunters had had their turn the geysh set
to with their big 5.5 inch artillery pieces from a position to the south of
us, and kept up a constant barrage of the city for ten straight hours. I
think it was probably this that made the adoo really angry, for that is
what they certainly became. On the following morning they launched a
massive bombardment of Simba, using mortars and Katyushas – Soviet-
built multi-barrelled rocket launchers.

The position at Simba was, roughly, a square of ground bordering
the edge of the plateau, each of its sides measuring about two
kilometres. There were a couple of major bunkers there, with twelve-
foot thick rock and sandbagged walls and corrugated-iron roofs, and
dotted around these strongpoints were a dozen or more smaller
machine-gun or mortar positions. The location was little more than a
mile from where the rebel supply route snaked around a sharply pointed
hill, known to us as 'Capstan', which overlooked the ancient camel-
caravan trail and gave us a commanding view of what was coming in. It
was from Simba that we would eventually move forward to cut off the
supply route. The date for that operation had already been set for
several weeks ahead, and we were still preparing the ground. What we

could not see from our positions, however, was where the adoo mortar teams were located. That morning they began to shell us.

I was with three other blokes putting the finishing touches to the sandbag defences of a substantial new sangar, in fact a sort of mini-bunker, when the mortar attack started. We were filling sandbags in order to strengthen further the walls of the sangar – which was about four metres long by two metres wide – when the first mortar rounds exploded near by. The adoo were using straight high-explosive mortar bombs, which made very little approach sound. If you were very lucky you heard a low swishing noise seconds before the round struck, and just about had time to crouch or throw yourself on the ground. If you were too close to the impact point, however, then crouching or chucking yourself down was not going to help you much anyway.

Which is exactly what happened to Chris Hennessey that day. He, 'Killer' Denis and a signaller were filling sandbags when the mortar landed among them. By sheer luck I was working alone about twenty-five metres away, filling another sack with sand and shale. I didn't even hear the bomb that caused the damage. One moment I was watching three fellow troopers, and the next I was looking at a scene of utter carnage.

The mortar round scored down Chris's side and exploded at his feet, killing him instantly. Yet although he took most of the blast, the signaller next to him was badly ripped by the shell splinters, and began screaming as though his lungs were going to burst. Denis, blown off his feet, vanished below the level of the sandbag wall, just as the blast hit me and knocked me flying. I was showered with stones and rock chips thrown up by the explosion but, mercifully, not by shrapnel. Shocked and disoriented, I managed to clamber to my feet and stagger the few yards to where the mortar had exploded. And then immediately wished I hadn't.

Part of the training for the SAS should be for recruits on Selection to go and work in an abattoir for a couple of days, and squelch about in the blood and gore and guts until the sight and smell no longer affect their stomachs or minds. The smell of fresh blood and splashed-about entrails is much stronger than most people could possibly imagine, and it is not only extremely unpleasant but also extremely unsettling. After a while – or, more accurately, after a number of such experiences – the sight of mutilated bodies eventually no longer sends the stomach's contents erupting mouthwards. But the smell – that's something you never, ever, get used to.

Chris could not have known what hit him, could not have felt the explosion that so violently took his life. But the signaller had. He couldn't stop screaming. The shrapnel had caught him everywhere, almost shredding him, and he was bleeding profusely from his legs, body and face.

I vaulted over the wall, snatched up the first-aid kit and started trying to plug some of the injured man's more obvious wounds with one hand while I scrabbled for a morphine hypodermic with the other. That's when I caught sight of Denis, who had been hurled backwards off his feet and ended up huddled inside against the base of the wall. What made the sight even odder was that, by some quirky effect of the blast, he was lying on the ground stark naked apart from his boots and socks. His only obvious injury appeared to be where his arse had been peppered by small shell fragments, rather like buckshot. He was bleeding a bit, but his wounds didn't seem to be life threatening. Given his near-naked state, I was able to tell this at a glance.

The sight was a pretty ludicrous one, and for some reason – perhaps a combination of reaction and relief – I began to laugh. I just couldn't help myself. 'Fuck me, Denis, that's not a very pretty sight,' I told him, and that was enough to set him off too. Our roars of laughter mingled with the signaller's screaming, until the noise must have sounded like the kind of row that would once have been heard only in the most insalubrious Victorian madhouse. Nevertheless, our laughter did us both the world of good. On the whole, the tougher the situation, the greater the need to preserve a sense of humour. Nor was there any disrespect to Chris. We knew he was dead – and later we would find a time to mourn him. Right then it was more important for us to keep our spirits up, and laughter is the greatest pick-me-up of all.

There was no point in our trying to fire back. The adoo mortar team might have been anything up to 4 kilometres away, the effective range of an 82mm mortar, which is what we later discovered they had been firing at us. If a mortar attack went on for any length of time you might guess the range by computing the time between the initial bang of the weapon firing and the moment of impact, and working out the range by multiplying the known speed of the projectile in feet or yards per second by the time of flight in seconds. It is a complicated and imprecise method, however, and in addition it won't tell you the direction from which the fire is coming. At night you can sometimes spot the flashes as a mortar fires, but this attack came in broad daylight.

All we could do was wait until the adoo had finished their bombardment for the day, and then whistle up a helicopter to take away the two wounded and what was left of Chris in a bodybag. It was a grim business, for parts of his body had been thrown more than twenty yards by the explosion.

You never get over the speed with which things can change during warfare. Half an hour earlier I had been sitting with Chris on the ground outside the bunker, smoking a fag and idly chit-chatting. We were looking down on Capstan, and I had asked him, 'Is it what you expected?'

'Yes, I think so,' he'd replied, but the truth is that he never had time to find out, really. He was quite new to the Regiment and had only been assigned to our squadron about a month earlier. Certainly, neither of us expected that he would be dead inside half an hour.

Despite the blood and the number of his wounds, the signaller was not as badly injured as we'd feared, and later made a full recovery. 'Killer' Denis spent a couple of weeks in the hospital at Salalah, where the regimental doctor picked a load of tiny shrapnel pieces out of his arse with tweezers. He later rejoined us on Simba, though he was pretty sore for at least a month – I hardly remember him sitting down during all that time.

Denis came from the south of England originally, but had moved to live in Hereford after he joined the Regiment. He had picked up his nickname during his early days with us, while taking part in a nuclear, biological and chemical (NBC) warfare course. At some point the instructor asked him to identify a powder commonly used in chemical warfare, only to receive the answer, 'I don't know. I'm only here to kill.' From then on he was known as 'Killer'.

After he and the wounded signaller had been evacuated we began clearing up the sangar, and it was then that I came across the tailfin of the mortar bomb that had killed Chris. It had come from Britain. The adoo were actually using British ammunition against us. Naturally enough the whole squadron was furious to learn this, although the irony of it did not escape them. We theorized later that the ammunition had got into South Yemen via Libya, but no one would ever have been able to prove it. What any member of the SAS will tell you, though, is that there are some people in Britain willing to sell anything to anybody in return for a fast buck. Yet it goes without saying that there's no point in making a fuss. The sale of British-made arms to hostile or enemy states is far too hot a political potato, and there are far too many influential figures with their fingers in the till, for there to be any chance of mere soldiers getting the trade investigated and stopped.

I was angry, however. In theory, if you could spot the enemy firing a mortar on a nearby hill, then by using a plotter board you could drop a mortar round on them. And of course they could do the same to you – especially if they used British ammunition. The adoo were equipped with Russian mortar tubes which the British 81mm ammunition fitted, and they were very accurate weapons. Yet sometimes we ourselves were forced to use mortar ammunition manufactured in India, which we found to be substandard and inaccurate, as well as dangerous in that the rounds would sweat and become unstable. To know that you are fighting with substandard equipment against the best of British would have made any British soldier angry. Yet all we could do, other than moan, was sit and take it, and try to make the sangar walls thicker with every chance we got in an attempt to defend ourselves against the mortars, rockets and machine-gun fire.

Two days after Chris was killed and the signaller wounded, a couple of replacements were sent in from Salalah. One was a fresh-faced guy called Ginge; the other, Ian, a stocky Northerner originally from the Paras, had been in the Regiment about as long as I had. We were still strengthening the walls of our sangar or bunker, which by this time had been given an official name – 'Green Five'. The aim was to make the sides at least ten feet thick, interspersing sandbags with boulders, with here and there a slit from which to fire the GPMG. Jimmy and I and a couple of other guys were filling sandbags when the chopper brought in the replacements. We greeted them briefly, and suggested they stick their bergens inside the partly built sangar and sort their kit out before setting to work with the rest of us.

I wish, now, that they had been set straight to work, for just ten minutes after they arrived we were hit by a rocket attack. The first rocket went way off to the left and exploded harmlessly against some rocks a couple of hundred metres away, but the second was already homing in. The Russian-built Katyusha rockets don't travel all that fast and they make a loud whooshing sound, which gives you about two seconds in which to decide what to do, and then do it. You can either drop behind cover, or run in one direction or another.

The four of us on the work detail were about five metres from the sangar, with no cover near enough that we would be able to reach in time. But in those few seconds of warning time I realized that the rocket was heading towards the sangar. The pair inside were in most danger.

I screamed 'Incoming!' but I think they had already sensed their danger. Ian ran towards the side of the sangar nearest us and Ginge ran the opposite way, further into the bunker – and, as it happened, right into the rocket's path. He just chose the wrong way to go. It was pure bad luck.

The rocket seemed to scoop him up and hurl him into the sangar's rear wall. Then it exploded, although by then, perhaps mercifully, he was already dead from the impact of the missile. When we ran forward, it looked at first as though Ian had been killed as well. But the blood was all Ginge's. Ian had been blown off his feet by the explosion, but was only stunned.

It was almost a replay of the incident with Chris two days before. In just forty-eight hours I had seen two mates meet the most horrific deaths imaginable – although at least they were mercifully quick – and another suffer appalling wounds, and I hadn't a scratch on me.

I am neither a superstitious nor a particularly religious man, but as I waited for the helicopter to fly in to pick up Ginge's remains and take Ian, who was in deep shock, to the field hospital, I reached for the rosary beads in the top left-hand pocket of my uniform top, where they were always kept, and muttered a couple of thankful 'Hail, Marys'.

I had been given the beads by an old lady whose father had carried them through the First World War, and whose husband had carried them through the Second. She had given them to me in 1970 with the words, 'Have these, love. They took my father and my husband safely through two world wars. Let them do the same for you.' I can't remember her name, if I ever knew it, but since then I've always carried them. They have been with me in every campaign I've been in, and I never go anywhere without them. On the day in 1982 when I left for the Falklands I couldn't find them, and became very anxious as a result. Then I remembered that I'd left them in my bag in the squash club, so I went back to get them. Did they help me? Well, I'm still here – though whether that is superstition or faith I don't know. I do know, however, that holding them in those moments after Ginge was killed brought me a certain degree of comfort.

Ginge had been wiped out with such violence that our immediate reaction was a furious desire to grab our weapons and rush down the foothills and try to avenge our pals. But this was the rebels' terrain. I didn't know where they were hiding, or even what they looked like. Nor could we send out choppers to locate them, for the adoo would shoot them down with SAMs or small-arms fire. This was the lesson the Soviets were beginning to learn in the rebellious Radfan area of Yemen, where they lost a number of helicopters, and they would later suffer even heavier losses in Afghanistan. All we could do was wait patiently for the big push. Then, we hoped, it would be time for revenge. Meanwhile, there was work to be done and a sangar to finish.

We could not escape the reality, however, that our losses on this tour were already starting to mount. Another member of D Squadron had been killed in Defa the previous week, and yet in two previous tours in Oman we had suffered no losses and only a few minor casualties. Now, in the space of a week, three men were dead and lying in the mortuary, waiting to take their last journey home. I wondered briefly what the public reaction would be when the bodybags started arriving at RAF Lyneham. Then I remembered: we were the SAS, and nothing was ever released to the media about us. No one but us would ever know about the bodybags – us and the next of kin of the dead men. Nor was anyone going to tell those relatives where their loved ones had been killed.

By January of 1976 the rebels' supply route out of Yemen had finally been cut off and the adoo realized it was time to call it a day. They retreated over the border into South Yemen, leaving most of their equipment behind. In the Wadi Dharbat we found hospitals built inside caves, huge ammunition dumps, and tons of discarded equipment, all of which had originally been brought in on donkeys and camels. Suddenly there was nothing left for us to do in Oman. So far as the Sultanate was concerned, having done the job we had been asked to do, we were redundant.

Not for long, though. Returning to Hereford, we discovered that the government of the day had found another hotbed of terrorism and nationalism against which to test us. This time, however, D Squadron was not going quite so far away from home. Instead, the Regiment was deployed to Northern Ireland – although that, as they say, is another story . . .

Chapter Eight

L IKE most soldiers, I have never had much time for politicians. The majority of them strike me as shallow, mouthy creatures who are in politics for what they can get out of it, or from an inflated sense of their own importance, or – more likely – from a combination of both. At least in this country they are prevented from abusing too greatly the trappings of power by all sorts of democratic checks and balances, but the same cannot always be said of some of the less democratic countries of the world. Politicians in such places often display a cynicism that would have disgraced an eighteenth-century pirate, and never more so than when they feel themselves threatened. To a foreign dictator who has trouble at home, there is nothing like a war to take the minds of the people off their lack of freedom, their country's soaring inflation, mass unemployment, or whatever else it is that is beginning to threaten the power base of their self-appointed leader.

So when, on 2 April 1982, the Argentinian military dictator President Leopoldo Galtieri ordered his forces to invade the Falkland Islands, a British dependency, I too, like a lot of others, reckoned that it was all a ruse to shore up his flagging popularity in Argentina and in its capital, Buenos Aires, in particular.

The Falklands – a group of two main and more than a hundred small islands – are little more than specks in the South Atlantic, 400 miles off the east coast of Argentina and 8,070 miles from Britain. English sailors first landed on the islands in 1690, and they have been under continuous British occupation and administration since 1833.

In 1982, there were fewer than 2,000 people living in the Falklands, most of them on East Falkland, which includes the islands' capital, Port Stanley. Almost all the inhabitants were of British descent. They drove on the left-hand side of the road; they spoke English with a distinct West of England burr to it; and, as far as they were concerned, they were as British as anybody living in Kent or Cumbria. The Argentinians, however, had long had their eyes on the islands, which they called Las Malvinas (from Les Malouines, after the French sailors from St-Malo who had first colonized them), and which they had indeed briefly occupied at one point during the nineteenth century.

By rights, or so most Argentinians believed, the Falklands should belong to Argentina. So when Britain announced that her already tiny Royal Naval presence in that part of the world was going to be removed almost entirely with the scrapping of the Antarctic survey ship HMS *Endurance*, the military junta, headed by Galtieri, which governed Argentina saw it as a good time to 'liberate' the Malvinas and score some popularity points at home, where savage inflation and popular disaffection with the often brutal government were threatening to erupt into widespread civil unrest.

Early on the morning of Friday, 19 March 1982, a gang of some forty Argentinian scrap-metal salvagers landed on the island of South Georgia, another British dependency lying some 800 miles east and slightly south of the Falklands – a wickedly cold, inhospitable island of mountains and glacier, scourged by blizzards and cloaked in ice. During the days of coal-burning ships South Georgia had been used as a bunkering port for the then vast Royal Navy. Moreover, when whaling was still big business, British whalers had regularly used the island as a drop-off point for their catches, which could be processed in the plants there.

All that remains of these long-defunct activities in the bays at the foot of the ice-capped peaks are a handful of ancient barges and the rusting machinery housed in sheds of corroded corrugated iron that long ago surrendered to the howling wind and the snow. It was this wreckage the scrap-metal workmen had supposedly come to dismantle. However, they had been brought to South Georgia aboard an Argentinian Navy transport vessel, and it seems almost certain that their presence there formed part of the Argentinian military's plans to take over the British dependencies in the South Atlantic by stealth. Within hours of their arrival at the old whaling station at Leith, they had raised the blue-and-white flag of Argentina on British sovereign territory.

The island's only occupants were a small scientific team at the British Antarctic Survey base at Grytviken, and two women naturalists who were making a natural-history documentary for Anglia Television; one of them was the daughter of Anglia's Chairman. The moment they learned of the Argentinian presence on the island the scientists radioed Rex Hunt, the Governor of the Falklands, who in turn contacted London. The diplomatic scuffle now started. Hunt instructed the scientists to order the Argentinians to strike their flag and seek proper

authorization for their presence on South Georgia; he also dispatched
HMS *Endurance* there after she had embarked a detachment of Royal
Marines from the small Falklands garrison.

Apparently in response to British pressure, on 23 March the
Argentinian naval transport left Leith with some of the scrap-metal men
aboard. On the following day, however, an armed survey ship of the
Argentinian Navy arrived and landed a strong detachment of marines,
ostensibly to protect the remaining workmen. *Endurance* also arrived on
the same day, but remained at Grytviken with her Royal Marines still
aboard, awaiting orders. Then, while the Foreign Office fired useless
paper broadsides at the Argentinian junta, on 31 March the twenty-two
Royal Marines from *Endurance* were ordered to provide a show of
strength on the island. Their primary task was to protect the survey
team and the naturalists, but they were also to keep an eye on the
Argentinian invaders at the same time.

While *Endurance* stood off at a safe distance, ships of the Argentinian
Navy arrived, and on Saturday, 3 April the Argentinians tried to
persuade the Royal Marines to surrender, informing their commander
by radio that the Falkland Islands had already been taken (which was
true). Naturally, the British troops refused. In reply, the enemy landed
two parties of their own marines by helicopter on both sides of
Grytviken harbour and opened fire on the British position at King
Edward Point. By now thoroughly annoyed, the Royal Marines shot
down one of the Argentinians' two heavy transport helicopters and
severely damaged another chopper that had been circling and observing
them. An Argentinian Navy corvette then sailed round the headland
and into the bay, whereupon the Royal Marines holed it beneath the
waterline with an anti-tank rocket. They then used anti-tank rockets to
knock out the frigate's gun turret, and poured heavy machine-gun fire
into the ship. In the fighting, four Argentinians were killed at a cost of
one Royal Marine badly wounded in the arm.

Nobody could say that the Marines had not put up a spirited and
brave defence, despite being heavily outnumbered and outgunned. But
having shown the enemy that they were not pushovers, and knowing
that there was no possible hope of escape, they were forced to negotiate
a ceasefire and then, wisely, surrendered. They were treated honourably
and well, and were swiftly repatriated to Britain.

The loss of South Georgia, coming as it did the day after the
Argentinian takeover of the Falklands, was splashed all over the British
papers. From the rhetoric of most British politicians, and the press, you

could have been forgiven for thinking that it was the Isle of Wight that had been invaded, rather than an ice-caked fragment of rock and glacier thousands of miles from Westminster, to which most of Her Majesty's subjects could not have pointed on a map of the world.

The same was true of the Falkland Islands, for at the time only very few people had any idea where they were. What almost no one in Britain knew, either, was the extent of Argentina's ambitions and the duration of her claims to British territory in the region: six years earlier, in 1976, the Argentinians had established a fifty-man garrison on the island of Southern Thule, one of the South Sandwich group, another British dependency lying to the south of South Georgia. The Foreign Office had recommended that no action be taken to eject the interlopers.

On the islands themselves, however, immediately after the British Antarctic Survey team had reported the Argentinian presence on South Georgia, the tiny British military garrison on East Falkland had been put on red alert. Normally there were only forty Royal Marines on the Falklands to look after the islands' defence in the interests of the islanders and of Her Majesty's government. When the trouble came to a head, however, there were nearly double that number, because one Royal Marine detachment had arrived from Britain to take over the six-month tour of duty from the outgoing garrison, although some of the Marines had been sent to South Georgia aboard *Endurance*.

In the light of the Argentinian presence on South Georgia after 19 March, and of increased activity by the Argentinian Navy, the Falkland Islanders had become increasingly afraid of being invaded. By 1 April the Governor, Hunt, had been informed that what was almost certainly an Argentinian invasion force was on its way to the islands, and that day the officer commanding the Royal Marines in Port Stanley sent his men to guard key landing sites close to the capital and its airport. He was perfectly well aware, however, that in the event of an all-out invasion his men could not possibly hold back a large enemy force equipped with heavy weapons, helicopters and vehicles, and backed by air cover.

Nevertheless, when the Argentinians landed in the early hours of 2 April, the Royal Marines were waiting for them. Massively out-numbered, they had not the slightest chance of halting the heliborne and amphibious landings, which the Argentinians had codenamed 'Rosario'. Yet for three hours the tiny detachment put up a tremendous fight around Government House until around 0800 hours, when the main enemy landing force bringing heavy support began disembarking in Port Stanley harbour. By 0830, as Argentinian guns and troop carriers began to come ashore, the Governor realized that further resistance could only result in heavy casualties among the Royal Marines, and possibly among civilians as well. He therefore ordered a surrender. The Marines had killed at least two of the enemy and damaged a landing craft, but had suffered no casualties themselves.

In Britain next day, the newspapers carried pictures of the Royal Marines who had defended Port Stanley lying face down beneath the weapons of their Argentinian captors. This marked the point at which the British people began to take Argentina's disgraceful military adventure seriously. True, few of those people cared much for the Falklands Islands, but they cared a great deal that British subjects, and in particular British troops, should not be attacked and humiliated by the servants of a despicable foreign dictatorship. This failure to understand either British anger or British resolve was probably the greatest single error made by Galtieri and his fellow members of the junta. The Argentinian government also gambled on the fact that Britain was too far away to be able to do anything effective to reverse the takeover of the Falklands, and certainly too far to take military action. In this they had not only seriously overplayed their hand, but had seriously underestimated the determination of the British Prime Minister, Margaret Thatcher, who felt keenly not only the national humiliation, but also the monstrous moral wrong done to British subjects and sovereign British territory. Finally, Argentina's ruling junta also failed to comprehend that success in a manifestly just war could only strengthen politically Mrs Thatcher and her government of three years.

One of that government's first actions, once the paralysis engendered by the shock of the Argentinian invasion had dissipated, was to agree to the immediate dispatch of a task force to retake the Falklands and South Georgia, something emphasized by the Prime Minister to the people of Britain and to the Falkland Islanders – indeed, to the whole world – in her statements on television. Galtieri had sown the storm; he was about to reap the whirlwind – or rather, his military forces were.

On 5 April, three days after the Argentinians had invaded the Falklands, the SAS was on its way to war. It had been decided to deploy two squadrons, D and G, with the former leaving immediately and G Squadron some time later, to join the Task Force at sea in the South Atlantic. As I sat trying to sleep the hours away aboard the RAF VC10 flight from Brize Norton in Oxfordshire to Ascension Island in the

South Atlantic, I couldn't help grinning. I had good reason, for if it hadn't been for British Army red tape and all the usual time-serving rubbish about having 'to go through proper channels', I would have been festering in a Birmingham drill hall, waiting to go back to Hereford in two years' time, where I was due to take over as troop staff sergeant of Mobility Troop. Instead, I was flying out to war in the company of my fellow professionals.

When the Falklands crisis blew up, I was stationed in Birmingham on a two-year posting to 23 SAS, one of the Regiment's two Territorial Army units, as a permanent staff instructor. It is a sad fact that the TA SAS tends to attract numbers of Walter Mittys: survivalists in camouflage gear, beer-bellied bouncers and muscle-bound thugs who think they are Kelly's Heroes and Rambo all rolled into one. Some of these characters arrive carrying combat knives in their socks, and boast that they are kung-fu experts and all the rest of the macho rubbish. The TA has its own Selection, however, and these headbangers who turn up could not run around the block, let alone successfully complete SAS Selection. A part of my job with 23 SAS was to make sure that they never again came through the drill-hall doors. I can't say that it was a job I was particularly happy in, but it would be two years before I could go back to Hereford and take over as a troop staff sergeant. There was nothing I could do about it.

On Friday, 2 April, the day when the Argentinians invaded the Falkland Islands, the 23 SAS unit I was with was on an exercise at Otterburn training camp in Northumberland. Back in the Birmingham drill hall on Sunday afternoon, I was having a shower when in walked the adjutant to tell me that D Squadron, 22 SAS – my squadron – was leaving for the Falklands on the Monday morning.

While we had been playing soldiers in Northumberland, the rest of my friends were being briefed by the commanding officer of the SAS, Lieutenant-Colonel Mike (now General Sir Michael) Rose. And next day an advance party was to fly out to Ascension, the equatorial island which was to become a halfway house and main base for the Task Force then being assembled. The really bad news, however, was that D Squadron had asked for Killer Denis, who was now the permanent staff instructor with the 23 SAS TA unit in Leeds, to be returned to Hereford so that he could go with the squadron to the Falklands. 'What about me?' I asked. 'Why him and not me?' The adjutant told me that D Squadron wanted Denis because of his Boat Troop experience. Ironically enough, he had only gained that experience because when he and I joined the Regiment, I persuaded the D Squadron commander to give me Denis's place in Mobility Troop.

I phoned Hereford and spoke with SSM Lawrence Gallagher, a good soldier and an even better guy, who was later to be killed during the Falklands campaign. He passed me on to the squadron OC, Major Cedric Delves, who told me that he already had eighty-four names for eighty places on the VC10 that was leaving the next day. He would, though, he added, see what he could do. I knew that the OC was quietly fobbing me off in a nice sort of way, but I was still determined to go.

As it happened, I had offered to drive the training officer and the RSM back to Hereford that afternoon. While I was waiting for them, I chanced to overhear the CO of 23 SAS speaking on the phone in his office. He was talking to Denis, who had just told him that he was leaving Leeds and going back to Hereford to join D Squadron for the Falklands. Spluttering with rage, the CO told him, 'You can't do that. I'm a colonel and I'm in charge. You work for me. You stay where you are.'

I was waiting outside the CO's office until he finished his telephone conversation with Killer Denis, at which point I was going to ask for my release from 23 SAS and to be returned to D Squadron. I was fairly confident that the answer would be 'yes', as I had established an excellent rapport with the CO. Then suddenly he charged out of his office, obviously seething with anger. Seeing me he exploded: 'Billy, Billy, it's not right. They shouldn't treat me like this. I'm a colonel.' To which I said, 'Quite right, Boss,' because I knew that it was neither the time nor the place to say what I wanted to say. Back in the office, the RSM had taken over the receiver and told Denis to stay put or he'd be in a whole bundle of trouble.

Once back in Hereford I went straight to the camp. By now Peter de la Billière, who was a brigadier at the time, had got wind of the squabble. He had found out from Birmingham that Denis had been directly ordered to Hereford, instead of the request going through the proper channels. What lay at the heart of this row over a piece of army bureaucracy was the fact that when a regular SAS soldier goes to the Territorial Army, he is actually posted to the TA unit. If he then goes to war, he goes with either 21 or 23 SAS, the respective TA regiments. Army formalities dictated that the CO, 22 SAS, should have approached the CO of 23 SAS and asked him if it was okay for them to get Denis back, because of his specialist expertise. If the squadron OC had then promised to send another man to replace Denis in Leeds in the morning, the CO of the TA regiment would certainly have agreed to let Denis go. However, when he learned from Denis himself about the transfer back to Hereford the CO of 23 SAS became extremely angry and called the Brigadier, de la Billière, who in turn had words with the CO of 22 SAS. As a result Denis's departure was categorically countermanded. Which in turn meant that I still had a chance . . .

All the guys were in the D Squadron Interest Room waiting for the briefings when I arrived in camp on Sunday afternoon. They all asked if I was going with them, and I told them that I didn't know. Then I happened to glance out of the window and saw Mike Rose talking to some of the men. So I went outside and just stood there, as close to him as I could get. Eventually he finished his discussion and, noticing me, turned and asked, 'All right, Billy?' I replied that I was, whereupon – because he knew I'd been posted to the TA – he said, 'What the hell are you doing here, anyway? You should be in Birmingham.

'Look,' he added. 'I've just had one rocketing over Denis and I'm not having another one over you. So just get into the aircraft tomorrow and go with your squadron.'

'I can't do that, Boss,' I replied, looking, I hoped, suitably crestfallen. He looked at me rather oddly and asked, 'Why not?' To which I craftily answered, 'Because I have to be approached and officially asked for by you.'

The CO looked at me for a moment. 'Offer me something,' he said, after a while.

'I'm a Spanish speaker.'

'Bollocks!' he said in disbelief. And with that he marched off to the office and asked the squadron second-in-command if I spoke Spanish. When the 2IC confirmed that I did, Mike Rose told him to contact the Brigadier and ask if Ratcliffe could go with D Squadron because he spoke Spanish. De la Billière cleared it immediately. So that was how I came to be aboard the RAF VC10 that carried the squadron on that long flight to Ascension Island.

On Monday, before we left for Brize Norton, we were given a send-off briefing by Brigadier de la Billière. His final words were, 'Don't forget to keep your bergen weight below forty-five pounds.' As it turned out, however, I was later to wish that I'd found some extra space, at least for food, because we were sometimes so hungry in the Falklands that I'd have eaten my leather belt. Furthermore, because of the atrocious weather conditions we had to face and the tasks we carried out, our kit seldom weighed less than 85 pounds, and more often than not 100.

There were eighty men aboard the flight to Ascension, sixty SAS and twenty support staff. In a sense it was a flight into the unknown, because we didn't know at the time that we were off to a real scrap. We each had a bergen and a canvas holdall. In the bergen was a sleeping bag, webbing (belt kit) and spare clothing, and there was more kit in the holdall. Also loaded into the aircraft were weapons, ammunition, rations, stores, and all sorts of other equipment. We had been issued with everything we might need. Not for nothing is the SAS the best-clothed and best-equipped regiment in the world.

And there, among the rest of the squadron and the mass of stores, was I, quietly grinning at the fact that army red tape and my ability to speak Spanish had got me a seat on the plane. Meanwhile poor Denis was stuck in Leeds playing soldiers with the weekend warriors. I had good reason to grin, for the real irony of the situation was that, in 1980, Denis and I had attended the same Spanish course at a technical college. As the cliché has it, it's a funny old life.

The last thing I remember before drifting off to sleep during that interminable flight was touching the top left-hand pocket of my camouflage jacket and feeling my rosary beads. The thread stringing them together had perished and finally broken, and I now kept the simple little black beads in a plastic packet. It didn't matter. It was enough that I knew they were there.

Chapter Nine

HARD tropical light lit up the inside of the VC10 as it dropped between puffballs of white cumulus to land on the seamless, black-tarmac runway the Americans had laid for the transports supplying their missile- and satellite-tracking station on Ascension Island. Outside, although it was early morning, the heat haze rose in shimmering lines from the rocks, and a covey of partridges whirred away to safety. It looked a barren, arid, miserable place.

The flight from RAF Brize Norton to Ascension, a 34-square-mile speck of volcanic rock in the South Atlantic, 1,400 miles off the coast of West Africa, had taken eight hours. The nearest land was St Helena, an island some 1,200 miles to the south-west which, with Ascension, Tristan da Cunha and several smaller, uninhabited islands, forms the British territory of 'St Helena and dependencies'. It was on St Helena that Napoleon Bonaparte was kept in exile after his final defeat in 1815 until his death in 1821. I remember thinking that if St Helena was as lively as Ascension, then the late Emperor could not have had much to occupy his mind.

Our aircraft taxied over to some grey and white prefabricated control buildings. There was no one there to meet us, and we did not know what we were meant to do now we'd arrived. There were no ships in the harbour, and neither had we spotted any out at sea as the VC10 had made its final approach to landing. We had arrived well ahead of the Task Force, and without direction from the overall command of that force there was precious little useful that we could do. In the absence of any orders, or anyone to tell us what to do, we established ourselves in an empty school hall at the US Air Force base on that Tuesday morning. The Americans fed us, which suited us fine since they really know how to eat, and how to keep their servicemen well supplied. That afternoon we went down to the beach, zeroed our weapons, and swam with the wild sea turtles that breed on the island. Some of the guys went for a run, despite the sun and the heat. There wasn't much to see, apart from sea birds and a few wild goats chomping on rain-starved scrub.

Our American hosts were friendly, but left us to ourselves. Nobody knew who we were, and nobody asked – which was also fine by us. For nearly three days we waited for something to happen, our boredom lessened slightly by the kindness of the Americans, who gave us quantities of beer each evening.

It was not until Thursday afternoon, 8 April, that the Royal Fleet Auxiliary *Fort Austin*, a fleet replenishment ship, came into the harbour. She had sailed as the crisis deepened on 29 March to provide support for HMS *Endurance*, and thereafter had been ordered to remain on station in the South Atlantic to resupply Royal Navy ships of the Task Force on their way to the Falklands. Our squadron commander, Major Delves, realized at once that getting us aboard the *Fort Austin* would be a good way of hitching a lift in the direction we were headed. He therefore went to see *Fort Austin*'s captain, Commodore Dunlop, and asked if we could bum a ride south until such time as Royal Navy ships of the Task Force should catch up and we could transfer to one of them. The commodore agreed, and we were ordered to gather up all our kit and go aboard. It was less than a week since the Argentinians had taken over the Falkland Islands and South Georgia.

'Bumming a ride' turned out to be an unfortunate phrase. Royal Fleet Auxiliary ships have Royal Navy officers, but the crews are primarily civilian, and of the crewmen aboard *Fort Austin* a large number were homosexuals. We, however, didn't know that when we boarded the ship on that Thursday afternoon. The effect of a squadron of SAS going aboard a ship with a collection of fairly overt gays giving them the eye was extraordinary, and occasionally extremely funny. We trained while at sea, running round the decks and around the edge of a massive lift shaft, which was used to bring cargo from the lower decks. The weather was glorious, and we ran in just our shorts and trainers. As we did so, gay crew members would line up to ogle us – jokily – so that above our gasps for breath we could hear them making comments like, 'Ooh, I do like him!' They thought all their Christmases had come at once. Eventually Commodore Dunlop had to ask our OC to order us all to wear tops and trousers when we trained, because his men were getting 'over-excited'.

One night during the voyage south, several of us were playing cards in the ship's bar when a civilian member of the crew walked up to the table. He was wearing a pair of pink hot pants with purple love hearts stitched across the seat of them, and he was clearly a man with a mission. The object of his desire was one of our guys, Al, whose lean face, aquiline nose and cropped hair, as well as the fact that he was very muscular and extremely fit, apparently made him a gay's dream of heaven. It turned out that two crewmen had been arguing over who had seen Al first, and the fellow in the pink hot pants had won. Tonight he was going to try his luck.

'Hiya, Al,' he said, at which Al looked up, said non-committally, 'All right,' and carried on playing cards. Whereupon Hot Pants said, 'I'll give you a blank cheque!' Al stared at him, hard. 'Listen, sunshine. You're starting to annoy me. I've been in the Merchant Navy. So fuck off.'

'*Ooh*, you animal!' said Hot Pants, not a bit perturbed, and wiggled away. He had not given up, however. After a few beers, Al went to the heads – which is what sailors call toilets – and Hot Pants followed him. Observing the SAS man as he relieved himself, Hot Pants remarked, 'Al, you piss like a gangster, and I want to be your moll.' Luckily for him, Al thought this was so funny that he just reached over and ruffled his hair. Hot Pants must have lived off that gesture for a week.

We were five days aboard the *Fort Austin* before meeting the advanced element of the Task Force, which was made up of the destroyer HMS *Antrim*, the frigate HMS *Plymouth*, and HMS *Endurance*. As luck would have it, the two former had been on exercise with the First Flotilla in mid-Atlantic when the Falklands crisis broke, and had been ordered to join *Endurance*. They had put in at Gibraltar to refuel and resupply, and had then steamed southwards at full speed. They called at Ascension, and were joined by the RFA tanker *Tidespring*, before all three ships sailed on for their RV with *Endurance*.

With our virtue still intact, the whole squadron was airlifted by helicopter from the deck of *Fort Austin* and split between the three warships. Squadron HQ, Boat Troop and Mountain Troop went aboard *Antrim*; Air Troop, the parachuting specialists, went to *Endurance*; and Mobility Troop, of which I was still a member, went aboard *Plymouth*. During the fighting that was to come, she was bombed three times by the Argentinian Air Force, on the last occasion being hit by no fewer than three 1,000-pound bombs, which caused severe damage, although her crew eventually managed to put out the fires and patch her up so that she was at least still seaworthy.

There was little for us to do aboard *Plymouth* except eat, play cards and drink beer. Much smaller than the RFA *Fort Austin*, but with a larger crew, there simply wasn't the room for us to run round decks, and there was even less space below. The hardest problem was finding a bed.

Since *Plymouth* had no room for us, we used the petty officers' bunks while they were on watch; when they came off duty they would tap us on the shoulder and say, 'Please can I have my bunk back?' We would then wander around until each of us had found another empty berth.

Most of the ship's crew were extremely young, many of them eighteen-year-olds, and the highlight of each day was when the tannoy screamed, 'Action nutty! Action nutty!' the announcement that the NAAFI shop was open so that the young sailors could go and buy their daily ration of one bar of chocolate. When the time came to fight, however, they proved as brave and enduring as veterans of more than twice their age. By contrast, all of us in D Squadron were much older than the crew. Our average age was thirty-three, which clearly must have surprised the captain of HMS *Plymouth*, Captain Pentreath, because he kept looking at us and saying, 'I had no idea.' He was very decent, and treated us as equals.

At that time, our Royal Navy 'mini-task force' was sailing two days south followed by one day north, in order to hold position within striking distance of the territories now occupied by the Argentinians. The force's commanders had no direct orders as yet, beyond holding station, although the general idea was that we were supposed to retake South Georgia before the main Task Force arrived to engage the principal enemy forces on the Falkland Islands. Our group, now grandly named the South Georgia Task Force and under the overall command of *Antrim*'s captain, Captain Brian Young, also now included M Company of 42 Commando, Royal Marines, which, like us, had flown out to Ascension, arriving on 10 April. M Company had then embarked in *Tidespring*, although its HQ and support elements went into *Antrim*, as did a section from the Special Boat Squadron (SBS, the Royal Marines' maritime equivalent of the SAS, now the Special Boat Service) which had also come aboard at Ascension. So it had been a very mixed military force that was crammed aboard the four ships when they had rendezvoused with *Fort Austin* on 12 April, and our squadron had come aboard. There were other problems apart from overcrowding, too. Both Captain Young and the Royal Marines' commander, Major Guy Sheridan, 2IC of 42 Commando, had expected an SAS troop to join from *Fort Austin*. Instead they got an entire SAS squadron, and with it our OC, Cedric Delves, also a major. The presence of a second major, unsurprisingly, raised uncertainties over the command structure, although Sheridan was later confirmed as having overall command of the group's 'Military Force'.

Above: Bradbury Lines (now Stirling Lines), Hereford, after passing SAS Selection, November 1972. In fact, as this was an all-arms survival course, only ten of those in the picture were going on to 22 SAS. The author is at far right in the back row; his friend Taff, who joined the Paras and then passed Selection at the same time, is seated at far right; 'Killer' Denis, who ended up in Boat Troop in the author's place, while the latter took Denis's in Mobility, is third from right in the back row. Three of the ten SAS members pictured here are dead: Phil Curass (back row, far left) died in the Sea King helicopter crash in the Falklands in 1982; Andreas Skrzpkowiak (*second row, second from right*), known as 'Jonesy', was murdered while filming in Afghanistan in 1987; Ron Cook (*front row, next to Taff*), who left the Regiment and joined the South African Army, was killed in an ambush in Mozambique in 1986.

Centre: On Operation Storm in Oman: Taff by the mortar pit on Diana One, Dhofar, 1973. Hanging from the bush at right is a chuggle, a cloth water bag that cools the liquid by evaporation. Taff was later wounded on Diana One when a 12.7mm armour-piercing round from a Russian-built Dargan heavy machine-gun pierced the roof of the sangar.

Right: The author (*left*) and Taff cleaning their SLRs on Diana One. Although heavy and cumbersome, the 7.62mm SLR was at least reliable, but the British Army's version proved to be hampered in action by the fact that it was not fully automatic.

Above: The author's sangar on Diana One, 1973, with Taff at right. The steep, rocky terrain made it all but impossible to locate the enemy; the gully in the background, about 200 metres away, was a favourite adoo machine-gun position (*arrowed*). Both troopers' SLRs have been placed immediately to hand, since an attack could come without warning at any time.

Below: The author deploying to a new location by Huey (Bell UH-1) helicopter during his third tour on Operation Storm, 1975. The officer at left is now a general, one of many senior officers in the army today who have served in the Regiment.

e author at Tawi Atair during his second tour in Oman, just after the end of the monsoon: 'It was always humid, with an endless ...vering of low cloud, swarms of mosquitoes and other biting bugs, a sea of mud under foot and a landscape that had suddenly become ...y green.' The photo also shows how poorly equipped the SAS were in those days.

A mortar pit at the Simba position in Dhofar, 1975: the author (*right*) with 'Jimmy'. The weapon is an 81mm mortar, but its ammunition, seen in the background, was a mixture of British-made rounds and unreliable Indian ordnance; the picture also shows the difficulty of building any kind of defensive position in such unforgiving terrain.

Green Five, the sangar at Simba shared by the author, under construction during the final push against the adoo, September 1975, with Killer Denis at right. With him is Chris Hennessey, who was killed the day after this photo was taken when he was hit by a British-made round fired by a Russian-built 82mm mortar. The sangar looks out over a steep drop to a hill known as Capstan, at the base of which ran the adoo's supply route from Yemen.

Two days after Chris was killed, another trooper, Ginger, died at Simba when he was hit by a Russian-built Katyusha rocket. The author holding up part of the rocket casing after the attack, September 1975.

A captured adoo coastal location near the Yemeni border during the final push in Dhofar, September/October 1975. The troops are geysh (soldiers of the Omani army), and in the foreground there is an unexploded bomb dropped by one of the aircraft of the Sultan of Oman's Air Force.

Captured adoo mortar rounds and other equipment being logged by SAS members during the final push in Dhofar. Seated at right are firqa - Dhofari irregulars, mostly surrendered adoo loyal to the Sultan - while a captured adoo AK-47 has been propped against the rock wall in the background.

Members of Mountain Troop, D Squadron, on the Fortuna Glacier, South Georgia, April 1982; in the foreground is one of the two Wessex helicopters that crashed in the attempt to lift the SAS reconnaissance party off.

The Wessex from HMS *Antrim*, piloted by Lieutenant-Commander Ian Stanley, holding in the hover position at full power just before landing, after returning from the Fortuna Glacier, 22 April 1982. On board the aircraft are the fifteen men from the SAS reconnaissance party and the crews of the two Wessex that crashed on the glacier.

The Argentinian submarine *Santa Fe* moored alongside the British Antarctic Survey base at Grytviken after the capture of South Georgia, April 1982. Severely damaged at sea by Royal Navy helicopters, she was forced back into harbour; a few hours later the Argentine garrison surrendered. The photograph illustrates well the island's bleak and inhospitable nature.

FIRST DAY OF ISSUE
FALKLAND ISLAND DEPENDENCIES

25 APR 1982

BRITISH ANTARCTIC SURVEY
KING EDWARD POINT
SOUTH GEORGIA
LAT. 54° 16 S LONG. 35° 30'W

VIEWS OF THE FALKLAND ISLANDS

One of the first-day covers franked by SAS members during their illicit raid on the post office at Grytviken; they set the date to that on which the Argentinian garrison on South Georgia surrendered. 'I was given one – I don't know what they are worth today, for I've never tried selling it. But, because of a disaster that was to come, their rarity value was tragically increased.'

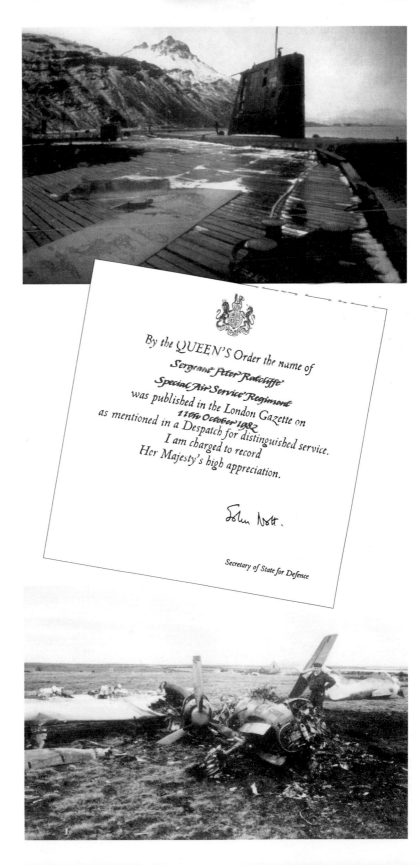

Another view of the *Santa Fe* moored at Grytviken after the capture of South Georgia, April 1982. Some of the damage inflicted on the vessel, which forced her back into harbour, is clearly visible on the conning tower (or 'fin'), which took a direct hit from an AS12 missile fired by one of the Wasp helicopters from HMS *Endurance*.

By the QUEEN'S Order the name of
Sergeant Peter Ratcliffe
Special Air Service Regiment
was published in the London Gazette on
11th October 1982
as mentioned in a Despatch for distinguished service.
I am charged to record
Her Majesty's high appreciation.

John Nott.

Secretary of State for Defence

The Mention in Despatches the author received for leading a four-man patrol at Fox Bay on West Falkland to observe and report on the substantial Argentinian garrison there. By the time this was gazetted, however, the author's name and unit and details of the award had already been published in the *Sun*.

The wreckage of an Argentinian Pucara ground-attack aircraft on the airstrip at Pebble Island after the raid by D Squadron on the night of 14 May 1982. In all the SAS destroyed eleven enemy aircraft, six of them Pucaras, for no loss to themselves.

D Squadron members checking Land Rover 110s at Victor, the main British holding base in the United Arab Emirates, prior to deployment to Al Jouf in Saudi Arabia, January 1991. Several LAW80s (hand-held anti-tank rockets) in their barbell-shaped cases can be seen on the ground.

An SAS trooper and off-road Honda motorcyle beneath the tailplane of a C-130 at Victor, prior to deployment to Al Jouf. The author found that the bikes and riders proved their value on patrol in Iraq: 'The bikes were used partly to check out the ground ahead and partly to carry messages between vehicles. Because of their greater speed across country, and the fact that they threw up much less dust than the 110s, they could go out in advance of the patrol to take a close-up look . . .'

An RAF Special Forces Boeing Chinook flying low over the desert during the Gulf campaign, showing the twin jet engines and massive tail ramp. Weighing 23 tons and capable of lifting up to another 15, the huge helicopters were often flown near their maximum speed of 188 mph only 50 feet above the desert – at night. Besides flying in and resupplying the SAS patrols, Chinooks were also used in the search for Bravo Two Zero.

During what proved to be a ten-day voyage, the seas became rougher and the weather progressively colder as we sailed further south. South Georgia lies some eight hundred miles east, and one hundred or so south, of the Falklands, placing it that much closer to Antarctica and with a wickedly cold climate to match. We couldn't go outside because the wind-chill factor sent the temperatures plunging well below zero. We played cards or read or watched porn videos, of which there seemed to be an inexhaustible supply but which at times bored me to tears, to the extent that I often nodded off to sleep in the middle of watching one. Still, sleeping helped to pass the time, an advantage since our greatest enemy so far was boredom.

On 21 April we came in sight of South Georgia and its attendant icebergs, and that day our formal orders came to retake the island from its illegal occupiers, using whatever force was necessary to do the job. D Squadron, 22 SAS, was to get the first close look at the enemy in the Falklands War.

Under Sheridan's command, the combat group was made up of ourselves, No. 2 Special Boat Squadron, Royal Marines, and M Company, 42 Commando. We would be supported by the guns and helicopters of *Antrim*, *Plymouth* and *Endurance*, the whole operation remaining under the overall command of Captain Young.

Unfortunately, however, although we had a rough idea of their numbers, no one knew exactly where the Argentinians were on South Georgia, or what they were up to. So, rather than risk sending his men blind into an amphibious operation, Sheridan decided, after discussing the problem with our OC, Delves, to put in a covert SAS troop to report on the enemy. At the same time, 2 SBS, which was to form the main advance party, would go ashore in Gemini inflatables to the southwest of the abandoned settlement of Grytviken, although how abandoned it was now, given the Argentinian presence on the island, was anyone's guess. However, if these reconnaissances showed that conditions were favourable for the operation to retake the island, D Squadron and the SBS would launch diversionary raids as the main amphibious invasion came ashore at Grytviken.

Where the recce by D Squadron was concerned, the idea was for Mountain Troop to be inserted by helicopter on to South Georgia's Fortuna Glacier, on the northern coast of the island some miles west of Grytviken. It was a wild and inaccessible place, but that meant that the Argentinians were most unlikely to see or hear the helicopters going in, or subsequently to spot the patrol. From there they were to march over the mountains and establish observation posts from which to watch and report the enemy's strength and movements in the derelict settlements of Leith and Stromness, which also lay on the island's north coast, between the glacier and Grytviken. We had no idea what was going on in these settlements, although the British Antarctic Survey people had, amazingly, furnished us with plans of them. These were so detailed that they even included room-by-room descriptions of the houses where the occupying force of Argentinians were thought to be living.

The weather was atrocious, but the use of poor conditions to screen the insertion formed part of the plan. At noon on 21 April, therefore, fifteen members of Mountain Troop under their troop commander, Captain John Hamilton, lifted off the deck of the command ship, HMS *Antrim*, in Wessex helicopters to be flown to the west of the settlement at Leith.

I have seen some terrible weather during my service, but nothing as bad as that on South Georgia – and I didn't even go to the glacier. Whiteouts – sudden swirling blizzards that reduce visibility to no more than a couple of feet – made the first two helicopter attempts to land the men impossible. Three times the naval pilots flew between the ships and the shore, before finally succeeding in setting down on the Fortuna Glacier at the third attempt.

Within minutes, however, the whiteout was back as gale-force winds whipped the glacier. Carrying their bergens, each weighing 77 pounds, and dragging four pulks (sledges) each weighing 200 pounds, in five hours Mountain Troop had covered about half a mile – and these men were the cream of mountain-warfare experts.

With the light fading fast, they tried erecting two-man Arctic tents behind an outcrop of ice in order to provide some shelter. But savage winds, by now gusting in excess of 100 mph, blew one tent away like a paper handkerchief and snapped the tent poles of the others. Five men crawled into one tent while the rest huddled for shelter under the pulks in sub-zero temperatures as winds that had now reached storm force clawed at the glacier. Next morning, 22 April, knowing that they could not possibly get through another night without the very real probability of some or even all of them dying of exposure, Captain Hamilton radioed *Antrim* to ask for an evacuation.

Three Wessex helicopters set out for the glacier, but couldn't find the SAS patrol and returned to refuel. On their second attempt they reached the men through a fifteen-minute, clear-weather window at 1330 hours, and embarked them and their equipment. But minutes after lift-off one of them crashed in a blinding whiteout, although, miraculously, of the seven men aboard only one was injured. They and the crew of the crashed aircraft were split between the two remaining helicopters, but in whiteout conditions one hit an ice ridge and also crashed, luckily again without serious injury. In one of the greatest single feats of the entire war the pilot of the third helicopter, Lieutenant-Commander Ian Stanley, embarked all the SAS and aircrew aboard his aircraft and managed to lift off the glacier, although most of the patrol's equipment had to be abandoned with the two wrecked Wessex. With himself and fifteen men and their weapons aboard, as well as the pilots and other aircrew from the two crashed machines, Stanley's helicopter was seriously overloaded. Because of the weight, he was unable to hover over *Antrim*'s deck, and he therefore decided to crash-land instead, slamming the aircraft down with the rotors at full power to slow the descent. For his skill and courage in bringing back the troop and the other airmen intact, and for his later actions, Ian Stanley was awarded the DSO, the only one awarded to a pilot in the campaign.

Unsurprisingly, any plans for further landings on the Fortuna Glacier were immediately abandoned. New schemes had to be hatched, and it was now decided to send in the whole of D Squadron, although Boat Troop and the SBS would make the initial recces. Next morning, under cover of the pre-dawn darkness, Boat Troop lowered five Gemini inflatables over the side of HMS *Antrim* into the waters of Stromness Bay. There was little wind and the sea was fairly calm. Each inflatable carried a three-man team, whose orders were to land on Grass Island in Stromness Bay, from where they were covertly to watch Leith and other areas around the bay and report enemy strengths and movements back by radio.

The specially silenced outboard motors had been warmed up in a tank on board *Antrim* only half an hour before the boats were launched. Nevertheless, once in the water, two of the engines wouldn't start. At the time it didn't seem any great setback, since the other boats could easily tow the unpowered craft to Grass Island – or so we thought. Once *Antrim* had departed, however, there was a swift and astonishing change in the weather. The wind that had, until then, been little more than a breeze rose to gale force in seconds. White-capped waves smashed over the Geminis and the troop was scattered in the Antarctic darkness all over Stromness Bay.

The two towed Geminis broke loose and were swept away. The crew of one paddled with their mess tins, but even so were in danger of being swept far out to sea when, next morning, Ian Stanley picked up the signal from their emergency beacon and winched them aboard his Wessex. The three troopers on the other drifting Gemini managed to paddle ashore on a headland, where they dug themselves in and remained concealed for several days to avoid being spotted by the enemy and compromising the operation. The others made it to Grass Island, where they set up camouflaged OPs from which to watch the settlements.

Launched at the same time, the Royal Marines SBS teams had also been hit by the severe weather. One section got ashore, but had then to be picked up by helicopter and reinserted at a different location. Another, using Geminis to infiltrate Cumberland Bay, at the head of which lies Grytviken, reported back that jagged ice had cut holes in their inflatables and that they were beginning to sink. They too were eventually picked up and taken to their observation points by helicopter, once more flown by the indefatigable Lieutenant-Commander Stanley.

By now, however, the odds against a successful amphibious invasion of South Georgia had lengthened considerably. On the evening of 24 April, Captain Young received intelligence from CINCFLEET HQ at Northwood, back in Britain, that an enemy submarine was approaching the area where the South Georgia Task Force was operating. Young immediately ordered *Tidespring* and *Endurance* to withdraw out of the danger area; with them went many of the Royal Marines whom Sheridan needed for his assault.

Then the British luck turned again. On the morning of the 25th, while he was on his way back from dropping off the SBS section, Ian Stanley spotted the Argentinian submarine *Santa Fe* on the surface off Cumberland Bay. He immediately attacked and succeeded in damaging her. Landing on the deck of HMS *Endurance*, he refuelled and returned to the fray. Three times he attacked the submarine, now supported by other helicopters from *Endurance*, *Plymouth* and the frigate HMS *Brilliant*, which had joined the task force the night before. This aerial assault by depth charges, missiles and guns proved devastating. Her hull plates buckled, critically damaged and unable to submerge, *Santa Fe* limped into Grytviken, where the Argentinians must have wondered where this powerful British force had come from.

With the submarine danger over, the ships carrying the bulk of the assault party could safely return to South Georgia. But the element of surprise had now gone out of the window, and it would be some time before *Tidespring* could come up with the warships – time in which the Argentinians would be able to strengthen their defences and make their dispositions against a British attack. In the light of this, there was nothing for it but to attack at once, while the enemy was still surprised at the British presence and demoralized by the attacks on the *Santa Fe* – before most of the Royal Marines could arrive to take a hand.

Thus, because the main assault force from 42 Commando's M Company was still miles out at sea aboard *Tidespring*, it fell to D Squadron, 22 SAS, to assault Grytviken in company with a composite force of SBS and those marines who had been aboard the warships, rather than the tanker. They would be supported by naval gunfire from the two destroyers. At 1445 that afternoon, therefore, the assault force of around seventy-five men under the overall command of Major Sheridan was ferried ashore by helicopters, landing about half a mile south of Grytviken. They immediately began to advance on the settlement.

At Sandhurst, officers are taught that, ideally, for an assault against defended positions to succeed, the attacking force should always outnumber the defenders by at least three to one. Not in my book, however, for success often depends on who's doing the attacking, as well as factors like surprise and the enemy's morale – as was proved in the retaking of South Georgia.

As the first of the assault force began to land near Grytviken, *Antrim* and *Plymouth* commenced the naval bombardment, directed by a fire controller in a Wasp helicopter. The noise was ear-splitting as they carefully directed their shells to land near the defenders without hitting them. Gradually they shifted their aim to drop their shells closer to the settlement, giving the Argentinians a fair idea of what they were up against. A naval gunner told me later that this was the first time that Royal Navy ships had fired in anger since the Korean War.

Meanwhile the warships' Lynx and Wessex helicopters were ferrying the assault party ashore, landing each group of men behind a ridge that screened them from the enemy's view. They took the men from HMS *Antrim* first, and we aboard *Plymouth* were to go in last. If there was going to be a big battle we wanted a lump of the action, but even while we were waiting to be picked up from *Plymouth* and ferried ashore the Argentinian garrison surrendered.

When Major Sheridan and his composite force reached Grytviken, the Argentinians were lined up in three ranks. Their national flag was flying over them and they were singing their national anthem, but white bedsheets of surrender hung from the windows of the houses. They gave in without putting up a fight and before the SAS and Royal Marines had even come within small-arms range, and without a single one of their side having been injured. Even as Sheridan was accepting the enemy's surrender, D Squadron's SSM, Lawrence Gallagher, ripped down the blue-and-white flag of Argentina and quickly ran up the Union flag in its place.

At the time, I was leaning on the rail of HMS *Plymouth* with our troop commander, Captain Paul. As we looked out towards Grytviken, wishing that we'd had a part in the action, he suddenly suggested that we get a Wasp helicopter to take us ashore, so that we could at least claim to have been in South Georgia. The choppers were flying to and fro between the island and the warships continually, and we had no difficulty in cadging a lift on a Wasp, which set us down at Stromness Bay. About half a mile along the coast we met members of Boat Troop who had gone in aboard their Gemini inflatables. The troop sergeant told us that the Captain Alfredo Astiz, the commander of the Argentinian garrison still at Leith, which we had not yet approached, had refused to surrender.

Back home in Buenos Aires, Captain Astiz was known as the 'Butcher of Argentina' for his part in atrocities against supposed dissidents during the military dictatorship; he was also wanted for questioning by several European countries over the disappearance of numbers of their citizens in Argentina some years earlier. In the light of his defiance and that of his troops still at large, Astiz was issued with an ultimatum by Captain Young: if he and the garrison at Leith had not surrendered by nine o'clock the next morning, then we would be ordered in to enforce their surrender, using maximum force, if necessary.

By South Georgia standards, the night was quite mild, so the troop commander and I put up a two-man tent on a little beach. Suddenly we heard what sounded like people singing, albeit out of tune. We could scarcely believe our eyes for, coming towards us over the hill was a gaggle of men all singing and carrying blazing torches of rags soaked in pitch tied to lengths of wood. They were making a tremendous row, and we watched them suspiciously as they approached, weapons at the ready. When they got a bit closer we realized that these were the Argentinian scrap-metal men who had been put ashore to salvage the old whaling ironmongery, thus helping to precipitate the whole crisis.

With the imminent threat of bombardment by naval gunfire and an all-out infantry assault, Captain Astiz had ordered the civilians to get themselves out of harm's way, telling them to carry torches and make a lot of noise so that the British would know they were not combatants sneaking up on them.

Moving forward, I counted thirty-nine men in all. They were a scruffy-looking bunch, and clearly both confused and frightened. Since there was nowhere for them to shelter on 'our' beach, I told them to walk round the bay to Stromness and wait there in the cookhouse of the abandoned whaling station, adding that they would be picked up next morning and taken to a British ship. My final words to them were, 'Don't worry. There is no one there and you'll be quite safe.' They were very relieved, and shouted 'Muchas gracias' as they walked off into the darkness.

We waited in our tent on the beach. About an hour after the scrap-metal merchants left us, there came the sound of gunfire and tracer bullets lit up the sky over Stromness. There were rounds flying all over the place. What the hell was going on?

Shortly afterwards, HMS *Plymouth* entered the bay and lowered a boat, which brought in the rest of our troop. As we greeted them, Bob, the troop sergeant, asked me, 'Where's Terry?'

'Terry who?' I replied, adding that I didn't know who he was talking about. He told me the man's surname and said that he'd come ashore with a patrol hours ago in a helicopter from *Plymouth*. I hadn't seen this Terry, who was a corporal, but I suddenly realized what all the firing had been about. Terry and his patrol had shot up the scrap-metal workers – the civilians whom I'd promised would be safe. The poor workmen, already frightened and bewildered enough, must have wondered what kind of soldiers we were to fire on innocent non-combatants.

Being nominally a Spanish speaker, next morning I went forward with the Boat Troop commander to meet Captain Astiz. He had considered the British ultimatum and obviously had not fancied being hammered by a naval bombardment and attacked by British soldiers and marines. As a result he and the remaining Argentinians at Leith agreed to the surrender terms.

Dressed in full naval uniform, Astiz came across as an arrogant piece of work. Haughty and dismissive, he looked at us from beneath the peak of his cap as though we were pieces of dirt. He refused to acknowledge the troop commander, an SAS captain, simply saying that he had come to surrender himself and his men. There were ten minutes left before the ultimatum ran out and our naval bombardment would start up again.

I had prepared a little speech for him in Spanish, which I had put together from my phrase book. I had been going to say 'Para usted, mi amigo, la guerra se un sobre.' As it turned out, however, Astiz spoke perfect English, so I didn't get the chance to air my skill as a linguist.

Still behaving as though it were he accepting our capitulation, he was taken aboard *Antrim* to sign the official surrender document. He was later repatriated to Argentina, without being questioned about his activities either by the British or by any of the countries whose nationals had disappeared after allegedly having fallen into his hands. As for me, it was just as well that I didn't have to try out my linguistic abilities, for it turned out that the sentence I had prepared in my limited Spanish meant, 'For you, my friend, the war is in an envelope.' I was unmercifully ragged by my friends in Mobility Troop when I foolishly told them of my mistranslation.

Back on board HMS *Plymouth*, I pieced together what had happened to the scrap-metal workers. After I had sent them on their way to the safety, as I believed, of the old whaling station, Corporal Terry, an ex-Royal Marine with a tendency to think he was God's gift to soldiering, saw them walking towards him, carrying their burning torches and still singing away. I have no idea why, but when they were about a hundred yards away in the darkness Terry shouted, 'Halt! Billy Ratcliffe?' He repeated my name a couple more times, to the bemusement of the scrap-metal men, who didn't know what he was talking about. They had never heard of me, and I had not given them my name when I had told them to make for the abandoned whaling station. Failing to get what he took to be a satisfactory answer, Terry and the rest of his patrol opened fire; nor did they aim over the heads of the workmen, but directly at them. Mercifully, not a single one of the Argentinians was wounded, despite having been fired on by an SAS corporal and the rest of this patrol.

Afterwards, on *Plymouth*, the three troop 'headsheds' – headshed is an SAS term for people in charge – held a debriefing with Terry about the incident. I asked Terry what he had been doing challenging civilians with my name, to which he replied that he thought the people were being led by me. 'And if they were not, then what were they supposed to say?' I continued. Not unnaturally, he had no answer to that, so I asked him how many times he'd been in action.

'You challenged in my name, you opened fire, and you missed every one of those Argies. Thank God you can't shoot straight,' I said, as quietly as I could, although I was seething with anger. 'You go around boasting about how good you are,' I went on, 'and there you were shooting at innocent civilians. What you did could have resulted in a major incident. Anyone would think we're a gang of psychopaths.'

Disgusted I may have been, but this was the Regiment, with its own code and its own way of handling matters. As a result, the four of us agreed that what had been said would stay within the confines of that room. Minutes later, however, while I was drinking a cup of tea, one of the other members of Terry's patrol suddenly came up and began to tear into me, asking me what right I had to call him a psychopath.

I told him to shut his mouth, grabbed Terry and shepherded him into a room. The troop commander and staff sergeant, anxious to know what was going on, saw us and followed. With the door closed I turned to them and, indicating Terry, said furiously, 'This guy has just repeated to another member of his patrol what we'd said to him in private. What's more, he twisted my words to make out that I'd accused all the troop of being psychopaths.' Then I told Terry, 'After my stint at the TA, I'm coming back as troop sergeant. And when I do get back, make sure you're not there. Because, if you are, I'll get rid of you. And that's not a threat. It's a promise.'

As things settled back down board we were fed and watered, and I went off for a shower. It was pretty primitive – we were allowed three pulls of a chain that released a measured amount of water through the shower head – but it was adequate. It was a pity, though, that the navy hadn't allowed the Argentinian scrap-metal workers a shower when they were brought aboard *Plymouth*. I went to practise my Spanish on them, and the stink from body odour and filth and unwashed clothing was so bad that it caught like ammonia at the back of my throat. When I told them that a big force was coming from Britain to take back the Malvinas, they stared at me for a few moments, dumbstruck. They simply could not believe that the British would come so far for a fight over some small and barren islands. When I reminded them of what had just happened on South Georgia they got the message, though.

Twenty-four hours later we were ordered to move across to HMS *Antrim* in helicopters, which ferried nine men at a time. Then the kit had to be shifted in cargo nets slung beneath the choppers. Other troops had moved across from the Antarctic survey vessel *Endurance*, with the result that, that night, all of D Squadron was aboard the South Georgia Task Force command ship.

It was on *Antrim* that we watched a satellite video of the Prime Minister, Margaret Thatcher, walking to a microphone outside Number 10 Downing Street and telling the nation, 'Rejoice, just rejoice. South Georgia has been liberated.' We didn't bother to cheer. We knew it was all political bullshit – good for morale at home, but also a good vote-catcher for politicians.

Before we left South Georgia, one of the guys in the troop came up with an idea which, he said, would make them all some money. He reckoned that if some of them got into the post office at Grytviken (which was maintained as a working post office because of the British Antarctic Survey base there) and found some first-day issue envelopes, they could postmark them with the date South Georgia was recaptured. Provided they didn't produce too many, these souvenirs would surely come to be worth quite a lot of money, especially given the interest in the campaign that was growing daily back in the UK.

Getting into the post office was not a problem – a crowbar took care of that. But though they found loads of first-day issue envelopes, no matter how many drawers they rummaged in they couldn't find an official rubber stamp. Finally they discovered a stamp which read, 'British Antarctic Survey, King Edward Point, South Georgia.' They set the date to 25 April 1982, to mark the day we'd taken back South Georgia, franked a whole batch of first-day issue envelopes and stuffed their pockets with them. I was given one – I don't know what they are worth today, for I've never tried selling it. But, because of a disaster that was to come, their rarity value was tragically increased.

Although recapturing South Georgia had proved no big deal in the end, it had been accomplished without the loss of a single British life, and despite initial, and potentially very damaging, disasters at the Fortuna Glacier and with the patrols sent in by Gemini inflatables. It had also achieved one very important objective: Britain now had a safe haven for the liner *QE2*, then making her way south with the Task Force. She had been requisitioned by the government from her owners, Cunard, and turned into a troop ship. Rather than put the great liner at risk from submarine and air attack nearer the Falklands, she was able to anchor in South Georgia's Stromness Bay and offload the troops she was carrying into landing ships, which took them on to the Falklands. As a result, *QE2* was never put in harm's way. Given that the loss of such a prestigious vessel to enemy action would have been a propaganda disaster of the first magnitude, quite apart from the loss of life that would have inevitably attended her sinking, the fact that she was able to anchor in safety in South Georgia was itself of inestimable value.

So far, we had achieved our objective and had lost no one. Morale was high. Ahead of us, however, disaster waited.

Chapter Ten

A FTER two days aboard *Antrim* we cross-decked by helicopter to HMS *Brilliant*, a new Type 22 frigate built mainly from aluminium. Cross-decking was not just a matter of picking up your own personal kit and weapons. Each time we switched ships we moved the equipment of the whole squadron. And I'm talking about vast amounts of ammunition, heavy weapons, rations, signals equipment and other kit, enough gear – about 15 tons of it – to have filled a C-130 or a giant sea container crammed to maximum capacity.

After being cooped up in *Plymouth*, life aboard the much larger *Brilliant* seemed like sheer luxury. She had full standing headroom and the companionways were wide and high. It was the difference between staying in a cramped seaside bed-and-breakfast and living in a five-star hotel. Even so, bed space was still the problem, so we bunked wherever we could, often having to wait until a sailor went on watch so that we could grab his berth for a few hours.

Unfortunately we were only in *Brilliant* for a little over twenty-four hours before we were ordered to cross-deck again. This time we were sent to join the aircraft carrier HMS *Hermes*, the flagship of the main Task Force, which had now reached striking distance of the Falklands. As a result, *Plymouth* and *Brilliant* had left South Georgia and steamed at full speed to join the main battle group under the Task Force's overall commander, Rear-Admiral John 'Sandy' Woodward.

On board *Hermes*, D Squadron was quartered wherever its soldiers could find a bed, with the officers going into the naval officers' quarters, and the NCOs joining the petty officers. Even on a massive aircraft carrier, there wasn't adequate room for another squad of men. I spent most of my time aboard the carrier sleeping, crammed between some pipework beneath the ship's low deckheads. The stench of human beings confined at close quarters was dreadful. We couldn't go on to the outside decks because it was freezing cold and the ship was rolling around in the almost constant gale-force winds that scourge the South Atlantic. Amazingly, of the eighty-four days the SAS was engaged in the Falklands War, fifty-four were spent on ships and just thirty on land.

For soldiers forced on to ships, it was difficult to understand what was happening, and we were given very little information about the Task Force's intentions. We seemed to be sailing aimlessly, although I imagine that Admiral Woodward knew exactly what he was about. Nevertheless, the lack of information and our apparently aimless course, coupled with the fact that we were cooped up in restricted quarters most of the time, added to an overall sense of disorientation.

We combated this by trying to keep busy, and especially by making plans for the kind of operation at which the SAS excels. Every day we had headshed meetings with officers and the troop sergeants. The OC, Major Delves, gave us hypothetical scenarios involving various Falklands locations, and we had to come up with viable plans of attack. The idea was to get us thinking of any possible eventualities that might arise in the weeks to come.

At some time at the beginning of May I was taken to one side by the OC, who told me that he had a job for me. And what a job . . .

As a prelude to one of the most daring operations of the war, six members of B Squadron, SAS, were going to parachute into the South Atlantic and come aboard *Hermes*. From the carrier, they were to be taken aboard a Sea King helicopter and flown into Argentina. Their role was to locate the main airfield on Tierra del Fuego from which Argentinian aircraft would fly to attack British ships and, once we had actually landed in the Falklands, British soldiers. All I was told by the OC, since the plan was highly secret and details were given out strictly on a need-to-know basis, was that once they had landed in Argentina, the six men, one of them an officer who had command, would leave the helicopter and walk to their objective. Despite the secrecy, it didn't take much to work out that the overall plan was for the patrol to locate the airfield and destroy the Argentinian aircraft on the ground, or to guide in a Special Forces C-130 with B Squadron aboard to carry out a raid similar to the hostage rescue carried out by the Israelis at Entebbe, Uganda, in 1976. It was an operation tailor-made for the SAS – exactly the kind of hit-and-run warfare for which the Regiment was founded and at which it has always excelled. And every man I knew in the squadron would have given his right arm to have had a part in it.

My role was to go with them. Once the six-man patrol under their officer had been dropped off, however, I was to stay aboard with the pilot and co-pilot, who were then to fly the Sea King to a nearby lake and deliberately sink it, since the distance to Tierra del Fuego from the Task Force was at the very limit of the aircraft's range. If we were successful in landing the patrol and then concealing the chopper, I was to report by radio directly to *Hermes* that everything had gone smoothly. After that I was to take the Royal Navy pilots, evading capture, along an escape route from Argentina, which I was to work out, and into Chile, where we were to be met by other members of the Regiment who would be waiting in hiding. Chile, which had long-standing bad relations with Argentina because of disputes over territorial waters, maintained close links with Britain throughout the war, and secretly provided material aid in a number of ways. General Augusto Pinochet, the President of Chile at the time of the Falklands War, encouraged his country's friendly assistance to Britain, which does much to explain the disgust of Lady Thatcher, as well as many British veterans of the Falklands, at the ageing general's treatment recently at the hands of the British government.

Aboard the flagship, I was weighed – as was everyone else who would be on the flight – and the Sea King helicopter was stripped down almost to the bare bones. Everything that was not required to fly the aircraft was stripped out of the fuselage – padding, soundproofing, seats, superfluous wiring and equipment – because the weight factor was critical if the helicopter was to carry sufficient fuel to fly from *Hermes* the massive distance to Argentina.

The plan was for me to spend up to two weeks ensuring the safety of the Sea King pilots, and I accordingly drew field rations for that amount of time for the three of us. Checking, for the hundredth time, my own weapons, ammunition and survival equipment, I was thoroughly geared up for the mission – although, if I'd had the chance, I would rather have been with the locate-and-destroy team. By then the selected members of B Squadron had parachuted into the sea and been picked up by and lodged aboard another warship. Early in May they were brought aboard *Hermes* and everything was made ready for take-off that night. Then Sod's Law took over, for at the very last minute I was pulled off the mission. Apparently Admiral Woodward had decided that I would not be needed; the pilots could escape to Chile without an escort, and one man less on the Sea King would mean that it could carry more fuel.

I watched the laden helicopter lift-off the flight deck and, within moments, vanish into the darkness. To say that I was miserable does not even come close to describing my overwhelming disappointment.

Some months later, we, and the rest of the world, learned that a Royal Navy Sea King helicopter had landed in the extreme south of Argentina – it had been discovered on 16 May – but had been found abandoned. Of its crew and passengers, if there were any passengers, there was no sign. The official line was that it had been making for Chile, but had mistaken its landing point. It was not until six years later, however, that I discovered what had really happened on that top-secret mission into Argentina.

In 1988 we were on Arctic-warfare exercises in Norway when I happened to meet the pilot of the Sea King helicopter again. We recognized each other straight away, and it quickly became clear that he was a man with a grievance to air. When we got a chance to talk alone, he told me that he was still disgusted by events of that long-ago morning. He had flown for hundreds of miles with the aircraft blacked out, and at low level to dodge the enemy radar. Having arrived safely and undetected over the landing point in Argentina, after an epic flight by anyone's standards, he had called the troop commander forward to tell him that they had reached their destination.

The officer, however, had refused to accept the location and demanded that they fly round again to get another positive fix on the ground. Once more the Sea King's pilot told him, 'Yes, this is definitely it. You are *here*,' emphasizing his point by indicating their position on the map. Yet the troop commander had again refused to believe it. 'Well, this is it,' the pilot told him, thoroughly exasperated. 'You've got to get out here – like it or not – because I'm running out of fuel.' And he set the chopper down.

So far as I know, the SAS patrol then simply took a compass bearing and headed due west – towards the safety of Chile, from where they were eventually repatriated to the UK. They didn't make the slightest attempt to locate the enemy airfield.

As for the pilot and co-pilot, they had ditched the helicopter, as ordered, in a nearby lake, where it was intended to sink and remain undetected for all time.

'But that's not the way it happened,' the pilot told me. 'Despite punching holes in it, the aircraft simply would not sink, so we left it half-submerged.' Then, having tried to destroy the evidence of their clandestine mission, he and the co-pilot had legged it into Chile, from where they too were repatriated to Britain. The SAS patrol had not even hung around long enough to help destroy the chopper and guide the two navy pilots to safety.

When the wreckage of the Sea King was discovered, there was immediate speculation about a covert raid into Argentina by British Special Forces.

But the government denied it totally, saying that the helicopter pilot had developed engine trouble with the result that its crew had become disorientated and had crash-landed in Argentina, mistaking it for Chile. Since Tierra del Fuego is divided roughly in half, and roughly north-south, between Chile and Argentina, this seemed plausible enough – even if the helicopter was an astonishingly large distance from any Task Force ships.

Six years later, that helicopter pilot was still not just angry, but absolutely disgusted by what had happened. Nor do I blame him for feeling that way. He and his co-pilot risked their lives to get the patrol into Argentina – and were then badly let down by men from the Regiment.

For a long time I have thought that while SAS Selection might be the toughest in the world, it doesn't tell you everything you need to know about a man. Only what he does in battle will ever show you what he's really like. The men of that B Squadron patrol threw away the chance of a lifetime. Here was an opportunity, not only to lessen British losses and perhaps shorten the war by severely hitting the Argentinian Air Force on the ground, but to go down in history as having pulled off the most daring exploit in modern warfare. Which is what the SAS is all about – or should be.

But that patrol blew it. Instead of heading for the enemy airfield, they hightailed it for Chile. They didn't even bother to look at the target and judge how difficult it would be to achieve a successful mission, deciding to call the operation off without taking a single pace towards the danger area. Anyone reading this can be forgiven for asking, whatever happened to 'Who Dares Wins'? Above all, can you hope to win if you are not prepared to dare at all?

In the aftermath and inevitable inquiry into what went wrong, the officer commanding the patrol quite rightly resigned his commission. The troop sergeant, who was nearing the end of his army career, was quietly sidelined until his time expired. To my mind, though, the damage to the Regiment was much more severe than the loss of two of its members.

I had overheard people talking about this operation – which was the brainchild of Brigadier de la Billière – saying it was suicidal, total madness. As it happens, I think just the opposite was the case, for we know the flight – the most difficult and dangerous part – was successful, and even a limited strike would have had a profoundly demoralizing effect on the Argentinians.

Over the years, I have watched too many people take the inflated pay and the even more inflated kudos of being part of the SAS mystique without trying to live up to its ideals and expectations. In the end, they simply didn't have what it takes and were not prepared to pay their dues, although many of them managed to complete their service with the Regiment. I believe that the command in that patrol in Argentina was made up of just such people.

I would have given absolutely anything to have led that patrol, and so would many of the guys I worked with. The winning was well worth the dare.

It was an incredibly expensive mission just in terms of the sacrificed helicopter. It also effectively took two very brave and skilful pilots, and an SAS patrol, out of the war, since they were in Chile as the Task Force prepared to invade the Falklands and eject its illegal occupiers. And who knows how many Argentine aircraft got through to damage or sink Task Force ships because the patrol was aborted, aircraft that might otherwise have been destroyed on the ground? Above and beyond all that, however, the lost initiative and the effect on morale was, in my opinion, far more costly to the Regiment.

In Argentina, if a man could not become a racing driver, then as likely as not the next thing on his wish list was to be a fighter pilot. As events were to prove, they were the cream of the Argentinian crop, very brave men whose courage and flying skill were to inflict terrible damage on the Task Force.

It was a lesson we were shortly to learn – the hard way.

Chapter Eleven

FROM a signalling position high above the flight deck of HMS *Hermes*, I watched the Sea Harriers come in to land after pounding the Argentinian positions at Port Stanley. They are magnificent machines, one moment hurtling at speed towards the ship and then suddenly slowing in mid-air, their jets swivelled downwards, to hover like helicopters before setting down on the deck with a kind of ungainly delicacy.

One of the Harriers had been crippled by enemy groundfire, which had shredded its tail fin. On the carrier, the flight controller ordered its pilot to come in last, so that if he crashed and burned, the wreckage on the flight deck would not prevent the other aircraft from landing. I kept my fingers crossed for the poor pilot as he slowed to hover alongside *Hermes*. Having crabbed sideways until he was over the flight deck, he brought his wounded plane down with a thump that shook the deck plates. But he'd made it. He climbed wearily out of his cockpit, shaken but not stirred.

It was then that the BBC's Brian Hanrahan made his famous radio broadcast from the observer's platform above the flight deck. For security reasons, Hanrahan was not allowed to tell his listeners how many aircraft had taken part in the raid on Port Stanley. Instead, he kept both the military censors and his audience happy with the remark, 'I counted them all out and I counted them all back.' It was a brilliant way of reassuring people in Britain that all our aircraft had returned safely.

The date was 1 May 1982, and the Task Force was still nearly three weeks away from launching the landings which, it was hoped, would liberate the Falklands. For the SAS, perhaps even more so than for the rest of the troops cooped up in ships, there was precious little for us to do. In the mornings we practised map reading, or worked out insertion points for use in forward aircraft control. We trained with our weapons and discussed anything we thought we might be tasked with carrying out. Every noon aboard HMS *Hermes*, D Squadron met in an enclosed area below decks in the stern of the ship. The place was known as '2 Sierra Flats', because that was what was stencilled on the steel walls, and it was just large enough to house the squadron if everyone stood. Our meetings lasted about thirty minutes, and once they were finished we were free for the rest of the day, which we would spend playing chess or scrabble or a few hands at cards, or trying to get our heads down somewhere.

In the evenings we always wound up in the bar of the Chief Petty Officers' Mess. In the Royal Navy drink is rationed and each CPO was only allowed two pints of beer or three shorts per day. As guests of the mess, however, squadron members could drink as much as they liked. So every night was party night, with us buying drinks and passing them on to our naval friends. We would pack up at three or four in the morning, completely smashed, having finished the night having a good laugh and a drink in somebody's cabin. Then we'd trundle off to bed. Bear in mind that the Task Force was operating on Zulu time – that is, Greenwich mean time. Deep in the South Atlantic, this meant that first light was not until eleven or eleven-thirty in the morning – by our clocks. And as most of us didn't have a regular bed, we were in no hurry to go off and find one. Indeed, I don't remember getting into a cold bed during that time. As on *Plymouth* and *Antrim* during the South Georgia operations, most often the bunk I chose had been vacated by its regular occupant only minutes before I climbed in. When its owner came back off watch, he would tap me on the shoulder and say, 'Can I have my bed back, mate?' and out I'd get and stumble off, half asleep, to find another place to kip.

The aircraft carrier was no floating Hilton and, as any confined area will when crammed with men, it always stank of rancid sweat, stale food, and wet socks drying on pipes. The sailors kept themselves clean, but with so many human beings jammed into what was really just a series of poorly ventilated steel boxes, often with condensation running down the walls, the atmosphere below decks had a cheesy ripeness to it. We could accept these discomforts, but most of the time, just as in Dhofar or Northern Ireland, we were bored, forced to wait until Intelligence had enough information to give us our next target – something for us to do.

In the event, we didn't have long to wait.

On the evening of Sunday, 2 May, we were drinking in the CPOs' Mess, as usual, when over the Tannoy came a metallic, disembodied voice from the control room telling everyone that the submarine HMS *Conqueror* had launched a torpedo against the Argentinian heavy cruiser *General Belgrano*. The place instantly erupted as all the navy guys began shouting and cheering. They were quite euphoric for a while, but when, about an hour later, there came a further announcement that *Belgrano* had been sunk, their din almost lifted the deckhead. The news was the cue for a tremendous party, with the ship's crew singing the praises of the Royal Navy to the high heavens. Everybody was in high spirits, and confidence about what lay ahead had never seemed stronger.

This Cloud-Nine high continued through Monday, but on the following day, 4 May, while we were halfway through our midday squadron meeting in 2 Sierra Flats, the Tannoy suddenly blared 'Hit the deck! . . . Hit the deck!'

We didn't know what the hell was going on, but everyone lay flat – difficult, in that cramped area. Seconds later, we heard the thumps of salvos of chaff and magnesium flares being fired from the carrier's launchers. (Chaff consists of thousands of strips of thin metal foil designed to deflect and confuse the homing devices on incoming radar-guided missiles, since the strips show up as countless images on any radar. The magnesium flares give off intense heat, and are fired to lure heat-seeking missiles away from their real targets.) We waited anxiously. Being trapped in a steel room below decks is not something any SAS soldier favours, but not knowing what was happening, and not being able to do anything about it, were the worst part of it. Yet after the first command there was total silence from the control room. Gradually everyone relaxed, although the ship remained at full action stations. It wasn't until an hour or more later that the Tannoy squawked into life again with a message from operations control saying that an Argentinian Super Etendard bomber had launched an Exocet, and that the missile was heading our way.

Once more we waited. After what seemed another endless hour a voice from the Tannoy told us that the Type 42 destroyer HMS *Sheffield* had been hit and that her crew were being evacuated to other ships. Our meeting broke up and, with nothing much to do, I pulled from inside my jacket a paperback thriller – oddly, I remember that it was *Eye of the Needle* by Ken Follett. Squatting on the floor of 2 Sierra Flats, I leaned against the grey-painted steel bulkhead, avoiding the iron rivets that were trying to put dents in my back, and settled down to read.

After an hour or so, a balding, stocky man of about forty came into the compartment and sat down opposite me. A forlorn figure in a white woollen pullover, denims and dark blue plimsolls, he said not a word but simply sat staring at the floor. I couldn't help glancing at him curiously from time to time. Even though he didn't volunteer anything, I knew that the clothes he was wearing were the standard issue given to survivors, and that his own must have been saturated by the sea – perhaps from having had to abandon a ship.

Later, one of the carrier's crew members told me that the man in the survivor's issue clothing was Captain Sam Salt, the captain of HMS *Sheffield*. As he sat there silently, his head bowed, he looked more like a beaten man than the captain of a Royal Navy warship. But by then, his command, a modern air-defence destroyer, one of only five Type 42s with the Task Force, was drifting and abandoned, smoke still pouring from the gaping hole in her port side.

Yet while I was with him, not a single one of the Royal Navy officers aboard *Hermes* came to where he sat silently brooding. Not one arrived to offer his condolences, or to say 'Sorry about your ship, Sam. You did your best.' Perhaps Captain Salt had found his way to 2 Sierra Flats because he wanted solitude. I don't know. To this day I find it strange, however, that none of the naval officers had any words of comfort for him during that hour and more while he was sitting opposite me, that not one of them put a friendly hand on his shoulder. It must have been the lowest point in that man's life. Yet the naval officers on *Hermes* simply ignored him. I remember reading that there was once a time when a Royal Navy captain who lost his ship could expect no mercy from the Admiralty. That was a long time ago, but maybe the Royal Navy still suffers from that kind of antiquated thinking.

Sheffield was the first ship the Royal Navy had lost to enemy action since the Second World War. In the Chief Petty Officers' Mess aboard *Hermes* that night the story of her tragic loss began to unfold.

During our time on *Hermes*, the carrier was in 'Zulu' state, which meant that all watertight doors and hatches were secured. When any of us, seamen or soldiers, passed through a door in a bulkhead we screwed or clamped it shut behind us. The idea was that if the ship was hit and the sea came in, the water would only get through to certain compartments, rather than flood the ship to such a degree as to threaten to sink her.

I was told that *Sheffield* had been on air-defence duty at the south-west corner of the Task Force, then lying some forty miles off the south-eastern tip of East Falkland. At the time, however, she had been at a state known as 'Yankee', which meant that, unlike state 'Zulu' on *Hermes*, doors and hatches were open. When the Exocet hit the destroyer, a ball of fire had instantly swept along the ship's 'Burma Road'.

Many ships have a Burma Road – a corridor which stretches the length of the ship from bow to stern. Clamped on brackets on the steel walls of *Sheffield*'s Burma Road was the ship's firefighting equipment. The super-heated fireball engulfed the corridor from end to end, immediately destroying all the firefighting equipment and making it all but impossible for the crew to fight the blaze. Within minutes, the fire had roared through the ship like a blast furnace, effectively ending the destroyer's life. After four hours spent trying to control the blaze, Captain Salt reluctantly gave the order to abandon ship as the flames threatened to engulf the magazine for the Sea Dart missiles. Twenty-one men were dead, and many more were injured, some with terrible burns. The Type 21 frigate HMS *Arrow* came alongside and took off most of the crew; others, including Salt, were winched off by Sea King helicopters.

In the CPOs' Mess on *Hermes* that night, one petty officer was walking about dramatically exclaiming, 'A ball of fire . . . a ball of fire . . .' It may be that he was in a state of shock, although I don't know why, since he was just a member of the carrier's crew and certainly hadn't been aboard *Sheffield* when she was hit. The squadron 2IC and I were drinking together at the bar as the ball-of-fire merchant walked up and down repeating his lines. We laughed – simply chortled into our glasses, and even mimicked him. This may seem callous, but the fact was that imminent death was nothing new to us. We'd lost men in action, and seen aircraft crash with friends and comrades aboard. To us, sudden, often violent death was simply a matter of occurrence.

In our business, we recognize that we can't deal in death without being able to accept the consequences. To the navy guys it was different, however, almost as though they couldn't understand how the Argentinians could have had the audacity to wipe out one of our ships. And this despite the sinking, two days earlier, of the *General Belgrano*, with the loss of more than 350 Argentinian lives. Now everyone in the Task Force had been made to realize that we were a fair target, and that the Argentinians had a sting in their tail. They had the assets, and they had the firepower; they also had the determination.

The loss of the *Sheffield* had brought home to us how vulnerable we were to enemy air or submarine attacks while floating about in the South Atlantic. We also all now knew it wasn't going to become any easier, and that the Argentinians were not going to go away.

If the sinking of HMS *Sheffield* was Argentina's revenge for the reconquest of South Georgia and the loss of the *General Belgrano*, the

Task Force's response was robust, effective, and not slow in coming. Quite early after the arrival of the Task Force in the theatre of operations, the pilot of a Sea Harrier, returning from a sortie over Goose Green, had reported that a radar lock had registered on his avionics as he had flown over Pebble Island, a barren place off the north coast of West Falkland. There was a small civilian settlement there, and it was known that the enemy had established a substantial outpost in and around it. Thinking that the signal might be coming from a ground-radar installation, he went for a closer look, and discovered that there was a grass airstrip on the island which the Argentinians were extending.

No one knew how much of a threat the strip on Pebble Island might be to the invasion ships, or to the land forces which, as the plan was even then, were to go ashore in San Carlos Bay on East Falkland. Once it was suspected that a radar installation had been set up on the island, however, the place became a very serious threat indeed. Admiral Woodward believed that the radar might be able to detect the British main assault fleet while it was out of range of radar on the Argentinian mainland or on East Falkland, while the airstrip was only a few minutes' flying time, even for piston-engined ground-attack aircraft, from the proposed site for the main landings.

Although they appear as mere specks on any map of the world, the Falkland Islands cover 4,700 square miles – about the same area as Northern Ireland. Distances between settlements are long and, outside the town of Port Stanley, population is sparse, and sparser still on West Falkland. Pebble Island is a narrow strip of land some twelve kilometres long, with the sheep-farming settlement and its grass airstrip lying at the eastern end. At its narrowest, the strip of water separating the island from the north coast of West Falkland is some 500 metres.

We had some intelligence that there was a force of between sixty and seventy Argentinian servicemen on the island, made up of engineers, surveyors, radar technicians and a guard force. There were also a number of civilians whom the enemy might be holding as hostages. This was why an early plan to bomb the runway was given the thumbs down. We didn't want any of the islanders to be hurt, and least of all as a result of British action. That was not what we'd come all this way for.

Some of our intelligence was conflicting, however, for other reports indicated that the Argentinian engineers might be there to prepare a new airstrip to receive Aermacchi light ground-attack aircraft which, among other armament, were equipped with Kingfisher air-to-surface missiles, representing a very real threat to any land force once it was ashore. But whatever the truth of these reports, it was absolutely clear that it was vital for someone to find out just what was happening on Pebble Island.

'Someone' turned out to be D Squadron, 22 SAS. Two four-man patrols from Boat Troop, led by Captain Ted, the troop commander, were to be sent ashore in inflatable boats for a close look at Pebble Island. By now, however, the weather was so poor that the plan was called off. Instead, the patrols were airlifted by Sea King helicopter on to West Falkland on the night of 11/12 May. Their orders were to get as close to the airfield as they could without getting caught, set up covert OPs, and radio back the information that would allow the Task Force's planning directors to make a proper plan of attack.

They took with them two five foot-long bags, each containing a Klepper collapsible canoe. Once they had been dropped, they laid low on West Falkland until nightfall and then 'tabbed' – the SAS (and Para) equivalent of the Royal Marines' 'yomping' – across country until they reached a point that was closest to Pebble Island. With them they carried the dismantled canoes in their bags.

Kleppers are constructed from willow frames which, once assembled, then have a rubber skin drawn tightly across them. Skilled hands can assemble them in a few minutes, and the Regiment's Boat Troops are nothing if not skilled. In pitch darkness, the patrols paddled their craft across the sound and beached them on Pebble Island. Then, while one patrol guarded the concealed boats and their escape route, Ted and the other three men crept towards the airstrip across land that had barely enough cover to hide a rabbit. Indeed, so sparse was the vegetation that to avoid detection during the hours of daylight, they had to lie completely motionless in the elephant grass. Given the close proximity of a much larger enemy force, they were in constant danger of being spotted and attacked, which would almost certainly have compromised any subsequent attack on the airstrip.

At about eleven o'clock on the morning of 15 May, the Boat Troop commander sent a signal which will go down in the annals of the Regiment. Coded and transmitted in Morse, once deciphered it read, 'Eleven aircraft, repeat eleven aircraft. Believed real. Squadron attack tonight.'

The timescale was very tight – clearly Ted saw the matter as urgent. In the light of this, the squadron commander and the senior planners got together and worked out that any attack launched against the aircraft on the Pebble Island airstrip would have to be completed by 0700 hours the next day to allow sufficient time for the raiding parties to be recovered by helicopter. The reason for this was because the Task Force ships closed up to the islands at night, but steamed away into the South Atlantic so that they should not be vulnerable to air attack when daylight came some time after 1100 hours. As they sailed out of danger, so the distance the helicopters would have to fly back to the ships increased.

The plan began to go wrong from the first. Because of bad weather conditions and *Hermes* miscalculating her run in to a position eighty miles offshore, which would bring Pebble Island within helicopter range of the ships, the operation started running late almost from the start. The South Atlantic lived up to its foul-weather reputation, and the aircraft carrier had to sail in fierce headwinds and mounting seas. Movement on board was risky, which meant that the Sea Kings on the hangar decks could not be safely readied by the technical crews in the time allowed. Once they were ready, there were more delays while the choppers were brought up to the flight deck for lift-off.

The helicopters were carried up from the hold of *Hermes* by huge lifts let into the flight deck, for all the aircraft, Sea Harriers as well as Sea Kings, were kept below deck at all times when they weren't flying. The mood and atmosphere among D Squadron was electric, with everyone raring to go. By then our faces were covered in cam cream and we were all tooled up. Each SAS man tasked for the raid carried an M16 rifle with three spare magazines taped to the butt, and another 200 to 400 rounds of 7.62mm GPMG ammunition in belts. Everybody carried two mortar bombs, one of high explosive and one of white phosphorus, which we were to drop off when we reached the mortar pits that would be established near the airstrip. Several of the guys also carried LAWs – M66 light anti-tank weapons – which are extremely effective against aircraft on the ground.

Adrenalin raged through our systems like rivers of fire, giving us an enormous rush. Armed to the teeth, forty-five of us boarded the Sea Kings; with us also went a naval-gunfire support team from 148 Battery, 29 Commando Regiment, Royal Artillery, whose task was to direct the bombardment from the 4.5-inch guns of the ships lying offshore. We all embarked on the hangar deck, and eventually the Sea King that my troop was to fly in was brought up to the flight deck. The helicopter's engines roared into life. We waited on deck for at least fifteen minutes, only to be told that one of the Sea Kings carrying another troop had developed mechanical problems and would have to be replaced. All in all, this took over an hour, leaving our time on the ground less than adequate, as everything had been planned on the basis of the distance between *Hermes* and Pebble Island and the range of the Sea Kings, making timing absolutely critical.

At last we lifted off, flying low level over the sea in blackout conditions, occasionally gaining fleeting glimpses of the waves below. I had never experienced surges of adrenalin to the same extent. To be part of the largest SAS raid since the Second World War was something that I would not have missed for anything, especially when I remembered that I should have been back in a Birmingham drill hall completing my two-year stint as an instructor.

The navy pilots were terrific, lifting off in the dark and, despite very high winds, flying only forty or fifty feet above the waves to dodge any enemy radar cover. For all their efforts, however, because of the atrocious weather we were already running an hour late when they dropped us off three miles from the airstrip. We estimated that it would take us about two hours to reach the target.

On landing we were met by Captain Ted, the Boat Troop commander, and his men. They had spent the last four days lying up on Pebble Island, watching the enemy without being seen; now it was their job to lead us to the target. The squadron commander and the headsheds of each troop were briefed by Ted. Once the briefing had finished, we were told that this was not a night for tactical movement; instead, we had to get our arses in gear and get to the target as quickly as possible, since otherwise we wouldn't have enough time to carry out the mission and rendezvous with the helicopters before the latter had to return to *Hermes*. The plan was for Mobility Troop to attack the eleven aircraft on the ground and destroy them with plastic-explosive (PE) charges. Air Troop was tasked to mask off the settlement, and Mountain Troop was to be held in reserve at the mortar pit, from where they would be able to go instantly to the aid of any troops that might be in trouble.

My troop, Mobility, was commanded by Captain Paul and his number two was Bob, a staff sergeant; I was number three in the pecking order. Considering the ground and the darkness, we got off pretty quickly. It was not quickly enough, however, for the going was against us. The ground was mainly of peat, spongy stuff that made walking difficult, especially in the dark, and there were lots of fences and walls to cross. Just the kind of thing you'd expect around a sheep settlement.

Realizing that precious time had been lost, the squadron commander decided to speed-march in single file, one man behind the other. As a result, rather than observing patrol procedures, which would normally involve a stealthy approach, we often broke into a run. But when we came to a wall or a fence, we adopted 'obstacle procedure', which dictated that each man should be covered by others while he crossed, and this slowed us considerably.

When moving in an extended single file, the soldier in front is responsible for the soldier behind. So as long as he can see the man ahead of him and the man behind, then everything is fine. That's the theory, anyway, but what we didn't know was that while we were painstakingly crossing obstacles, the squadron OC and the other troops were leaping walls and fences and racing towards the target as though their boots were on fire.

Inevitably, we lost contact with the troop in front. They were travelling much faster than we were, and before long the man at the head of our troop could no longer see the last man of the troop ahead. Going over undulating ground at night, you can simply disappear into the darkness, and once the chain is broken you are as good as lost. In the pitch blackness we couldn't see a thing, even through our night scopes, so our only means of contacting the leading troops was by the radio carried by the troop signaller. When Captain Paul realized our predicament he radioed the OC, who was somewhere up in front of us in the dark, and asked him for a steer. The squadron commander came back on the radio and said he didn't have time to wait for us – if we didn't catch up with him by the time we reached the rendezvous position, we were to stay in reserve by the mortar pit, the task originally given to Mountain Troop.

We didn't catch up. However, a contingency plan had been agreed before we left *Hermes*. Under this, if anything happened to Mobility Troop prior to our reaching the target, then Mountain Troop was to pick up the baton and lead the attack. Its members were carrying enough explosives to complete the mission.

By the time we reached the mortar pit, we knew we had lost our starring role in the attack. Almost beside ourselves with anger and disappointment, we realized that we had been relegated to being just a bunch of extras.

Looking back on that night, the troop sergeant should have detailed someone to be in front as the lead scout. Captain Paul was a good officer and was trying to do things properly, and it was not his fault that a gap had developed, for on this particular night there was drifting mist that continually came and went. To make matters worse, we were the only troop that didn't have a member of Boat Troop attached to us as a guide – a mistake, since by then they knew the way to and from the airstrip better than the backs of their hands.

Nevertheless, there can be no excuses. Mobility Troop's delay in arriving at the target was the result of incompetence, and it should not have happened. The important thing to remember, however, is that the Regiment is not infallible. We do sometimes make mistakes. In this respect the SAS is like any other regiment, and its solders are not immune from sometimes getting things wrong, especially in the confusion of war.

The attack started at 0700 hours Zulu when, miles offshore, the 4.5-inch guns of HMS *Glamorgan* opened up. Guided on to coordinates signalled by the naval-gunfire support team and based on information from Boat Troop, the destroyer's gunners laid down a precision barrage, shelling the Argentinian positions but carefully avoiding the islanders' houses. At once our mortar began firing, the phosphorus rounds whumping down, turning the night sky into near daylight. Then, led by John Hamilton, Mountain Troop went in to destroy the aircraft, which were spread out all over the lengthy runway.

Split into seven two-man teams and carrying their PE charges, they also used their machine-guns and LAW rockets to smash the grounded planes to bits. It wasn't easy, for military aircraft are built to withstand bullets. Nor is it anything like the movies, where aircraft blow up when a bullet hits their fuel tanks. But then, there are a lot of things that aren't like the movies – such as highly trained soldiers getting lost on a tiny island like a bunch of novice Boy Scouts.

It was a race against time. Not only was the raid late in starting, but we had to be back at the drop-off point bang on time for the Sea Kings to come in and pick up us. They couldn't risk waiting for us because as soon as dawn broke they would either become sitting ducks for enemy fighter aircraft, or *Hermes* would by then be out of their range.

On the airstrip, meanwhile, it rapidly became apparent that the Argentinians had effectively abandoned any attempt to save the aircraft and were lying low, looking out for their own safety and hardly firing back at all. A single brave enemy officer and one of his soldiers did try to stop the raiding teams, opening fire on them, but they were quickly shot down. It was then that Mountain Troop began using the few explosive charges they had to wreck the rest of the aircraft. To reach the wings of some of the machines they had to stand on each other's shoulders; once the first man had scrambled up he would reach down and pull the other guy up after him. The Pucaras – twin-turboprop ground-attack aircraft – were the tallest planes and caused the demolition teams the most trouble.

By this time the pre-dawn sky was glowing orange from fires raging in the Argentinians' fuel store, which had been hit by *Glamorgan's* guns. Then the destroyer's gunners found the range for the enemy's ammunition dump and blew it to smithereens. As the final charges shattered the last of the aircraft, the squadron began to withdraw.

Once the attack had finished, we all regrouped by the mortar pit in all-round defence. I was still pissed off by what had happened to my troop, but at least the squadron's casualties were almost non-existent. One man had been concussed by the blast from a landmine, which had been triggered by the Argentinians just before we left the airstrip, and another had been hit by shrapnel; his wounds had not stopped him from doing his job, however.

Despite my fury that we had missed the main action, I still felt a sense of pride and elation in knowing that the boys had carried out a successful mission. The squadron commander and Captain Ted had planned the raid to perfection. Nothing had been left to chance or overlooked, and the result had been a triumphant success.

As we waited, suddenly, out of nowhere, four Sea King helicopters appeared, flying in formation and hugging the ground. It was a remarkable sight. They touched down simultaneously. We all knew by the formation in which they had landed which helicopter to get on, and we were airborne within thirty seconds. Two and a half hours after the first shot had been fired, we were again aboard the Sea Kings and heading back out to sea.

Behind us on the airstrip lay the wreckage of six Pucaras, a Short Skyvan light transport and four Mentor trainer aircraft. Naval gunfire had taken care of the rest of the enemy installations with such effect that the whole of Pebble Island appeared to be on fire. It must have been the warmest it had been for several million years.

It was still dark just ten minutes before we reached *Hermes*, but by the time we landed first light had broken – the timing had been that critical. Our Sea Kings landed us back on the flagship's flight deck nicely in time for breakfast. News of the raid's success, with virtually no casualties, had arrived before us and the sailors, who had shown us nothing but kindness from the moment we had come aboard, couldn't do enough for us. That night, in the Chief Petty Officers' Mess, they congratulated us over a drink. Now they realized what the SAS really did for a living, when we weren't laughing and joking and drinking beer. More than that, however, everyone from the most senior naval officer all the way down to the most junior rating also knew that, working together, the sailors, soldiers, marines and airmen of the Task Force could knock seven kinds of hell out of any enemy. As for us, we had had a great night out, and it had been wonderful to get our feet on dry land once again, if only for a few hours.

On Pebble Island, there was now nothing left to interfere with the British landings in San Carlos Bay. The mission had been an enormous success. Apart from the recapture of South Georgia nearly three weeks earlier, it was the first major operation against the enemy on land, and one that triumphantly showed what the Regiment could do.

Above all, we had delivered a huge blow to the Argentinians' morale, while at the same time massively boosting the Task Force's. Even if some of us had got misplaced . . .

Chapter Twelve

I T has often seemed to me that Fate puts a price on moments of triumph. Sometimes this can mean men paying with their lives in the final minutes before victory; at others, Fate's charge for having earlier smiled upon some venture comes a few days later. But whether it comes within hours or days, there is always a payback time.

We didn't have to wait long before Fate delivered her bill after our highly successful raid on Pebble Island. On 18 May, three days after the raid, the ships carrying the main British invasion group – known as the amphibious force – linked up with the aircraft carriers and their escorts. It became clear that the attempt to land in the Falklands was imminent. What emerged from the planning directives was that the SAS was tasked with four separate attacks designed to make the Argentinians believe that a much bigger force had landed, and to draw them away from San Carlos, where the real landings were to go in.

The role of my squadron, D, was to be offensive action, while G Squadron, which had arrived with the Task Force, via Ascension, some time after us, was to report information on enemy positions, strengths and movements from observation posts set up behind, and even in, the enemy lines. In preparation for these operations, the two squadrons were ordered later that day to cross-deck from *Hermes* to HMS *Intrepid*, an assault ship specifically equipped for amphibious warfare.

Cross-decking a squadron involves shifting a vast amount of kit. Cross-decking two is like moving a circus. *Hermes* and *Intrepid* were steaming about a mile apart, so we initially sent a lot of the guys over to the assault ship to act as movers for all the equipment as it arrived. The rest of the men were to stay on the carrier and load the gear into nets, which were then slung beneath the bellies of Sea King helicopters and ferried across.

There was the usual howling wind, and the sea was fairly choppy. When there were only two helicopter loads left on *Hermes*, I leapt aboard one of the aircraft as it completed loading. I figured that the last helicopter would be very crowded, and that there would be more elbow room in the one I had chosen.

As we hovered above *Intrepid* with the cargo net slung beneath us, I could see our equipment piled high on the deck. There seemed to be a miniature mountain of the stuff. I jumped on to the deck after the helicopter had dropped its pallet, and walked from the flight deck into the ship through open landing doors rather like those on cross-Channel ferries. I looked at my watch. It was 2130 hours Zulu, just after last light.

There was so much stuff aboard the last Sea King that the remaining men simply piled their gear in and sat on top of it. None of them were wearing survival suits because they wanted to get the job over with as soon as possible; besides, the flight between the ships only took about five minutes.

Waiting to come in, the last chopper was hovering about seventy-five metres away from *Intrepid* when one of our guys on deck suddenly shouted, 'She's gone down!' In the gathering dark he saw the Sea King plunge into the sea. Immediately klaxons began to blare all through the ship, and from the Tannoy came the shouted order, 'Crash teams, action stations! . . . Crash teams, actions stations!'

The Sea King hit the waves and capsized. Damaged from the impact, it rapidly filled with water, but for a few moments it stayed on the surface with the sea pouring in on the men inside. The pilot and his co-pilot punched their doors clear and climbed straight into their rubber dinghy, which had automatically inflated when the machine hit the sea. One of our guys inside the downed helicopter was wearing a lifejacket, but he couldn't find his way out. Finally, in sheer desperation, he pulled the tags on his self-inflating lifejacket. Suddenly buoyant, it shot him straight out of the hole where the Sea King's tail had snapped off on impact. He got out alive to find men clinging to the sides of the pilots' rubber dinghy. As the stricken helicopter slowly slipped beneath the waves, the survivors could only think of their mates on the inside of the aircraft. It was a horrible way to die, and it affected us all pretty deeply.

There were thirty men on board that Sea King, including the pilot, co-pilot and a crewman. Twenty-two of them died that night in the freezing waters of the South Atlantic, all but two of them members of D and G Squadrons. We lost good friends in that terrible accident. They lie at the bottom of the South Atlantic, for their bodies were never recovered. Their wives back in Hereford were not told of the deaths until three or four days later, after the landings at San Carlos had taken place. Nor were the public. I suppose that, had the bad news been known back home in Britain before the success of the landings had been announced, then it would have dealt a body blow to public morale.

The deaths of twenty members of the Regiment hindered us, but the disaster didn't jeopardize our mission. It would have been much worse had the men all been from the same squadron, but as the losses were split between two squadrons, in practical terms the soldiers who died were easier to replace. Put bluntly, the show had to go on regardless of the deaths of so many good men.

In emotional terms, and while it might sound callous, we very quickly got over the disaster. The reason was simple: on the following night we ourselves were going into action, something which really concentrates the mind. Nevertheless, I had lost many friends in the crash. One of them had been among those who raided the post office at Grytviken. His stamped covers went with him to the bottom. How much they were worth didn't matter any longer.

The following morning, I was pulled aside by the squadron OC and told, 'Look, we want you to take over as troop sergeant of Mountain Troop.' It was promotion of a kind, although it was a very depleted troop that I now joined. Because of the crash, there were only eight of us in the troop: Captain John Hamilton, who had led the mission to the Fortuna Glacier on South Georgia and the demolition party on Pebble Island, myself and six others. Putting the Sea King crash to the backs of our minds, we immediately began to prepare for the task ahead of us, since there were just forty-eight hours to go before the main landings were to go in at Port San Carlos. We were to go ashore twenty-four hours earlier at Darwin, fifteen miles or so south of the actual landing areas, to make the Argentinians think that the invasion was taking place there instead of at the main beachhead.

Aboard *Intrepid* on the night before our diversionary attacks, I bumped into an old friend of mine whom I hadn't seen in ten years. I had known and soldiered with Sergeant Ian McKay when he was with Support Company in 1 Para. Ian was a thoroughly nice guy and a good soldier, but I was surprised to see him, since 1 Para hadn't come out with the Task Force. So I asked him what he was doing there on the assault ship with 3 Para, and he told me his story. Apparently he had been in Berlin with 1 Para some years earlier, and had become involved with another man's wife. When the affair was discovered, he was given twenty-four hours to get out of Germany. He went back to the Para depot in Aldershot and became an instructor, after which he was posted to 3 Para as a platoon sergeant. We sat having a mug of tea together and talking until it was time for me to gather my kit and go. As we shook hands I told him, 'Best of luck. I'll see you again.'

And, sadly, I did – one Saturday morning back in Hereford, after the war was over. A picture of him suddenly came up on the television screen in my bedroom. The sound was down and when I turned up the volume it was to hear the announcer say that Sergeant Ian McKay of 3 Para had been posthumously awarded the Victoria Cross, one of only two awarded for the campaign. He had been killed on Mount Longdon, one of the final battles of the campaign, single-handedly storming an Argentinian machine-gun post. He was a very brave man, and it seemed a double shame that he should have died just three days before the enemy surrendered.

That night, D Squadron was landed on East Falkland, and made a forced march, weighed down with extra ammunition and mortar rounds, until we were able to take up our positions around the settlement of Darwin, where there was a strong Argentinian force that might be deployed to counter-attack the main British landings. We put a lot of fire down on the enemy in our diversionary raid, hitting them with mortars, Milan AT missiles and GP machine-guns, as well as small-arms fire. At the time, I wondered if we had achieved much, but it later turned out that the Argentinians in the settlement had radioed their main HQ that they were being attacked by a full battalion – 600 men, rather than the 40 or so we actually numbered. Since this had been the purpose of our raid from the first, we had obviously achieved what we'd set out to do.

By morning, however, the Argentinians knew exactly where the real landings had taken place. From 0400 hours on 21 May, 3 Para and 42 Commando, Royal Marines had come ashore in landing craft launched from the ships in San Carlos Water, and established themselves at Port San Carlos. A few miles to the south, 2 Para and 40 and 45 Commandos had safely landed at San Carlos, and all were now working frantically to consolidate the beachhead. In response, the enemy had their Pucara ground-attack aircraft sweeping the landscape and, as we prepared to move off, one of them headed straight for our position near Darwin, dropping down low and opening up with its 20mm cannon.

Unlike the other units, which were equipped with a largely ineffective hand-held anti-aircraft missile called Blowpipe, we were carrying with us a Stinger missile launcher which had been given to us on the quiet by the US government. The American-built surface-air missile was then virtually unknown and untried in the Regiment; indeed, none of us had even seen a Stinger before, let alone fired one. Nevertheless, as the Pucara flew overhead Kel, who had been in the

New Zealand SAS before joining us, got the Stinger launcher to his shoulder and squeezed the trigger.

The missile streaked after the aircraft and whacked it straight up the tail. There was a huge explosion. The pilot ejected and we watched his parachute coming down as the Pucara exploded into a hillside. The sight made us all feel good, and Kel was whooping with delight. Then, minutes later, another Pucara came over and Kel, full of his success, decided to have another crack. Once more he put the Stinger launcher to his shoulder and aimed it at the aircraft.

Unfortunately, the Stinger expert had been killed in the Sea King crash. Of the rest of the squadron, only a handful had seen the instruction book for the weapon. Kel had slotted a new missile into the launcher, but forgot that the weapon should have been recharged with compressed gas before it could be successfully fired again. All unaware, he took aim at the Pucara and pressed the trigger. The rocket ignited, flew about twenty yards and then nosedived on to the ridge we were following, twisting and turning as it hurtled along the ground with smoke and flames pouring out of it. We threw ourselves out of the way as it went past like a rattlesnake on fire. Then it went off with an almighty bang, luckily without hitting anyone. Kel put that down to a faulty missile, and at once reloaded and fired again. We all dived for cover once more, everyone shouting expletives at him in a good-natured way. At this point the OC called a halt to Kel's brief career downing Pucaras

Stingers are expensive bits of kit. We had just watched more than fifty thousand quid's worth of missile go up in a puff of smoke. But apart from the waste, it was a pity Kel had forgotten to recharge the gas, for he might have downed a few other enemy aircraft – certainly more than the British-built Blowpipes managed to get. Still, he had done well to bring down that first Pucara.

The whole squadron was now together, tabbing north to San Carlos. We covered nearly twenty miles that morning and we were all pretty exhausted by the time we linked up with the main force. By then the Paras and Marines were all off the ships and on to the surrounding hills, so we sat on a slope overlooking San Carlos Water and had a brew, knowing that the beachhead was secure.

Or secure against enemy land forces, at least, for sitting on that hill was like being in the front row of a cinema showing a war movie. From the hillside, we watched as wave after wave of Argentinian Air Force Skyhawks and Mirages bombed and strafed British ships. The trouble was, there was not a thing we could do about it.

From the first, the enemy targeted the warships in San Carlos Water, and several were hit and damaged. Then, as we sat there, helpless, HMS *Ardent*, a Type 21 frigate, was hit. That afternoon, in what mercifully proved to be the day's last air attack, a wave of Skyhawks came over and one of them sent two bombs into her stern. The little ship simply disappeared under a great mushroom of smoke. We all thought she was a goner, but five minutes later she limped out of the obscuring cloud, trailing smoke from her superstructure.

It was a false hope. Two minutes later a Mirage came over and hit her again with another bomb. It was a direct hit, striking her in the middle of her superstructure. Engulfed in flames and smoke, she began to sink. It was a desperately sad sight, made worse by the fact that we could only sit there and watch a warship die.

The Argentinian pilots were incredibly skilful and desperately brave. They always came in at low level, screaming over the hills before dropping down to hug the surface of the sea as they streaked towards their targets, pursued by missiles and fire from every ship's gun that could be brought to bear, as well as hundreds of hastily mounted machine-guns. Luckily, many of their bombs failed to go off – *Plymouth*, for instance, the frigate we had been aboard in South Georgia, was hit by three 500-pound bombs, of which only one detonated.

It had been a day of triumph, but also one that gave us much to worry about. As for us, from the settlement at San Carlos the whole squadron was airlifted in dribs and drabs back to HMS *Intrepid* as soon as Lynx helicopters became available. It took a long time and we were all extremely weary by the time we were back on the assault ship in the late afternoon.

The two assault ships, or landing platform docks (LPDs), that accompanied the Task Force, *Fearless* and *Intrepid*, were large vessels of some 12,000 tons and with crews of nearly 600 men. They were equipped to take four large and four smaller landing craft as well as four Sea King or five Wessex helicopters, and had a dock within them that could be flooded to act as a floating harbour for the landing craft; they could also accommodate 400 men for an extended period or 700 for a shorter time. Yet despite their size, once back on board I couldn't find anywhere to sleep. As usual . . . I did have a camp bed, but I'd nowhere to put it, so in the end I dragged it into the ship's chapel and set it up there. As I lay there, just beginning to doze off, a naval padre came in through the chapel's sliding doors. When he saw me there he went berserk.

'You can't sleep in a church!' he bellowed. I blinked up at him from my camp bed and said, 'Why not? It's a place of worship and I'll start praying while I'm sleeping.'

He didn't like my answer one little bit. 'Get out,' he ordered, and I realized that I wasn't going to get any rest here. I was so dog tired that I could hardly keep my eyes open, but I picked up my camp bed and stumbled out into the companionway.

As one of the ship's officers, the padre had his own bed in his own cabin. Yet on an overcrowded ship he was not going to allow an exhausted soldier to bed down in the chapel. One of the things I learned during the time we spent on warships was that there is still a good deal of snobbery in the Royal Navy. That padre, I realized, despite his Holy Orders, was a fairly typical immature naval officer.

I was wandering around the ship trying to find somewhere else to put my camp bed when I bumped into the OC, who asked me what I was doing dragging the bed around. When I told him that I'd been turfed out of the chapel he said, 'I'm going for a drink. Use my bunk and put that camp bed on the floor in my cabin.' I didn't need further encouragement, and within minutes I was dead to the world.

A couple of hours later, I was woken when the metal door slid open and in walked a lieutenant-commander, a naval rank equivalent to that of an army major. He asked for Major Delves, and when I told him that the OC had gone to the wardroom, he looked at me as if I was something unpleasant that he'd brought in on the sole of his shoe.

Then he demanded to know what I was doing in the Boss's bed. He was completely flummoxed when I told him, 'I'm having a kip,' because the idea that an officer would allow a senior NCO to sleep in his bed while he wasn't using it was totally alien to most naval officers' way of thinking. Even when I told him that Major Delves knew all about my being there – had suggested it, in fact – he still looked at me as though I'd come from the moon. The situation seemed to be beyond anything his class-conscious mind could grasp.

'And where is Major Delves going to sleep?' he asked. When I replied, 'On the camp bed,' he just looked blank. Without another word he walked out, sliding the door to behind him.

In my experience the Royal Navy – with the honourable exception of the Fleet Air Arm – is to a large extent officered by snobs. There is a much greater divide between officers and men than there is in the army or the Royal Air Force. Even the food the sailors eat doesn't begin to compare with the food the officers get in the wardroom. It's not like that in the army or the RAF, where the officers take a great interest in the food served to the men in the mess halls, and are constantly striving to raise the quality. And almost as though to rub it in, the décor of the seamen's mess is atrocious when compared to that of the wardroom.

The same them-and-us attitude applies to naval discipline, even today. The lash may have gone, and with it the rum ration, but many of the officers are still living in Nelson's time, which perhaps explains why the Royal Navy is always court-martialling men, and women, too, nowadays, for the most trivial offences. Its officers don't know anything about modern man-management, but cling instead to an outmoded notion of the 'Senior Service' that vanished for ever after the First World War. The stooge who had walked into the OC's cabin clearly couldn't get his institutionalized mind around the idea that a commissioned officer might lend his bed to an NCO.

With the land force safely ashore and plans well advanced for the operations that would defeat the Argentinians, headshed meetings aboard *Intrepid* sought more work and more targets for the SAS. The G Squadron OPs ashore – some of which had been in place for three weeks – were keeping a sharp eye on enemy strengths and movements, and soon reported that despite the fact that the Argentinians had invaded the islands some six weeks earlier, they had failed to occupy some of the high ground that guarded the landward approaches to Port Stanley. As a result, D Squadron was tasked to go to Mount Kent, set up an OP there and then secure the ground for the arrival of the Royal Marines and the artillery, whose gun position was to be established below the mountain.

On 25 May the squadron commander took three men and set up the OP on Mount Kent, to reconnoitre the area before the rest of the squadron arrived. Mount Kent, with Mount Challenger to the south, is the most westerly of the mountains on the direct route from the beachhead to Port Stanley. Beyond it lies Two Sisters and then Mount Tumbledown, after which the ground slopes down to the capital some five kilometres to the east.

The squadron was to rendezvous with the OC on 26 May. In the event, however, the Sea King helicopter pick-up was cancelled that night because one of the British invasion force's main ammunition dumps had taken a direct hit from an Argentinian bomb and every helicopter was needed to ferry the injured to the field hospital at Ajax Bay, near San Carlos. Incredibly, somebody with more braid on his cap than brains in his head had sited the ammo dump right alongside the main hospital. A lot of damage was done by the Argentinian Air Force that night – there were explosions and huge fires, but by the grace of God none of the hospital patients was injured by the bombing. However, the patients all had to be ferried to other hospitals, together with the burns cases among those who had been caught in the fires when the dump went up.

There were some tremendously good and dedicated medics in the Falklands campaign. Of those injured in the ammo-dump blast, the surgeons did not lose a single man. It is a fact that during the war not one injured man, British or Argentinian, taken to a field hospital died there. No matter how horrific the injuries, the navy and army surgeons did not fail. In their treatment of trauma and gunshot wounds, and many other types of injury besides, they proved themselves to be simply the best.

Eventually, the squadron and all the equipment we needed to rendezvous with the OC and secure Mount Kent was reassembled to be lifted in by four Sea King helicopters the following night. We took off and flew low towards the landing site. As we neared the area, the lead pilot began to look out for the signal to land we had previously agreed. Whether he thought he'd seen the signal, or simply calculated that he had reached the correct location, he landed and the other three choppers followed suit. We all got out and unloaded the gear, whereupon the Sea Kings lifted off and disappeared into the night.

Watching your transport depart always leaves a lonely feeling, but what made matters worse was the fact that there was nobody there to meet us. We had been dropped in the middle of bloody nowhere, though God alone knew where. We had not the least idea where we were, and whatever the lead pilot might have thought he had seen, it quite certainly wasn't the signal we had agreed earlier.

Almost the entire squadron was there on the ground, completely lost. The night was getting more and more misty and we could not see a thing. Wondering where the hell we were, we sent people out to different compass points to try to get a fix while I stayed on the 320 radio, desperately trying to establish Morse-code communications with the ship.

The four compass-point parties returned just as I eventually established contact. We had a meeting to decide where we were, and the men we'd sent out said that they thought – only thought, they didn't actually know – that we were in an area which on the map was marked 'Obscured by cloud'. This made it sound more like somewhere on a reservation for North American Indians, but the description on the map was certainly accurate, for it was extremely cloudy. It was also marshy and wet underfoot, and we didn't know where any Argentinian positions might be.

I got through to *Intrepid* again and told them where we were, or at least where we thought we were. About four miserable, damp hours later the helicopters came back to collect us. It turned out that we were miles away from Mount Kent, and about twenty kilometres from where we should have been dropped off. The Sea Kings ferried us back to the ship, and twenty-four hours later, on the night of 28 May, we were flown to an area east of Mount Kent, to the spot where we should have been landed in the first place. The lead pilot received a severe reprimand for that cock-up, although no one ever found out why we landed where we did.

This was the day on which 2 Para won their astonishing victory at Darwin and Goose Green, after a long night-and-day battle against a much larger Argentinian force. The news, when we learned it, heartened us, although we'd never really doubted the outcome. Now there we were, finally, at the base of Mount Kent, with each troop occupying a different position round the foot of the mountain. We had no intelligence as to how many Argentinians there were in the area, and it didn't really matter. Our job was to clear the mountain, and that was what we would do.

We moved up to the summit in troop formation, clearing the ground as we went. When we reached the top it was obvious that the enemy had been there in some strength. They had established five positions, but for some reason had abandoned them and cleared off, leaving masses of equipment behind. There were rucksacks, belt packs, rations and other equipment, although they had taken their weapons and ammunition. We couldn't understand it, because their positions had occupied the most westerly high ground overlooking the plain along which our forces would have to advance.

We were reasonably certain that the four-man OP established earlier had not been compromised, so the enemy's flight was a mystery. It is possible that they had seen the Sea King helicopters ferrying in the artillery to a position west of Mount Kent, and had assumed that there was a large British force waiting to attack. Since they were probably only young conscripts, they almost certainly decided to bug out while they still had the chance.

While we were on the summit, discussing the situation and trying to spot the Argentinian positions on Two Sisters, five kilometres to the east, we watched a Sea King with a 105mm field gun slung beneath it fly right past us. It was heading towards Two Sisters, the pilot mistakenly believing it to be Mount Kent.

Someone got on the radio and tried frantically to contact the pilot, but he flew steadily on until, suddenly, the Argentinians on Two Sisters saw the Sea King coming their way and opened fire. There were tracer rounds flying all over the place, which soon began to converge on the aircraft. Realizing that the fire was aimed at him, the pilot put his machine into a steep bank and headed back in our direction.

Amazingly, he got away with it. To manoeuvre in mid-air like that, with a heavy field gun slung underneath while dodging incoming machine-gun fire, was magnificent flying. He must have been a brilliant pilot to have dodged all that fire, but he managed it – minutes later we watched him land his cargo safely beneath us at the foot of Mount Kent. It was damned near miraculous.

Mount Kent was secure. The artillery was coming in and the Marines would soon be moving up, for on the following night K Company of 42 Commando was to be ferried to the landing site in the Task Force's sole remaining Chinook twin-rotor transport helicopter (five other Chinooks had been lost when the container ship *Atlantic Conveyor* was sunk by an Exocet on 25 May). The rest of the commando was marching from the beachhead to join up with K Company, which they did on 4 June. It was time for us to move on.

Mountain Troop had been allocated a location to the south of Mount Kent, but because of the scant amount of ground cover the area wasn't large enough to accommodate the whole troop. As a result, John Hamilton, the troop commander, took three men and I the remaining three. We then split up and found our own separate hiding places.

We lay up all day and into the night. Away on our flank we heard gunfire as Air Troop made contact with an Argentinian patrol. Then we suddenly heard our troop commander scream, 'Contact!' I wondered what was happening, because there had been no sound of firing from his position. We grabbed our belt kits and weapons and ran down the mountainside to meet him. We found him running towards the landing site where the helicopters had come in.

We carry a type of night scope known as PNGs, which stands for passive night-vision goggles. They are pretty good, although they require considerable experience in order to make sense of the green tinted, two-dimensional image you get through them. The troop commander now put them to his eyes, and immediately exclaimed,

'Fucking hell! . . . There's hundreds of them! Look at them.' I grabbed the goggles from him and put them to my eyes, only to find that I couldn't see anything. So I passed them to 'Bugsy', a member of the troop who was very short-sighted as well as extremely deaf.

Bugsy was a decent guy, with a tremendous sense of humour, and he was extremely popular in the squadron. Everyone was fond of him, and I personally liked having him in my patrol; with Bugsy around life was never dull. He put the goggles to his eyes, scanned the darkness and said he couldn't see anything either. Given his eyesight, this was hardly surprising, but it was too much for the Boss, who grabbed Bugsy and shouted at him, 'Are you blind, man? Are you blind? There's hundreds of them. Look at them!'

As it turned out, however, the Boss's hundreds of Argentinians proved to be just rocks sticking out of the ground. Yet he had thought they were enemy troops coming forward, because at the time, Air Troop had just made contact with the enemy patrol. Alerted by the noise, he had run down to the landing site, scanning the ground through the PNGs as he ran.

Anyway, after having a few words with the troop commander, we had a good laugh and went back to our location. He was a fine officer, and had simply become confused and disoriented for a few minutes. As we all knew, it can happen very easily when you have been crouched, motionless, under a rock pile for hours.

The next morning, Sunday, 30 May, we climbed on to the ridge overlooking open ground to the south of Mount Kent. We could see for miles, and almost at once spotted a four-man Argentinian patrol working its way towards us. I was leading our own four-man group, and signalled that we should crawl forward to our OP among the rocks and wait for the enemy to approach. None of us said a word. All communication between us was by hand signals. Apart from the buffeting of the wind, there was complete silence.

Through my binoculars, I watched as the Argentinians came steadily towards us. Wearing green uniforms and carrying packs on their backs, they were walking in single file at normal patrol speed, holding their weapons at the ready. When they were 100 metres away we opened fire with our M16 rifles, a far better weapon than the heavy and cumbersome 7.62mm SLR with which the rest of the British forces were armed. They immediately took cover behind a big boulder, although we knew we had hit two for certain, because we saw them go down and we could hear screaming. Somebody was in a lot of pain.

Moments later, a little bit of white cloth fluttered out from behind the boulder. I moved forward, followed by Johnny, an Irishman. We saw that we had in fact shot three of the enemy, though fortunately they were not badly wounded. They had caught the rounds in their arms, and one had also been hit in the leg. I say 'fortunately', because I had not wanted to kill them. They were just young conscripts, and they probably hadn't even wanted to be there. Only eighteen or nineteen years old, they had been drafted into the Argentinian Special Forces and dispatched to these barren islands hundreds of miles from home. Apart from being hurt, they were terrified. We gave them some chocolate and, in my basic Spanish, I asked them where their radio was. They said they didn't have one. Special Forces without a radio? I could hardly credit it, but it was true. Some Argentinian officer with a warped sense of humour had obviously led them to believe that they were Special Forces, and that belief was about as near as they had come to being the highly trained, self-sufficient troops the term implies.

We searched their packs and found that they were carrying brand-new equipment which included US-made PNGs. Their kit must have been bought from the Americans just prior to their deployment, since most of it was unused. They had little in the way of rations, however, although each of them had two or three miniature bottles of whisky in his pack. It was a brand I'd never heard of called 'Double Breeder', and on its label was a picture of two cows. We passed it round and everyone, including the prisoners, had a swig. It tasted fine, despite its weird name.

The young enemy soldiers, once they'd recovered from the shock of being fired on from ambush, wounded – most of them – and captured, told me they were on a reconnaissance mission aimed at gathering information about British dispositions. They didn't seem to have gathered much, however, because they didn't know that the area was now thick with British troops. Apparently they were on their way back to Port Stanley, having made their reconnaissance. 'Do you realize,' I said, 'That between here on Mount Kent and Port Stanley there are masses of British troops?' They shook their heads in despair, having been totally unaware that they were cut off.

Since one of the wounded Argentinians couldn't walk we carried him on a stretcher back to the base of Mount Kent and radioed for a carry-back procedure to get medical attention for him and the two walking wounded.

Soon after that I had my first introduction to Max Hastings, who had come out to the Falklands as a war correspondent for the London

Evening Standard. He had flown forward to Mount Kent in the Chinook with K Company of 42 Commando; the CO of 22 SAS, Mike Rose, had also flown in on the same helicopter, as had the CO of 42 Commando. Wherever Mike Rose went, Max Hastings seemed to follow, and it appeared likely that the journalist was getting good information from the CO. A day or so after we had ambushed the Argentinian patrol I was standing by the CO's two-man command tent at the foot of Mount Kent. Mike Rose had satellite-communications equipment that allowed him direct access to high command in the UK, and I listened in astonishment as Max Hastings spoke directly to his newspaper office in London, using the satellite link with the CO's blessing. He was dictating his story. When he had finished, I heard him say, 'And can you ring my wife and tell her I'm OK?'

I thought admiringly, You clever bastard! There were we ordinary soldiers, with no decent communications, and here's a reporter using our equipment and, what was more, giving his story to his newspaper. The radios used by the troops on the ground in the Falklands were often unreliable or insecure in that the enemy could listen in to them. The CO's satlink, however, allowed him instant and secure access to the people running the war back at Northwood, without his having to go through his senior officers in the Task Force. While this was a good thing for us, it undoubtedly got a good few backs up among some of the officers of the infantry and Royal Marines, as well as among the senior commanders with the Task Force.

D Squadron stayed on and around Mount Kent for a further two or three days, and by that stage the campaign had begun to move fast as preparations went ahead for the final assaults towards Port Stanley. Our task there was finished, and we deployed back to HMS *Intrepid*. The wounded Argentinian soldiers and their unwounded comrade were airlifted out from the base camp and I never saw them again. Their injuries weren't that bad, and no doubt they were repatriated glad to be alive.

Chapter Thirteen

O NCE back on board *Intrepid*, I was tasked with a new mission. I was to establish an OP at Fox Bay on the east coast of West Falkland, and Captain Hamilton was to establish a similar position near the settlement at Port Howard, some twenty kilometres to the north-east on the same coast.

One of my patrol had developed conjunctivitis, and although he pleaded to be allowed to come with me, I wasn't prepared to take him. I told him the state of his eyes made him a liability and that I might have to casevac him out, leaving us a man short. I then went to see the OC to tell that I needed a replacement. Major Delves told me to take my pick from the squadron, and I chose a big Northern Irish lad called, to no one's surprise, Patrick. He looked rather like the comic-book character Desperate Dan, but he was an excellent soldier in the field. I took him for that reason, and also because I reckoned he'd be good to have around if there was any bother with the Argentinians, since he was extremely tough. The other two members of my patrol were Bugsy and the radio operator, Dash.

Weighed down with weapons, ammunition, bergens, radios, night-vision equipment and rations for the seven-day mission, both four-man teams went in on the same Sea King on the night of 5 June. My patrol was dropped off at Two Bussoms, about twelve kilometres from our target. Then the chopper ferried Captain Hamilton and his three men to a landing site some distance from their location.

We had been issued with a report on our area of operations compiled by a patrol from G Squadron, which had had a team at Fox Bay. When we arrived, however, we found that the report bore no resemblance to the terrain ahead of us. Something was very wrong. This is not to say that the G Squadron patrol had not been there, merely that the report did not fit the ground – in any way.

Carrying 90-pound packs, the four of us moved out. The ground was almost flat, and so barren that we were completely exposed. Yet the report I'd read had said that there was plenty of cover. It was a cloudy night, so at least the darkness concealed us, even though it made movement difficult. After walking for some hours we crossed a grassed strip, and I suddenly realized that we were on an airfield. We had walked right on to the airstrip at Fox Bay, then in Argentinian hands. We looked at our watches. They showed 0930 hours Zulu time. First light was due at 1130, which meant that we had only two hours in which to find somewhere to lie up where the enemy couldn't see us.

Moving away from the airstrip we found a shallow, waterlogged hollow thick with reeds. It was wet, but we put down our ponchos and I said, 'Right lads, it isn't the Hilton but, with a bit of luck they won't spot us.' Settling down in the wet, we lay flat and went into our 'hard routine', which meant no movement, no smoking, no cooking, and no hot drinks. We just lay there, almost motionless, and waited. If we wanted a piss, we rolled on our sides, very, very slowly, and hoped the hint of steam wouldn't give our position away to some Argentinian patrol we had failed to see or hear approaching.

It was miserably uncomfortable, but we'd had plenty of practice at being uncomfortable. We lay there, very still, until last light, then moved out. We were very stiff and cold, but we had to find a place where we could dig in, so that we could watch the enemy positions without being compromised. Eventually, just as the darkness closed in, we found a sloping bank – it must have been the only sloping bank for miles – and we began to dig a two-man trench. A half moon came up and we dug like demented badgers all through that Sunday night, camouflaging the OP with nets and tufts of grass. I went into the trench with Patrick, and Bugsy and Dash, with the radio, hid themselves in a natural dip in the ground in front of our position.

When dawn broke next morning we realized that the Argentinians were only about two hundred metres away. We were right on the edge of the forward line of their defensive position. And the beauty of it was that they had no idea that we were there. I thought, Hell, a few more feet and we'd have been sharing their trenches. I was surprised, too, that they hadn't seen or heard us digging, although we had been pretty quiet about it. Presumably they were too busy getting their heads down to notice us, and no doubt it never crossed their minds that there were any British soldiers within thirty kilometres of them.

From the OP we had a clear view of Fox Bay. The area was bristling with enemy soldiers and their gear. They were at least a battalion strong – perhaps as many as 1,000 men – supported by artillery pieces and plenty of vehicles. There was also a lot of movement among the troops and their supporting arms. They were in defensive positions, holding

Fox Bay for whatever reason they thought it was of value, and had taken over the islanders' settlement. This was the size of a small village, and the Argentinians had requisitioned the houses for accommodation and cooking. They had also dug long trenches for the infantry, and had positioned three 5.5-inch field guns as part of the defences.

The enemy sent out foot patrols throughout the day, and one morning we spotted one heading straight for our positions. We kept our heads down – and then one of them suddenly fired a round. Alarmed, we couldn't work out what they were doing, for they clearly weren't firing at us. Then there were a few more shots, and we realized that they were shooting sheep for the larder. We watched as they carried the creatures back to their cookhouse.

They didn't know that we were within spitting distance of their lines, and that we were radioing their positions and strength, as well as details of their equipment and movements, back to *Intrepid*. Indeed, they could hardly use the latrines without our knowing about it. Mind you, not having latrines ourselves, we had problems of our own. All we could do was roll quietly into position, crap, and then just roll away from it and live with the smell.

One night we received a radio message telling us that the enemy had surveillance equipment that could pinpoint our position by picking up and monitoring our movements. If that happened, things were going to get very interesting for us at Fox Bay. Nevertheless, we stayed in our location until Thursday night – five days in all without the enemy having discovered that we were there – and then I decided that we were overplaying our hand, taking unnecessary risks by remaining. The longer we stayed the greater the odds that we should be compromised. It could only be a matter of time before our presence was discovered by an Argentinian patrol. Since we had radioed back all the useful information that we could gather from our OP, I reckoned it was time to move out.

We left, as we had come, like thieves in the night, and walked back westwards about eight kilometres until we found a small area that was slightly higher than the surrounding land. It wasn't big enough to accommodate the four of us in one location so we split two and two in the same formation as before – I remained with Patrick, while Dash and Bugsy took the other OP fifty metres or so away. Each night I crept forward to speak with them, listening to their reports of enemy movements, telling Dash what to send on the radio and reading any messages that had come in for me. We were carrying a Swift Scope, a powerful telescopic single-lens monocular. Through it, though we were now a fair distance away, we could still see almost every movement the enemy at Fox Bay made.

It was during this time that we heard over the radio that John Hamilton, the troop commander, had been killed at Port Howard, where he had been doing the same sort of job as ourselves. He had taken three men to establish an OP near the settlement, where there was another substantial Argentinian garrison, and report back any information they could gather. Because of the nature of the ground, they could not establish a position large enough to accommodate them all, and so, like us, they opted for the two-man split. Unlike us, however, instead of remaining in their positions, they rotated each two-man team at night to give people a break.

It was while they were in the OP that John Hamilton and a trooper named Ron were compromised by an Argentinian patrol consisting of approximately twenty men. Realizing they'd been spotted, and despite being outnumbered, they made a break for it to give the two men in the other location a chance. But in this heroic attempt to draw the enemy's attention from their friends, John Hamilton was shot and wounded. They continued to fire back, until the troop commander told Ron to make a dash for it. Hamilton was shot again and killed, and Ron was eventually captured when he ran out of ammunition. He was taken back to Port Howard, where he was stripped and questioned. Quite what the Argentinians made of him isn't known, but he was apparently well looked after, and was repatriated soon after the Argentinian surrender. Eventually, he joined us aboard the RFA landing ship *Sir Lancelot*. He was the only British soldier to be captured during the war after the Argentinian seizure of the Falklands and South Georgia. The other members of the Port Howard patrol managed to get away. John Hamilton was awarded a posthumous Military Cross.

Meanwhile, away to the south-west, the cold was getting to us. It was particularly bad for Dash, the radio operator. He had to encode the messages and then tap them out in Morse. This is a tricky enough task when your fingers are warm, but when they are freezing it becomes extremely difficult, and on several occasions I took over from Dash. You have to rub your fingers together inside your gloves to stop them from freezing, but the real worry is that if you make a mistake while decoding, you have to start all over again. Encoding and transmitting messages is also very time consuming, and more so when you're freezing. If a message became garbled in transmission, we had to spend hours trying to get it right.

By Saturday, 12 June, our seven-day mission was up and we received a message which read, 'Stay in your location. Helicopter arrival to be advised soon.' We waited and waited, listening out for the flap-flap sound of the Sea King coming for us. I liked their idea of 'soon'. We lay there for another five days, by which time the rations we'd brought to last us for seven days were all but exhausted.

We were down to eating the stuff in our belt-kit emergency packs – a bar of chocolate, powdered soup and tea bags – which was supposed to be enough to last for a couple of days. These and the leftovers from our original rations – boiled sweets, apple flakes and foul-tasting packet soup – had to last us five days. Patrick and I had almost come to blows over the apple flakes even before we ran out of rations. He had wanted to put them in rice pudding, but I objected because I can't stand the horrible things. And since I was the boss, that ought to have been that – end of argument.

Actually, I bribed him not to put the apple flakes into the rice pudding. It happened to be his birthday, and I just happened to be carrying a hip flask full of rum. So I gave him a tot for his birthday, which not only made him happy, but at the same time resolved the problem over the apple flakes.

We received good news over the radio, when we were informed on 14 June that the Argentinian forces on East Falklands had surrendered that day, just before the final British assault on Port Stanley. Nevertheless, we were ordered to stay in position and to continue observing the enemy, since at the time it was not known what the Argentinian forces on West Falkland would do, and there was a chance that they might determine to go on fighting.

By 16 June our seven-day stint had stretched to twelve days, and the helicopter still hadn't arrived. That day, however, we received a radio signal that we would be picked up at 1200 hours the following day at the landing site designated in our orders. Since it was only about a kilometre away we didn't leave our location until 1100, arriving at 1145. Then we sat on our bergens, awaiting pick-up. Noon came and went, but still no helicopter, and by 1300 hours we were freezing. The wind-chill factor meant the temperature was around minus 10 degrees Celsius, so I told the others to get out their sleeping bags and wrap themselves up against the wind. We were chilled to the bone, and our hands felt cold enough to drop off. Much more exposure to that icy wind and we might easily have had frostnip problems.

We were a little weak from having had no proper food for at least five days and the cold saps your energy like nothing else. At 1400 hours, with still neither sight nor sound of the helicopter, I told Dash to get on the radio and ask where the helicopter was. Back came the reply, 'To you shortly.' Apparently the pilot had been given the grid reference for the landing site, but no one had told him it was on West Falkland. Since almost all the British land forces were on East Falkland, he'd been searching for us there.

The helicopter finally arrived at 1600 hours, by which time we had been waiting for four and a quarter hours and were almost frozen stiff. We saw the Sea King flying in at low level when it was still about ten kilometres away, and I told the lads to stow their sleeping bags in their bergens and Dash to put away the radio. The chopper landed, but because of the extreme cold we were stiff-limbed and movement was very difficult. After a real struggle, we managed to throw our kit on board and climbed in after it.

I asked the RAF load master, who sits at the rear of the helicopter during flights, if he had any food, and without a word he threw me a tin of corned beef. To open it, we had to break a metal key off the lid and use it to unwind a strip of metal running round the tin. Sounds easy – after all, thousands of people do it every day – but not with frozen fingers. After a struggle we eventually managed it and wolfed the cold, fatty meat down. You'd have thought the load master would have offered to help, but he just sat there with his headset on, looking at us. Mind you, after nearly two weeks in the open without washing, we must have stunk like nothing on God's earth.

We landed not on *Intrepid*, which we'd left twelve days earlier, but on *Sir Lancelot*, an LSL (landing ship logistic) manned by an RFA crew. She had been struck by two Argentinian bombs on 24 May, and though they had not exploded, she had been abandoned until they had been made safe and removed. Even then, the damage to her was such that she was now being used solely for military accommodation. In the last week of the war SAS troops had been stationed aboard her as a rapid-reaction force, to be deployed at a moment's notice when and where they might be required.

I dragged my kit out of the Sea King and trudged below. The circulation was coming back into my numb fingers, a feeling like having pins-and-needles, and I sat at a table and cleaned my M16 before handing it in to the armoury. What I really wanted, though, was to stand under a hot shower for hours. I had been thinking about that shower for days and days, so I stripped off my filthy clothes, wrapped a towel around my middle, pulled on a pair of flip-flops, and found the shower room.

There was no hot water. There was no lukewarm water, either. In fact, if the water had been any colder, it would have come out of the showerhead as snowflakes. They must have pumped it straight out of the South Atlantic, and you would have needed a survival suit to stand it for any length of time. Unfortunately, I didn't have a choice, for I needed more than a few minutes to wash away the grime and fifth I'd accumulated on West Falkland. That done, it took me hours to get warm afterwards, but eventually we managed to get some food inside ourselves, which helped. By now some of the other members of the squadron were trickling back from whatever operations they'd been tasked with. One team had a hilarious story to tell of what had happened to them while patrolling a few miles from Mount Kent before the Argentinian surrender.

While on patrol they had come across a hut that they thought might be occupied by the enemy. The squadron commander decided that this was a mission for Mobility Troop and, never one to miss a bit of action, he went with them. After lying low and watching the target for some time, they decided to go in fast and grab whoever was inside. So they silently surrounded the place and then smashed the door in with a sledgehammer and threw themselves through it. The door burst inwards with such violence that it flew off its hinges. But the only living thing in the room was a single Argentinian soldier, and he was in bed. It was so cold in the hut that, under the bedclothes, he was wearing a quilted duvet jacket, denim trousers and a pair of thick woollen socks.

When the guys charged into the room with their weapons ready to blast anyone who offered the slightest resistance, the terrified enemy soldier sat bolt upright in the bed. They dragged him out, and at once a terrible smell filled the hut. The poor sod was crying and was so scared that he'd fouled himself.

On the floor by the bed was a well-thumbed pile of dog-eared porn magazines. One of the patrol sat on the floor, leafing through the magazines, while another took off the captured soldier's socks and put them on his own feet. Then someone else took the prisoner's quilted jacket. Just then the OC walked in. He looked at the Argentinian, who was still sobbing – by now he only had his shitty trousers left on, because nobody wanted those – and shook his head in amazement.

'Give the poor lad his kit back,' he said. So the guys handed the terrified soldier his gear and sat him down on a chair. The OC then told

Jock, one of the patrol members who spoke Spanish, 'Ask him where the barracks are.'

Jock looked down at the Argentinian and demanded, 'Donde esta la estación?' At this the soldier, who turned out to be a cook, cried and sniffled even more, and said, 'No se, no se.'

'Donde esta la estación, you lying dago fuckwit,' said Jock. The question was repeated again and again, with Jock getting increasingly irate, shaking the cook and shouting at him. And still the Argentinian, by now almost gibbering with terror, said that he did not know.

Things might have got completely out of hand if somebody hadn't suddenly realized that Jock's Spanish wasn't all that it was cracked up to be. He had been demanding to be told where the railway station was – not the barracks. It was little wonder that their prisoner didn't know the answer, because there wasn't a station anywhere between there and South America.

Since he clearly had no information, and was equally clearly no threat to anyone, the cook was taken away to a helipad. When the chopper arrived, however, he had to be physically dragged on board. Later we learned that he thought he was going to be taken up a few thousand feet and then thrown out. Nevertheless, he was delivered safe and sound, although still smelling strongly of shit, to the JSIW – Joint Services Intelligence Wing – where he was debriefed.

Having willingly given up what little information he possessed, he was given a job behind the hotplate in the galley aboard *Intrepid* until he could be repatriated to Argentina. When he wasn't serving food he washed pans, and whenever anyone walked in whom he recognized from the raid, he would wave and smile. He was good at his job and worked hard; what was more, he was living in better conditions than he had been in that hut near Mount Kent. All things considered, he seemed a good deal happier as a PoW than he had been as a soldier.

It was a further twenty-four hours before all the squadron was back together again. Then, during lengthy debriefing sessions aboard *Sir Lancelot*, we stood up and spoke of what had happened during our various missions exactly as it had happened, warts and all. If there had been a cock-up, then we said so, with the result that we all learned from the experience, and with a very good chance that our mistakes would not be repeated. The same went for a successful mission, in that everyone learned something from it that might be of help in future operations.

That June also saw the start of the 1982 World Cup with England's first game against France. We listened to the match on a big radio with the commentary relayed from Spain on the BBC World Service. I remember Bryan Robson scoring the first goal in the opening forty seconds of the match, which cheered us all greatly. England won 3:1, which was poetic justice on a country that had supplied Argentina with Exocet missiles.

Although it was some days since the formal surrender of all Argentinian forces in the islands, we didn't go ashore. We had seen enough of the Falklands to last us a lifetime. I had made friends with the Chinese cooks aboard *Sir Lancelot*, and every night, myself and a pal called Geordie would eat Chinese food with them, instead of the lousy navy slop. They were a good lot, those cooks, especially considering that they were civilians who had sailed into a war zone and been put in considerable danger.

On 25 June, nine days after we returned from Fox Bay and eleven after the enemy surrender, Rex Hunt, the Governor of the Falkland Islands, returned to Port Stanley from London, to which he had been repatriated by the Argentinians after their invasion, just eighty-four days earlier. Our CO, Mike Rose, was adamant that D and G Squadrons were not going to have their time wasted on a long sea voyage back to the UK. Instead we would wait for RAF C-130s to airlift us back. The aircraft that had brought in the Governor took the first wave of thirty men.

On the following morning, Saturday 26 June, another RAF C-130 flew in to Port Stanley airport. Long-range fuel tanks had been fitted in the rear and a few hours later it took off again, carrying thirty SAS men on the fourteen-hour flight to Ascension Island. This was the second SAS flight out to Ascension, and I was on it. A party of logistic support personnel from Hereford met us on arrival and gave us a proper English breakfast. There was time for a mug of tea and a shower before we boarded another C-130 homeward bound for RAF Lyneham in Wiltshire. The aircraft touched down for refuelling only once, in West Africa, and then it was non-stop all the way home. We landed at Lyneham at around 0500 hours on 28 June, and three hours later I was back in Hereford.

The first thing I did was go to the squash club and book a court for that afternoon, so that I could have a game with a friend of mine who, like me, was a member of the county squash team. Quite apart from other, more serious, considerations the Argentinian occupation of South Georgia and the Falkland Islands had rudely interrupted my playing. I was determined to become the Herefordshire County Champion. And I had a fair bit of catching up to do.

The Falklands campaign caught up with me again later that year when, one Sunday evening in September, the 2IC telephoned me at home. He told me that the following morning the *Sun* was publishing the names of all the recipients of honours and decorations awarded to those who took part in the campaign. I was not to be alarmed, he said, when I discovered that 'Sergeant Peter Ratcliffe, Special Air Service' was among the names, awarded a Mention in Despatches for leading the patrol on West Falkland.

Chapter Fourteen

THE self-styled 'hard men' of Scotland's toughest maximum-security gaol turned out to be about as tough as newborn kittens when faced with really hard men from the SAS.

In October 1987, long-term prisoners in Peterhead's D Wing rioted, all but destroying the building and taking a warder hostage. Although many prisoners gave themselves up to the prison authorities, a group led by three of Scotland's most notorious prisoners held out defiantly, threatening to kill their hostage, a fifty-six-year-old warder, Jackie Stuart, who had only one kidney and urgently needed medical care and drugs to stabilize his condition. The three ringleaders were all men with nothing left to lose, for each of them was looking at the wrong end of a massive sentence for violent crimes. Twenty-four-year-old Malcolm Leggat was serving life for murder, as was Douglas Matthewson, thirty, who had murdered a former beauty queen, while twenty-five-year-old Sammy Ralston was a convicted armed robber.

They and the remaining rioters had barricaded themselves into the area beneath the roof of D Wing. Pushing the captive warder through a hole they had made in the slates, the convicts placed a noose round his neck and threatened to set him on fire, yelling their threats to the prison authorities and police who stood below watching helplessly in the unwinking gaze of the media who had been drawn to the drama. Exhausted, ill and terrified, Mr Stuart, who had six grandchildren, stretched out his arms towards the watching television and press cameras and pleaded for help. The hard men of Peterhead simply laughed at him. One of them threatened him with a hammer, and others warned that if anybody tried to rescue the hostage, they would hurl him from the roof into the yard 70 feet below.

Angered and sickened, the Prime Minister, Margaret Thatcher, watched the poor man's ordeal on the television in her flat at No. 10 Downing Street. Seeing that the police and prison officials were powerless, she telephoned Malcolm Rifkind, the Secretary of State for Scotland. Mrs Thatcher had been triumphantly re-elected in 1983, her reputation, and that of her Tory government, greatly enhanced by the victory in the Falklands. That campaign had also increased the Prime Minister's respect for the SAS, a process that had begun in May 1980 when men of the Regiment stormed the Iranian Embassy in Princes Gate, London, and freed the hostages being held there by a terrorist group.

Trouble had been brewing in Scottish gaols for weeks, and there had been sporadic outbreaks of violence in some of them. At least fifty prisoners had gone on the rampage at the grim maximum-security gaol at Peterhead, a seaport which lies some thirty miles north of Aberdeen, protesting against what they claimed was a harsh regime. Most surrendered after a couple of days, but before doing so they had taken over three floors of D Wing and smashed the place to pieces. Meanwhile several of the most violent men had grabbed Warder Stuart and refused to give either him or themselves up. Both the Scottish Secretary and the Chief Constable of Grampian Police warned the Home Secretary, Douglas Hurd, that the position was extremely serious and that neither the prison staff nor the police were able adequately to cope with the situation.

They requested military help, and by 'military' they obviously had in mind the SAS, especially given the Prime Minister's well-known regard for the Regiment. Both Hurd and the Director of Special Forces were dead set against sending us in, however, claiming that to do so would set a precedent for future gaol sieges. For twenty-four hours after Mrs Thatcher's call to Rifkind it had been an off-and-on situation as to whether the SAS became involved or not.

By October 1987 I was squadron sergeant-major, and now lived in my own flat in Hereford. I was there one evening when the telephone rang. It was Major Mike, the D Squadron commander, a tall, tough, no-nonsense kind of man with the distant blue eyes of a deep-water sailor. He was both liked and respected by the men – something that's tough to achieve in our business. On this occasion he was also a man of few words. 'I'm going north', he told me over the phone. 'By helicopter. Turn on your television set.' Then he hung up. For once the Boss didn't have much time for idle chit-chat.

Switching on the television, I read the latest headlines from the Peterhead Gaol siege on Ceefax. The situation there didn't look good. By early next morning the CO had become involved, and had talked over the telephone with both Malcolm Rifkind and the Ministry of Defence.

The SAS Counter-Terrorist team, known as the SP (Special Projects) team, was on permanent standby, as it always is. At the time D

Squadron was doing its tour as the SP team, which is why the OC and I were involved. But, apart from Major Mike, now in Peterhead giving the local prison authorities on-the-spot advice – and in my opinion there was no one better able to tell them what was what – it still wasn't certain whether our services would be needed. Margaret Thatcher, however, apparently had no such doubts.

Formed in the 1970s, by 1977 the SP team had expanded to full squadron strength, all four of the Regiment's squadrons forming the team in rotation. Each team did six months' standby duty based in Hereford, but with periods of SP training, deployments to Northern Ireland, and training abroad, to cope with any hostage or terrorist situation within the United Kingdom, or anywhere else in the world where Britain had an interest.

I spent the day hoping that we wouldn't be called in to Peterhead, for the truth was that I would much rather have been playing squash, since I was due to play for the army in a tournament on the Friday and Saturday. In addition, a good friend of mine and his wife had arrived from Germany, and were staying with me in Hereford. Throughout the day, we were constantly told the operation was on, then off, then on again. This became quite tedious after a bit, leaving us wondering why the authorities couldn't make a simple decision, one way or the other.

At around eight o'clock that evening I drove the CO home from the camp in my car. He invited me into his house for a drink, and as I was leaving I joked, 'I'll see you in half an hour.' Smiling as he closed the door, he said, 'I hope not.' I drove home and walked into my flat to find the phone ringing. This time it was the operations officer. 'It's on,' he said.

I raced back to the camp. Earlier that morning I'd had a telephone conversation with the squadron OC, and together we had selected which team would deploy to Peterhead, if required. The SP team consists of two twenty-man teams, known as Red and Blue, although otherwise there is no difference between them. We had selected Red Team, in readiness against our being called in to rescue the warder and quell the Peterhead riots, which by now had been running for four days.

The guys came in to the camp fast. Taking some of them, including the CO and the ops officer, in two Range Rovers while the rest of the men boarded a motor coach with all their equipment, we set off for RAF Lyneham. Blue lights flashing in the darkness, a police car escorted us all the way, clearing the roads ahead of us of slow-moving traffic. At Lyneham, Royal Air Force Police with more flashing blue lights, escorted us directly to the runway, where the C-130 Hercules was already warming its engines. The two Range Rovers drove straight up the tailramp of the aircraft and were chained to the deck. Then the rest of the guys from the coach, hauling their equipment and their weapons, piled aboard. Everyone was in the C-130 in less than a minute, and the vehicles were still being lashed down as the aircraft began taxiing down the runway. We were airborne within five minutes of driving through the gates.

Flying time to Aberdeen was an hour and fifteen minutes, and when we landed in the very early hours of the morning another police escort was waiting at the airport to guide us to Peterhead and the maximum-security gaol. The CO, the ops officer and I rode in the police car, while the rest of the team followed in a big police van and our two Range Rovers.

Camped at the front gates of the gaol were television crews, press photographers and journalists. The cameramen had their long focus lenses trained on the roof of D Wing. To avoid being spotted by them, we left the vehicles out of sight and went the back way into the gaol, picking our way along the fence flanking the houses where the warders lived.

Each man carried his green canvas holdall, containing a gas mask, black leather gloves, fireproof black coveralls, black, rubber-soled Adidas boots, a 9mm Browning High Power automatic pistol and a Heckler & Koch 9mm submachine-gun, body armour, belt kit, ammunition, riot baton and personal radio. Additional equipment, including explosive charges, stun grenades, more ammunition and ladders, was rapidly and stealthily ferried into the gaol by our guys using the same route.

We slipped through a gate, crossed a yard to a building and entered a room measuring about twenty feet by thirty, which some prison-authority wit had chosen to call the gymnasium. There was scarcely room to swing a cat and the place filled up rapidly as we piled in with our gear, to find the squadron OC waiting for us.

When the civil authorities call in the army and formally hand over control of a situation, that situation or emergency, regardless of what it may be, becomes entirely a military matter. All decisions are taken by the military involved, although this does not mean that there will not have been discussions with other authorities, and notably government ministers. Now the gaol seige, and its resolution, was in our hands.

The OC had a mind like a steel trap. No detail escaped him as he rapidly briefed everyone. He had a map of the prison laid out and, on a blackboard, detailed drawings of the roof and the landings at each level of D Wing. The plan Major Mike had devised called for a four-entry approach involving a total of sixteen SAS men. The prisoners had taken over three floors of D Wing and the warder was being held hostage in a cell beneath the roof, which they had barricaded off.

Four of our men were to climb out of a skylight in another part of the prison and then creep along a narrow brick parapet flanking the roof, with a drop of 70 feet to the ground – in the dark, which took some nerve. The parapet was very narrow, which meant that the men would have to walk along it in single file, while at the same time trying to avoid being spotted by prisoners locked up in another wing of the gaol across the yard. To make matters worse, it had rained, and the parapet was slippery as a result.

When the OC gave the word over the radio, the guys on the roof were to ease themselves down through the hole the prisoners had made in the slates and then crash through the ceiling into the room where it was believed the hostage was being held. Simultaneously, shaped explosive charges would be electronically detonated to blow three metal doors on the D Wing landings clean off their hinges, and the other three SAS teams would charge in.

In the gymnasium, we put on our fireproof black coveralls, Adidas boots for stealth, body armour and gas masks. We were to carry batons, stun grenades and canisters of CS gas. The OC told us that we were going in for hard arrest, meaning no firearms were to be drawn unless absolutely necessary – the CS and stun grenades would do most of our work for us.

Silently, the four teams got into position and made their preparations. But, as the guys edged their way along the slippery wet parapet, they were spotted from across the yard by prisoners in B Wing, which held several hundred men. They shouted warnings and banged pisspots on the bars of their cell windows to alert the hostage takers. By now, however, everything was in place for the rescue and the OC didn't wait a moment longer.

'Standby, standby . . . go!' he shouted over the radio. It was exactly 5 am.

And in we went. The prisoners didn't know what had hit them. The moment the stun grenades exploded and the CS-gas pellets released their fumes, the fabled hard men of Peterhead were no longer in the game. Indeed, they had never had a prayer from the moment we were called in.

It was all over within three minutes. Reeling around, stunned by the bangs and choking on the gas, they were grabbed from the room they'd barricaded in D Wing and dragged down the iron stairs from one landing to the next. Other SAS guys in black overalls and gas masks gently led the prison officer to safety.

I had been tasked along with a guy called Johnny, an Ulsterman, to go through the door on the first-floor landing. When the simultaneous explosive charges blew the hinges off the door, I charged in. It was extremely difficult to see anything, owing to the gas and the amount of smoke from the flash-bang grenades. The rioters had wrecked or ransacked everything in sight, hurling the debris on to the walkways outside the cells, which further impeded our progress. Johnny and I cleared each cell, but there were no rioters on this floor. Then, over the radio, the OC reported that the hostage had been rescued and the rioters seized.

I was still on the first floor with Johnny when our guys brought Mr Stuart down the stairs to our landing. He was wearing a donkey jacket with orange flashes on the sleeves, and was utterly bewildered. He had been sitting at a table in the cell beneath the roof when our guys burst in, and it was obvious that he didn't know what was happening to him.

Other teams cleared any remaining resistance from the landings. Apart from a thundering great racket from the rest of the prisoners in the other wings, who were locked in their cells and rioting, it was all over bar the shouting. The prison warders, the same warders who had been unable to cope with the rioting convicts, suddenly became very brave. They had entered the wing after we'd freed the hostage, and I watched as they dragged the ringleaders down the metal stairs.

Peterhead was a typically forbidding, Victorian-built prison, with galleries – metal walkways with iron railings – round the landings, which in turn ran round a hollow lightwell in the centre. Strung across the lightwell between each landing were wire nets, put there to break the fall of any prisoner who tried to kill himself by jumping off one of the walkways. It was one of the most horrible places I'd ever seen in my life. If I had spent any time banged up there as a prisoner, I'm certain I'd have been up on the roof myself.

D Wing was a shambles. The prisoners who had rioted earlier had made a good job of wrecking it, and anything they had not managed to destroy or use for barricades had been finished off by the hostage takers.

In the aftermath of our assault, wraiths of CS gas began creeping into the cells in which the other prisoners were locked. They banged their pisspots and set their bedding on fire, or clung to the bars on their windows and yelled out, demanding to be released. From the prison yard, the newly brave warders hosed down the open cell windows with water jets. Meanwhile, Mr Stuart was examined by the prison doctor and then taken to hospital and reunited with his wife. His captors were locked up in top-security cells. And we returned to the gymnasium, in the darkness still managing to keep away from the prying cameras of the media.

Under Scottish law, after a crime has been committed full statements have to be taken by the police from every person concerned before anyone may leave the country. As we slipped out of our kit in the prison gymnasium, the police arrived, looking for statements from each of us. They were swiftly told to forget it.

After a quick chat with the OC, who had so brilliantly planned and executed the whole rescue operation, I told the lads to finish changing out of their kit, pack up and start moving out. There was a very simple reason: we didn't want to be still hanging around when dawn broke, which would not be long now. There was no point in advertising our presence, especially not with the press and TV there. We slipped quietly out through the back gate, the same way we had arrived. The entire operation had taken less than an hour from our arrival to our departure. No wonder, as we learned later, Margaret Thatcher was said to be pleased.

The lads were driven immediately to Aberdeen airport, where they had to wait for the pilots and crew of the C-130, who were on enforced rest. The earliest time they could depart was midday. Meanwhile the Colonel, the OC, the Operations Officer and I climbed into a police car and were also driven to the airport, where a helicopter was waiting to take us back to Hereford. Six hours later, having refuelled at Glasgow and Liverpool, we were back in the camp. The flight back was slow, but I passed the time thinking about the events of the pre-dawn hours, and reflecting on my luck that, once again, I had been involved in the action and another piece of the Regiment's history.

It was a Saturday, and having been up all night and taken part in the operation at Peterhead, I was looking forward to getting my head down. Only a quarter of an hour after walking into my flat, however, the telephone rang.

The caller was Chris Wilson, captain of the British Army squash team, of which I was a member. Every year there is a squash tournament between teams from the police, army, navy and fire service. It is called the Quadrangular, and I had been selected to play for the army on Friday and Saturday. When the Peterhead job blew up, however, I had called Chris and told him that I was working and wouldn't be able to make the team. He had no idea what was happening, but he had the good sense not to ask. The fact that I was a squadron sergeant-major in the SAS was enough to tell him all he needed to know.

But now he was asking if, after all, I could get down to Portsmouth, where the Quadrangular was being held, by 3 pm that same afternoon. I still stank of CS gas, as well as being unshaven and badly in need of a shower. Nevertheless, I promised that I'd be there by 4 pm, which would at least give me time to clean myself up a bit.

That afternoon, I drove to Portsmouth and, ten minutes after arriving, found myself on court playing Sean Hobbs, a police inspector from Nottingham. The matches between the police and army teams would decide the overall winners, and it would be nice to be able to say that I won. I didn't; I was so whacked out that I barely even saw the ball, and Sean completely slaughtered me. Even so we won the Quadrangular overall, so at least something of my pride was saved.

The tournament ended at 5 pm, and I then drove all the way back to Hereford. And neither Chris Wilson nor anyone else involved had any idea where I had been between Friday night and Saturday morning. For me, though, it was all in a day's work.

Seven months later, when the three ringleaders of the Peterhead riots appeared in court, they were sentenced to a total of a further twenty-seven years in gaol. In the course of hearing evidence, the court heard that Peterhead prison staff had never been told who ended the siege and freed the hostage unharmed. Giving evidence, one prison officer, David Guthrie, remarked in a masterpiece of understatement, 'Some unidentified gentlemen came and took the matter to a conclusion.'

I couldn't help wondering what the 'hard men' in the gaol might have said.

Chapter Fifteen

WITHOUT warning, on 2 August 1990 the President of Iraq, Saddam Hussein, launched his country's sneak invasion of its oil-rich neighbour, Kuwait. Yet although Saddam issued no ultimatum or any other notice of his intentions, all the danger signs had been there, plain to see, and still he had taken the West by surprise.

At that date Iraq was in debt to the tune of tens of billions of dollars, largely as a result of its eight-year war with neighbouring Iran, which had proved immensely costly not only financially, but in terms of men's lives and destroyed material. In addition, the Iran-Iraq War of 1980–8 had left Saddam with a vast battle-trained army which he could barely afford to pay; he also had easy access to a weak, immensely rich little emirate on his southern border to which he owed most of his throttling debt. On 28 August Saddam declared Kuwait to be Iraq's nineteenth province.

The sudden and, as it turned out, brutal invasion brought the immediate censure of the United Nations. What sent shudders down the spines of most Western leaders, however, was not the immediate fate of Kuwait but the threat to Saudi Arabia and its vastly rich oilfields. For, once Iraq had mobilized, there was little to stop Saddam's forces from sweeping straight through what was, to the West, the most important of the desert states to the Red Sea. With the prospect of Saddam in control of the oilfields of Kuwait and Saudi Arabia, the threat to the West became not just very real, but very immediate.

George Bush, one of America's most decisive presidents since the war – perhaps not surprising in a former head of the CIA – did not wait to see whether the United Nations would take action. He ordered a rapid-reaction force to Saudi Arabia to bolster the existing defences there, and placed the whole of the mighty US military machine on red alert.

By then I was the Regimental Quartermaster Sergeant to 22 SAS, responsible for over four hundred ammunition accounts, and with not a hope in hell of firing a single round of any of them in anger myself. But suddenly Bush was wielding a big stick, Margaret Thatcher (in what would prove to be the last three months of her time as Prime Minister, for she was ousted as leader in a Tory Party coup in November) was talking tough, and to a long-service soldier like me it meant just one thing. The Regiment would be going to war.

This was what we were there for, what all the years of training were about. However useful we had proved ourselves in dealing with terrorists, only in a war could we ever put that training to full use, and only in a war would we get the chance to prove conclusively that we were worth our pay.

The buzz around Stirling Lines was almost tangible. People were smiling. Everyone seemed to be walking with a lighter step. There was a sudden sense of urgency about the place. War was definitely coming – it was only a question of time. And somewhere in that war there was going to be a role for the SAS. Even though it was not immediately obvious to any of us exactly what that role might be, we were all utterly certain that one would be found. Behind enemy lines? Almost certainly. Extremely dangerous? Undoubtedly. But then, we were the best, and as the best could only expect the most hazardous assignments.

When the Iraqis swept into Kuwait 22 SAS had G Squadron undergoing desert training six hundred miles south of the action, at the other end of the Persian Gulf. They were operating out of our permanent base in the United Arab Emirates (UAE) in a huge desert wilderness in southern Saudi Arabia known as the Empty Quarter (Rub' al-Khali), which extends along the country's borders with Yemen and Oman. The Regiment's secret training there falls under Britain's military assistance commitment to the UAE and Oman. What G Squadron was doing there at the time, apart from training, was testing a new fast attack vehicle (FAV), as well as a few other tricky items which no one was supposed to know about.

The FAV had originally been developed for the US Special Forces, but a British company had built a modified version based on SAS specifications. They were tough enough to travel across country at up to 60 mph carrying two men and their equipment as well as a mounted weapon, and yet light enough to be inserted deep behind enemy lines by helicopter. Unfortunately, the G Squadron guys who put the FAVs through their paces in the desert found that the suspension wasn't quite as tough as the rest of vehicle, and they were not deployed by the SAS during the Gulf War. This prototype fault was later rectified and the FAVs are now in favour with the Regiment, two being issued to each four-man patrol for certain desert operations.

News of the invasion of Kuwait brought these desert tests to a halt, and the CO decided to rotate each of the Regiment's remaining three Sabre Squadrons to the UAE in turn. Once there, they would concentrate on mobility training, navigation, desert survival, vehicle maintenance and weapon training.

Meanwhile, in Hereford everything slipped smoothly into top gear as the Regiment was put on standby. One section – the Intelligence Corps unit permanently attached to 22 SAS – went into hyperdrive. Intel spewed out of their office twenty-four hours a day. There were endless written and verbal briefings on every aspect of the impending fight, as well as on what we could expect to face in Kuwait and Iraq when we were deployed. Knowing your enemy's strengths and weaknesses may not be half the battle, but it's a very important part of it, and what we had hammered into us time and again by the intel experts was that Saddam's forces had considerably more strengths than weaknesses.

Like most of us, I had more or less dismissed the Iraqi Army as an ineffectual rabble of jabbering clowns in cloth headdresses, but that idea was quickly jettisoned after just a couple of intel briefings. One I Corps officer told us at an early briefing, 'You may be tempted to think of them as mere camel dung, but that would be a big mistake. These particular dungheads are battle-hardened veterans with eight years' war experience under their belts.

'They fought Iran, which is a well-armed country five times Iraq's size, to a stalemate and forced the Ayatollah to throw up his arms and sue for peace.

'They are a ruthless, well-trained and highly disciplined force – especially Saddam's personal bodyguard troops, the Republican Guard – and they not only enjoy killing their enemies, they are very good at it, as well.

'These guys are not at all squeamish about using nerve or poison gas, either. They found out, while screwing Iran, that these gases are both effective and indiscriminate killers, and you don't even have to be a sharpshooter to get them on target. They just go off and everyone in the area simply falls down dead.'

We were certainly getting to know our enemy, although what we were learning was nothing like what any of us had expected. Saddam's soldiers had suddenly become a fighting force to be reckoned with, and jokes about 'towelheads' and camels rapidly went out of the window. The message was clear: there would be no easy rides. Yet that was not the biggest problem we faced once it became clear that the West and its

Arab allies would fight to liberate Kuwait. For the SAS, the most important question now was whether or not we would get a chance to test our skills against Saddam's forces at all.

Soon after the invasion the UN Security Council passed its resolutions supporting Kuwait and giving Iraq a deadline of 15 January 1991 for the complete withdrawal of all its forces from the emirate. As a result, Desert Shield was created – a coalition spearheaded by the United States and with Britain and France heading the other thirty nations which eventually provided troops and other aid.

The SAS was just one of a number of Special Forces outfits to be dispatched to the Gulf, and all were left kicking their heels because of the attitude of just one man. He was, unfortunately for troops like us, the top man, the Commander-in-Chief of the Allied forces in the Gulf, US General H. Norman Schwarzkopf. As a highly experienced Vietnam veteran he had seen Special Forces in operation during that war, and had been distinctly unimpressed. In fact, he repeatedly let it be known that he thought Special Forces stank, maintaining that other, more valuable, resources had been jeopardized in Vietnam pulling the specials out of trouble on too many occasions.

Desert Shield, he emphatically declared to all and sundry, was going to be principally an air and missile war, backed up on the ground by massed armoured and infantry divisions. 'What the goddamn hell,' he was fond of asking those around him, 'can a goddamned Special Forces unit do that a Stealth bomber or F-16 can't do a darned sight better?'

And of course, when you think about it logically it's not a bad question, given the sophistication of modern aircraft and missiles, and the payloads they can deliver. Nevertheless, it meant that our prospects of getting into the war looked distinctly bleak. In the months leading up to the Coalition making its first aggressive move against Iraq, however, two lucky breaks occurred. One was personal, but the other affected the whole Regiment.

In September it was announced that I was to be appointed Regimental Sergeant-Major, with effect from December. This meant that I would have a substantial personal involvement in directing and planning any operations in which we might become involved. The second lucky break was the news that Lieutenant-General Sir Peter de la Billière, that much decorated SAS hero, had been appointed overall British commander in the Gulf, and effectively Schwarzkopf's deputy.

In the end it all came down to personalities. The American and British generals swiftly established a rapport, so that by October our secret weapon, DLB, had become one of Schwarzkopf's most trusted colleagues. Among Sir Peter's priorities was finding a worthwhile role for his former regiment, still languishing in Hereford, and he got rapid results. The order came through from the Allied Coalition HQ in Saudi Arabia: the SAS was to examine ways of rescuing the thousands of British, other Western and Japanese citizens trapped or held hostage in Iraq and Kuwait, all of whose lives were at risk from Saddam's regime. In order to deter any Coalition attack on Iraq and Kuwait, Saddam had already ordered most of these hostages to be dispersed to military and other strategic locations throughout the two countries to act as human shields.

In theory, of course, this was an ideal task for the SAS. We had practised just this kind of extraction exercise, in combination with RAF helicopter squadrons and the Royal Marines, on numerous occasions. Even if teams had to be sent deep behind enemy lines there was still a high probability of success – provided the operation involved the rescue of just a single group, or very few groups. In the case of there being several groups of hostages, the rescues could be carried out simultaneously.

In the scenario we were talking about, however, which took in some 3,500 hostages split into groups in hundreds of different locations scattered across two countries, we faced the very ugly reality that even with the best possible intelligence, we could not expect to trace the places where even 50 per cent of the hostages were being held. This in turn would mean launching a vast, half-cocked operation involving all the troops in British and US Special Forces, as well as units and even whole battalions from some of the other countries involved in Desert Shield, plus hundreds of helicopters. And all of these must go deep behind enemy lines, to a hundred or more different locations, with no proper backup available other than a degree of air support. Casualties among the human shields and their rescuers would be horrendous, and those hostages who were not located would probably be slaughtered by their Iraqi guards at the first sign of any rescue attempt.

It was a wonderful, almost romantic, dream of an idea, but it didn't have a snowball's chance in hell of succeeding. Those of us who had the facts recognized this from the start. I felt extremely sorry for all those hostages, and for their worried relatives, but I can now admit that, however desperate their situation, the plan to rescue them was never realistically considered by any of us as being even a remotely feasible option. As a plan it gave the troops something definite to train for, and that was about all that could be said for it. It also caused Schwarzkopf to think about us – if only briefly – as participants in his war. Among the US Special Forces, Delta Force – roughly the American equivalent of the SAS – were also going crazy trying to carve out a role for themselves in the Gulf. Most of them were still back in the States and, like us, rehearsing the liberation of the human shields, while being just as certain as we were that it was an absolute non-starter.

Luckily, on 6 December Saddam released most of the hostages and we were able to drop the ridiculous rescue charade which, had it been attempted, could only have ended in bloody nightmare, and many of us being shipped home in bodybags. The only trouble was, with the operation now cancelled, we were once more left without a meaningful role in the coming conflict.

We had good cause, though, to bless our luck in having General de la Billière as the British commander. He was not to leave us kicking our heels for long. On 12 December new orders came through from Coalition HQ in Saudi Arabia. We were to start planning deep-penetration raids into Iraq, the type of operation on which the fledgeling Regiment had cut its teeth after its formation in the Western Desert in 1941. Saddam had been given a deadline of 15 January to get out of Kuwait. DLB gave us the same deadline, by which time we were to be ready to go in to Iraq. What we didn't know at the time, however, was that DLB had not cleared these plans with General Schwarzkopf. So far as we were concerned he was the man in charge of the British forces in the Gulf, and we were a British regiment – so we would do whatever he ordered. At least preparing for operations behind enemy lines would get us up to full battle readiness.

Within a week of my taking over as RSM the Regiment was officially committed to going to war in the Gulf, or at least believed itself to be, which in the end came to the same thing. The announcement to move came in a special meeting convened by the CO in Stirling Lines. The entire staff of regimental headquarters was present. This included the regimental 2IC, the ops officer, adjutant, intelligence officer, quartermaster and myself, as well as the squadron commanders and sergeant-majors and all heads of department. In addition, the motor transport and signals officers and the masterchef were also present. There was an air of expectancy, even excitement, although, typically, every thing was understated. The CO's message was equally brief. With the exception of G Squadron, who were to man the SP team, the whole Regiment would deploy to the Gulf between 27 December and

3 January. It was to be the biggest gathering of SAS personnel in a battle zone anywhere in the world since the end of the Second World War.

There was a quite mind-boggling amount of planning and preparation to get through before we could move out, and I spent virtually every waking hour – including Christmas Day – until our departure in my office at the camp. For myself, I couldn't wait to get to the Middle East, although the last formality for everyone in the Regiment – to make out a will – tended to focus the minds of us all on the fact that we weren't shipping out for a vacation. Indeed, there was a very good chance that some of us would not be coming back, something the Intel guys drummed into us at every available moment – just to keep us on our toes, of course, they explained gleefully. Wills could either be drafted by the documents office on base, by a private solicitor in the town or by simply filling out a suitable will form. It had also become compulsory for each of us to take out an army insurance policy, which pays on death only. There is no limit as to how much one can insure oneself for, but there is a minimum, which is the estimated cost of supporting a soldier's family until his children come of age. For SAS men without families, the policy pays out a lump sum to his next of kin or some other named beneficiary.

The pay sergeant-major also issued each man with twenty gold sovereigns, and a piece of paper printed with a text in both English and Arabic. The sovereigns were intended to be used to bribe Iraqi citizens or military personnel if the need should arise. Since gold sovereigns are an internationally accepted currency, and since each one is worth, not its nominal £1 face value, but around £80, they are an extremely useful and compact way of carrying a large sum of money. The statement printed on the paper was to the effect that after the war the British Embassy would pay the bearer £50,000 or its equivalent in Iraqi currency if he or she helped the owner of the paper to evade capture. This was supposed to benefit an SAS man if he had been stranded or even captured behind enemy lines, but ignored the fact that many Iraqis, and most of the nomads and bedouin, could not read or write. It also seemed to take for granted that any Iraqi was prepared to sell out his country to a hated enemy just on the dubious promise of riches to come at some unspecified date in the future. The sovereigns had to be handed back after the war unless you could prove to have had a legitimate use for them. No one did use them. We tended to steal or hijack what we needed, rather than barter for it. Better to rely on our own, admittedly rather anti-social, tactics among the indigenous population than on some Iraqi's possible greed. I might add here that, contrary to what has been said in several accounts of the SAS in the Gulf War, most of the sovereigns were accounted for after the end of the war.

I deployed with the second wave on Sunday, 30 December, from an RAF base aboard a United States Air Force C-5 troop carrier, a monstrous aircraft known as the Galaxy. We flew out via a base in Germany, where we refuelled and picked up a group of American servicemen before carrying on to our initial destination in the Middle East, Abu Dhabi, one of the seven emirates that make up the UAE.

I was sitting with the Regiment's MTO (motor transport officer) and the Quartermaster. The MTO had told us how he had become the first proper casualty of the war by walking into a marble stairway in the officers' mess at the RAF and cutting his head. As proof, he showed us his bloodstained handkerchief. 'I want this to go down in the records,' he insisted. 'At least I'll be first in one aspect of this war.'

I knew that on the airbase at which we landed there was one of the legendary American PXs – roughly equivalent to our NAAFIs, but usually larger and much, much better – where drink is sold at rock-bottom prices. I also knew that the MTO had a quantity of US dollars about his person. 'Why not go for a Mention in Despatches, as well?' I suggested to him. 'It's extremely underhand and strictly against regulations, but there are two of us here who will swear you performed an act of great heroism and saved two suffering companions at considerable risk to yourself.

'All you have to do is leap off the plane and use some of your US cash to buy wine in the PX.'

So far as the Quartermaster and I were concerned, the MTO earned his MID. He managed to get back on board with a couple of 2-litre cartons of red wine tucked away out of sight. It made the next seven hours much more enjoyable than they would otherwise have been. The three of us were on the upper deck and would be visited every half-hour or so by one of the American load masters handing out soft drinks or coffee. They never noticed that every time we were offered more coffee our paper cups were still always half full. To drink on a military aircraft, British or American, is a serious offence, but we managed to sink all four litres of wine right under their noses before we reached Abu Dhabi.

Three of us may have fooled the load masters with our illicit drinking, but the rest of their SAS passengers hadn't fooled them over another illegal act, namely the theft of twenty-eight of Uncle Sam's airline pillows. These pillows, handed out at the beginning of the flight, had proved so comfortable, and were of just the right mini dimensions, as to be irresistible. Their disappearance was not going to wash with the senior load master, however, a giant black USAF sergeant who was refusing to let his Galaxy take off again until he had his pillows back.

Of the men standing on the tarmac – some one hundred and fifty of them – not one of the culprits was prepared to give up his bounty willingly. Having asked the sergeant to step back into his aircraft for a moment, I told my grinning mob, 'These Yanks are our allies. They give us a nice ride down here and we thank them by robbing them blind.

'I am going to take a short walk – for five minutes – and when I get back I want to see twenty-eight pillows. If not, I am going to search every man's kit and if I find a pillow in anyone's gear, then that person will immediately be RTU-ed.' With that I turned and walked off.

When I returned after having smoked a cigarette there were twenty-eight pillows neatly stacked on the tarmac. They may have been comfortable and a handy size, but that was nothing compared with the threat of being RTU-ed.

What we had not expected to find in Abu Dhabi in winter was that it was extremely cold there in the early mornings. By the time we had appeased the sergeant and unloaded our personal equipment from the Galaxy the sun had edged a little higher and the temperature had begun to rise, but we were still freezing. While we waited for our RAF transport to arrive we must have looked a sorry sight. Here was the whole of the headquarters staff and the support team from 22 SAS standing on the edge of a windswept runway on New Year's Eve 1990, shivering like a bunch of vagrants abandoned in the Arctic.

At the designated time an RAF C-130 came in to land and thundered across to where we were waiting. Once we had loaded ourselves and our gear aboard it flew us the short hop to the main British holding base in the area codenamed Victor. Lying near to Abu Dhabi city, Victor was a newly built parachute-training establishment which was still unoccupied. It had a runway system large enough to accommodate big jets and, surrounding this, a vast, twenty-square-mile secured area where paratroops could be housed and trained. Within the Victor perimeter were numerous camps, up to a mile apart, and one of these, close to one of the perimeter fences, was ours. The buildings were all brand new and, though basic, were adequate.

A small SAS advance party had been sent out before Christmas to establish our camp within Victor. The main operations room, the offices and a major part of the accommodation were all in a giant hangar, originally designed to allow paratroops to practise their descents from high up near the roof. I say offices, but in reality they were desks set a few feet apart from one another. The desks, six-foot wooden jobs with metal legs, were all identical, as were the plastic chairs. They were grouped in a wide, roughly semi-circular, arrangement – the CO, the adjutant, the intelligence officer, the signals officer, me, and the other department heads. It was lucky that they were close together, because the telephone system was very basic, and most of the time we communicated by shouting to one another. If anyone wanted to speak to Hereford, where the second-in-command and G Squadron were holding the fort, he went to the satellite communications desk from where there was a direct link.

On the hangar walls behind the desks were huge maps of Iraq and Kuwait, and on the floor were piles of cardboard cartons containing hundreds of smaller copies printed on paper or silk. These were to be issued to the troops. The silk maps were for evasion or escape purposes. They wouldn't tear if they became wet, as paper would, and they remained readable even after being stuffed damp into a pocket.

Everybody slept on camp beds – even the CO, though he had yet to arrive. Rather than sleep in the hangar with the rest of the HQ staff, however, I requisitioned a very cramped extension on the side of the camp barber shop, about the size of a fifth-rate broom cupboard, where I was able to keep my kit. At night I moved my camp bed into the barber shop to sleep. It had mosquito netting on the windows – though this was rarely needed because of the cold – and a sink and a mirror which were ideal for my morning ablutions. I could even shave while sitting in the leather-covered barber's chair.

The CO had been allocated a small room in one of the buildings outside the hangar, but the rest of the HQ party slept in the huge construction. Our three squadrons of fighting personnel, A, B and D, were either billeted in neighbouring hangars or under canvas. When we first arrived, however, A Squadron was still at the Regiment's training camp in the United Arab Emirates, being the last of the four squadrons to undergo the special desert refresher course.

G Squadron remained at Hereford on counter-terrorist duty. Combating terrorism was still the Regiment's first priority so far as the British government was concerned, and had become more so because of fears of terrorist attacks in the UK by Iraqi or pro-Iraqi agents. Even though Britain was at war we had to leave an adequate special-projects team or anti-terrorist squad in Hereford to deal with any threat that might arise. As has been said, it fell to each squadron, on six months' rotation, to form the SP team; it was G Squadron's bad luck that it happened to be their turn during this period.

Also camped in Victor were sixteen members of the Regiment's R (reserve) Squadron, who were civilian volunteers also based in Hereford. In addition, there was a squadron from our Royal Marines sister service, the SBS, as well as the Special Forces flights from 7 and 47 Squadrons, Royal Air Force. Apart from three C-130s, the RAF had brought in four Chinook helicopters with extra pilots, navigators, flight engineers and load masters as part of their contingent.

We also had a small group based in the Saudi Arabian capital, Riyadh, led by the Deputy Director, Special Forces. He and his team came from Duke of York's Headquarters in Chelsea, London, which among other functions is the regimental headquarters of Special Forces. They were in Riyadh to work closely with General de la Billière, and to pass on the latter's directives to the rest of us in Victor.

Unfortunately, the Deputy Director was as different from DLB, who was worshipped throughout the SAS, as chalk is from cheese. He had commanded the Regiment some years earlier, during which time he had sacked all four squadron sergeant-majors and his adjutant. He was not a man to be messed with; indeed, I can remember only one other squadron sergeant-major being sacked during the rest of my twenty-five years with the Regiment.

I was to get a first-hand view of the Deputy Director's setup when our commanding officer arrived and sent me to Riyadh. He was planning to get us to our forward operating base (FOB) at Al Jouf in north-western Saudi Arabia, 200 kilometres south of the border with Iraq. I was asked to meet up with two RAF staff officers and work out with them just how long it would take us to move 600 men with equipment and vehicles from Victor to Al Jouf, a distance of some 1,700 kilometres as the crow flies. A and D Squadrons were to be broken up into half-squadron units of about thirty men apiece. Each unit would have eight long-wheelbase Land Rover 110s, a Unimog (roughly equivalent to a Bedford 3-ton truck) and whatever motorcycles they required. B Squadron would be split into one half-squadron subdivided into four eight-man units, with sufficient Land Rovers, trucks and motorcycles for their needs. The other half of B Squadron would remain in Victor as an anti-terrorist unit, there being considerable, and justified, fears of terrorist attacks on British targets, notably embassies, in other Gulf states that had joined the Coalition. All this, together with weapons, stores, personal equipment and backup staff, had to be shifted just over a thousand miles north-westwards.

On the way to Riyadh the aircraft I was flying in stopped off at Dhahran on Saudi Arabia's Gulf coast, the principal base for the Coalition air forces. There, for the first time, I realized the sheer power of the forces ranged against Saddam. If I had needed any evidence to convince me that the Americans were taking this war seriously, it was to be found at Dhahran. On that vast airfield there were rows of helicopters and military aircraft stretching literally for miles. Many of the helicopters were still coated in grease beneath a protective layer of brown paper.

Meanwhile, there we were at Victor with four RAF Chinook twin rotor helicopters, one Army Air Corps Gazelle light helicopter, and the use of three RAF C-130 transports. By contrast, the firepower the Coalition had at Dhahran was unbelievable, and there were waves of fresh aircraft coming in all the time. Schwarzkopf had said he saw this as an air war. He clearly meant what he said.

In Riyadh, the British and US headquarters had been established in an office tower block cleared by the Saudi Arabians for the Allies' exclusive use. Adequate for its purpose, though certainly not luxurious, it stood in the bustling centre of the city. At the entrance US Marines and British military police checked everyone in and out. I was cleared through and located the people I needed to see on one of the upper floors. That place became my home for the next two days while we worked out the best way to split up the loads. In the end it was decided that each flight would carry three vehicles and the men who would use them, with all their kit, and that we would try to keep the three C-130s operating in a continuous roll-over movement. This, of course, had to fit in with the RAF pilots flying within their time frame, for I discovered that they were not permitted to fly for more than eight hours without taking the required rest period in between – even in wartime.

I told the air force planners that I thought this was completely unreasonable; after all, our guys had to go without any sleep, sometimes for days on end, while harassing the enemy deep behind his lines. That, I was told by one RAF wit, was our problem. 'Next time round work a bit harder at school and pass your exams, and then you can join the RAF instead,' was his only advice.

'If that's the level of humour that goes with the job, I'll stay where I am,' I replied. 'At least we get to laugh, even if it's only at you glorified taxi drivers.' But it was all good natured, and I found the two staff officers very helpful and extremely professional.

With less than a week to go before our jump-off date to our forward operating base, the CO asked me to fly down to the Regiment's desert-training camp and run an eye over A Squadron. They had been the duty SP team during the three-month run-up to our move to the Gulf, and as a result had not had an opportunity, unlike the other three squadrons, to undergo special desert training. They had been among the first to leave Hereford on 27 December, however, and on arrival in Abu Dhabi had been transferred directly to the training camp.

The camp was a forty-minute helicopter ride from Victor. The Gazelle has little more seating capacity than a sports car. Besides its pilot, it can take four people without kit, or just two men kitted out. None of which mattered to me that particular day, since I was the only passenger, and therefore riding in rare comfort.

A Squadron was nearing the end of its training period and the guys were prepping their vehicles in anticipation of pulling out – possibly for immediate insertion into Iraq. Morale seemed high and the men were in peak condition. It was clear that the squadron was now a highly trained and highly motivated desert fighting force. In anticipation of coming operations, it had already been split into two half-squadrons, each divided into two sub-units: Alpha One Zero and Two Zero, and Alpha Three Zero and Four Zero. The squadron's four troops, Mountain, Boat, Mobility and Air, had been split between the two main units. Two Zero had half of Mobility and Air Troops and all of Mountain Troop, while Four Zero had the other halves of Mobility and Air and all of Boat Troop.

That afternoon the CO flew in to the training camp with the Deputy Director from Riyadh. When he asked if I had unearthed any problems I was able to tell him, 'No. Everybody seems fine. There are no problems at all that I can see.' It was true – I couldn't see any problems. At least, not then; not until we met the men who were to command the two half-squadrons in the field and arranged a private briefing with them later that day.

Alpha Three Zero and Four Zero – codenamed Alpha Three Zero – were commanded by the squadron sergeant-major, because the two troop commanders were fairly new officers and didn't have the experience to be given overall command. To a certain extent, therefore, they were going along in a learning capacity. It is a unique feature of the SAS that units will often be commanded on operations by an NCO, even though there may be an officer present. It is a system that has been proved time and again, partly because the man in command will discuss matters with, and take advice from, other members of his patrol.

The setup for Alpha Three Zero and Four Zero was excellent. It was the command of Alpha One and Two Zero – codenamed Alpha One Zero – which caused immediate misgivings. The squadron commander was a Royal Marine major who had come to us on a two-year secondment from the Special Boat Service. He had already served with the Regiment for a year, but this was the first time he had been charged with anything more difficult than a routine exercise. He didn't seem to relish the prospect of leading his unit into the dangers lurking in Saddam Hussein's unwelcoming back yard. During the briefing, in which the two commanders explained in turn their concepts of the operations to come, it soon became apparent that the OC of A Squadron was not at all happy. He seemed hesitant, apologetic, even timid, and appeared to lack any confidence in what he was supposed to be doing.

When we arrived back at Victor that evening, the CO asked me to join him for a cup of tea and a chat. He seemed very ill at ease, and I didn't need to be a clairvoyant to work out what he wanted to talk about. As always, he came straight to the point.

'OK Billy,' he said, 'the Deputy Director has severe misgivings about OC A Squadron, and to a certain extent so do I. What do you think we can do about it? The balance is all wrong. Alpha Three Zero and Four Zero have most of the senior ranks with the experience and the strength of character to cope. Looking at the other half-squadron, there's a serious imbalance.'

I had already come to a similar conclusion, but I had also come up with a possible solution. I explained to the CO that while in Riyadh I had met up with an officer, an ex-Guardsman named Jeremy who was a member of the Regiment's headquarters staff, who not only appeared to have the right stuff, but had asked me if I could try to get him into the field in the coming fight. A captain in his late twenties, he was due to take over as officer commanding G Squadron in December.

'Perhaps he's the answer,' I said. 'We could put him in as second-in-command of Alpha One Zero, which would give the squadron OC some really positive support.' The CO agreed that this was not a bad idea.

'Well, there's your chance,' I said. 'Put Jeremy in and say it's because you want him to have experience of active service before he takes over his command.'

'Mmmmm,' the CO mused, staring into his half-empty mug of tea, 'I like that. But I'm going to sleep on it.'

When we met again the following morning, however, he told me, 'I've thought about it and I'm going to let them run. We'll make no changes.'

'Okay, Boss, that's fine by me,' I said. He was the CO. He knew the facts and he'd taken his decision, based on those facts. For me personally, that decision was to mean that eventually I would be catapulted from the sidelines into the sharp end of the war against Iraq. At the time, however, there were a hundred other things to occupy me. Matters that required more urgent attention and involved countless instant decisions, and most of them to do with our move to Saudi Arabia.

In the event it took just under four days for the Regiment to complete the move from Victor to Al Jouf. On our jumping-off night, 16 January, the Deputy Director and half a dozen members of his staff turned up. For the life of me I couldn't work out what the hell they thought they were doing there. Everything that could have been arranged by that stage was already well in hand. Furthermore, they were no better informed than we were. It turned out that they didn't even know that the night we had chosen to move up to the front was also the night that General Schwarzkopf had chosen to launch his air war – and they had just come from his HQ in Riyadh.

Between midnight on 16 January and dawn on the 17th, a total of 671 Allied sorties, involving God only knows how many thousands of aircraft and cruise missiles, were launched against Iraq. Somewhere in among them were three RAF C-130s lumbering north-westwards at 350 miles per hour, carrying some of our men and their gear. Aircrew and SAS alike marvelled at the number of F-117 Nighthawks – the so-called 'Stealth fighter' – zipping past them just overhead. They had come from Khamis Mushait airbase, in the far south-west of Saudi Arabia, and were on their way to hit Saddam where it hurt – right in his own back yard.

At Victor, the first that we and, I'm sure, the Deputy Director's party knew of the start of the Gulf War was when we heard it announced on the BBC World Service the next morning. One result of the launching of the air bombardment of Iraq was that only one of our C-130s got back that morning. Its pilot said that during the return flight from Al Jouf all three aircraft had been ordered to land at Dhahran because of the number of Allied attack planes in the sky. He had refused and had continued on to Victor, but the other two C-130s were at Dhahran, waiting for clearance to fly again.

They arrived back that afternoon, and were immediately reloaded and, each with a fresh flight crew, were quickly on their way back to Al Jouf. By midnight on the 17th the Allies had flown 2,107 sorties and the SAS had moved a quarter of its force to the front line. Yet the air war already seemed to be going the way Schwarzkopf had predicted. Who needed Special Forces?

Al Jouf, like Victor, was a brand-new airfield which had never been used, although it was intended for civil use. It was about the same size as Luton airport, and had a runway long enough to take jumbo jets. As each SAS group arrived the mobile fighting patrols unloaded their vehicles and moved directly to a point south of their start line, which was approximately a hundred miles north-west of Al Jouf. They were to wait there until the order to cross the boarder into Iraq should be given.

The rest of us – signallers, intelligence and other headquarters staff, regimental personnel, the quartermaster and storemen, logistics personnel, and support staff from 7 Squadron, RAF, who were there to look after the Chinook helicopters – about a hundred people in all, remained at Al Jouf, where we were located under canvas around the terminal building. Most of our administration offices were to be in the luggage-collection hall inside the terminal, with some of our desks actually positioned on the luggage conveyor belt, but that was still being organized when we arrived. The CO and I moved up to Al Jouf on 18 January.

The whole regiment was now on ration packs. There was no fresh food to be had, only the boil-in-the-bag field rations. You simply placed the tinfoil pack into a mess tin full of water and boiled it. Then you used the water to make your tea. The meals served a need, but that was all. The RAF, however, who were camped next door to us, had a proper mess and proper food. The air force's powers that be had decreed that pilots could only be expected to carry out their jobs if they had decent chefs preparing decent meals.

For once, the CO and I were all in favour of this junior-service favouritism, because we used to sneak into their mess without telling any of our boys where we were going and enjoy a first-class breakfast of eggs and bacon with toast and butter. The RAF put up with us, but swore us to secrecy; 'We can't accommodate any more of you poor, half-starved characters,' we were told. That was fine by us. We would stroll back to our area, pretending we had just been eating our boil-in-the-bag rations. Being in charge had its distinct advantages. Perhaps it's true, and there's no point in having power if you don't occasionally abuse it. To be fair, among the rest of the Regiment, apart from a few regular whingers who would have moaned whatever food they had, there were no complaints about the rations. They went with the job.

The cold was a different matter, however, and one that was to have severe consequences once we were actually operating in Iraq. Everybody was complaining about what they mostly referred to as the total ineptitude of our weather forecasters and intelligence officers. At night it became very cold indeed. Some people wore their desert camouflage outfits with their nuclear, biological and chemical warfare (NBC) suits on top and a jacket over that. The charcoal-coloured lining of the suits would run off on to the camouflage outfits underneath and turn them dark, but the suits were windproof and did keep you warm, which is what mattered.

Fortunately that was all the NBC suits were needed for, as Saddam never resorted to using nerve gases or other agents against us. At the time, however, it was a very real danger. As well as the suits, we also had our gas masks, pre-loaded hypodermics with which to inject ourselves in case of a nerve-gas attack, and Naps tablets, which were kept inside the gas-mask container. One of these was supposed to be taken daily as a defence against nerve gas and other chemical poisons, but I never took any of mine. I don't like popping pills at the best of times, and I simply didn't trust the things. Nobody could put his hand on his heart and say that there would be no contra effects after taking Naps tablets, and I just wasn't prepared to risk it.

To this day I wonder whether this 'Gulf War Syndrome' that has affected numbers of servicemen who took part in that war, and which successive governments have denied exists, might not be related to Naps tablets rather than anything else. Very few of the men in the Regiment risked taking them. The British Army had not faced NBC weapons since the First World War, and most of us decided that the risk of taking the tablets, with their unknown side effects, was greater than the risk of coming under NBC attack.

At Al Jouf we were much more concerned about being blown to Kingdom Come by one of Saddam's Scud missiles, which we had been warned to expect at any time, night or day, from the moment we arrived. As the airfield was less than 150 miles south of the Iraqi border, we were well within range of even the antiquated and inaccurate Scuds, and it was known that Saddam had plenty of them. There would be early warnings, but since the Soviet missiles, which the Iraqi's had developed further to improve their range, were very fast, only a few minutes at the most.

The first warning, when it came, left me none the wiser. It happened just after dawn on 20 January. I was enjoying my breakfast of a fried-egg sandwich and idly watching the B Squadron OC briefing his men some distance away. The squadron had arrived that morning on the last C-130 from Victor. Suddenly they all started moving, grabbing for their kit and generally running around like headless chickens. I worked out that the meeting must be over and that they were grabbing their packs to go and put a brew on.

Then I noticed one guy who was walking around saying something to them. As he came closer I heard him calling out, 'Good morning. Good morning.'

'You're a jovial little bastard,' I said. 'Have a good morning yourself.'

'He's not saying "good morning",' the RQMS said from behind my shoulder. 'He's saying "Scud warning"!' The men of B Squadron hadn't been dashing off to make a brew, they were trying to locate their kit in order to get out their gas masks.

As it turned out, the Scuds fired that day came nowhere near us, but the danger was very real. Obsolescent it may have been, but since the Scud could carry high-explosive, chemical, biological and even nuclear warheads, its inaccuracy was not necessarily a hindrance. In addition, it could be fired from mobile launch pads, which were difficult for Allied aircraft to locate and destroy.

The Iraqi missile attacks had started two days earlier, on the 18th, which was to prove a significant date for the SAS. On that day the Iraqis had fired their first Scud missile of the Gulf War – at Dhahran, the main marshalling base for US aircraft. The Americans had predicted this, and as a defensive measure had ringed the base with MIM-104 Patriot surface-to-air (SAM) missile launchers, specifically designed to destroy incoming surface-to-surface missiles (SSMs).

The way the Patriots worked was very simple. As the Scud hurtled towards its target at just under 4,000 miles per hour and came within range, the radar-guided Patriot would be launched in its path. In the fraction of a second when they were passing one another the Patriot's radar would trigger it to explode, hurling hundreds of gobstopper-sized metal chunks into the immediate vicinity that would detonate the Scud's own warhead. As a principle it was almost childishly simple, but it worked as long as the timing of the Patriot's launch was spot on. Which it was at Dhahran that day. The Americans were justifiably cock-a-hoop with their success, and deserved to be.

What they had not anticipated, however, was that Saddam's small, easily concealed mobile-launcher teams would scuttle to positions in the western Iraqi desert and, that same day, fire off seven more Scuds towards Israel. Three landed in Tel Aviv, two in Haifa, and two in open country. On the following day two more hit Tel Aviv, wounding seventeen people, and two others fell in unpopulated areas. Thus far all the Scuds launched had been armed with conventional warheads – but the Israelis feared, not unnaturally, that future missiles might carry chemical and biological payloads. In a brilliantly calculated move, Saddam had substantially upped the ante and now had an almost unbeatable ace on the table.

The Knesset, Israel's parliament, has never been famed for its moderate reaction to terrorist attacks. The policy of 'eye for eye' is not only religiously correct to Jews, it is politically correct in Israel. Now the Israeli people, angered by the Iraqi attacks, were baying for blood, and they expected their leaders to order swift retaliation. The Allies, however, emphatically needed the opposite. For the Coalition, it was vital that the Israelis do nothing; indeed, that their country be kept entirely out of the war. If Israel attacked Iraq, then many of the Arab nations in the Coalition would almost certainly pull out, led by Syria and Egypt. It was paramount that Israel should be kept out of the conflict, and the only sure way to achieve this was to put a stop to the Scud missile attacks.

With its solid-fuel propellant and crude targeting devices, the Scud was a dinosaur in 1981, let alone 1991. The Iraqis, however, had themselves extended the range of the basic Soviet weapon with Israeli targets in mind, and though the missiles were highly inaccurate over long distances, enough were landing on target to ensure that the Israelis continued to press vehemently for retaliation. Anxious to defuse the situation, America's diplomats made frantic efforts to keep Israel out of the conflict. At the same time, Schwarzkopf ordered hundreds of Patriot missiles to be dispatched to Israel – the first of them arrived on 20 January – along with the launchers and the crews to operate them. Meanwhile, from Saudi Arabia he launched continuous air sorties by several squadrons of F-15E Strike Eagles into the southern and western Iraqi deserts, tasked solely with seeking out and destroying the Scuds and their mobile launchers.

The Iraqis, however, turned out to be far better at hiding or disguising their Scud launchers than Schwarzkopf had bargained for. The F-15s returned from sortie after sortie with negative reports: no Scuds found or destroyed. As a result, Schwarzkopf was finally forced to concede that this was one task his beloved air jockeys were technically incapable of handling. 'It looks,' he finally told an exultant General de la Billière, 'like a job for those SAS guys of yours. Send 'em in.'

DLB snapped back a quick, 'Yes, General,' but neglected to explain that he had anticipated his supreme commander's reaction by some thirty-six hours – and that we had already prepared for insertion into Iraq. By the time Schwarzkopf's orders had been relayed down the chain of command to the CO at Al Jouf, A and D Squadrons, in 4 mobile units totalling 128 men, had already been dispatched to the edge of enemy territory – the start line – on DLB's earlier instructions, ready to ferret out the Scud launchers, mobile and fixed, and destroy them.

By midnight on 20 January the first four fighting units were heading across the Iraqi border. The SAS was officially at war.

Chapter Sixteen

In the space of just forty-eight hours the Regiment had gone from having no part at all to play in the Gulf War, to being responsible for taking out the greatest single enemy threat to Allied victory. We had been hurled in at the deep end with a vengeance.

Singlehandedly, 22 SAS had been tasked with saving the Coalition, which would undoubtedly fragment if Israel struck at Iraq. To achieve this, we had to locate and destroy Saddam's remaining Scud missiles and their mobile launchers, and cut the concealed fibre-optic and other land communications that linked Baghdad with both the static launch sites and the elusive mobile launch teams. It seemed almost as though we had been suddenly placed on a countdown to save the world.

The American pilots had done their damnedest, but had proved incapable of finishing the job from the air. Now the Scuds had to be cleaned up at ground level, and we were the outfit that loved getting its hands dirty.

In essence, the SAS had now had thrust on them the task of keeping the people of Israel safe, and their country out of the war. It was a race against time, for the decision for us to go in on the night of the 20th came even as the Israelis threatened to send troops and aircraft into western Iraq to sort out the missile threat themselves.

'We are supposed to defuse the situation,' the CO told me. He had been receiving constant sitreps (situation reports) fowarded from London and Washington, and shared the latest intelligence with me. The lines between the White House, Downing Street and Jerusalem must have been at melting point as President Bush and John Major begged Yitzhak Shamir not to take action against Iraq. The Israeli Prime Minister was as furious as the rest of his countrymen, however, and was making no promises. Far from it, for the Israelis could well go in that night with a couple of parachute battalions and air support. Whether they took any action depended on whether Schwarzkopf could satisfy the Iraelis that we would do their dirty work for them – and just as efficiently.

Everything apparently hinged on whether or not the Israelis were sufficiently aware of the Regiment's reputation to trust us to handle it alone. We were not altogether convinced that they would leave us to do the job. Furthermore, if the Israelis did go in, then it would be into the 'Scud box', an area that started twenty-five miles over the same border that we were to cross that night. (Because of the missile's limited range, Scuds targeted on Israel could only be launched from western Iraq.) That in turn meant that our patrols might well have been attacked by Israeli troops and supporting aircraft, in mistake for Iraqis. As a result, the four half-squadrons were ordered to cross into Iraq but to hold at the twenty-five-mile line that night and hole up there until the next day. By then we would know just what course the Israelis intended to follow. All we could do was hope that, for all our sakes, they decided to leave the Scud threat to us.

We were the best hit-and-run outfit in the world, the purpose for which the Regiment had been founded. Now we were to take on the role once again. Spearheading the assault and taking on the most dangerous and difficult missions were the men of A and D Squadrons. Split into four elusive, heavily armed and highly mobile fighting columns, they would crisscross the western Iraqi desert in a campaign of destruction intended to annihilate Saddam's secret missile force.

At last light they were given the go-ahead to leave their holding positions on the Iraqi border and head out into enemy territory. No one was there to see them off. Everything that needed to be said had already been said. It was no time for heroic speeches or jingoistic bullshit; besides, we had already had some of that from the Deputy Director when he visited Al Jouf. It was time to get going.

They would cross at varying locations, to give more direct access to their particular areas of operation, in whichever parts of the western Iraqi desert that had been assigned them. We had received reports that it was bitterly cold up on the border, and in their open Land Rovers – even wearing their NBC gear – these men were going to feel half frozen by the time they had crossed into enemy territory, established a lying-up position (LUP) and bedded down for the day. I fervently hoped that they would not find a hot reception waiting for them on the Iraqi side. To go into instant action when your fingers and face are numbed and cracked with cold is no picnic, as I knew only too well.

For their part, they were probably saying that it was all-bloody-right for us, safe back in Al Jouf and heading for our camp beds. But as stupid – and as clichéd – as it may sound, I did wish I had been going with them. I had never had to sit out a hostile situation before. It felt very strange – as though I was not pulling my share of the weight. I knew I would do my bit at Al Jouf, just like everyone else. But I'd much sooner have been out there with them than waiting at our forward mounting base for news.

After twenty years of the toughest military training in the world I was absolutely in my prime as a soldier, with a wealth of operational experience. I was ready, willing and more than able to take on Saddam's soldiers, Republican Guard and all – and unable so much as to fire off a single round in the enemy's direction. It was extremely frustrating. I was simply not used to kicking my heels while somebody else did the fighting, and there were many others around me who felt the same.

Yet, although I didn't know it, Fate was already preparing to step in and scatter a few wild cards around. And one card had my name on it, although, had I seen it at the time, I would not have believed what it predicted. So when I slipped into my sleeping bag on my camp bed that night it was with one enormous regret: that by the time I woke up in the morning the men of 22 SAS – my men – would be in Saddam's back yard, about to start kicking hell out of the Iraqis. And I would not be with them.

As it turned out, I was only 75 per cent right. When the morning's sitreps came in I was at the CO's side in the ops room, which was packed with electronic listening and transmitting devices, screens, satellite-communication decoders, and a dozen other humming, crackling bits of complicated machinery.

One by one the half-squadron units reported in. Alpha Three Zero and Four Zero had crossed the border without incident. Both Delta call signs were also comfortably laid up in enemy territory. (Each half-squadron used one call sign for both sub-units; thus Delta One Zero and Two Zero would use the call sign Delta One Zero.) But Alpha One Zero and Two Zero were still in Saudi Arabia. The squadron OC reported that a large berm (man-made sandbank) was blocking their area of infiltration. Recce patrols were being sent out to look for a gap in the berm or a place where it was lower, and the half-squadron would probably try to cross further along the border that night.

Knowing my own, and the CO's, serious misgivings about A Squadron's OC, commanding Alpha One Zero, I felt the first flutterings of anxiety tweak at my stomach. I glanced across at the Boss, and found him staring at me with a look on his face which told me that he wasn't completely happy with the situation either. Nevertheless, at this stage he wasn't ready to make any sort of comment or criticism. It was not unusual, particularly during the early stages of a mission, for one unit to experience greater difficulties than the others.

Next to the ops room was the intelligence setup, where the duty I Corps officer and his staff collated, dissected and interpreted all the information coming in. At that time this came mainly from the Americans, and included which targets had been hit by air attacks, which were intended, and which identified, so that we could advise our units on the ground what to avoid and what to investigate. Known Iraqi locations were being plotted on a huge map on one wall of the intelligence room.

From that day on our men in the field would be adding our own intelligence information to the mass of incoming data. This morning, though, the patrols were simply represented by four small stickers on the map. Three were behind enemy lines. A lone sticker still remained south of the border. I hoped for the best, but my gut feeling, which began to grow stronger as I stared at that little sticker on the map, was that Alpha One Zero was in no particular hurry to join the war.

What was so special about the berm in his sector, I wondered. According to Intelligence the whole of the southern Iraqi border was protected by a berm except in a few isolated places, where there were border posts.

A berm is a man-made sand dune, anything from 6 to 16 feet high and, in the case of the berm along the Iraqi-Saudi Arabian border, often extending for many miles. The sand had been pushed into place by bulldozers, and there was a wide trench dug out on the side from which an enemy might approach – in this case, the southern side – to prevent vehicles from taking a run at the slope. Yet even if digging away the berm itself was a major undertaking, filling in a section of the trench with hand shovels, though backbreaking work, was hardly difficult. What was more, in that weather it might even have been a welcome way of keeping warm. Once a length of the trench the width of a vehicle had been filled, the 110s could have taken enough of a run at the berm to carry them over the crest. Besides, three of the units had somehow made it across and into Iraq. Why not Alpha One Zero?

At least there was one piece of good news that morning. The Israelis had agreed not to retaliate against Iraq – 'for the time being' – which meant that there was now nothing to stop our men streaming northwards across the desert to their designated areas – except the enemy. It was possible, too, that the next morning's sitrep might bring us better news from Alpha One Zero, although something told me it wouldn't. Meanwhile we received orders from headquarters in Riyadh that three eight-man patrols from B Squadron were to be sent in to Iraq to observe movements and installations along three of Iraq's main supply routes (MSRs; the main east-west routes across Iraq passable to vehicles – some are tarmac) roughly two hundred miles west of Baghdad and report back information to our location.

Only half of B Squadron had been transferred to Al Jouf. The other half had remained at Victor on counter-terrorism duty, in case the Iraqis tried to bomb the British Embassy in Abu Dhabi. Those in Al Jouf were put on standby and told to check over their equipment. They could be going in on the following day, 22 January, or at the latest on the 23rd.

The next day dawned dull and cold – almost all of us had been misled by the supposed joys of a Middle East winter – and found the Boss in a foul mood. The OC A Squadron and his band were still fumbling their way along the border like nomads, with little promise of a crossing, and the sergeant in charge of one of B Squadron's eight-man patrols, Bravo Two Zero, seemed to be playing silly buggers.

The CO had just come back from a frustrating conference with this sergeant, who would go on to write an account of his abortive mission in Iraq under the pseudonym 'Andy McNab'. I believed then – and I still do – that most, if not all, of Bravo Two Zero's misfortunes resulted from 'McNab's' refusal to take advice before he even left base. Some of that advice had come from the CO, and he was as mad as hell.

'Get over there and try to knock some sense into him, Billy,' he told me as soon as he came into the office. 'I want them to take a vehicle and they are refusing. They say the ground will be too flat and they will be compromised. But it will give them a means of escape if they get into difficulties.'

They proved to be prophetic words.

Both the CO and I were aware that 'McNab' was only judging the ground by satellite pictures, which show height but not depressions. Once you're on the ground, as I knew from experience, you can usually find depressions to hide a vehicle in. To be fair, the reliance on satellite photos was not his fault, since the maps we had of western Iraq were aerial charts showing very little ground detail.

The most important reason for taking a Land Rover is that it provides a rapid means of escape from a contact, and the chance to return to the objective at a later date. Retreating on foot with full kit on your back is never fast, or easy. And that means that in a situation where your patrol is threatened the only way out is to ditch most of the gear and run, fighting a rearguard action as you go. Even if you manage to get clear, however, there is no way you can ever make another attempt to fulfil the mission because you have had to abandon your gear, as well as thoroughly alerting the enemy in that area. There is nothing for it but to call to be evacuated.

It was also highly relevant to Bravo Two Zero, or should have been, that A and D Squadrons were operating in four half-squadron mobile fighting units within twenty to thirty miles of their North Road Watch operational area. With a vehicle at their disposal the possible solution to a multitude of problems was pretty obvious – and only a couple of hours' drive away. But 'McNab', a London lad with an engaging Cockney accent and seven or eight years' service with the Regiment, was having none of it, and his face showed it when I sauntered over to where his patrol was gathered round him.

I didn't bother with a preamble, simply telling him, 'I'm strongly advising you to take a vehicle. If it comes to a firefight it could well save your arse. So take the Boss's and my advice and don't be a fool.'

'No way,' he retorted. 'We don't need it and we're not taking it. It's a sure-fire way of getting compromised.'

'But at least you'll have a means of escape,' I said. 'We've got our own guys working to your rear. And if you do get inserted successfully then you'll know the ground has been cleared by the chopper and you'll have plenty of time to select a decent LUP for yourselves and the vehicle.'

But 'McNab' was adamant; indeed, I wondered if he was even hearing me. 'You can forget it,' he said. 'I'm telling you what I've already told the CO. It's not for us.'

I looked around at the faces of the other members of his unit and saw only defiance there as they began to chip in in support of their patrol commander.

'It'd be like dragging a bloody great albatross around with us,' said one comedian.

'We don't want it because there'll be nowhere to hide it,' said another.

One man who also supported 'McNab' was 'Chris Ryan'. He had been a part-time soldier with the Territorial Army when he decided to try for Selection – and passed. Like 'McNab' he was destined to survive the war, and like 'McNab' he found success as an author, under the pseudonym 'Chris Ryan', with an account of his adventures in the Gulf entitled *The One That Got Away*. That book gives the impression that he disagreed with 'McNab' on a number of points, while 'McNab's' own book also indicates that the two did not always see eye to eye. Nevertheless, 'Ryan' joined 'McNab' and the others that day in vetoing any suggestion of taking a Land Rover. I personally believe that after coming under fire in Iraq, and with three of the eight-man patrol dead and four captured, 'McNab' and the other survivors later deeply regretted not taking the advice of the Boss and myself. However, at the time I realized that they had obviously hammered this out between themselves and were set upon a course which I, like the CO, couldn't comprehend. Nor was there anything I could do about it.

We had reached an impasse, and we all knew it. I could easily have ordered them to take a vehicle, as could the CO, because what the Colonel or the RSM says will be obeyed, reluctantly or otherwise. But I also knew, from my long experience in the Regiment, what would happen as a result. They would have gone on the ground – with a vehicle, admittedly – and almost certainly got themselves compromised in some way. They would then have come back and said, 'Up yours! If you hadn't made us take the vehicle we wouldn't have failed. It's all your fault.'

That may appear incredibly childish, but it's what could happen. These tough-as-nails, highly trained soldiers, who would go to hell and back if their CO asked them to, could also act very stubbornly if they felt that they had been slighted in any way, or that their professionalism had been questioned, however lightly. Objectivity would fly out the window, to be replaced by a macho pride. It is in order to avoid such self-defeating, even damaging displays, therefore, that the SAS has for many years had a rule that the man in command on the ground is always right, whatever his rank. In the end you do not question his decisions before he goes into the field because it is his patrol, and he has got to live with it – and with the consequences.

Having lost that discussion, I then tried to get Bravo Two Zero at least to reduce the amount of kit they were taking. Everything was spread or piled around them: weapons, ammunition, bergens, rations, water containers, sandbags, communications equipment, lay everywhere.

'What's all this, Andy?' I asked.

Deadpan, he replied, 'It's the kit we think is essential to the mission.' From the look on his face, I could tell that he wasn't going to take any advice about reducing the amount they would have to carry. Still, I had to try, so I asked how long they were going for. I admit to being the traditional kind of practical soldier who believes that you don't need much equipment to operate efficiently and that you should go in as light as possible. But they were taking twenty or thirty bulging sandbags in addition to the rest of their gear.

'Tell me, Andy, what's with the sandbags?' I asked.

'They're full of kit. We've got water, ammunition, batteries, rations. They're going to be cached.'

Their bergens were already stuffed almost to bursting point, as were their belt kits, with rations, water, radios and spare batteries, ammunition, personal equipment, sleeping bags, waterproofs, medical packs, survival kits, and much more. On top of all that, of course, they had their weapons, as well as grenades and, for each man, a single-shot LAW 66 anti-tank rocket-launcher weighing nearly 10 pounds.

I knew to a certainty that they were taking far too much. I couldn't accurately guess the weight load for each man, but when they pulled out the next night 'McNab' estimated that each of Bravo Two Zero's men was carrying 150 pounds. That's the same as hefting a 10½-stone man around with you. I gave them a dozen paces – maximum – yet 'McNab' expected them to move freely, as circumstances demanded. An SAS unit, to misquote Muhammad Ali, should be capable of floating like a butterfly and stinging like a swarm of killer bees. The guys in 'McNab''s patrol were carrying far too much equipment, and far too much weight, to be able to operate effectively.

They were not going to reduce their load, however, either on my say so or the commanding officer's. So I returned to the CO's office in about the same foul mood as he had been in when he sent me to talk to Bravo Two Zero – and for much the same reasons.

'He won't take a vehicle and that's the end of it,' I reported back. 'He gave me the same cock-eyed justification he gave you.

'And he won't cut back on kit either. Short of ordering him to do it, I don't think anything either of us says now is going to change his mind.' I paused before adding, 'And in my opinion it's best not to force him.'

The Boss nodded 'I agree, Billy. But thank you for trying.'

I left the CO's office hoping that my conclusions about Bravo Two Zero were wrong. Because, given the way the patrol was being mounted, I didn't think it was going to work.

Having heard the official debriefing of the survivors of Bravo Two Zero back in Hereford after the war had ended, I was surprised by several of 'McNab's' anecdotes as he recounted them in his book. What I found most surprising, however, was that, in the book, he made no mention at all of the two meetings he and his men had had with the Colonel and myself, meetings during which we tried our damnedest to persuade him to take a vehicle and to cut down on the amount of kit they would be carrying. His sole reference says that I came over to them, wished them luck, told them to get the job done and to come back safely. Considering what were, I'm convinced, the results of not following our advice, I find it odd that he didn't feel the meetings worth mentioning. After all, the failure of that mission ultimately cost the lives of three men, and led to four others being captured and tortured. That's a casualty rate of nearly 90 per cent.

To add to our problems, Alpha One Zero checked in next morning with what was rapidly becoming the 'usual' progress report: they were still on our side of the border.

'This is ridiculous,' the CO said. 'I'm going to have to do something pretty damned drastic to get them sorted out.'

First, though, we had to get our three B Squadron units away. Bravo Two Zero and two other eight-man patrols – Bravo Three Zero, which, like Bravo Two Zero, declined to take a vehicle, and Bravo One Nine (which did take a Land Rover), which were to observe the southern and central MSRs from Jordan to Baghdad while 'McNab's' patrol watched the northern one – were going in on separate helicopters.

Bravo Three Zero's mission was of extremely short duration. When the helicopter landed the patrol commander jumped off, looked at the ground, which was flat and featureless in every direction, and said, 'It's not good enough.' The chopper took them off again and put down a few miles from the original site, where exactly the same scene was re-enacted. The patrol commander inspected the immediate area and decided that it was untenable to set up an observation post on a flat gravel plain, and that to do so was asking to be compromised. He aborted the mission there and then, as was his prerogative, and he and his men returned to Al Jouf in the same helicopter. His report read simply that there had been nowhere to hide.

All credit to 'McNab', at least when the helicopter carrying Bravo Two Zero arrived at their landing site he deployed, which was what I would have done myself. I would not have come back and said that my patrol could not deploy because the terrain was unsuitable. Nevertheless, no shame attaches to the patrol commander who pulled Bravo Three Zero out. That was his decision, and he believed that his reasons for making it were perfectly valid. The commander of Bravo One Nine took his team in as planned.

The following morning, I had just showered and shaved and was heading for the ops room with a mug of hot water in one hand and a sachet of hot chocolate in the other when I was almost run down by the CO. His mouth was clenched tight shut, and his eyes were glaring. The

Boss was furious. I guessed, even before he spoke, what had got him so het up.

'I was coming to look for you,' he said. 'Alpha One Zero still hasn't crossed the border.'

I said nothing.

'I have two options,' the CO continued. 'I can bring up Jeremy from Riyadh, which would take two days, or I can send you in.'

The last part of the remark really did grab all my attention. He had not dropped the slightest hint over the previous few days that his mind was working in this direction. To join one of the fighting patrols behind enemy lines was more than I could have hoped for in my wildest dreams, and to say that I was surprised would be a huge understatement. All I could think of as a reply was, 'What time am I going in?' meanwhile trying to stop the grin spreading across my face.

'Ten hundred hours,' said the Boss. It was then 0830.

Leaving the ops office for my tent, I quickly gathered up my kit, and then took time out to write a letter to a girl I had been seeing. I wanted to explain that I would not be able to write for a while, and that she was not to worry if she didn't hear from me for a bit. With the letter finished – it's curious how long letters like that take to write – I handed it in, unsealed, to the censor's office, where all outgoing mail was read by an officer. Because I was the RSM, however, I was told to seal it myself and place it directly in the mailbox. By then it was time to rendezvous with the CO, who was also flying forward with me in order to talk to the commander of our reluctant patrol. He had a signaller in tow, who would in addition act as his driver for the return journey, which they would make by road and track in the short-wheelbase Land Rover so that was also being flown in with us.

In the brief time it took to drive over to the far side of the airfield, where the helicopters were parked, the Boss explained that he had signalled Alpha One Zero's commander and ordered him to drive to a rendezvous point on the Saudi Arabian side of the border. His signal also read, 'New 2IC to you.' This had been worded by the ops officer, dreadfully badly in my opinion, since it would act like a slap in the face to the patrol commander and his 2IC. It should have been worded to read, 'RSM to your location to act as 2IC,' or some equally tactful phrase.

While the vehicle was being lashed down inside the Chinook's big belly the CO, his signaller and I boarded the chopper and took our seats on the deck behind the pilot. The Boss intended that after his meeting with the OC A Squadron his driver would bring him back to Al Jouf before nightfall. He would not, he assured me, be leaving the patrol commander in any doubt about his position. I was being sent in as 2IC to get the show moving, and to crush any signs of negativeness on the part of the patrol commander or anyone else.

'Anyone else' included the current 2IC, a staff sergeant named Pat. Based on my very brief acquaintance with him during my visit to the desert-training camp, however, I figured that Pat could be one of the primary causes of any negative thinking in Alpha One Zero.

He was a large guy, about six foot three, extremely fit and very articulate – clearly a well-educated man, and someone, frankly, one would have expected to be an officer rather than a senior NCO. But at that initial meeting – the A Squadron briefing at the desert-training camp, which was also attended by the CO and the Deputy Director – I had noted that it took him a long time to reach a decision, and that, generally, he came across as being very negative. As curious as it may seem, that was the first time I had ever had dealings with him, and I had been in the Regiment, by then, for nearly twenty years. That can easily happen, as in general we tended to socialize with members of our own squadron or even just our own troop, and rarely mixed with others. On top of that, I had only been RSM for a few weeks and, with all the hullabaloo over the Gulf crisis, had not had the time to get to know everyone in the Regiment.

The Deputy Director, however, had been Pat's squadron commander when he was OC A Squadron in the early 1980s, and during our visit to the training camp had casually asked the tall staff sergeant how things were going. Surprising all of us, Pat had replied, 'Can I be candid, Boss?' When the Deputy Director nodded, he immediately launched into a whole list of complaints.

'What you are expecting us to do is ridiculous,' he began. 'Trying, in ten days, to train men for mobile warfare who are not mobility trained is ludicrous. We are also short of the mounts that the Mk19* sits on, and we are even short of pen-torch batteries.'

Having seen A Squadron at the camp that day, I had formed a good opinion of their morale and mood, as well as their readiness for action. Listening to Pat's catalogue of moans, however, I had scarcely been able to believe what I was hearing. I looked across at the CO and shrugged my shoulders. But Pat had been in full spate, and I had stood there,

---

* A fully automatic weapon, not unlike a machine-gun, that fires different types of 40mm grenades. It is usually mounted on a 110, and, with its high rate of fire, is a very effective weapon. Also referred to as an M19.

feeling increasingly embarrassed, while he'd reeled off a long list of other personal judgements and petty complaints, before simply walking off.

'Well, he gives a totally different impression to the one I gathered from the rest of the guys today,' I had told the Deputy Director and the CO. 'Morale was good. They were full of enthusiasm and in good spirits.' To which the Deputy Director had casually replied, 'Well, that's Pat for you. He's always been the world's worst eternal pessimist.'

I couldn't help thinking back to that remark, and my own opinion of both Pat and the A Squadron commander, as I waited aboard the Chinook that was to take me to join them in the desert. These two together – the one negative and pessimistic, the other hesitant and indecisive – were a bad mix. Perhaps a good shake-up, as was now being put in hand, would sort them out. Within two hours I would be ramrodding this unit, and whether the squadron commander and his 2IC liked it or not, I was simply not going to tolerate any negative comments from either of them.

In addition, I also had a wild card tucked away in the map pocket of the right trouser leg of my DPM (disruptive-pattern material – i.e. camouflage) trousers. Instinctively, perhaps half recalling an occasion during my jungle training when I had lost the code books while crossing a rain-swollen river, I reached to check that the button on the pocket's flap was secure as the pilot started to wind the engines up to full revs. This 'failsafe' was a letter, which the Boss had dictated and ordered to be typed that morning. It authorized me, at my own discretion, to take over full command of the half-squadron whenever I felt it necessary, 'to ensure that the unit was operating to its maximum efficiency'.

Unfortunately, one thing that was certainly not operating to maximum efficiency was the Chinook. As the aircraft began to shake preparatory to take-off, the pilot suddenly decided to shut down. The racket and vibration suddenly began to diminish and the rotors began to slow. We looked at each other questioningly, though not for long.

'We have a problem,' the pilot announced. 'It's either a fuel blockage or it's the hydraulics. If it's fuel we'll be thirty minutes. If it's the hydraulics we'll be here for at least another two hours. Probably much longer.'

Since there was not a thing that we could do, the Boss and I climbed down from the chopper and walked off a dozen paces or so to the side of the helipad. He lit up a cigar and I put together a roll-up. We stood there smoking and chatting while the RAF engineers tried to work out what was wrong, peering in remote parts of the machine and muttering technical questions. As we stood there, the CO told me that he, and headquarters, were happy with the progress the two D Squadron units and the other Alpha half-squadron were making. Alpha One Zero we knew about, and we were trying to take steps to get the patrol moving. However, everyone was deeply concerned about the status of Bravo Two Zero, which had failed to make radio contact with RHQ at Al Jouf.

It is always worrying when a patrol behind enemy lines fails to make radio contact – especially when, as Bravo Two Zero did, they have two separate radio sets with them. Additionally, the reservations we had both felt prior to 'McNab's' patrol going in didn't make their silence any easier to accept. Our frustration was further increased when the Chinook's pilot strolled over and told us that the trouble was definitely hydraulic. We wouldn't be going anywhere for a few hours.

'OK,' said the CO, 'we'll leave it until tomorrow night. Let's go back to the ops room.'

Back in the terminal, there was still nothing from Bravo Two Zero. There was a new problem in the form of a signal from Alpha One Zero, however. It was an answer to the CO's earlier signal, and was a double refusal: 'Not for us. Not for this location.' What it meant was that the patrol commander was not even going to attempt to make the rendezvous with the CO. And he was also telling his commanding officer, 'I'm not accepting a new 2IC.'

I looked over at the Boss, waiting for his reaction, and thanking whatever fate had caused our helicopter to malfunction just before take-off. If it had not done so, we would have been waiting at the rendezvous like a couple of idiots for an officer who had no intention of showing up. I could tell that the CO was fuming, but whatever the thoughts inside his head, he kept them to himself.

On the following day, 25 January, the CO was again unable to send me in because of a shortage of helicopters. What he did do, however, was to arrange for Alpha One Zero to rendezvous on the border that night with a certain Major Bill, one of the Regiment's most experienced officers. In a day when the Iraqis launched eight Scud missiles against Tel Aviv, the CO could no longer tolerate the fact that one of our spearhead units was still swanning about in Saudi Arabia, unable even to cross the border, let alone start knocking out Scud launchers.

In Israel, the US-donated Patriots had brought down all eight Scuds, but debris from the detonating missiles had killed two civilians and injured sixty-nine, and the Israelis were getting more furious, and more belligerent, by the hour. I felt that each Scud attack on their country would be taken by them as evidence that we weren't doing our job properly. In the case of Alpha One Zero, of course, we weren't doing it at all.

Then in his fifties, Major Bill had come up from the ranks. Years earlier he had served in A Squadron, and had then done time with B Squadron. A very experienced member of the Regiment, he had seen active service in the Radfan, Aden, Borneo and Dhofar. In short, he was a no-nonsense, get-up-and-go sort of soldier.

I can't say that we got on particularly well, however. But that would not have caused a problem had we had to work together in the Gulf, although as things turned out we never had to try. This was the man the CO had tasked with the job of getting Alpha One Zero over the border and into the war. It was now Friday, and that patrol had been hanging around on the border since Sunday.

The CO had simply told Major Bill, 'Pick the right spot and get them over.' Bill had set out at once, travelling to the border to RV with our stalled patrol. His choice of crossing place was beautifully simple. He picked an old border post watched over by a medieval fort garrisoned by about a dozen Saudi Arabian regulars. On the Iraqi side there were probably half that number of troops holed up in a watchtower-like structure more than a quarter of a mile away across the border. Being Major Bill, he probably assumed, and almost certainly correctly, that the Iraqis would be asleep after midnight – the time at which he would send Alpha One Zero across.

And that was exactly what he did. On the morning of the 26th we heard, finally, that Alpha One Zero had successfully crossed the border and was heading north. Less happily, that morning – three days after they had been flown in – there was still no contact from Bravo Two Zero. The CO therefore ordered a helicopter to go in after dark to try to locate his missing men.

That night, an RAF Chinook lifted off from Al Jouf to begin the search. It was accompanied by a US Air Force helicopter fitted with sophisticated electronic and other equipment for locating people in the dark. But despite flying a search pattern around the spot where Bravo Two Zero had been dropped off, the choppers didn't pick up so much as the whisper of a trace of anyone. It was as though the patrol had vanished into thin air. Either 'McNab' and his men were moving very fast and covering a lot of ground, which told me that they had already ditched most of their equipment and were racing for the border, or they had been captured or killed. If they were trying to get back, however, we had no way of knowing until we could establish radio contact – if we ever did.

As for me, I seemed to have been left in some kind of limbo. There was no way that I could get forward to join Alpha One Zero in Iraq, even if that were still thought necessary, because the CO now needed every available Special Forces helicopter for searches. Then, early the following morning, I was again summoned to the Boss's 'office' – still a desk on the luggage conveyor belt in what would one day be the baggage-reclaim area of the terminal building. 'I've seen the sitrep,' I told him at once. A report from Alpha One Zero, now over the border at last, explained that they had established their first LUP in enemy territory, in the midst of an Iraqi division's position in Wadi 'Ar Ar.

'You're going in tomorrow,' said the CO, without preamble. 'Definitely. Have you got that?'

I nodded, then added, 'OK Boss,' for good measure. I was still carrying the letter he had written for me to give the patrol commander in my pocket, and my gear was still packed and ready to go. There was nothing else to say. The die was cast.

Or at least it seemed to have been, until four o'clock that afternoon, when I walked into the ops room and found the CO standing there with a broad smile on his face.

'What the hell's going on? Is the war over?' I asked.

'Better than that,' he chortled. 'We've had our first contact with the enemy.' Contact meant a firefight, and from the CO's antics it looked as though it had been a successful one.

'That's great,' I said, then added 'Any casualties?'

'Not on our side. But guess who had the contact?'

'I've no idea,' I replied – after all, we had a fair number of patrols out there. 'Share the big secret.'

'It's Alpha One Zero,' he said. And as he gave me the details I knew straight away that I would not be going out to join them. Three enemy killed and one captured meant success; indeed, they had even captured intact the enemy soldiers' vehicle, a Russian-built Gaz jeep. The contact indicated that the patrol commander had found his feet and had started to get his act together. The patrol was some fifty kilometres north of the border, and they would soon be heading for their designated area of operation. That, of course, was the logical assumption, and the CO agreed. 'It might just work after all,' he murmured. 'Let's see how they get on.'

Above: Half of an SAS half-squadron mobile patrol just prior to moving forward into Iraq for operations against enemy Scud missiles and their launch sites and communications. The 110 second from left mounts a Mk19 automatic grenade launcher at the rear; the vehicle third from left has a Milan anti-tank missile system mounted on the rollbar, while that at far right has a covered Browning M2 ·50-inch heavy machine-gun mounted at the back. 'Not all the Land Rovers carried the same assortment of weapons – other than the GPMGs and personal weapons – equipment or explosives, but all were a variation on the theme of "mobile but heavily armed".'

Centre: The Special Forces CH-47 Chinook of the RAF's No. 7 Squadron landing in Iraq at 0125 hours local time, Tuesday, 29 February 1991. On board is the author who, as RSM of 22 SAS, was just about to sack the officer commanding Alpha One Zero and Alpha Two Zero and take over command himself. This action set two precedents in the Regiment: the first time an SAS RSM had been sent into action; and the first time an officer of the Regiment had been relieved of his command in the field.

Right: A member of I Corps (*right*) questioning the Iraqi officer captured by Alpha One Zero when the patrol ambushed his Gaz jeep and killed his three fellow officers. The prisoner was well looked after, as can be seen from the fact that he has been given a British tunic; he was flown out of Iraq on the Chinook that brought the author in to take over command of A10.

SAS 110s camouflaged in an LUP during operations in Iraq: nice and cosy, but not conducive to going into action or moving quickly - hence the author's decision that Alpha One Zero should not use cam nets while behind enemy lines.

A 110 and a member of D Squadron under a cam net in Iraq. A GPMG can be seen on the vehicle at top right, with a burnous - a locally made Arab coat - hanging beneath it. With their thin issue clothing, the SAS patrols in Iraq all initially suffered from the extreme cold, something that didn't improve until the author flew in with a load of burnouses the RQMS had bought in the local markets around Al Jouf.

An RAF Special Forces C-130 taking off from a primitive back-country earth landing strip. 'The RAF pilots in 47 Squadron really were brilliant flyers . . . Give them a short, narrow strip of more or less level ground and these characters would set a Hercules down on it - even at night . . . They would fly in at low level and land these huge monsters on grass, gravel, mudflats, even a frozen lake . . .'

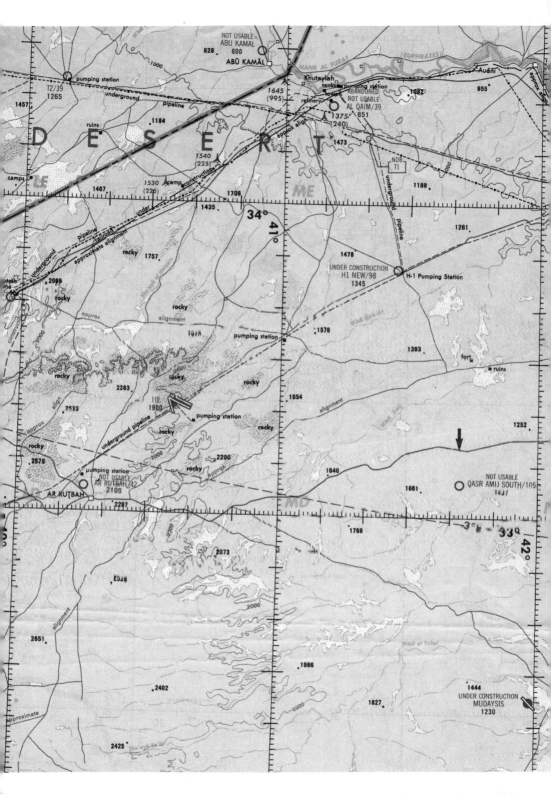

Part of the escape map with which the SAS were issued while still at Al Jouf. Being silk, the map could be folded very small, and wouldn't turn to pulp if it got wet, as a paper map would; as a tool for navigation, however, it was far from ideal. The Iraqi airfield at Mudaysis reconnoitred by Alpha One Zero is in the south-eastern grid square, the northern extremity of the Wadi Tubal lies slightly to the north-west of that, and Victor Two lies further to the north (*indicated by a red arrow*).

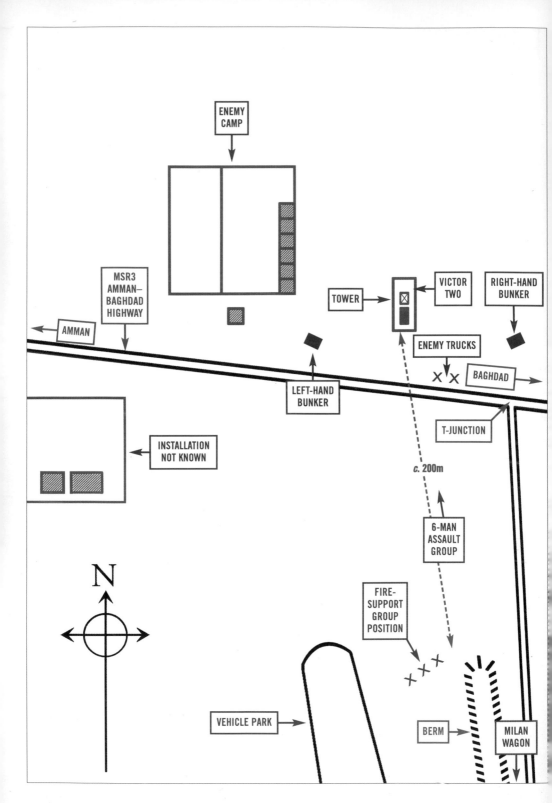

ENEMY CAMP

MSR3 AMMAN–BAGHDAD HIGHWAY

AMMAN

TOWER

VICTOR TWO

RIGHT-HAND BUNKER

ENEMY TRUCKS

BAGHDAD

LEFT-HAND BUNKER

T-JUNCTION

INSTALLATION NOT KNOWN

c. 200m

6-MAN ASSAULT GROUP

FIRE-SUPPORT GROUP POSITION

N

VEHICLE PARK

BERM

MILAN WAGON

Sketch map, to scale, of the Iraqi communications installation at Victor Two, annotated to show the various enemy positions (red) and those of Alpha One Zero (blue) during the latter's attack. As the author discovered just before the assault 'went noisy', the site had already been attacked by Coalition aircraft.

Above: A USAF A-10 in action over Iraq during the Gulf War. The Fairchild A/OA-A10A twin-jet, single-seat close-support aircraft, officially designated the Thunderbolt II but more usually known by its nickname of 'Warthog', proved its value in the conflict; it was an A-10 that overflew Victor Two and confirmed that the author's patrol had successfully destroyed the 250-foot communications mast.

Below: The 'Wadi-Bottom Wanderers': an SAS Bedford 4-tonner, part of the supply convoy that drove from Saudi Arabia into Iraq to resupply the Regiment's mobile patrols, in the Wadi Tubal. The legend in insulating tape on the front of the vehicle is a dig at the relatively advanced ages of the members of the convoy. There is a machine-gun and ammunition track on a mount on the cab roof.

Above: The Sergeants' Mess meeting convened by the author in the Wadi Tubal during the resupply, 1224 hours local time, 16 February 1991. The author, Chairman of the Mess Committee, is seated in the front row; on his left is the RQMS, President of the Mess Committee.

Below: A rather different view: a cartoon by JAK of the same subject, with Saddam looking distinctly nervous (probably with good reason). The author and the famous cartoonist were later to become firm friends.

Above: Mess Meeting at Wadi Tubal, Western Iraq, by David Rowlands, the painting commissioned by the author after the Gulf campaign. Four hundred limited-edition prints of the painting, signed by Generals de la Billière and Schwarzkopf, as well as the author, the CO and the artist, are sold to members of the Regiment. The author and the RQMS are at far right.

Right: The last page of the minutes of the Sergeants' Mess meeting held behind enemy lines, signed by the RQMS, the author, the CO, the Deputy Director of Special Forces, and Generals de la Billière and Schwarzkopf. The 'Afternote' above the signatures adds a dash of typical SAS humour.

There being no further business to discuss the Extraordinary Mess Meeting was closed at 1224 hrs LOCAL, 0924 hrs ZULU 15 February 1991.

AFTERNOTE:

The PMC wished it recorded that if he was to be in a nonsense whilst returning to the Saudi border he would be compelled to eat the minutes of the Mess Meeting!

Signed:

President of the Mess Committee ....

Regimental Sergeant Major *Pete Ratcliffe* ....

Commanding Officer ....

Colonel, UK
Force Commander

Pete de la Billière

P E de la BILLIERE
Lieutenant General, UK
General Officer Commanding
Free Mesopotamia

H Norman Schwarzkopf

H NORMAN SCHWARZKOPF
General, USA
Commander in Chief
Free Mesopotamia

Above: Resupply at Wadi Tubal, 11-17 February 1991. The RQMS, Gary, is reclining at centre, while Major Bill, the officer who led the supply convoy in, and who had earlier helped get the dilatory Alpha One Zero patrol over the border into Iraq, is second from right. Personal weapons are, as always, close at hand

Below: The author with the Prince of Wales during the latter's visit to Stirling Lines, the SAS HQ in Hereford, in April 1991. The Prince arrived by himself and spoke at length to the widows and children of the four members of the Regiment killed during the Gulf War, as well as to the rest of the men who had taken part in the campaign.

We didn't have long to wait. Half an hour later a message came in from Alpha One Zero: 'Moving south towards the border. Will advise rendezvous location in morning for prisoner pickup and resupply.'

I thought the CO, who was always ultra-cool, was going to explode. This time he completely lost his rag, and his comments about Alpha One Zero and its commander, though extremely succinct, didn't make pretty listening. He ended his outburst by telling me, 'There's no question about it, Billy. You will *definitely* be going in tomorrow evening.'

Alpha One Zero's actions had become not just erratic, but increasingly ludicrous, almost like something from a comedy sketch. Now, after days of delay, they seemed to be running around the Iraqi desert like headless chickens. Having had time to mull it over, I didn't reckon the Boss's idea of sending me in as 2IC was going to work. Not now. Time was short, however, so I told him there and then that I wasn't happy with my brief.

'I don't want to add to your problems at this stage, Boss, but I don't think I can operate like this. Not in the way you want. I don't need all this aggro that's being lined up.

'I can't go in as 2IC knowing that I can take over full command at any time just by producing your letter from my pocket. I can stage a mini-coup whenever I want if I have this joker. That's exactly what it's like – having a wild card that will trump everyone else's hand.

'The patrol commander is obviously getting very negative advice from somebody – and I have a good idea who that person is. Whatever I advise as 2IC, the OC is going to have this bloke telling him the opposite, and he's going to end up like a piggy in the middle. And at that point I play my joker – and ship him out.

'I can't work like that. I could never expect to have the men's confidence and trust after pulling that kind of stroke.'

The CO may have been angry, but he had lost none of his decisiveness. He looked at me for a moment, then said, 'You're absolutely right. Give me the letter back.'

Reaching down, I unbuttoned the map pocket on my trousers, pulled out the letter and handed it to him. He went over immediately to where the staff assistant was sitting at a nearby desk and dictated a new letter, which he signed as soon as it had been typed. He brought it back and handed it to me.

'Read it,' he said.

Looking down at the paper, I scanned the brief message. It was addressed to the A Squadron commander, and read:

You are to comply with this order. You are to hand over your command to the RSM. He can take whatever action is necessary to ensure that you leave your present location. You are to get on board the helicopter. You are to speak to no one and report to me directly on your return.

It was signed 'Commanding Officer, 22 SAS'.

When I had read it, I sealed it in its envelope and slipped it into my map pocket, buttoning the flap. I would go in on the following night, 28 January, in the Chinook that was scheduled to make the first resupply delivery to two of our four mobile fighting units.

Against all my expectations, I was going to war.

Chapter Seventeen

As I approached the gaping rear doors of the huge, twin-engined, twin-rotor Boeing Chinook, I was acutely aware that I was about to become the central character in a piece of regimental history. This was the first time ever that an SAS squadron commander had been relieved of his command in the field, and also the first time that the RSM had been sent in on active service to replace an officer.

Unsurprisingly, I had spent most of that day killing time before my flight, turning over in my mind what was likely to happen when I reached Alpha One Zero. I would, I think, have to have been rather less than human if I had not wondered about my takeover of the patrol, although I knew that no amount of thinking before the event could possibly prepare me for the reality.

Furthermore, my destination lay behind enemy lines, so quite apart from any problems that might arise with men whose patrol commander I was to replace, or with informing that officer that, in effect, his career was in tatters, I was also having to adjust to the recognition that, from this night on, every move I made could lead to an incident that might well become a matter of life or death. Nor was it just my life or death; I was about to become responsible not only for the successful outcome of a vital mission, but also for the lives and wellbeing of thirty-three soldiers, most of whom were married and had children.

On the Chinook's tail ramp I paused and took a look around me. It was an impressive scene. The two great rotors were already spinning and shimmering, turning silvery in the bright moonlight. The sky was clear, the night dry but bitterly cold. We had heard that day from the weather men that this was the coldest winter ever recorded in Iraq. Perhaps the meteorologists should have forewarned the Intelligence donkeys back in the UK who had briefed us to expect mild, even warm weather. As a result of this advice, a lot of the guys hadn't even bothered to bring sleeping bags.

Still, I knew that at least one aspect of my arrival was going to cheer up the lads in Alpha One Zero and Two Zero no end. With a lot of pushing from the CO and myself, the RQMS had investigated the local *souks* (bazaars or markets) and had managed to get his slippery palms on a good supply of burnouses, Arab goatskin overcoats, known to us as 'bedous' or 'Al Jouf coats'. They stank more than a little and were none too elegant, but they were surprisingly warm – which was all that would matter to the men.

I had taken only a few steps up the ramp when I felt a tug on the yoke of my belt kit, the strap that goes over the shoulder to support the weight of equipment in the belt. It was the CO. As I turned he put an arm around my shoulder and, leaning forward, yelled in my ear, above the noise of the engines, 'What I have done is a first. What it won't stand is a major contact in the first twenty-four hours.'

I could barely hear him. Even so, I knew that what he was telling me, in the nicest possible way, was, 'Don't do anything stupid, because at the moment my head is on the block.' I gave him what I hoped was an encouraging nod, shouted, 'OK, Boss,' and strode up the ramp with my mind firmly focused, and my fingers just as firmly crossed.

Top whack, a Chinook can carry nearly fifteen tons of equipment. This flight was stretching that capacity to the limit, since the aircraft was taking enough fuel, water, rations, ammunition and other equipment to resupply the two Alpha half-squadrons in the field. In addition to the three-man crew, it was reassuring to find an RAF corporal manning the forward pintle-mounted machine-gun should there be a hostile reception committee waiting when we landed. The only others on board were the RAF load master, me, and two SAS SNCOs who were there on my orders. They could help offload equipment at the landing site, but the main reason for their being on the flight was to assist me in case I had trouble with the squadron commander.

I waited until after we were airborne to tell them what was going on – that I was flying in to take over command of Alpha One Zero. They were even more stunned – 'gobsmacked' would be more accurate – by my announcement than I had been when the CO first told me. Their jaws dropped, and they were clearly having a struggle getting their brains to accept the message from their ears.

'You're joking, Billy,' one of them finally managed to blurt out. 'We thought you were just coming along for the ride.' That dragged a laugh out of me, albeit a cynical one. 'Do you honestly believe I'm so stupid that I would climb aboard one of these things of my own free will without a good reason?' I asked them. 'You may both be daft enough to do it – but I'm not.' I looked hard at the two of them for a moment, my mind still turning over what might happen when we reached the patrol.

Then I gave them their orders. When we landed they were to wait on, or very close to, the helicopter, and be prepared for my call. I paused again, then dropped the bombshell:

'If I decide that it is necessary, you are physically to restrain the OC A Squadron and put him aboard the helicopter, using whatever force is needed, and no matter what he does or says.'

This time the shock almost bowled them over. I waited a few moments until I thought it had sunk in properly, then confirmed, 'And also' – they sat rigid, waiting for further revelations – 'don't go shooting your mouths off all over camp when you get back.'

Now, their looks said, I was the one who was being stupid. They had just had handed to them on a plate the juiciest item of gossip of the war so far. There was nothing in all God's earth that was going to keep them quiet. Only the chopper crashing on the way back was going to keep this mega story from bursting out. I knew it, and they knew it, but I had to go through the motions.

The load master was hardly less surprised when I told him what was about to happen. Utterly dependable, Flight Sergeant Jim was a first-rate guy who had been with the RAF's Special Forces flight for a long time and had operated with the Regiment on many previous occasions. We had built up a good rapport over the years, and got on extremely well.

The load master of any aircraft is in complete control while it is on the ground – and that means that the pilots, however senior, cannot take off without his say-so. That, of course, was my reason for telling him. Having let Jim know the score, I briefed him on just what I needed from him at Alpha One Zero's location. It was quite simple. I didn't want him sanctioning take off until I had given the all-clear with a thumbs-up signal.

The first leg of our flight took us to 'Ar Ar, a Saudi Arabian town on the border with Iraq, where the Americans had established a base. We would land there to refuel before flying on into enemy territory.

When we put down I strolled about a hundred yards away to enjoy a quiet cigarette – smoking is never allowed on RAF flights. Still contemplating the immediate future, I felt apprehensive, not knowing quite what to expect. Finally I stubbed the half-smoked fag out on the tarmac with the heel of my boot and headed back to the helicopter. Even my favourite tobacco seemed to have acquired a bitter taste. I suppose the tension was beginning to have its effect.

Within minutes of taking off again we were over Iraq, flying near the

Chinook's maximum speed of 188 mph only 50 feet above the undulating desert terrain. The ground below, clearly visible in the bright moonlight, looked barren, cold and inhospitable.

I was sitting on top of a pile of the goatskin burnouses, idly looking out of the window and trying to relax, when there was a sudden, dazzling red flash outside and off to the right. 'Shit, we're being attacked,' I thought, as I grabbed a rail on the side of the fuselage and braced myself for impact. My other hand went immediately to my rosary beads in the breast pocket of my windproof. At that moment there came another bright flash close to the helicopter and we banked violently to the left. As my body thudded violently into the fuselage wall the aircraft banked even more sharply to the left. Had I not been hanging on I would have been hurled across the cargo bay into a stack of lashed-down jerry cans on the opposite side.

Convinced that we were about to be shot down, my heart was pounding wildly as I clung on. I am not a good passenger on aircraft at the best of times, but now I was facing one of my worst nightmares turned into reality. I have an absolute horror of being burned to death, the kind of not always rational fear that sometimes brings panic attacks in the dead of night. Rigid with dread, and powerless to prevent what might be about to happen, I held on to the rail as the machine levelled out. My mind turned over images of enemy jets stalking us, missiles hurtling towards us, locked on to this fat, slow, juicy chopper, radar-controlled ground batteries waiting for the right moment to send a stream of tracer into our flying deathtrap . . .

Minutes passed, but nothing else happened and I began to breathe more easily. After fifteen minutes, however, just as my heart had resumed a normal beat and I was beginning to relax my grip on the rail, exactly the same thing happened again: two incredibly bright flashes outside, followed by violent banking to the left and right. This time I wasn't quite so surprised. Not quite – but still too rattled to be able to sit back comfortably and enjoy the rest of the flight. At least the flashes and violent manoeuvres took my mind off the coming takeover of Alpha One Zero, though.

Shortly after the second incident we made our first landing on enemy turf – a rendezvous with Alpha Three Zero. I immediately went up to Jim, the load master, and asked him what the hell was going on. He looked puzzled. 'What do you mean?' he asked.

'All the flares and swerving about the sky,' I yelled. 'What do you think I mean?'

Jim actually laughed. 'You poor sod,' he grinned, looking most unapologetic, 'I'd forgotten. You weren't wearing a headset were you?' I shook my head and he went on, 'We got locked on by a couple of F-16s. What happens is they send down a message to the chopper and the chopper sends back an automatic answer so they know we're one of the good guys, and the plane goes away. That's the theory.

'In practice, and to be on the safe side just in case the nasty F-16 didn't receive our friendly code, we take all the action necessary to prevent a missile ramming us up the backside.

'We fire off magnesium flares and duck about a bit, the general idea being that if there are any heat-seeking missiles coming at us with evil intent they will happily chase our fireworks and not us.'

By now I'd calmed down a bit, so I thanked him for the lesson, but couldn't resist adding that I wished I had known all that before it had happened, since then I might not have been so concerned – if 'concerned' is the right word for having been almost paralysed with dread.

At that first rendezvous I advised the commander of Alpha Three Zero that I was about to take over the other Alpha patrol from its officer. He was visibly shaken by the news, but accepted the deal without asking questions. Then, as the supplies were unloaded from the Chinook, I stood with him inside the aircraft, bringing him up to date on Bravo Two Zero. It was now five days since 'McNab' had taken his patrol in and we hadn't heard a peep out of him. We knew that they had with them several surface-to-air rescue beacons, known as TACBEs, a piece of equipment weighing only half a pound which is used to make direct contact with aircraft flying overhead. The pilot then relays the coordinates for the position from which the TACBE signal has come to HQ, which can then take action to rescue the man or men who sent the signal. Extremely dependable, TACBE had several times saved the lives of SAS men who had got into difficulties in the jungle. The fact that Bravo Two Zero had not used it to summon help looked bad for the safe outcome of the mission, we concluded.

Alpha Three Zero was the most northerly of our mobile patrols, and we had therefore flown to resupply it first. Now it was time to fly southwards for our rendezvous with Alpha One Zero and, for me, an appointment with my own immediate destiny. Once more the engines roared and the airframe vibrated as the Chinook lifted off in a cloud of sand and turned on to its heading. Within thirty minutes we had reached the RV point. We approached the landing site only some twenty feet above the ground, and were still moving fast as the pilot deliberately overshot before banking round and setting us down on the hard desert surface. I grabbed my rifle, left my seat and made for the rear of the aircraft. Nothing would be served by hesitating now.

As I walked down the tail ramp I found myself buffeted by a strong wind that had sprung up from the north and which, because of the wind-chill factor, had sent the temperature plummeting well below zero. I could see at once why the men running down the nearby slope towards the Chinook didn't look much like the crack desert patrol I had last seen in Victor. They were mostly wrapped in their chemical-warfare suits with extra jackets on top, and had *shemaghs*, Arab headdress of the kind favoured by Yasser Arafat, wound around their heads and the lower parts of their faces. The noise from the two rotors, which continued to turn and had formed twin dust halos from the sand being sucked up from the desert floor, was almost deafening. RAF aircrew never switch off their engines during a supply run or insertion into hostile territory, in case they come under attack and have to make a quick getaway.

I grabbed one of the men as he trotted past, put my mouth close to where I thought his ear should be beneath the shemagh, and yelled, 'Where's the OC?' He pointed up the slight incline down which they had come and shouted something I couldn't make out. I set off in the direction he had indicated, and on the way passed a strange-looking vehicle that had been parked with a couple of its wheels in a kind of natural ditch. It was giving off an awful stench which I vaguely recognized, but which I didn't have the time to investigate right then.

At the crest of the slope I came across another small gang of troopers gathered around two Land Rovers. They looked amazed suddenly to see the RSM, but I didn't give them time to ask me what I was doing there. Without preamble, I said, 'One of you go and find the OC and bring him here to me.'

A few minutes later the commander appeared. He looked at me quizzically, but before he could say anything I said, 'I'm sorry,' and handed him the CO's letter. There was enough moonlight for him to read it without a torch. When he'd finished he looked up, his face working with some powerful emotion which he somehow managed to keep bottled up. Then he walked away. I set off back for the chopper, wondering what he would do.

I needn't have worried. He fetched his bergen and rifle and joined me at the tail ramp of the helicopter. The unloading had been completed. The Iraqi officer the patrol had captured the previous day was brought down and I went across and walked with him over to the helicopter. I could guess what he must be feeling, especially after seeing three of his fellow officers killed, and even felt a pang of sympathy for him.

While this was happening the outgoing OC had located his number two, Pat, and was explaining to him that he had been relieved of his command. Then the two men hugged each other as though they were brothers.

The worst part of my job was over. The pilots needed to get on their way as soon as possible, and I wanted to get started. Recognizing that there was no point in wasting more time, I hustled the patrol's former OC aboard the helicopter and gave Jim the thumbs-up signal. Now the handover was complete I couldn't help feeling sorry for the departing major. He had accepted the order without argument, and his behaviour had been impeccable.

Moments later the tail ramp winched shut, and with enough racket to wake every Arab – not to mention his goats, dogs and camels – within three miles, the engines wound up to full power and the Chinook was away into the star-studded sky.

As soon as the noise had dwindled sufficiently so that you could speak without shouting, I went back to Pat. I had no intention of wasting time or words on long explanations.

'I'm in charge now, and that means a whole new ballgame,' I began. I paused to let that sink in, then continued, 'I'm going to let you lead in the front vehicle on what's left of tonight's run because I'm a bit rusty on mobility tactics and I'm told you're one of the best. But by first light I want to be fifty kilometres north-east of here. That's where we'll make our next LUP.'

Pat could be stubborn, especially when it came to procedures. He looked at me sullenly and said, 'We can't make that far.' I had been expecting a negative answer, and was ready to jump on it.

'You're not listening to me, Pat. Understand one thing: I'm not asking you for an opinion, I'm telling you. And what I'm telling you, if you need reminding, is fifty kilometres north-east.

'Opinions are like arseholes – we all have them. I'm not here to listen to yours. I'm here to tell you what to do, and you're here to do it. Is that plain enough?' He nodded. 'Good. Now tell me, what's the strange vehicle in the ditch up the slope?'

'That's the Iraqi soldiers.'

'What Iraqi soldiers?'

'The ones we shot yesterday. The dead ones.'

'What the hell are they doing here?' I asked.

'One of the guys drove them here.' I guessed from Pat's attitude that, with me now breathing down his neck, bringing the truck and its grisly load all this way no longer struck him as such a good idea. Now I knew why I remembered that foul stink. It was the smell of putrefying flesh.

'I can't believe you would actually drive three stinking corpses all this way,' I said.

'Well, we didn't want to be compromised,' he muttered.

'What does it matter about being compromised?' I asked him. 'This is not Northern Ireland, this is Iraq. We are behind the enemy's lines. What were you planning to do with them now?'

'I thought we could blow them up and destroy their vehicle,' he said.

'No you won't – we're not in the game of blowing up people and scattering their remains all over the desert. We haven't got time to bury them now. We'd be here all night if we did that, and then we'd never make our fifty kilometres.' I thought for a moment, then said, 'Right. Get all the burmoils left over from the resupply which we're not taking with us and put them around that vehicle, and then have Mugger come here. We'll cremate the bodies, and their jeep at the same time.' (Burmoils are steel 45-gallon drums used for fuel.)

Mugger, who had driven the patrol's former commander and would now drive me, was an expert demolitionist – one of the best in the unit. He arrived a few minutes later – Pat had made himself scarce – and I briefed him on what was needed. He suggested an incendiary device wired up to a thirty-minute fuse, which would effectively cremate the three Iraqi corpses, their vehicle – a Russian-built four-wheel-drive Gaz, not unlike a jeep, though with a closed cab and body – and the leftover burmoils. Some of these still had plenty of fuel sloshing about inside, which I ordered poured into and over the Gaz.

'Leave it to me, Billy,' said Mugger. 'It'll only take a few minutes.'

I left him to apply his special kind of magic to the truck and its gruesome cargo and made sure my own gear had been stowed aboard what was now my Land Rover. As I did so a figure suddenly emerged from the darkness and shook me by the hand.

'Thank God you've arrived, Billy, it's been a nightmare,' came a voice I recognized. It was Des, the troop staff sergeant of Mountain Troop, who, like Mugger, was one of the few members of A Squadron I knew. What he said next, however, confirmed my worst fears about Alpha One Zero, even if it didn't altogether surprise me.

'I was about to take off with my guys and our own four vehicles,' he confided. Des was one of the most reliable and experienced men in the half-squadron patrol, but as I gathered from the outburst that followed, he had been excluded from the decision-making process. Furthermore, he had, from the sound of things, heartily disapproved of the course of action so far adopted by the patrol's former commander and Pat. Yet I didn't have time to listen to everyone's gripes – we had fifty kilometres to make before first light, across pretty inhospitable terrain. So I put a hand on his shoulder and told him quietly, 'It's good to see you, Des. We'll have a chance to go through all of this tomorrow, I promise you. But for the moment I can tell you that there are going to be some major changes around here. As I told Pat, it's a new ballgame now – and we have to be positive.'

Just at that moment Mugger came up to report that the charges were in position. At once I shouted across to Pat, 'OK. Let's go.' With a roar of engines our convoy – eight 110s, three motorbikes and the Unimog support vehicle – moved out, leaving behind a more or less serviceable Gaz and three very dead Iraqi officers.

In my Land Rover there wasn't a lot of chat. Mugger, driving over difficult terrain without lights, needed all his concentration to follow the vehicle ahead and keep an eye out for rocks and holes, and the third member of the crew, our rear gunner, Harry, couldn't really make himself heard over the din. I was preoccupied with the task ahead of me, endlessly turning over in my mind the problems we faced. There were some positive aspects. Temporarily, at any rate, the men's spirits had been lifted by the arrival of the burnouses. But I knew that, in terms of morale, it was going to take a lot more than a few warm goatskin overcoats to put this unit back in top shape. In addition, Des's comments had unsettled me far more than I was prepared to admit. The morale in this unit seemed to be right on the floor. The men's pride and confidence – even, I was to learn, their basic belief in the Regiment – had taken a hell of a drubbing. Most of them were really positive guys and were champing at the bit, but had found their leader's indecision very frustrating. It was up to me to raise their spirits and get the patrol operating professionally and effectively.

Still, I wasn't out there for a picnic, I told myself, or for a touring holiday of Iraq. I had been sent in by the CO to sort things out, and that's what I intended to do, no matter how many feathers I ruffled.

As well as now being the half-squadron's OC, I was also the commander of one of its two sub-units, Alpha One Zero. Because of the way the patrol was divided, I knew that I would tend to use the guys in my own section for the most difficult and dangerous tasks ahead. As a result, Alpha Two Zero was destined to play a supporting role throughout the time we were behind enemy lines, which in turn meant that they would not have the opportunity for either virtuosity or glory, and the kudos that goes with both. This was probably very unfair on those among them who were first-class soldiers, but it was a natural result of my commanding one of the sub-units, as well the entire patrol.

Alpha Two Zero was led by Staff Sergeant Pat, albeit under my overall control. However, my decision to ride roughshod over everybody and to take all the command decisions myself, made clear by the way I had spoken to Pat, meant that I would not be seeking much advice from my 2IC. That, I felt, was the mistake the previous OC had made. He had initially solicited the views of most of the sergeants, and when he discovered which of them advocated the course he himself wanted to adopt he concentrated just on them – and principally on Pat. Des, whom I knew to be extremely positive in his manner and outlook, had clearly not been telling the patrol commander what he wanted to hear. Des would have wanted to forge ahead and get to grips with the mission and, if needs be, with the enemy. His OC's inclination had been to hold back.

I was also not an advocate of so-called 'Chinese parliaments' – meetings at which everyone chips in until a decision is reached – about which so many books on the SAS have made such a lot of noise. Indeed, it's possible to get the impression from some of these memoirs that command of 22 SAS relies on a democratic process in which the opinions of the lowest trooper have equal weight with those of senior officers and NCOs. True, some commanders believe in consulting all their senior ranks before making a decision, and by tradition these heads of section get together for their conflabs in what is called the 'head-shed'. (Which is why the commanders of units and sub-units, from the CO and his HQ staff at Hereford downwards, are known as headsheds.)

Don't mistake me: I have never been against constructive ideas – people throwing in positive suggestions that will help an already formalized plan to work more efficiently. But in my opinion these Chinese parliaments are largely a waste of time, tending merely to provide an opportunity for the waverers to be negative and for others to voice unwanted opinions, both of which more often confuse rather than help matters.

Every commander should take all the relevant factors into account and find ways to work with or around them – not use them as excuses to abort. The commander is there to command – in essence, to tell the other guys what to do. Otherwise you end up with people all voicing their opinions at once, and often getting into heated discussions which can easily turn into arguments, or worse. Everyone feels he has a right to add his twopenn'orth and you get absolutely nowhere, one of the many reasons why I was not going to adopt the system in Alpha One Zero.

I intended to go in hard from the outset. The men might not agree with my tactics, but that didn't matter. Only then would the patrol begin to come together and start doing its job properly, rather than swanning around and withdrawing the moment someone raised his voice to say that something was too difficult or risky. After days of inaction, I had been sent in to grab the patrol by the scruff of the neck and set it back on course. Given that situation, I was the Boss – the RSM – and these guys knew that I had a reputation as a hard-liner. It was the only way I knew of getting things back to normal SAS operating level.

I knew, too, that some of them were going to resent deeply my way of doing things. But I was equally certain that no one was going to come out and say so. In some of the more fanciful personal memoirs of service with the SAS in the Gulf War, the authors describe how they would approach me for what seem to have been cosy little chats, often offering advice or telling me where I was going wrong. There are detailed accounts of the arguments they had with me and mention of almost coming to blows when I failed to act out their wonderful plans. I may as well state here that these accounts are as fictional as their authors' pseudonyms.

The truth was rather different. Almost invariably when I told them during the patrol what we were going to do, they would nod their heads and say, 'OK, Billy.' A few would go away and talk behind my back with others who shared their views, telling each other that a nutter had been put in charge of them. There is nothing either new or surprising in this – it is something that happens in every regiment of the British Army. The crucial point, however, is that I was the Regimental Sergeant-Major – a revered rank. No one in his right mind would dream of arguing with the RSM, far less even think of squaring up to him, either in peacetime or when at war.

Undoubtedly, there was real resentment in some quarters. I was fully aware of this. To most of these men I was virtually a complete stranger. I had served with D Squadron for almost all of my service with the SAS.

Of the thirty-three men in this unit I knew only three of them other, perhaps, than by sight. Nor, that first night – for me – in Iraq, could I help wondering how many would survive long enough for me to get to know them better.

Half an hour after leaving the resupply area I sent a motorcycle rider forward to tell Pat to stop. One by one the vehicles halted. We all waited, swivelling round in our seats and gazing back the way we had come. Sure enough, right on time, below the horizon and in the far distance behind us a massive explosion erupted into the sky, full of red and yellow starbursts that momentarily turned the night into day. The sky had already returned to star-speckled blackness before the dull, rumbling blast had caught up and rolled over us. In the passing of a moment the three Iraqi corpses and their vehicle had become flames and smoke and dust and widely scattered scrap metal. My thoughts were immediately of their families, of their wives and children they'd left behind. I wondered, too, how many of my call sign would be in the same situation over the coming weeks.

Mugger, the demolition man, sitting behind the Land Rover's wheel on my right, wore a satisfied grin.

'Nice one, Mugger,' I told him.

'I haven't lost my touch, then,' he replied and turned the key in the ignition. I had a feeling that we were going to need Mugger again, both for his calm approach and his expertise.

Pat drove the lead vehicle because, despite my other reservations about him, I knew him to be the top guy in Mobility Troop and a superb navigator. He was particularly expert with a piece of equipment called Trimpack, a satellite-navigation device. His performance while we were behind enemy lines was nothing less than excellent, but unfortunately his naturally cautious, by-the-book way of handling things didn't suit my way of operating at all.

Our order of march was Pat in the lead, then my vehicle, then the other six Land Rovers and the Unimog support vehicle strung out in a straight line behind at thirty-yard intervals. The three motorcycles kept station to one side or the other. The bikes were used partly to check out the ground ahead and partly to carry messages between vehicles. Because of their greater speed across country, and the fact that they throw up much less dust than the 110s, they could go out in advance of the patrol to take a close-up look at something we might have spotted through the night glasses. Since we were observing radio silence, however, they were used as a communication service most of the time, riding up and down to pass messages between the vehicles, rather like mounted cowboys escorting a wagon train in the Old West. I would just raise my hand and shout to one of the riders, who would come in closer and check with me, then zoom off and pass the message. Very simple, but it worked.

The rocky terrain made the going extremely difficult, and that first night we covered a maximum of twenty kilometres in an hour, and sometimes less than half that. We didn't talk much. All the equipment in the 110s and on the Unimog that wasn't bolted on had to be secured or it would have been bounced out of the vehicle or damaged beyond repair in seconds. The noise was horrendous, with all our kit banging and rattling and vibrating like things possessed. After a few hours of being thrown around in this din, thinking became almost impossible.

Even though the Land Rover Defender 110s we were using gave a much better ride than their predecessors, since they had the coil-spring suspension used in civilian Range Rovers, it was still one hell of a bumpy trip over that patch of desert. Moreover, having no windshield, which meant that we took the full brunt of an icy wind interspersed with long periods of sleet, did nothing to make it any more comfortable, let alone enjoyable.

In my vehicle, even with all the gear we were carrying, we were not pushed for space with only three of us aboard. In a pinch this 3-ton baby can carry a driver and up to eight passengers. Apart from the name, however, our 110s had little in common with the commercial Land Rover. The spare wheel was carried flat on top of the bonnet, there were no windscreen, doors or roof, and the whole vehicle was painted a desert-camouflage shade, a sort of light sand. All the lights, including the brake lights, were painted out so that not even a flicker would show at night by accident.

Lashed to the vehicles' sides we carried sand channels, steel-mesh runners for crossing soft sand or ditches, and mounted at the front were powered winches to drag other vehicles, or even people, out of tight spots. Stowed inside and outside were jerry cans of petrol and water, rations, ammunition, spades and shovels, and a host of other pieces of essential equipment. Then came the weapons – enough weaponry, in fact, to start my own little war.

Mounted on the bonnet directly in front of me was a 7.62mm GPMG, and on a mounting behind me, facing rearwards, was a Second World War-vintage 0.5-inch Browning M2 heavy machine-gun, an air-cooled, belt-fed weapon with a high rate of fire and a tremendous punch. We were also carrying an 81mm mortar, a Mk19 grenade launcher, our personal weapons – M16s – and a Milan anti-tank-missile launcher. The Milan, a wire-guided Euromissile useful against prepared defences as well as armour, was mounted on the 110's roll bar and had a range of 2 kilometres. On top of this we would place a thermal imager called a MIRA, a very useful piece of kit that could 'see' through clouds and mist, allowing you to spot people and vehicles in poor visibility several kilometres away. Besides all the different kinds of ammunition, we were carrying various types of explosive, detonators and anti-personnel mines.

Not all the Land Rovers carried the same assortment of weapons – other than the GPMGs and personal weapons – equipment or explosives, but all were a variation on the theme of 'mobile but heavily armed'. Multiply the contents of my 110 by eight, and it is immediately apparent that we were a force to be reckoned with. We could take on an enemy or a target face to face or at ranges of up to 4 kilometres. With the vehicles in line abreast on flattish terrain, the Brownings – each capable of firing some 1,000 rounds a minute – could decimate a vastly superior force up to 1.5 kilometres away, and became even more terrifyingly effective as the range shortened. Arguably the finest machine-gun ever made, these weapons were both reliable and accurate, and it was not for nothing that they had become the SAS soldier's favourite support weapon.

As we halted an hour before dawn to lie up for the day – having made our fifty kilometres – it was not our firepower which concerned me, however, but the readiness of the men who would man the weapons. It was up to me to do something about their morale and give Alpha One Zero the direction and aggression it seemed to have lost.

The site chosen by Pat was ideal, with plenty of cover and a good escape route. I watched while he allocated areas to the 110s, which were separated into pairs, and selected four sentry positions. These were positioned for all-round defence, with each sentry a short distance away from one of the pairs of 110s. A sentry's stag lasted two hours and the men in the two nearest vehicles would be responsible for manning one of the posts nearest them throughout the day. The sentry's job was to stay hidden and report back any enemy movements or unusual activity. Since we were observing total radio silence, this meant that either one of his mates back with the vehicles had to stay on watch for any signals, or the sentry would have to crawl back to report in person. On flat ground when operating close in, the sentry could tug on a length of string or wire running back to 'his' two Land Rovers to attract attention. The unarmed Unimog was laid up in a central position, protected by the outer ring of Land Rovers.

Having watched Pat make his dispositions I told him I was completely satisfied with the arrangements. The moment was spoiled, however, when I saw that the lads had cammed up – that is, camouflaged the vehicles with netting staked down to the ground. Turning to Pat, I told him, 'There's no need to hide the vehicles. We have total air superiority over Iraq. The Allied planes are all flying around at night with their lights on in case they bump into one another. We don't need cam nets. There's plenty of cover here to keep us hidden from ground forces, and if any do spot us then they're close enough for us to have to fight or make a break for it anyway.

'What we do is lay Union Jacks on the ground, weighted down with stones, so that any aircraft flying over will see we're British and not mistake us for a disguised mobile Scud-launching site. Let it go for today, but pass the word that tomorrow there will be no cam nets.'

A look of dismay crossed his face. I could almost hear his thoughts out loud, 'This idiot doesn't know what he's doing. He's going to get us all killed.' But in the end his army training won out and he accepted my order, stomping off without another word.

Later, when I popped my head under the cam net covering one of the pairs of 110s, I found a home from home. The crews had their Peak stoves going with pots simmering away and were sipping their brews, cuddled up out of the wind and cold and feeling nice and cosy. When they saw it was me they all stopped talking and looked rather guilty I didn't need to guess who they had been talking about. There's a strong temptation to get all pally with the men in such circumstances, especially if you're that rather isolated figure, the RSM. I resisted it. Alpha One Zero had to get back on course, and that meant its members needed gingering up.

'Well, this is all nice and bloody cosy,' I said. 'Enjoy the moment, because there's going to be a shake-up around here. This patrol is about to find out what it's really like to be involved in a war.' I walked off, getting ready for the moment when I would have to address the whole unit.

I called the meeting for 1600 hours that afternoon, by which time every member of the patrol had managed to get some food down him, as well as a few hours' sleep. Everyone who was not on sentry duty was told to be there, and at the designated time the whole gang, less the four keeping watch, were gathered around my vehicle. I stood facing them with my back to the bonnet, and I gave them a long, hard stare. The afternoon sun did nothing to dispel the arctic cold, and in its harsh, probing glare the group of SAS soldiers gathered around were starkly lit against the desert landscape that surrounded us.

They were a typical bunch – typical for the Regiment, that is: extremely varied in size, and probably the best-trained fighters and saboteurs in the world. A mean-looking, unwashed, unshaven crew, these were the men who would at times piss me off, but who would also fill me with pride, and never more so than when accomplishing the impossible against overwhelming odds.

In short, from a chaotic, badly bungled and almost amateurish beginning, a fighting unit was to emerge that would flamboyantly carry out the most daring Special Forces action behind enemy lines of the entire Gulf War.

These events, and the transformation of Alpha One Zero, still lay ahead when I got up to speak to them that afternoon. What I did know at the time is that a few of them, the most easily influenced, resented my takeover of command. They feared that their safe and comfortable routine was about to be disrupted and that danger – perhaps rather more than some of them were ready for – was to become part of our daily diet.

I was not about to disappoint them.

Chapter Eighteen

D URING our stopover to resupply Alpha Three Zero on the flight in the previous night, I had told the OC that I would join him at his patrol's LUP by the following night, 29/30 January. It meant a 160-kilometre drive over difficult terrain and in poor weather conditions, but I was determined to make it. By now Alpha One Zero had already been behind enemy lines for four days, yet had still to reach its area of operation on Main Supply Route 3, the road from Amman in Jordan to Baghdad, which lay to the north of where Alpha Three Zero was based. The ten days since they should have crossed had been wasted, and Scuds were still threatening Israel and the entire delicate balance of the Coalition. We urgently needed to crack on.

Apart from geeing up the boys and communicating with RHQ at Al Jouf, I had spent most of the 29th trying to get a feel for the ground. There's nothing mystical about this process. It's an instinct you have to acquire in order to be fully in command, and comes from experience, a good assessment of your area of operations, and your own and others' judgement of the enemy's movements and capabilities. In fact, I found it took only a short while to get a good feeling about being in Iraq. That might sound ridiculous – being seventy clicks inside enemy territory and about to move much deeper into it – but I felt there was nothing immediately life-threatening about our position. It was a rather *Boys' Own* notion, I suppose, but I knew I had the men, the weapons and, collectively, the ability to cause Saddam's forces a lot of grief.

With the meeting over, I decided then and there that we would not wait until after dark to move out. By grabbing the last couple of hours of daylight we could make much faster progress. The chances of one of the very rare sorties by Iraqi aircraft coming this way and actually identifying us on the move as an enemy patrol were virtually non-existent.

The men were already drifting away after my little pep talk. I called after the troop sergeants to come back.

'It's now fifteen hundred hours,' I told them. 'I want you to get everyone packed up and be ready to leave at seventeen hundred. We'll be pulling out then, and we won't be stopping until we team up with Alpha Three Zero. It's a hard push but we can do it.

'So let's get cracking.' Pat hung back as the others went off to join their vehicles, and I turned to address him.

'Pat, you'll be in the lead Land Rover again tonight,' I told him. 'You did a good job last night. We must get to that rendezvous with Alpha Three Zero by the early hours of the 30th. Then we'll be in position tomorrow night, finally, to get where we're supposed to be.'

If you hold a position of some authority, to be talked about behind your back and generally slagged off is a fact of life in most outfits – and especially in the British Army. A part of this is the common human reaction to people in authority; another part is the fact that everyone wants to be promoted, and wants to be in charge. Where the SAS is concerned, with everyone in the Regiment vying for the top job, the more of those ahead of them who drop off the ladder the better they like it, since it means that they have moved one place closer to the top. As a result, there are far more schemers in the SAS than an outsider might think. Guys just hoping you'll fall, and not at all unwilling to give you that little shove if they can get away with it. They all want to get there – to the top – which is only understandable. It can be quite comical sometimes, though, having seen these characters all slating the guy in charge, because the moment they are put in charge themselves they have to go on the defensive in order to guard their own backs against the pack they have just emerged from. Knowing all this, I expected to take plenty of stick before this war was ended.

I spent the rest of the time before we pulled out on the radio to HQ at Al Jouf. That was the worst thing about being in command – the length of time that had to be spent on communications, encoding and sending signals or receiving and decoding them. The radio systems we were using were supposed to be state-of-the-art, but in fact they were nothing like it. We operated on a 'burst-transmission' system, which was at best inefficient. Under this method we sent our encrypted messages by 'bursting' them into the ether, which allowed the receiver at the other end to pick them up at any time; in effect, either to pluck them in straight away, or leave them floating about in limbo for up to several days.

The same system was used for HQ's messages to us. Sometimes at the end of a night drive the counter on the radio set in my vehicle would advise that I had four or five messages waiting to be 'sucked in', as it were. These had to be taken in order, first one first, second one second, and so on. Since some of the codes were very complex it could take four or five hours to decode all our waiting messages, of which the last one, almost inevitably, would prove to be the most relevant.

What we really needed was a mobile phone, but the Royal Corps of Signals, which has a unit at Hereford attached to the Regiment, is obsessed with, even paranoid about, electronic warfare (EW), whereby an enemy using direction-finding techniques and equipment can locate your position by getting a fix on your transmission. This is understandable where a large formation like a battalion or armoured unit is concerned, but we were small, fast-moving patrols operating behind enemy lines. What should also have been taken into account was the fact that Iraqi radio-defence systems were made inoperable within a few days by American jamming operations

We had satcoms, which gave us direct voice-to-voice access to Al Jouf, but initially we had been ordered not to use them except in dire emergency. After a short while, however, we knew that we had the upper hand over the Iraqis, and could safely use our more efficient, and far easier to operate, satellite equipment, which saved us from spending many tedious and unnecessary hours on exchanging and decoding a few simple messages.

Eventually the time came for our departure, and in the weak, late-afternoon sunlight we set off. We made slow but steady progress over the rocky desert during the night. It was still bitterly cold, but we were spared further rain and snow.

Once again there was little conversation in my Land Rover. Because of the constant noise it was next to impossible to exchange any but the briefest shouted comments with Harry, the rear gunner, while my driver, Mugger, wasn't strong on chat himself. If he and I talked at all it was usually about the extension he planned to build on to his house, or what he intended doing after he left the army. Mugger had a marvellous temperament and manner for an SAS sergeant – calm, easy-going and humorous, he was a good counterweight to more volatile and temperamental members. A big, fair-haired man, over six feet tall and well-built with it, his nickname came from his days as a boxer, and although he had given up fighting he had kept in great shape.

Besides Mugger's natural quietness, though, there were other barriers to our nattering away like some of the other lads. One was that I was of a different generation, having joined the SAS ten years before he went through Selection. The second, and probably more telling, hurdle was that I was the RSM. Chit-chatting with the boss can be hard going in any job, and soldiering is no exception. Mugger probably felt that he had drawn the short straw in having to sit next to me night after night, although he never let it show in his manner. He was an out-and-out professional, and I came to rely on him completely as the mission unfolded.

Personally, I was equally happy not having to make small talk. I had a lot on my mind, and was to spend most of our long night rides making plans for the following day. During the whole of our four weeks together I rarely exchanged small talk with the men, and they, wary of my rank, equally rarely tried to initiate a conversation. Since I preferred it that way, I was glad of their reticence.

Eventually, after eleven solid hours of driving, we arrived in the vicinity of Alpha Three Zero's temporary base. It was 0400 hours on 30 January, and we had been on the go since 1700 the previous afternoon. We had averaged just 15 kilometres an hour, which is as good an indicator as any of what night driving over that sort of terrain was like.

As we had agreed earlier over the radio, the 2IC of Alpha Three Zero, Captain Guy, had walked south about a kilometre from their base to rendezvous with us. When he made his first sighting of Guy and two of his men, Pat had stopped our convoy and sent a message back to me with one of the motorcyclists that we had a possible enemy contact. Even though we had an arranged rendezvous and were in the designated area, he was right to be cautious. I told Mugger to close up on Pat's Land Rover ahead and kill the engine. Looking through the MIRA, the thermal-imaging device mounted on top of the Milan on the roll bar, we could clearly make out three people on the brow of a small mound about two kilometres ahead of us. They were in the right place and at the right time to be ours, but just the chance that they could be the enemy sent the adrenalin racing through our veins and sharpened our senses.

Now halted alongside Pat's 110, I told him, 'I'm going to take us in about another click, then I want you to lie up with all the vehicles while I go ahead on foot and check them out.'

We took the convoy to a point about halfway from where we had spotted the figures, and stopped again. I got out, selected three men from another crew, and went forward with them on foot. The party ahead must have been watching us as we had been watching them, for when we were about three hundred metres away I spotted the prearranged signal we had agreed over the radio. I immediately sent our reply. Minutes later I was standing face to face with Captain

Guy. He grinned a greeting and said, 'Nice to see you again so soon, Billy.'

We had last met at Victor, when I had waved him off on one of the C-130s that took the squadrons to Al Jouf. But I had spoken with his OC less than thirty hours earlier when I had landed at their position in the resupply Chinook. Everything we had needed to discuss had been said then, and there was no reason to hang about now.

'Do you have an LUP picked out for us?' I asked.

Guy nodded. 'About two kilometres north of here. I scouted the area myself yesterday and this will do you fine,' he said.

After that exchange there was nothing more to say. Unless there was some major rethink at HQ, we would not be linked with Alpha Three Zero again on this mission.

Captain Guy gave us directions to the LUP he had pre-selected for us, after which I thanked him and ordered my column to move out, while the three members of the other patrol vanished back into the night. We reached our LUP co-ordinates within fifteen minutes, and I silently congratulated Alpha Three Zero's 2IC on his choice. The tallest hills in that area of Iraq are no more than a hundred feet high, but in our immediate vicinity there were lots of small hillocks all around us. Their presence allowed us to conceal the vehicles easily, and meant that we could walk about and stretch our legs without risk of being overlooked by shepherds or bedouin.

Pat and I picked out the best defensive positions and the men began settling in for the day. When I reminded them that we would not be using cam nets, however, their faces momentarily dropped. But apart from a little unintelligible grumbling they got on with it, placing a large Union jack, pinned down with stones, between each pair of Land Rovers. Only Pat tried to change my mind. He had obviously given the matter a lot of thought since I had announced my decision the morning before, and had decided to approach it from another angle.

'Can I have a word with you?' he asked.

'What's wrong, Pat?' I said.

'I'd like to remind you about SOPs.' SOPs are standing operational procedures. Every regiment in the British Army has SOPs. They are guidelines, but that is all they are. They are not carved in stone.

'Yes?' I replied, unhelpfully.

'Well, we're not using cam nets, and SOPs say we should be.'

'Well, Pat,' I said, 'I'm not interested in cam nets and I'm not interested in SOPs. They are simply guidelines.' He thought about that for a moment, but obviously believed that he could take it just one step further. There was nothing wrong with his determination, but he picked the wrong argument this time.

'The Deputy Director won't like it if we ignore SOPs,' he ventured.

'I don't give a toss what the Deputy Director thinks,' I told him. 'He's tucked up in bed in Riyadh and not here. I also don't give a damn about SOPs. *I* am the SOP as far as you're concerned. Now drop it, and let's get on with the job.'

A few days later we were to hear by radio that a unit of D Squadron elsewhere in western Iraq, hidden under cam nets while lying up, had been attacked by one of our own aircraft. The pilot had spotted two Land Rovers under their camouflage nets and mistaken them for a Scud missile. He had launched a Maverick air-to-ground missile which had exploded beneath the front wheels of one of the vehicles, causing major mechanical damage but, fortunately, no casualties. After hearing that titbit of news my own unit brightened up considerably, and there were no more protests about my decision not to use cam nets.

I tried on other occasions to explain to Pat how necessary it was to ignore an SOP in specific circumstances. For example, it states in Regimental SOPs that a soldier operating as a signaller must carry his codes in the map pocket of his trousers. Clearly, however, if you were wading across a river and the codes were inevitably going to get wet, you would transfer them to your shirt pocket. What was more, as I had learned after an experience during my jungle training that might have got me RTU-ed, I had good reason to know that map pockets were not necessarily secure. But Pat would never agree. To him SOPs were the Bible. You just had to comply with them. Our arguments – differences, really, to be fair – would always end the same way, with me telling him, 'Pat, we're at war. We can do what we like. *I* can do what I like.'

Nevertheless, Pat preferred to work within the rules, and was often egged on to approach me by others in the patrol. It was extremely frustrating, but I couldn't make him understand. In the end, whenever he came to me moaning about some SOP or other that I had contravened, I had to tell him to leave it alone – hardly a very constructive argument.

Most of the other members of the patrol were more flexible, especially after the Allied pilot's attack on the D Squadron Land Rovers. When I first banned the use of cam nets, however, they didn't like it one little bit, and I found the usual banter noticeably absent as I made my rounds of our new LUP.

By then everything was in place and the men had lit their stoves and were heating food and water for a brew. I would normally have expected one or two of them to have invited me to share a mug of hot, sweet army tea at their vehicle, but all I received were sheepish looks and averted eyes. Just like children, I told myself, and hurried back to my own stove and mug, on which I was soon warming the feeling back into my fingers as I sipped the tea I'd made.

We were camped that day in a place just to the south of the small Iraqi town of Nukhayb, and from the following night would be operating in an area north of an east-west line drawn through that town. Alpha Three Zero's operational area was to the south of the same line. The reason for allotting patrols completely separate areas of operations is not just perfectly logical, but essential. It is to avoid any form of contact between units that could lead to a 'blue-on-blue' situation, a euphemism for occasions when friendly forces end up firing on one another. No SAS patrol will ever stray over the borders of its area of operations without first notifying the unit into whose area it will move.

The Regiment had been involved in a blue-on-blue in the Falklands, when a member of the Special Boat Squadron had been killed by a patrol from the SAS. It was a tragic accident, but the SBS had been operating outside their designated area of operations. A firefight had started, and it was only when someone shouted and the other side heard English being spoken that the mistake was realized. By then, however, one SBS trooper had been killed.

At our new LUP that morning I spent the whole of my free time on the radio while the off-duty men settled down to sleep. The news was not good. Bravo Two Zero had still not made contact, and a unit of D Squadron operating some fifty kilometres south-west of us had been compromised and involved in a heavy exchange of fire with the enemy. Seven men had become separated from the main unit and were missing, with one of them known to be injured. On top of this, an eight-man patrol, Bravo One Nine, who deployed on the same night as Bravo Two Zero but had sensibly taken a vehicle, had also been compromised and was now out of touch, heading, it was hoped, for the Saudi Arabian border.

On a lighter note, RHQ also passed on to me the response in London to my having been sent into action. The Director of Special Forces, a very jovial brigadier, had refused to believe the report given to him by the duty officer in the ops room in London. The Director was a real character, a genuinely funny man who was both very gregarious and extremely good company.

'You must be fucking joking,' was his first comment to the ops officer. 'The RSM's role in war is ammo and POWs. What the hell are you talking about?' So far as I could gather, when his ops officer insisted that I had indeed been sent into Iraq to take over a patrol, the Director told him, 'Don't be so damned stupid. RSMs don't fight in wartime. It's an outrageous suggestion. Either that, or they've all gone stark raving mad out there.' In the end, it took a special signal from Al Jouf to convince him that I was not nursing the ammo in Saudi Arabia, but leading Alpha One Zero behind enemy lines.

From the radio I also learned that our massive 160-kilometre push during the night had reduced some of the pressure on the CO, since it had already begun to justify his decision to replace the patrol's original OC with me. Most of that pressure was coming from the Deputy Director in Riyadh, who could behave at times like a frustrated commanding officer, and who would occasionally meddle and criticize, without necessarily offering constructive alternatives.

So far as I – and a great many others – was concerned, however, and whatever the pressure the Deputy Director was trying to exert we had a CO who was performing absolutely brilliantly in very difficult circumstances. He never became rattled even when under extreme pressure; that night alone he had twenty-three men missing in action, but simply carried on performing as a commanding officer should. Well liked throughout the Regiment, he was also well respected – which is not always the same thing. Our CO bothered to communicate with his men, and took pains to learn their names and their worth. By trusting me he had stuck his neck out, and I was determined not to let him down. I didn't give a damn how difficult it might be, I was going to do my utmost to pull off any mission thrown at me.

Nevertheless, one of my first duties was to the men under my immediate command. They had a right to be told some of the news I had received, and it was only fair that they should know that some of their friends and fellow soldiers were missing, and that the Regiment had already suffered at least one casualty. Early that afternoon, therefore, I called an O-group – orders group, in this case a briefing of all vehicle commanders – and brought them up to date on regimental news. Their faces became very sombre as I spelled out the bare details of the D Squadron patrol's skirmish with the enemy.

It didn't make for cheerful listening. One member of that patrol was known to have been shot in the stomach, and was missing with six other men who had become separated from the main unit during the fighting which, even with the sparse information I had been given, sounded as though it had been pretty fierce. At the moment there was no report of other casualties, but during the contact one vehicle had been completely destroyed and a second badly damaged. As the news sank in some of my guys began to look really upset, and there were a number of groans and impromptu exclamations of sympathy.

'But it wasn't all one-sided,' I told them. 'Our guys also managed to knock the stuffing out of Saddam's people.' They perked up at this, and I continued, 'There were forty Iraqis in the enemy force and our patrol killed ten of them, wounded others, destroyed three vehicles and eventually drove the rest of them off.'

This lifted my vehicle commanders' morale considerably, and I decided to grab the opportunity to remind them of our own concept of operations. 'First, to locate and destroy Scud missiles and launch sites. Second, to gather intelligence. And third, to take offensive action. Which means dealing with any enemy forces or enemy locations we come across.' The last raised an appreciative grin on most of their faces, and brought a chorus of ribald suggestions about appropriate measures to be taken against any Iraqi troops we might stumble over.

I gave them a moment, then motioned to them to quieten down. 'Tonight we will head north another fifty kilometres,' I said. 'Which means that our LUP in the morning will be in our centre of operations.

'I intend to stay there for thirty-six hours, which will give you all a chance to rest up. We'll also start with foot patrols, which will give you a chance to develop a better feel for the ground. We move out at seventeen hundred again this afternoon. So let's start packing everything away.' It seemed that, for the second day running, we were going to start our night trek in a positive frame of mind. The men were now itching for a fight, and several of them came up to me to ask when we would see some action.

'Don't worry, it'll happen soon enough,' I told them. They certainly seemed enthusiastic, but watching them disperse towards their vehicles I was acutely aware that I hardly knew any of them at all.

I was getting to know the two other members of the crew of my 110, however. As I have said, Mugger was the ideal driver, a quiet type with whom everybody got on well and against whom no one had a bad word to say. He didn't have a strong accent or, beyond his size, any notable mannerisms or characteristics; he was simply solid and dependable and decent, with a great sense of humour. If he couldn't say something nice about a person then he wouldn't say anything about them at all. During the whole time I knew him I never heard him slag off anyone.

It was in his role as demolitionist, though, that Mugger really came into his own, for the moment he had explosives in his hands he became like a man possessed. His eyes would light up and he would grin from ear to ear at the merest hint of there being something that needed blowing up. The bigger the potential bang, the happier Mugger became. Indeed, I have never known another soldier quite so in tune with his work, and it was wonderful to watch the transformation that came over him whenever his fingers came into contact with plastic explosive, fuses, detonators, timers, mines, and all the other tools of his lethal trade.

The third man aboard our Land Rover, Harry, my signaller and the vehicle's rear gunner, was also a quiet type. He looked as though he needed six good meals a day to put some weight on him, but contrary to appearances he was incredibly fit and tough, and was a superb long-distance runner. Apart from the fact that he was an expert signaller as well as a first-class soldier, I liked having Harry aboard because he was happy to eat nothing but hardtack biscuits and bacon grill. The latter, which came in small tins, was a substance like luncheon meat which, when fried, tasted like bacon. Harry loved to eat it cold, and would happily swap his other rations for our bacon grill. Since both Mugger and I loathed the stuff, we were very glad to have him with us.

The senior vehicle commander in my section, Alpha One Zero, was Des, the troop staff sergeant who was one of the few A Squadron members I'd come across before the patrol. I knew him to be someone who could be trusted absolutely and relied on in all situations. I also knew that he was incapable of saying one thing to my face and another behind my back. Of medium build, he had a very dark complexion and was beginning to lose his hair. He was normally quiet, unless made angry, and he and I seemed to be on the same wavelength, perhaps because, like me, he too was a former Para. Two members of the patrol who wrote books about their experiences in the Gulf War described Des as a brown-noser, constantly sucking up to me. Not only was this not true, it was extremely unfair to say such a thing about an excellent, positive and professional soldier. It was because of Des and others like him – and I was to discover that most of the other guys were, like Des, also on the same wavelength as me – that our mission was able to stay on track.

I had retained Pat as my second-in-command and in charge of one half of the unit and four of the Land Rovers. I had the other four Land Rovers and the Unimog, while the motorcycles worked with either group. The only times these two groups would ever split was when we were travelling in parallel formation, operating on either side of a large wadi or wide valley.

The other senior NCO in the patrol, Sergeant 'Spence', was also in Pat's section, Alpha Two Zero. I had known him for several years and always thought of him by his nickname, 'Serious'. He had earned this not only because he had a serious manner, but because everything he did he referred to as being serious. If you saw him smoking and greeted him, 'All right, Spence?' he would reply, 'Aye. I'm just having a serious smoke.' Or I might spot him leaving the mess on a Saturday carrying a bag, and if I asked what he was up to he would say, 'All right, Billy. I'm just going to do some serious admin.' This meant he was going into the town centre to do his laundry, or to buy something from Boots, or some other mundane errand. Everything was 'serious' to him, and it became a standing joke among the lads. He was 'Serious' to one and all.

This was not meant unkindly, for he was a pleasant enough individual. Of medium height, he had dark, slightly curly hair, and during the course of the patrol had grown a black beard and moustache. He had joined up as a boy soldier, and I think that that was the cause of everything being serious to him. In my opinion, all the lads who signed on for the army as boy soldiers and then progressed to regiments as adults tended to be far more institutionalized than the recruits who came in from Civvy Street aged eighteen, nineteen or twenty. The boy soldiers had joined straight from school, and most had been thoroughly brainwashed by the system. They somehow lacked the all-round, more abrasive experience the rest of us had enjoyed – or endured – during our late teens before we had opted for the Queen's shilling. Some years after our experiences in the Gulf I came across a book by one 'Cameron Spence' called *Sabre Squadron*, which seemed to be an account of the author's experiences in Iraq with Alpha One Zero. I had never heard of 'Spence' and was surprised to find on reading the book that he was none other than Serious. Perhaps I should not have been surprised, for *Sabre Squadron* certainly contains some serious untruths, which I will come to later.

Pat also had an officer in his section. Captain Timothy was a thoroughly nice guy who had come to us from an infantry regiment. Having only recently passed Selection he was with the patrol primarily to gain experience, and so had only a limited role to play. I found him a tremendous asset when it came to making constructive suggestions, however. On the occasions when I called the senior men together, after deciding on a course of action I would ask for suggestions, and he could usually be relied upon to come up with ideas that could be incorporated into the main plan. Rather than being put at the back and told to shut up he was invited to offer his own contributions. He understood the part he had to play in the patrol, but equally understood that his ideas were welcome. I could have wished that everyone had been as positive and constructive.

Pat's driver was a case in point. For someone whom I found so negative in the field, I was surprised by how gung-ho Corporal 'Yorky', as he was nicknamed, made himself out to be in his book *Victor Two*, which first appeared under the pseudonym 'Peter "Yorky" Crossland'. As with Serious 'Spence's' book, I will deal with some of Yorky's claims later. He was a big man with a shock of dark hair and a rather bland face. His broad Yorkshire accent, coupled with a slightly gormless expression, especially when wearing his steel helmet, made him appear harmless enough, but later I learned from some of the other patrol members that he seemed to have a great deal of influence over Pat, which in turn may have contributed towards some of the previous OC's poor decisions. For myself, I found Yorky's behaviour erratic, and it was clear to me that the situation – being active behind enemy lines – had got to him. Not much fun for him, I agree, but also potentially dangerous for the rest of Alpha One Zero.

Active service affects different people in different ways. Soldiers can be exceptionally good during training and in exercises. When it comes to reality, however, matters can be completely reversed. No one knows how he will react to battle until he's been in a firefight. Training, discipline, a sense of self-worth, loyalty to one's fellow soldiers and one's unit, all these and other factors have a part to play in making a good fighting soldier, but he is still an unknown quantity until he has been in action for the first time.

Once you have been in a firefight then you are confident of your own reactions in future situations. To the seasoned soldier, as I then considered myself to be, there was only one way for Alpha One Zero to go, and that was forward. No order, no task, no mission was impossible. To some extent I was able to use that confidence in myself to influence other people, and so boost them into a positive frame of mind, after which their own character and training took over.

Sometimes soldiers who had not experienced action, and hence did not know how they would react, were led into aborting missions without even attempting them. This was what had happened all those years earlier in Argentina. The team that was helicoptered in to Tierra del Fuego did not attempt to reach the target because, in their eyes, the task was impossible – and thus unacceptable. Having convinced themselves that they were on a suicide mission, they came to believe that since they had no chance of survival, they therefore had no chance of success. In fact, the reverse is often true – as Pebble Island or the Iranian Embassy operation had proved, success and survival go hand in hand.

Nevertheless, it is very easy to portray people in films and novels – or even autobiographies – as cheerfully accepting suicide type missions. It is not so easy to undertake such missions in real life. Some SAS guys in Iraq, now faced with the prospect of a real firefight for the first time in their lives, had been in Hereford for many years. They had wives and children and a life outside the service. It is much more difficult to face enemy fire when you have all that going for you. If life has become comfortable and attractive, the risk of dying becomes very much harder to face. I was to see this manifest itself in various different ways as our time behind enemy lines in Iraq lengthened into weeks.

Another through-the-night drive in miserable, near-Arctic conditions brought us, on the morning of 31 January, to the centre of our initial area of operations. Once we had established a new LUP I took stock of our situation. We had by now driven for three nights in a row and were some two hundred kilometres inside Iraq, but the men were very tired, and not only physically. This kind of driving, apart from the toll it took of the drivers, meant keeping extremely alert, permanently on the lookout for any kind of enemy activity or location. Such constant vigilance was mentally exhausting, however. As a result, that morning I confirmed that we would be staying at this LUP for thirty-six hours and that I would be sending out foot patrols, partly to reconnoitre the surrounding territory, and partly to give the men some exercise. The vehicles had also taken a battering from the rocky terrain, and I charged our Mobility Troop members with servicing them and carrying out any necessary repairs.

The first radio message of the morning contained good news. The eight men of Bravo One Nine were back in Al Jouf. They had crossed the border the previous night and returned through 'Ar Ar, where they had been stopped by the local Saudi Arabian police for driving without lights. They were exhausted but uninjured, although four of them had needed treatment for frostbite. My thoughts immediately turned to Bravo Two Zero. If they had been less stubborn, and had heeded the CO and myself and taken a Land Rover, we might have been cheering their return through 'Ar Ar as well as that of their mates from the same squadron.

Twenty-four hours later came more good news. The missing seven members of D Squadron had made it back to 'Ar Ar and were en route by chopper to Al Jouf. The injured man, a trooper, was being airlifted to hospital. When I issued the news to the men a few minutes later I was also able to tell them that although the trooper had suffered a gunshot wound to the stomach there was an exit point. This was received with obvious relief, for they were all aware, through their medical training, that it was much more dangerous when bits of metal were left scattered in the body.

I waited for the comments to die away.

'Now for our own news,' I told them, with a broad grin. 'We've been given our first specific mission outside our main task.'

I watched most of the upturned faces light up with eagerness – and some with a look of apprehension. Time to worry about that later, I thought, before continuing, 'We are to carry out a recce of the Mudaysis airfield, which is a large Iraqi fighter· base about twenty kilometres west of the main supply route. That will be our destination tonight. I hope I don't need to remind you that we will be approaching a manned target with the likelihood of there being other enemy positions in the area. So keep your eyes peeled – and no unnecessary noise.'

That last remark raised a few chuckles from the more relaxed members of the patrol, for a stiff afternoon breeze had already begun rattling anything aboard the Land Rovers that wasn't securely tied down or wedged against the sides. No matter how hard we tried, we were always going to sound like a mobile breaker's yard.

That night, travelling slightly north of west, we encountered several bedouin encampments. We were able to pick these out on our MIRA thermal imagers and skirt around them. Apart from a lot of barking from the bedous' dogs, our passing appeared not to produce any noticeable reaction.

After weeks spent behind enemy lines during the Gulf War, I can never picture bedouin villages without coupling that image with the sound of barking dogs. The two things go together, and it would be fair to say that where you find one, you'll find the other.

As a result, I was highly amused by some of the things 'McNab' wrote in *Bravo Two Zero*. In one scene, he describes him and his men hearing dogs near a bedouin village. According to 'McNab', if the dogs approached the patrol, he and his men would use their 'fighting knives' to kill the creatures and carry the corpses away with them, for disposal later. Elsewhere in *Bravo Two Zero* he mentions that, since they had no silenced weapons with them, he and his men might well have to use their knives to take out any enemy manning a Scud launch site, so as not to attract unwelcome attention from other Iraqi forces in the area.

The fact is, however, that no man in his right mind would go anywhere near any dog, anywhere in the Middle East – let alone a bedouin dog. There is a very high probability that it would be rabid, quite apart from the fact that dogs are tough animals, especially semi-wild dogs. The chances of someone killing a dog silently and quickly with a blade are very slight indeed.

More tellingly, I repeat that there is no such thing in the British Army, never mind the Regiment, as an official fighting knife. The only knives issued are small clasp knives which are mainly used for opening ration packs and removing or replacing screws in your rifle. I have known a few SAS guys who carried slightly larger knives, but only for doing ordinary things – not for stabbing people and dogs or slitting sentries' throats. There are no instruction courses in the SAS involving the use of knives, fighting ones or any other kind. Even training in unarmed combat is only rudimentary, and the only time knives are involved is during instruction on how to defend yourself against an antagonist armed with a blade. Finally, if you have to kill someone, or some animal, in combat or otherwise while on active service, then you use your rifle or pistol. There is no unit of the British Army which uses knives – other than bayonets – garrottes or crossbows to dispose of the enemy. Any soldier who asks you to believe differently is either lying, or has himself been taken in by some of the nonsense written about the Special Forces.

What does ring true in 'McNab's' account of hearing the bedou dogs, however, is the sheer tension of being on a mission behind enemy lines, and especially in such an unforgiving landscape. I think that at first none of us felt completely at ease in the desert, for all our training and, for some of us, years of experience. Certainly spotting that first desert settlement must have rattled Pat and Yorky, because they pulled up abruptly. Mugger stopped and I jumped out and walked forward the fifty or so paces to the lead Land Rover. As I came level with Pat I asked, 'What's up?'

He jerked his head towards the front. 'There's a lot of movement about a kilometre ahead. It could be an enemy patrol.'

I lifted my rifle and took a squint through the Kite sight, a night-viewing scope which attaches to an M16 or SA80* and works the same as a normal telescope sight – only in the dark. Then I took a long look through the MIRA, listening hard at the same time. I began to smile.

'There appear to be a group of tents or other quarters over there and what might be a cooking fire,' I said. 'Which means they could be anybody. But I can also hear dogs barking and you don't often get the Republican Guard taking pets on manoeuvres.

'That means bedouin to me. Aim to clear the village by about five hundred to a thousand metres and they won't give us any trouble.

'Now let's get moving or we won't make our LUP by dawn.'

True, there was a certain element of risk, but it was a risk I was prepared to take. The chances were that if whatever lay ahead was a military unit, then its sentries would probably think we were Iraqi troops on the move. And even if they did sight us and become suspicious, I counted on them waiting until dawn before trying to confirm those suspicions.

If they were bedouin, however, as I was convinced they were, then they wouldn't give a damn about us anyway. Most of the desert tribesmen almost certainly had very little idea of what was going on in the country, cared nothing for politics, and had no strong feeling of loyalty to country or leader. If aircraft were to start dropping bombs near them then they might move out of the way, but whether soldiers driving quietly by in the night were Iraqis or somebody else generally didn't interest them in the slightest.

We must have passed half a dozen such encampments during the night, some so close that a few of the villagers waved to us in the moonlight. We waved back. I suspect that, if they could make us out at all, then seeing us in our shemaghs and burnouses probably convinced them that we were Iraqis.

'Who dares wins,' I muttered our regimental motto to Mugger as we

---

* The army's standard-issue rifle, a British-built 5.56mm automatic. It is disliked by the SAS, who distrust its reliability, especially in harsh conditions, among other faults – hence their preference for the US-built M16. Early in 2000 it was reported that some 300,000 SA80s and their derivatives in service with the British armed forces were to be recalled and modified, because of serious problems in certain conditions.

bumped and rattled past another village. 'It's amazing how many times that saying proves to be right.' He gave me a quick grin and carried on driving. I am quite certain that if one of the villages had turned out to be a massive Iraqi ambush mounted by a full regiment of tanks, Mugger would have remained just as unflappable.

At one point, just before midnight, when we were moving over higher ground, I ordered the convoy to halt and, using my Kite site, looked towards Baghdad. The sky was alight with the flash of explosions. Bomb after bomb, hundreds upon hundreds of them, made the sky to the east a spectacular sight, even at that distance.

I almost felt sorry for the poor Iraqis who were getting such a royal pummelling that night. The chances were that most of the unlucky ones were civilians anyway. That, however, seems to be the pattern of modern warfare.

Chapter Nineteen

A T 0200 hours on the morning of 2 February we arrived at the top of a long, undulating slope that led down to the vast and sprawling military complex that was the Mudaysis airfield. In the thin moonlight I could make out through my Kite sight a number of massive, oval-shaped hangars, whose concrete sides and metal roofs and doors had been very effectively camouflaged, so that the huge structures seemed to blend in with the runways and aprons. They were probably extremely difficult to make out from the air even in daylight. There were other buildings on the airfield, which I assumed were admin and sleeping quarters, and these too were camouflaged.

Headquarters had requested a daylight recce of all movements and an aircraft count, so I decided to send in a two-man team to establish a forward observation point (FOP). Meanwhile, I would keep the main unit well out of sight of any patrols the Iraqis may have had checking the perimeter and the areas around it. We fired up the vehicles and cut round to the north-west of the airfield. I selected an LUP for the patrol about three kilometres from the base, then detailed two men to use motorcycles to get down to within 1,000 metres of the perimeter fence and find a concealed spot from which to carry out a daylight observation of the complex.

I chose Des and a corporal named Ken to carry out the recce. Ken was an ex-Para in his early thirties, not tall, but stocky and very fit; he was also, like Mugger, a first-class demolition man. Des had recommended him, which was good enough for me, but just watching him over the past few days I had noted him as a cheerful sort. I had marked him down as very 'wilco', meaning that he had a positive attitude and was likely to do anything I asked him to do quickly and competently.

The two of them rode off on their bikes just before first light, each carrying a day sack of rations, a sleeping bag and their Ml6s. They established their OP within a kilometre of the airfield. It was a good choice, for the site had a panoramic view which allowed them to see all aircraft and vehicle movements on the base.

When the Allies established air superiority – which they did almost immediately with the launch of the air offensive – the Iraqis decided either to leave all military aircraft in their hangars, which were bomb proof to a certain extent, or move them to hidden airfields; indeed, many front-line Iraqi aircraft were flown out to Iran and interned there for the duration of the war. Saddam had clearly decided that there was nothing to be gained by risking expensive warplanes in a one-sided contest against a vastly superior enemy. RAF Tornados had partially bombed Mudaysis in an attempt to destroy the airfield, but had caused little damage, and I later learned that they had lost one aircraft during the attack. Since we'd been tasked with the recce, it was clear that another bombing mission was under consideration at Allied HQ.

When Des and Ken returned just before last light, however, they reported very little activity on the base. Apart from a couple of light aircraft there were no others to be seen. It was almost like a ghost airfield. Since we had done what we'd set out to do, I radioed in our sitrep and informed HQ that I intended to return to MSR3, which the Iraqis were using to bring supplies in from Amman in Jordan. In reply I learned that Corporal 'Ryan', one of the missing members of Bravo Two Zero, was safe in the British Embassy in Damascus. He had become separated from the others and had successfully escaped over Iraq's border with Syria, after an epic journey on foot through heavily guarded areas. The news gave the guys something to smile about, and once again we left our LUP on a high note.

The first part of our drive that night was uneventful – except for a minor disaster that struck one unfortunate member of our team. He had failed to make sure his bergen was securely strapped to the back of his Land Rover, and somewhere along the way it had fallen off, unnoticed. In it were his sleeping bag, his personal kit and almost everything he needed in the field except weapons. It meant that until we were resupplied he was going to have to go without most of his kit.

Still, the incident probably served to make the others more careful when it came to tying their bergens on the Land Rovers. Luckily for the trooper we had a resupply due in three days' time, and over the radio I was able to order him up a new bergen and kit.

Shortly after midnight we hit a major road. Running roughly north-south, it proved to be the road that linked MSR3 with Nukhayb. Since I couldn't imagine that much Iraqi traffic would be heading down into Saudi Arabia at the moment, I figured it was safe to use the road for a few kilometres. Travelling on a surface that didn't cause the Land

Rovers to buck and lurch every second or two was pure bliss. So too was the silence, for without all the bumping the constant din we had all grown used to disappeared.

All too soon it was time to strike off into the desert again and return to our usual punishing form of travel. As we went to turn off, however, Mugger suddenly pointed off to his right. We could just make out a square shape, visible only because it was a different shade from the surrounding surface, lying flush with the ground about twenty metres from the road itself. I told him to stop and sent a message forward by one of the motorbikes to Pat, ordering him to turn back. By the time his 110 had turned around and the other vehicles had closed up from behind, Mugger and I were out of our wagon and looking down at what turned out to be a four-foot-square steel manhole cover. A steel bar ran across the cover from a heavy metal hinge at one side to an equally sturdy bracket at the other, where the bar was secured by a large padlock. I stared at this arrangement, wondering what on earth could be underneath that needed to be protected like that.

'They obviously don't want our kind taking a sneaky look at their sewage,' I said to Mugger. 'I've never seen a manhole cover sealed up like this before.'

'It must be protecting a fibre-optic cable,' he replied. He was tugging at his earlobe, obviously deep in thought. 'Which means,' he continued, 'that there should be another little darling just like this one down the road a-ways.'

Telling the others to stay put with the vehicles I walked with Mugger along the roadside, which was clearly lit by the moon. After I had paced out exactly 200 metres we came across another of the manhole covers, just as securely sealed.

'That clinches it,' said Mugger. 'The cable probably links that airfield, and other places, to Baghdad.'

'OK,' I said. 'We'd better locstat this location on the Trimpack so we can inform HQ. Meanwhile let's get clear of this road while our luck holds out, and before the whole Iraqi Army comes rolling down it.'

We hurried back to the others, mounted up and quickly got moving again, slipping northwards across country, away from the deserted road. As we clocked up the kilometres I noticed that the going gradually became easier, the landscape becoming less rolling and the surface less rocky. By the time we reached the site I had picked out the previous afternoon we were on a huge plateau, almost completely flat, from which we could see for about five to ten kilometres in every direction.

After the last of the Land Rovers had joined us I told the lads, 'This is our LUP. We'll spread the vehicles out in pairs as usual, where I tell you, and post the usual sentries.'

I could see, though, that some of the others were none to happy about lying up in a location with so little cover.

'What if any Iraqi armour comes along?' someone asked. 'What happens then?'

'Simple,' I told him. 'We call the jets in to wipe them out. In an emergency we can use our satcoms and have the aircraft here in under half an hour. So let's get on with it.'

'What about cam nets?' came a final question. 'Surely we're going to use them when we're this exposed?'

'When we're this exposed is all the more reason to let our chaps know who we are,' I told them. 'Now, I've already told you once what we're doing, so let's do it.'

Up to this time, with the exception of Mudaysis, we hadn't spotted any enemy locations. As has been said, the Iraqis were no longer capable of putting more than a handful of aircraft into the sky, if that, and had no reason to be moving troops across country this far away from a major road and in this direction. As far as I was concerned we were as safe on that beautiful gravel plateau as we would have been in a twenty-foot ditch. Nor was I going to worry about it – it was far more important to pass our information on to Al Jouf as quickly as possible. As soon as I had set the Land Rover pairs heading into their positions I told Harry to get the radio cranked up. When that was done I gave HQ our sitrep on Mudaysis and our new location, and then informed them that we had located a probable fibre-optic cable and asked their OK to cut it. The answer came back within minutes. Mission granted. Give it priority.

To carry out the operation meant splitting my unit into two, since it would be foolish to risk compromising the entire patrol for a simple demolition job, and we would be very exposed down by the manhole covers on the road. I would take care of the fibre-optic cable along with Mugger and Harry, Des and his wagon, and Ken on a motorcycle. I told Pat to take the Unimog and the other six wagons and motorcycles and locate an LUP and a desert landing area for our resupply chopper, which was due in either the following night or in the early hours of Tuesday morning.

I took out my air map, which clearly defined the wadi system, and picked out a spot on one of the wadis. Having made sure that Pat had copied the coordinates on to his own map I told him to rendezvous with me there at 0400 hours the following morning.

'If I don't show up on time, go to the LUP without me and return to the rendezvous location at eighteen hundred hours tomorrow.'

'Yes, okay,' he said. He moved off towards his vehicle.

At last light that evening I pulled out with my two vehicles and the motorcycle and headed back towards where, about thirty kilometres to the south, we had located the access covers for the buried fibre-optic cables. I had told Des to lead the way – for a very good reason. He had with him a Magellan global-positioning system (GPS), a satellite-navigation device which is both extremely accurate and very reliable. I didn't have a clue how the thing worked, never having trained on it, but Des was able to work its magic, and within a couple of hours brought us to the section of the road where we had spotted the manhole covers.

My plan was to blow two of the manholes and the cables beneath them. We parked a few metres away from the first and while our demolition experts, Mugger and Ken, prepared a charge, Des and I used crowbars to break the padlock and remove the security bar that held the metal cover down. Once the cover was lifted clear we were faced with a hole some six feet deep and four feet square. By the light of my torch we could see three cables running across the bottom of the hole from a pipe on one side to an identical pipe on the other. Another wire, separated from the three main cables, also ran through the pipes.

I called Mugger and Ken over to take a look and check if the charge they were preparing was big enough to do the job. Mugger carefully examined the cables in the torchlight and told me, 'The three larger cables are fibre optics. I don't know what the other one is. But the charge we're putting down there is not only going to cut the command link, but will fuse it back along the tunnels for hundreds of yards in both directions. They're going to have to do a lot of digging to reconnect these beauties.'

'Perfect,' I grinned at them. 'In the words of the song, "Who could ask for anything more?"'

We had already agreed to a thirty-minute delay on the explosive charges to give ourselves time to get well clear of the area. The charge comes in a plastic-covered case, which makes it easier to handle, and within a couple of minutes Mugger and Ken had the first one ready. As timers we were using time pencils which, when broken, start a chemical reaction. Depending on the pencil you have selected, that reaction lasts for a carefully computed length of time before it produces a spark. At the end of the selected delay this would ignite the safety fuse, which would then ignite the detonator cord, which in turn would ignite the detonator pressed into the explosive charge. It sounds complicated, but once the time pencil has produced a spark, the chain reaction that follows is pretty much instantaneous.

The two demolition men decided between them that Ken, who was the slimmer, had better be the one we lowered into the manhole to place the charge. We did this using a loop line which I fetched from my Land Rover. A loop line, as its name implies, is a piece of strong nylon cord some thirty feet long with loops at each end. Using our karabiners, which are small metal clips with spring-loaded gates used by mountaineers, we could string these lines together to form a rope which we could abseil down. We could even use them to tow vehicles, since they are immensely strong. Ken put a foot in one of the loops, and we lowered him down to the bottom of the shaft. He placed the charge alongside the cables and snapped the pencil timer, whereupon we hauled him out.

Immediately Des and his crew, with Ken, sped to the next manhole cover, 200 metres away, while Mugger, Harry and I replaced the cover on the first one, snapped the security bar back in place and carefully arranged the forced-apart padlock so that it would at least pass a casual inspection. We then brushed the area around the cover with sacking to obliterate any signs of our having been there and headed after Des.

He and his team already had the cover off the second manhole, Ken had prepared the charge, and we were able to lower him down straight away. In less than three minutes the cover was replaced and we were cleaning off the area. Then Mugger grabbed my shoulder.

'We have company, Billy,' he said quietly. I looked up and immediately spotted three sets of headlights zig-zagging slowly down the road towards us, about a kilometre away.

Suddenly we were all on full alert. There was no chance of our visitors being bedouin this time. This was the enemy, and they were heading straight for us. We were almost certainly outnumbered, although I doubted we were outgunned. I was weighing up the odds and risks involved when the three vehicles stopped. Then, within a couple of minutes, they came on again at the same steady pace.

'They're checking the manholes,' said Mugger. 'That spare wire must have been a trembler. We've tripped the alarm system and they've come to see what's going on.'

Between where we had left the vehicles and the edge of the road there was a small berm running parallel to the roadway. If we brought the bike and Land Rovers across it, we would be able to use the metalled road to make a fast getaway. Even though we would then be on the roadway with the enemy vehicles, I decided that this was our best option.

'Over the berm,' I pointed across the road. 'You first, Des, then Ken, and we'll bring up the rear. Now go.'

Des's driver revved up, took a fast run at the berm and bounced over the top easily. Ken on the motorcycle was only seconds behind him, doing a great impression of Evel Knievel as he leapt the top with a foot or more to spare.

Then it was our turn. Mugger revved up and we charged towards the berm and raced up the side. Then, just as we reached the top, Mugger let the revs drop and we stalled right on the crest, rocking slightly backwards and forwards.

'For fuck's sake, Mugger, what are you messing about at?' I hissed in his ear.

'Oh shit,' he said.

By this time Des had realized what had happened and had driven back to the bottom of the berm on the far side.

'I'll tow you off,' he shouted.

'No you won't,' I yelled back. 'All you'll manage from that side is to pull us in up to our axle. Come back over here and pull us off backwards.'

Our position was beginning to get slightly hairy. From our excellent vantage point in our Land Rover on top of the berm, I could see the three sets of headlights creeping ever nearer. They were now less than 800 metres away. 'Better be prepared,' I told Harry in the back, and within seconds was reassured to hear the double thud of a grenade being loaded into the Mk19 as the weapon was cocked.

Getting a good purchase from the metalled road, Des made his return run over the berm with ease and within thirty seconds had a winch line attached to the back of our 110. Thirty more and we were free and back at the foot of the berm. Mugger reversed some distance to give us a good run-up, and Des's driver did the same once the winch line had been recovered.

By now the enemy were no more than 600 metres away and time was getting a bit tight. Once more Des's vehicle managed to sail over the berm without difficulty, and then it was our turn again. I half-turned in my seat, grinned at my driver and said, 'Mugger, don't stall it again – *please*?'

It was his turn to grin. 'Piece of cake, Billy,' he said, 'piece of cake.' And with the revs rising to a howl we surged forwards and then up the side of the berm. At the top the 110 leapt the crest, flipped nose down, and we were suddenly rushing and sliding down the far side and on to the road.

'All right,' I said. Then, after a quick glance back along the road to where the oncoming Iraqi vehicles were now less than half a kilometre away, I told them, 'Let's get out of here before these guys get any closer.'

But we had little to fear. I figured that as the enemy were using headlights their night vision would be so poor that they'd need to be within a hundred metres to spot us. The noise of their own engines would more than mask the sound of ours at this distance.

When we'd put a good kilometre between us and the enemy I signalled Des and Ken to follow me off the road and into the desert, where I pulled up. The other Land Rover and the bike stopped alongside me, and for a moment silence reigned. I told Des and Harry to stand down the grenades from the Mk19s and then gave the go-ahead for a cigarette break.

We didn't have long to wait. Some ten minutes later, when the search vehicles were almost opposite the first of the manholes we had doctored, the charge blew, sending a huge gout of red and yellow flame high into the sky. I couldn't see what the reaction was aboard the enemy trucks, except that their headlights were suddenly stabbing in all different directions. We waited just under five minutes for the other charge to blow, which it did with an equally spectacular display of pyrotechnics, the heavy boom of the explosion reaching us a few seconds later.

'Saddam won't be launching any more Scuds using that command line,' I declared. 'Well done, lads. Now for the RV.' Cigarettes crushed out under foot, we mounted up and set out to drive the thirty kilometres or so to the rendezvous I had agreed with Pat. I didn't know it, but I had a couple more hours in which to enjoy the success of our mission before all my high spirits would be knocked out of me.

We arrived at the RV shortly after 0330 hours, to find no trace of the other group. After half an hour and still no sign of them I asked Des to give me the latitude and longitude of the spot I had picked out. When I plotted the reference against our position on the map I saw at once that we were not at the location I had selected, and where I had told Pat to meet us.

'You've brought us to the wrong place,' I told Des bluntly.

'No I haven't,' he replied, somewhat sheepishly.

'Des, I'm telling you that this is not the place where I told Pat to meet up with us.' I was rapidly running out of patience.

He looked at me even more sheepishly and said, 'I think I'd better tell you what happened. After you told Pat the RV location he called me over and told me he was changing it to the place we're at now.'

I was absolutely stunned. For a moment I couldn't speak. Then I said incredulously, 'You mean, if my vehicle had become separated in a firefight and headed for our rendezvous we would have been the only ones there, because for some reason known only to him, Pat has changed the location?'

Des didn't answer, probably wisely, since I was furious. I made up my mind there and then that, come that night, Pat would be shipping out on the resupply helicopter. Meanwhile it looked as if my 2IC and the rest of the patrol weren't even going to make the changed rendezvous, and we needed to find an LUP. This time I made Des follow me. I hadn't decided how I was going to deal with him yet.

We drove through the night for a few kilometres, until we came across a site that looked ideal for an LUP, especially since we only had two 110s and a motorcyle to conceal. Having disposed the vehicles and detailed a couple of sentries, I went straight back to my Land Rover, where I contacted Al Jouf on the radio and reported a successful mission. In return, HQ advised me that a new second-in-command was flying in that night with the resupply. He would take over from Pat, and would stay with us for approximately two weeks; however, he would be under my overall command throughout his allotted time with the patrol. HQ didn't name him over the radio, but described him as 'the new OC designate of A Squadron'.

There was a further message, forwarded from Pat, which told me to meet him and the rest of Alpha One Zero at 1800 hours that evening. You are forbidden to use foul language over the radio, but had I been able to I surely would have used it then. Instead, I had to content myself with sending him a return message, through Al Jouf, telling him, as a direct order from me, that he was to meet me at another location at 1800 hours, and giving the map coordinates. And that, until I met up with him, would have to be that.

From our LUP during that morning we detected enemy activity on a hilltop some three or four kilometres away on our right flank. Since we could see them I was sure that they could see us, but they caused us no bother. I was in no position, with only six guys and two Land Rovers, to do anything about them there and then, and after briefing Des and his crew to keep an eye on them during the day, I tried to put them out of my mind. Before pulling out at 1730 that evening, however, I sent a brief message to Al Jouf giving them the coordinates of the Iraqi position. If the enemy troops stayed there for long after we left, then they were going to have a very unpleasant extra dish for dinner in the shape of a few air-to-ground missiles.

The RV I had selected was only thirty minutes' drive away, and we arrived at almost the same time as the rest of our unit. The moment all the vehicles had come to a stop I walked straight over to Pat and told him to come with me. I was still seething, but I managed not to say another word until we had walked about a hundred metres away from the men and were out of earshot. I then gave him one of the biggest bollockings I had ever handed out.

'What the fuck do you think you are you playing at?' I began. 'I told you where you were to meet me, and the moment I walked away you told Des you were changing the location.

'You deliberately countermanded my order. You had no authority to do so, and on top of that you jeopardized the lives of the people in my vehicle. If there had been a contact and a split, we would have gone to a completely different location from everyone else.'

Pat said nothing.

'I've had enough of you and your negative attitude,' I went on. 'You're out of this location on the resupply helicopter tonight.'

He was shocked, so stunned that he couldn't say a word. He knew, though, that he was completely in the wrong. Without a word he just turned away and walked slowly back to his vehicle with his head down. He looked utterly dejected, but I didn't feel the slightest pity for him. I was still fuming. Not just because he had ignored my order, or even because he had put my life at risk, but because he had risked the lives of Mugger and Harry.

Having dealt with Pat I went back, found Des and took him on one side.

'All right,' I demanded, 'I want to know why you didn't tell me that Pat had changed the RV location.'

'I'm sorry, it was my fault,' he said. 'But I was between a rock and a hard place. Pat's senior to me. It's as simple as that.'

And of course, it was – the damned seniority system. In the Regiment we have a kind of batting order among people of the same rank. This is based on the date at which a man was promoted, and everyone knows where they stand in this order, just as batsmen do in a cricket team. You can have six guys who are all staff sergeants, but each one knows who is senior to him – and who is junior. It doesn't take a genius to work out whether someone was promoted before you were. Everyone knows this is how things work, and everyone accepts it. The Regiment is a very small one, and that's the way it has always operated.

Des had naively thought that Pat's change would make no difference. And had I not asked for the lat. and long., or if we had arrived at the location and Pat had been there, I would never have known about the switch, since I would not otherwise have checked the coordinates.

There was no point in chewing Des out further. I simply told him, 'If anyone countermands any of my orders in future, I want you to tell me the moment it happens. No matter who it is, or how senior he is. This time we were lucky and nobody got hurt. I don't want there to be a next time.'

I went back to the convoy and told the men to get aboard their vehicles. Then I walked over to Pat's Land Rover.

'Okay,' I told him. 'I trust you picked out a decent landing site last night. We should have plenty of time to get there before midnight. Even so, let's get moving.'

Whatever his other failings, Pat was still the best navigator we had. He just lacked the qualities I needed. It was obvious, too, that he didn't like me or the way I ran things. Later I was told that he thought me much too laid-back to command a patrol behind enemy lines and bring it home safely.

I will admit that that's the impression I like to project. It's both my nature and the way I operate. Faced with a choice I will always go for positive action, but I would never risk people's lives unnecessarily. Nevertheless, the SAS is a regiment whose motto is 'Who dares wins', and that's what our job is all about – going forward and actually trying to achieve a mission or a goal. Pat seems to have found me a bit too blasé, even careless; I found that he lacked what I was looking for in a 2IC to drive the patrol on to complete its tasks.

The distance to the landing site was only thirty kilometres, and we should have been there well before midnight – giving us a couple of hours in which to make the site secure before the chopper came in – if Yorky hadn't driven Pat's Land Rover over the edge of a sheer drop into a ravine, something which, in those conditions, can happen to anyone. How nobody was killed or badly injured God only knows, for the 110 dropped about six or seven feet and then rolled over, landing upside-down in the ravine. I think the three of them were saved by the roll bar, which took the main force of the crash, but they had all suffered some hard knocks and were badly shaken up. All the fuel had spilled out of the vehicle's tank, and ammunition, fuel cans, weapons, equipment and rations were scattered along the bottom of the ravine.

It took us nearly an hour and a half to get the Land Rover out, but we were forced to work with great care so as not to cause any sparks that might ignite the fuel. Eventually we managed to winch the thing upright, hook it up to the Unimog and drag it backwards out of the ravine.

They were amazing vehicles, those Land Rovers. We refuelled Pat's battered 110 once it had been checked over and it started first time. In fact, in our whole time in the field, during which we covered thousands of kilometres over some appalling terrain, we didn't experience a problem with any of them. I would endorse Land Rover's product any time.

Pat and his crew were so badly shocked that I actually relented in my decision to ship him out. Pulling him to one side, I told him that I had decided to give him one last chance. But, I added, he had received his final warning. I think he appreciated it. He damned well ought to have done, charity not coming high up on any RSM's list of priorities, least of all mine. He mumbled some kind of a thank you, though he was still pretty shaken from the accident. By some miracle Yorky was also unhurt and, to his credit, declared himself fit enough to drive. We were able to resume our journey in our earlier formation, delayed but still more or less in one piece.

In the event we arrived at the landing site with a good two hours to spare before the rendezvous, set for 0200, and immediately set about securing the area. We had to make sure it was completely sterile – free of the enemy and of any civilians – and this was done by sending out patrols for several kilometres around. If there was no sign of the enemy we would arrange the vehicles in defensive pickets around the site, and station members of the patrol in the centre to guide the helicopter in. Since we had to maintain complete radio silence, the pilot wouldn't land if he didn't get the correct signal from the ground.

Right on time the Chinook came clattering in, flying just thirty feet above the ground. It made a sweeping pass overhead, turned within a hundred metres and landed, noisily but gracefully enough, exactly where planned. Dust blew up in great clouds from the downdraught and the noise was horrendous, since the engines were kept running.

The first person I saw when the tail ramp came down was the load master, and I went forward beneath the spinning rotors to greet him. Then I handed him a confidential report I had written to the CO, explaining the situation with Alpha One Zero. Some things I couldn't trust to the airwaves. In that report, after giving the CO my appraisal of the men I urged him under no circumstances to consider splitting the unit into two patrols. I'd heard over the radio that one Delta half-squadron had split, but I felt that we would be a more effective fighting force if Alpha One Zero remained intact, not least because Pat's way of operating gave me cause for concern. It was imperative they remain together under my command until we quit Iraq.

While I had been talking to the load master another man had disembarked, carrying an M16 and a bergen. This must be my new 2IC. Having safely handed over my report I turned to the newcomer and we shook hands. I still didn't know who he was, but I yelled in his ear for him to follow me away from the noise of the engines. As we moved off my men clambered aboard the Chinook and began rolling everything off. The helicopter had already resupplied other patrols on that run, and the fact that we were the last unit to be resupplied on that flight meant everything left aboard was intended for us, which made the unloading simple.

When we were a couple of hundred metres from the helicopter the new arrival set his bergen down and put out his hand again.

'I'm Major Peter,' he said. 'It's a pleasure to meet you, Billy.'

I took a moment to look him over carefully. He was in his early thirties, about five feet nine inches tall, stocky, with a thick mop of fairish hair and a steady, confident gaze. He seemed like a nice guy. This was the first time we had met, for he had been on a staff posting in Riyadh and our paths hadn't crossed during the couple of days when I had been there. When the previous patrol commander had been pulled out Peter had been designated as his replacement. He was not due to take over as OC A Squadron until November, but the CO thought that sending him in to join us for a few weeks would give him a chance to meet half his squadron and set him on a very good learning curve. A very steep learning curve, if you had asked me, but I was confident the CO knew what he was doing.

I quickly brought Peter up to date on the mission so far, and briefed him on my future intentions. For a couple of days I had been mulling over an idea in my mind, and while waiting for the helicopter had finally decided to go ahead with it. I intended to start moving during the day as well as at night, and to carry out operations in daylight, where that was possible. There was no hesitation from my new 2IC – he was in full agreement. 'It'll give us a chance to see what the enemy is up to,' he said. 'I'm all for it.'

I warmed to him even more a few moments later when he produced a familiar-looking bottle from under his coat. 'This is for you,' he said, glancing around to make sure no one else was watching. 'I feel as though I shouldn't be giving it to you, in view of the CO's orders, but I'm told it's purely for medicinal use.'

I laughed. 'Give the thing here,' I said, taking the bottle of dark rum, 'it will come in very useful. A little tot in hot chocolate or coffee will do wonders for the guys' morale.' Then a thought struck me.

'Where's the rest of it?' I asked. I had put in for half a dozen bottles.

'That's it,' he told me. 'I only brought the one bottle.'

Well, there goes the guys' morale booster, I told myself. I was damned if I was going to share the one bottle around. It was going to stay in my pack and provide an occasional solo nightcap in the days to come.

By this time everything had been unloaded from the helicopter, including a replacement motorcycle for one that had packed up, and I went down and gave the load master the all-clear to pull out. Within forty-five minutes of the Chinook clattering off into the night sky the vehicles' tanks and all the jerry cans had been replenished with fuel, and we had our maximum supply of water stowed aboard. As usual we had a lot of fuel left over in the burmoils that the chopper had brought, but I knew from earlier experience in the Middle East that if it was left where it was then the bedouin would eventually find and make use of it. They weren't our enemies, however, so good luck to them.

Our other cast-offs, mainly the cardboard boxes that had contained our ration packs, were all placed in a pile and set on fire the following morning. I wanted to make as much smoke as I could so as to attract a little attention to ourselves in an attempt to draw out the enemy. The Union jacks were spread out as usual, so that friendly pilots could identify us from the air as British if, attracted by the smoke and flames, they flew by for a closer look. A few of the lads got a bit nervy about giving away our position, and once again wanted to know what would happen if we attracted enemy tanks.

'Then we call in the RAF,' I explained to them. 'We're on a plateau and can see one hell of a long way. A tank doesn't just appear out of nowhere. It blows up a great cloud of dust which can be seen twenty miles away. Just relax. Settle down and enjoy the fresh grub.'

It was a real treat to have fresh fruit and vegetables – and even meat – again, although we knew we'd be back on the rations soon enough. I had noticed that I had already begun to lose weight. A different way to diet, perhaps, but very effective.

I decided that the patrol would stay put that day, which would allow the men to cook themselves a couple of decent meals and catch up on a bit of personal maintenance. Just after midday, however, we received orders from Al Jouf that we were to try to find them a usable airstrip somewhere in our territory, and safe from prying Iraqi eyes. In the coming month, February, we would be without moonlight from the 14th to the 20th, which meant that the helicopters would not be flying and so would not be able to resupply us. Someone at HQ had suggested, as an alternative which had been backed by the CO, that a C-130 fly in at night to make the resupply. In other words, an aircraft 30 metres long with a wingspan of more than 40 metres and weighing, when fully loaded, over 75 tons, would put down in absolute blackness on an unknown airstrip 200 miles behind enemy lines.

The RAF pilots in 47 Squadron* really were brilliant flyers, all of them. Most were former fighter pilots who had flown Harriers, Tornados, Jaguars, Buccaneers and the like before being switched to the Special Forces flights because of minor medical problems or something equally trivial. They and their aircrew were a great bunch of guys; they were also extremely brave men. Give them a short, narrow strip of barely level ground and these characters would set a Hercules down on it. I have never encountered their like anywhere. They would fly in at almost zero altitude and land these huge monsters on grass, gravel, mudflats, even a frozen lake – anything that was just long enough and wide enough, and more or less level.

For night flights we would mark the runway ourselves. We would set markers at each end and in the middle of the runway – that was all these pilots needed to set down in the middle of nowhere, unload or collect men or gear, turn round and get back in the air.

That evening I took part of my group on a recce north-west of our location and sent Pat with part of his group to the north-east. Our task was to find a suitable landing strip for the C-130 and, if we were lucky enough to locate one, to try to pinpoint and assess any enemy activity in the area. It must have been our lucky night, because after some twenty

* The RAF squadrons operating Special Forces flights are Nos 7 and 47, the former operating Chinooks, the latter C-130s.

kilometres we came across a disused airfield; better still, it wasn't even marked on the map. Like dozens of others, it had probably been built during the Iran-Iraq War and then abandoned after the armistice.

It was a clear night with barely a cloud in the sky, and even though there was only a slight moon it was very light. The scrub-grass runway was sharply etched by the moonlight, looking for all the world like a worn, pea-green carpet. Peter and I walked its length to check that it was still level and free of any craters, then sat on the centre line to have a cigarette.

'If you think about it,' he said after we'd smoked in silence for a while, grinning across at me, 'this is really quite bizarre. Here we are, sitting in the middle of a grass runway, in the middle of Iraq, having a fag. There's nobody here who gives a damn, or who is going to stop us or check our passports. It's quite surreal, actually – but it gives me a damned good feeling.' I could see what he meant, although being in strange situations in remote places is so much a part of SAS life that I probably wouldn't have even thought about it if he hadn't said something.

In the early hours of the next morning, having caught a fascinating glimpse of the new motorway, still under construction, which would soon replace the main supply route out of Amman, we returned to our LUP, where I'd left half our force with the Unimog and some of the Land Rovers. We waited for Pat to return. He was back just before dawn, reporting that his unit had found only one possible landing strip, which would in any case need a certain amount of clearing.

The disused airfield seemed our best bet, and I therefore radioed headquarters to give them the exact coordinates, which would then be passed to the C-130 pilots. Once that minor task was out of the way I could give time to planning our way forward. I intended to move north again that night, 5 February, and take up position near the main supply route so we could begin observing the enemy's movements along it – including, I hoped, movements of mobile Scud missile launchers.

The morning of the 6th found us in position close to MSR3. It was drizzling and bitterly cold. Around us the desert was a dun and dirty grey, studded with low black hills and huge grey boulders. It looked and felt fiercely inhospitable. Early that afternoon, while I was trying to catch up on some sleep under the Land Rover, I found myself being shaken awake by Harry, my radio operator.

'Sorry to wake you, Boss, but it's your call sign coming in from HQ. They have an immediate signal for you.'

'Probably only routine,' I groaned, rolling from under the vehicle and staggering to my feet.

But the message, when I had finished decoding it, proved to be not at all what I had expected.

Alpha One Zero was ordered to penetrate and destroy a microwave Scud-control station known as Victor Two, the mission to be carried out by no later than 0600 on Friday morning, 8 February – just under thirty-nine hours away. We had to take out the major switching gear and fibre-optic cables contained in a fortified underground bunker. The control station, situated right on the MSR, was in a key staging area used by civilian convoys, and was defended by a minimal enemy force of about thirty soldiers, according to the signal.

All of a sudden we were going in at the sharp end. Just from the sparse information I had been given in that first order I knew we were being sent into action.

Chapter Twenty

I had a gut feeling from the very outset that we would be walking into a heavily defended location, from which perhaps not all of us could expect to walk away.

It was almost certain that we were being sent into a situation that must result in a firefight. Even from the few details I had received so far, it was plain to me that Intelligence was only guessing at the enemy's strength. Indeed, I was also very dubious about their estimate of the number of enemy troops we were likely to encounter. Right from the start I realized that the figure thirty, which so conveniently matched our own strength, somehow failed to emit that much desired – and hoped for – ring of truth.

For obvious reasons we would try to make this a covert operation, which meant we'd be going in at night, but if the target was defended by the enemy in any great numbers, then the chances were that the mission would 'go noisy' on us – our euphemism for all hell breaking loose – before we could even get the explosive charges into position. Furthermore, no matter how difficult sneaking in might prove, getting out again promised to be even more of a nightmare.

I already had a number of burning questions buzzing around in my head, all of which needed answering before I could plan the mission with any accuracy. It was certain, too, that there were a few more I hadn't even thought of yet. I therefore decided that this was one of those rare occasions when several minds were better than one. I called Mugger over and told him to seek out Major Peter, Pat and Des and have them rendezvous at my wagon in ten minutes.

Meanwhile I brewed myself a strong mug of tea, carefully rolled a cigarette and sat in the sunshine with my back against one of the Land Rover's rear wheels. After a few minutes the others drifted over and I suggested they sit down facing me. When they were all settled I took a long swallow of my tea, looked at each of them in turn and announced, 'We've had a signal giving us a target – known as Victor Two – which HQ want taken out. According to them it's a microwave station which is only lightly defended. There's a civilian parking lot near by but no major enemy presence.

'I've signalled Al Jouf that I want a direct satcom voice link with the ops officer in half an hour so I can get some more info. I've already come up with a bunch of questions myself, but if you three can think of any others then let's hear from you. The more we know, the better prepared we can be.

'Which, of course, doesn't mean a dicky bird if they don't actually know anything else. In fact, let's face it – they could come back with a "don't-know" response to all our questions, leaving us with just the info we can pick up ourselves.

'But there is a deadline on this one. They want us to complete the mission by zero six hundred hours on Friday.'

That grabbed their attention and gave them something to chew on, and for the next twenty minutes or so we sat by my vehicle weighing up the pros and cons. By the time the satcom link was established and Harry had called me over, the four of us had come up with a dozen very relevant questions. I was told by the ops officer, however, that most of our queries – particularly those concerning the enemy's strength and their deployment, for which we were most eager to get replies – could not be answered until the following day.

What Intel could tell us was that the main target – a bunker about forty metres square – was completely surrounded by an eight-foot-high wall of prefabricated concrete slabs slotted into concrete posts. Between this wall and the target bunker was a six-foot-high intermediate chain-link fence. Having reached the main building we would find steps leading down to three underground rooms, one of which contained the vital switching gear. Just behind the bunker was the secondary target, a 250-foot-high mast. About a quarter-kilometre south-east of the military installation was a lorry park, which was used by civilian drivers as a night stop.

And that, apparently, just about covered all the information the ops officer back in Al Jouf could give us. Having made an arrangement to speak with him again at the same time the following day, I replaced the radio handset. Then I turned to face the other three and repeated all the details given in the ops officer's briefing. They were silent for a moment; then Pat said, 'If the stuff we've got to destroy is in one of three rooms, how the hell will we know which one? Does anyone know what communications switching gear looks like?'

The others looked as blank as I did. Time to take a hand, I decided.

'OK, let's not worry ourselves about that,' I told them, far more cheerfully than I was actually feeling. 'We'll blow up all three rooms to make quite sure we've got the right one. The tricky bit is going to be the getting in and the getting out. Compared with that, the demolition side of it is a complete doddle.' I paused to let this sink in, then went on, 'I want a bit of time to myself to work out a plan, but let's meet back here in one hour. Meanwhile,' I added, 'let's try to build ourselves a model of the target.'

As they dispersed back to their vehicles I wandered off about twenty yards from the Land Rover until I found a rock to lean against. Sitting down, I rolled myself another cigarette and turned my mind to the coming operation.

From the location HQ had given me, Victor Two was situated about ten kilometres north of the new motorway being constructed to the south of the main supply route from Jordan, and which we had stumbled across on our way back from the airstrip recce the night before. This put the target about thirty-five kilometres from our LUP.

Our first problem was how to cross the motorway. It was most probably of British design and construction and, just like the motorways at home, consisted of three lanes each way with crash barriers lining both sides of a central reservation. According to Intelligence, the road needed only the finishing touches before its official opening.

Once over the motorway our next major hurdle, other than approaching the target without being spotted and challenged, would be making our way through the wall and fence protecting the main bunker. I worked out that the only way the demolition team could successfully breach the target was by blowing a way through both obstacles with instantaneous shaped charges, then rushing through the gaps and heading straight down the steps. Once below ground we could use similar charges to remove the doors, if any, to the three rooms, and place charges with two-minute fuses in each of them. The team would then make a dash back to the main group, which would be laying down supporting fire and otherwise responding to any enemy threat that might arise.

The mission was already exhibiting signs of being difficult, even dangerous, but certainly not impossible. I decided I could do the actual job with just three demolitionists, with two men assigned to each both to help carry the gear and to cover them. That meant just nine men in all for the most dangerous part of the operation. I would be one of them, while the remainder of the half-squadron would act as fire support and provide any additional backup that might become necessary after the primary task had been completed.

Having mentally sketched out the bare plan, I returned to the Land Rover and summoned all the senior NCOs and Major Peter and Captain Timothy. When they had all arrived I outlined the plan to them. 'The final details depend a lot on the recce I want carried out tonight, and on the one I intend to lead myself just before the actual job,' I told them. 'But essentially that's it.

'It's certainly not going to be easy,' I continued. 'I expect there to be guards on duty, and other additional troops floating around. In fact, I think we can take that as almost certain. But it's just as certain that HQ want this little task carried out by zero-six-hundred Friday.'

Although details on the target were still sketchy, the others had managed to put together a model based on the little information we had and on what we could gather of the target area from our own maps. We had no photographs or imagery of any kind – what wouldn't I have given just then for a portable fax machine – so we had to try to picture the target using the bare description we had been given over the radio, and from that build a very basic model. Between them the guys had come up with a selection of objects – some of the hexamine blocks, the white, one-and-a-half-inch cubes of solid fuel we used in our cooking stoves; small squared-off stones; sweets; cigarette packets; odd scraps of wood; matches; even some buttons – out of which to fashion a model. It may seem strange, but if you give the guys a look at even a crappy model before they attack a target, it boosts their confidence tremendously. They feel they have a far better working knowledge of what they're getting into, and as a result are much more assured about the tasks that face them.

We knew that the base lay on the north side of an east-west road – MSR 3, soon to be superseded by the new motorway – and that fifty yards east of the main bunker and mast another road led off at right angles to the first, running towards the south. It would be alongside this north-south road that we would be making our approach. Having scraped the outlines and the relative positions of the two roads on a flat, sandy surface the guys had found conveniently near my Land Rover, they had created a square model of a building with a mast just behind it and ringed by both a fence and a wall. Squatting down by the model, I took them through the plan detail by detail.

'The attacking unit will cross the east-west road directly in front of the target building,' I told them, pointing the way with a stick. 'The main fire-support group – at least half our total force – will be positioned south-west of the junction where the north-south road joins the first one. The rest of the men will be given their positions nearer the time – when, I hope, we know a bit more.

'The reason we should know a bit more is because Pat and Serious here are going out tonight with their section to do a recce of the motorway and locate a decent crossing point.'

'When do we leave?' asked Pat.

'Just before last light. We went that way last night and the going was good. It's about thirty kilometres maximum to the motorway. Your job is to find us a place to cross, either underneath the roadway through one of the culverts, or across the middle where there's a break in the crash barriers.' Both NCOs nodded, and I continued, 'There was no military presence there last night; in fact, there wasn't a sign of anyone at all. It was like a ghost motorway. Even so, what I don't want is you drawing any attention to yourselves or, worse, getting compromised.'

Our briefing ended, and it was a thoughtful group of NCOs who made their separate ways back to their own Land Rovers. Oddly enough, though, I was the one who felt uneasy, and for all the time that Pat's unit was gone I found myself unable to relax. I was usually good at waiting, but now I had an uncomfortable feeling that the target wasn't all that it seemed; that there was a lot more to it than I was being given by HQ. Throughout the night my gut feeling, and the knowledge that the main target was on a major junction, told me that we were in for an interesting time, to say the least. There was one thing I was certain about – we were going in come what may. Even so, I was standing on the edge of our LUP, waiting, when Pat and his recce group arrived back. I hadn't been anxious about their safety because, having been in the area they'd just visited the night before, I knew that there was no Iraqi military presence there. But I wanted to have their intel – indeed, I needed it urgently.

It was about 0630, just on first light, when the vehicles returned. I walked over to Pat's wagon and immediately asked him, 'How was it?'

'There's no simple way across the motorway,' he told me.

'Does that mean we can cross, or that we can't cross?' I pressed him.

'Well,' he said, looking at me hard, 'you could probably cross under a culvert, but it would be a tight squeeze. Plus you wouldn't get the Unimog through, and if you came back the same way you'd have it all to do again.'

'Did you go into a culvert to check the ground?'

'I'm sorry, I didn't check,' he confessed. 'Time was against us. But further down the road we found a gap in the central crash barriers.

There's a continuous concrete-sided storm drain or open culvert running right along the central reservation between the two carriage-ways, about three feet wide and four feet deep. If we could get across there, at the gap, then right opposite is a service station, which didn't appear to be manned. Though it could be used at any time by the Iraqis as a military base,' he added.

'Forget about that,' I told him. 'Tell me about getting across.'

Pat had obviously given the matter some careful thought. 'Well, as I said, it won't be that easy. But if each vehicle carried two sandbags inside the spare tyre on the bonnet, then when we get to the gap in the barriers we could fill in the central culvert with the sandbags, lay a couple of sand channels down on them and drive across.'

I thought for a moment, trying to visualize the site. Off the top of my head I couldn't see any obvious problem with the plan.

'That's a good idea, Pat,' I said. 'We'll do it that way.'

From the look on his face, however, my approval didn't please him one little bit.

'Me and some of the guys think you should call the whole thing off,' he said sheepishly. 'It's an impossible mission.'

'Forget it,' I said. 'No mission is impossible. We're going. Now get some kip. We're leaving tonight at seventeen-thirty, and I'll be holding an O-group at fifteen-thirty.'

It worried me that some of the men might not be fully committed to our task, but I still reckoned that the majority would be hoping to be given key roles, and to be put in the thick of the action when the time came. After all, this is what we had spent so many years training for. It was why we were in the army and not pushing pencils in a bank, or doing something equally ordinary. Above all, it was why we were in the SAS, and not in some other regiment or corps. I only hoped that when it came to it none of them would let me – or their mates – down. For the time being, however, I had to put all that out of my mind and get on the radio. I had to find out what further intelligence I could squeeze out of HQ.

In the event it wasn't much. I was told by the ops officer that we could expect to find only three or four Iraqi technicians on duty in the middle of the night, and Intel reckoned no more than a couple of dozen troops would have been assigned to protecting the relay station. But whether this was based on fact or just inspired guesswork, HQ wasn't saying. To me, it sounded much too good to be true, and I felt the sharp teeth of suspicion and foreboding gnawing away at my innards. Even the photos taken by the high-flying American spy planes must have told them more than this. Yet if they did know any more, then for reasons best known to themselves they were not letting us in on it.

Not that I would have approached the problem any differently. With the force at my disposal I didn't have many options. I had only thirty-four guys, and whether it turned out to be thirty against thirty or thirty against three hundred, I wouldn't – indeed, couldn't – have changed things. We still had to go in. It would just have been nice knowing, that's all. I brooded on all this as the day wore on, until, at 1530 hours, I gathered the entire half-squadron around me for orders.

In giving military orders for an operation, the commander talks about the intelligence, the ground, the execution and the general outline. It didn't take long to cover the intelligence. We knew where and what the target was, and had an estimate of the enemy strength. The ground took little longer. I explained our model and where the target stood in relation to the motorway, then told them that it was my intention to lead a final recce – a CTR or close-target recce – to the edge of the target just before we went in, and that the intelligence we gathered from this would be given out at the last moment before the attack. In the meantime we would travel in single-file convoy to the motorway, locate the gap in the crash barriers on the central reservation, and use sandbags and sand channels to bridge the central storm drain. We would then move to within a kilometre of the target.

In the first stage of the attack I would enter the target building with three demolitionists and five other men, so that each demolition man would have two men to cover him and help carry the explosives. The rest of the patrol would be deployed to give fire support, or on other tasks which I would detail later.

I had already decided to take Mugger with me on the final recce. As the lead demolitionist I wanted him to have an advance look at the target. Des would also be on the team, as would Ken, who was to be second demolitionist. He could help Mugger work out beforehand what explosives they would need. I left the choice of the final recce-team member to Pat, who knew the men far better than I. I did ask him, though, who was our best man on the spy glass, an extremely compact thermal-imaging device used mainly for night reconnaissance, which allows you to identify objects, and especially people, at night or in poor visibility by producing an image of anything that is a heat source.

Pat considered for a moment or two, and then replied, 'Yorky's your man. He's the best we've got.'

'Okay Yorky,' I said, looking towards the large figure of Pat's driver where he stood in the loose circle of men surrounding our model, 'you'll be on the recce with me tonight.'

Just before I dismissed the men I told them to check over their weapons, spare ammunition and vehicles and be ready to move out at 1730. Everything else, including surface-to-air missiles (we were carrying Stingers with us) and spare fuel and water, would be left in, or stacked alongside the Unimog which, having first been boobytrapped and camouflaged, would remain otherwise undefended at the LUP.

While Mugger and Harry did the checks on our wagon and transferred additional ammunition from the Unimog, I radioed HQ for the last time before we went into action. I informed them of my intentions for the night ahead, and advised them not to expect further radio contact until after we had completed the operation.

At exactly 1730 hours our convoy – eight Land Rovers led by Pat 's vehicle and accompanied by all three bikes – pulled out of the LUP, leaving the Unimog under its cam net. Anyone who tried to mess with it was going to get a horrible shock in the fraction of a second before he was atomized. We headed northwards in the gathering twilight, and I don't suppose there was a single one of us who didn't reflect on the night ahead, and whether he'd see the dawn.

Some hours and about thirty kilometres later we reached the deserted motorway and began searching for the gap in the central reservation that Pat and his team had spotted the night before. Having found the right place, we packed the sandbags in place in the storm drain, unhooked the metal sand channels from the sides of two Land Rovers, and carefully arranged them in position on top before slowly driving across to the north carriageway. I ordered the guys to leave the sandbags in position, so we could beat a fast retreat if we had to, and we began the last leg of our journey to the target. When we were approximately a thousand metres short of it Pat stopped, as he had been briefed to do, and I closed in on his vehicle. From here I would take my team – Mugger, Des, Ken and Yorky – forward on foot for the CTR. The rest of the guys were to stay with the vehicles until they heard from me or until I got back. I would give my final confirmatory orders after the recce.

We had pulled up about thirty metres west of the roadway – a main supply route linking MSR3 with the town of Nukhayb – that ran north to its junction with the east-west road fronting the target building and mast. To our left, some thirty metres further west and running parallel with the road on our right, was a massive berm about ten feet high.

Slow going meant that we were already behind schedule, and the moon was well over the horizon and rising. It was less than a quarter full, but as bad luck would have it we had been granted a clear night for our mission, and there was already quite a lot of light. We could see the road and the berm quite clearly – a pity, since I had hoped to launch our attack before the moon came up.

I checked my team. There were Ken, Des and Mugger, and finally Yorky, coming round the side of Pat's wagon. Everyone except me was wearing a steel helmet, which we call a pot. I find them cumbersome and have never felt comfortable wearing one. Perhaps this was not a good example to the other men, but it was my head and I preferred to leave it bare.

In his big steel pot, Yorky, all six feet three inches of him, looked rather like an understudy for one of the Flowerpot Men. He was wearing a flak jacket, which is supposed to stop shrapnel and at least to slow a 7.62 round, tightly buttoned to the top, and over this he had his belt kit, with full yokes and extra pouches, as well as bandoliers of extra ammunition criss-crossed from his shoulders. His weapon, an M16, was across his back on a sling, and the spy glass hung from a cord around his neck.

On a recce, and especially a CTR, it is vital that you should be able to move stealthily, quickly and with the least possible noise. The rest of us were in light order, which is ordinary desert gear with sleeves rolled down, standard belt kit and our weapons. Yorky, however, reminded me of one of those one-man-band buskers you used to see in London, hung about with drums and cymbals and trumpet, and other instruments as well. It was too late to tell him to change, but I remember thinking at the time that I was probably going to have problems with this one. For now, though, we had to get moving, so I pointed north to where, in the moonlight, we could make out the mast and said, 'OK, Yorky, off you go.'

He looked shocked. 'What? Me? At the front?'

'Well, you'll be no fucking good with that spy glass in the rear,' I replied. 'Of course you go in front. Now get going, we're late.'

It was obvious to me and the rest of the party that Yorky was not exactly overjoyed at being given the honour of leading, but it was equally obvious that he couldn't think of a good excuse to get out of it. After a few tense moments he led off slowly in the direction of where the main target ought to be, beneath the huge, skywards-pointing finger of the mast. I followed on, three or four metres behind, with the others strung out behind me at similar intervals.

However, we had only gone about fifty metres when, without a word of warning, Yorky suddenly dived full length on the ground. I walked up and, looking down at him curiously, said, 'What's wrong?'

'There's an enemy bunker about fifty metres ahead of us,' he answered in a loud stage whisper.

'Is it manned?' The spy glass ought to tell him this, since it can detect heat signatures from bodies even through a wall.

'No – at least, I don't think so.'

Our CTR, already delayed, was in danger of becoming a farce. I kicked him quite sharply on the ankle and said, 'In that case get on your feet and keep moving.'

By the time we had covered another hundred metres we could visually identify the target building. Behind it the lights showed like pinpricks over a considerable area, almost the size of a small town, and, just beyond the main supply road, the relay block and steel mast were etched in silver moonlight. To the right of these buildings and on our – southern – side of the supply road was a large enemy bunker, built mainly of sandbags and timber, which looked to have been constructed by proper engineers rather than ordinary Iraqi soldiers. Through the slits in its sides we could see, outlined against the bright interior lights, a good deal of movement. It was clearly manned, and probably in some numbers.

As we stood watching a large vehicle, which seemed to be brightly lit from front to rear, drove along the main road from the east and passed in front of the relay station and mast before turning south, towards us, on the road to our right. Although it was still some eight hundred metres away Yorky again dived full length to the ground.

'Now what's wrong?' I asked. What little patience I'd had with him was rapidly wearing thin.

'Vehicle, vehicle, vehicle!' he replied.

'I can see the fucking vehicle,' I said.

I slowly sank down until I was on one knee. You always get down very slowly in white light and keep one eye closed so that at least the night vision in that eye won't be wrecked. That way you can take a look at whatever it is that passes without being seen and without throwing any shadows. Behind me, the other three had also slowly crouched down.

As the vehicle drew closer I began to recognize the shape. It was a coach with all its interior lights switched on, as well as its headlights. The driver appeared to be the only person aboard. It was probably a very wise move to have all the lights on, since any Allied pilot who saw it would be unlikely to think that it posed a threat; no Iraqi military vehicle would dare drive along at night lit up like a Christmas tree.

As it drew level we could see that it was a brand-new luxury coach, of the type that football teams take to their away games and which, as a kid, I had used to call a 'charabanc'. It was not until 1996 that I heard General de la Billière explain that the Iraqis had used this kind of coach to transport Scud missiles. At the time, however, we had no idea, but I now realize that the driver must have been collecting or moving a Scud that night. In any case, with what we already had on our plate there wasn't very much we could have done about it, even had we known it was carrying half a dozen of the missiles.

When the coach had thundered on past us – with not so much as a glance in our direction from the driver – I told Yorky to get up and carry on towards the target. We were about five hundred metres from it when he dived to the ground yet again. I turned to Des, who was immediately behind me, and said, 'Is this guy for real, or what?'

Des just shrugged his shoulders and smiled. My problem, he seemed to be indicating. My patience was exhausted, however. 'What the fuck's wrong now, Yorky?' I demanded.

'An enemy bunker!' His voice came out as a sort of croak.

'Where?'

'To the left,' he said, pointing.

'Is it manned?' Since the spy glass worked by thermal imagery, he should have been able to tell me that.

'I don't know,' he said. 'And before you ask, I'm not fucking looking.'

I walked past him and took a careful look around the scrub and rocks that partly screened the enemy position. There was an L-shaped dugout bunker ahead, but it was in complete darkness. I edged forward as quietly as possible until I was able to see over the low sandbagged wall. The bunker was obviously well built, probably by engineers. It was empty. That did it. What was the point of having an expert with a thermal-imaging device if, in the end, you had to go and find out for yourself using the MkI eyeball?

I returned to the corner and motioned with my arm for Mugger, who was behind Des, to come forward. As he came up I told him, 'I want you to take this clown' – indicating Yorky – 'back to where the others are waiting. Then tell them that I want all the vehicles and the rest of the half-squadron down here in half an hour.'

As soon as they had gone I led the other pair to the bunker. From there we had a good view not only of the main target but also of what appeared to be, from the dark shapes and dozens of lights, some kind of encampment about half a kilometre further north. It was clearly military, and it was equally clearly manned. So much for there being only thirty or so Iraqi soldiers at the location. Every few minutes the impression was strengthening that this target was going to be a sight more difficult to crack than I'd first imagined when I got the brief over the radio. For now, however, I would have to take into account the enemy dispositions we had so far discovered during the recce.

'I'm going to sit here and work on our plan,' I told Des and Ken. 'Meanwhile I want you two to go forward another couple of hundred metres and see if there are any more nasty surprises for us down there. Don't worry about the camp to the north. By the time those guys get involved, we'll either be out of there, or never going to come out.

'And for God's sake don't take any chances and get compromised. Just take a good look and then rejoin me back here.'

'OK, Billy,' they chorused, grinning like a pair of Cheshire cats. Then they slipped out of the bunker and were gone. These were exactly the sort of guys I wanted for that kind of patrol – stable, positive and reliable, they were also first-class soldiers. The right stuff, if ever there was any.

If the rest of the men had all been like Des and Ken I wouldn't have been feeling so anxious. I had serious doubts about Yorky, however, who had become erratic in his behaviour to the point of being a liability. Not something I would have expected from an SAS soldier. To add to the problem, I also believed that most of the others were expecting me to call the mission off now that we were within the target area and could see the size of the problem.

Certainly we were heavily outnumbered, and possibly outgunned as well. I knew that, ideally, I could have done with the whole Regiment to handle this attack, instead of just thirty-four of us – a number that included the few doubtful types who thought the whole mission was suicidal. But we also knew that there was no chance whatever of reinforcements streaming down the slope, like the US Cavalry in Western movies, to join us if things started going wrong. I had no other choice than to make the most of what I'd been given. None the less, I remained certain of my objective: this mission was going ahead as ordered. Calling it off was simply not an option.

Sitting down in the empty bunker, I covertly cupped a cigarette in my hands and sucked the smoke deep into my lungs as I turned over the problems we faced. One thing that would have to be taken out straight away if things went noisy was the large manned bunker ahead of us and to the right of the target. The best way to achieve that was with a Milan anti-tank missile. These weapons are extremely effective not only against armour but also against fixed defences. All the operator has to do is to keep the target in his sights after launch and the missile is guided through a trailing-wire system, which stays with it until impact. The launcher had to be at least 400 metres away from the target, so if we moved up one of the Milan-carrying wagons to close to where I was sitting, it would be perfectly placed to take out the bunker.

Having decided this, I went outside, and was studying the relay building through my ordinary night glasses when Des and Ken came back. I asked for an immediate report on what they had seen.

'Well, apart from the bunker which we know about on the right, there is another, identical one, on the left,' said Des. 'The end of the berm is obscuring our view from here but it's about fifty metres west of the road junction, on the far side of the main supply route.'

As 'Spence' might have said, this was getting serious. I hadn't catered for having to take out two bunkers in my revised plan. After a moment's thought I asked Des and Ken, 'If we set up a team in front of the relay block on this side of the road will they be able to take out the left-hand bunker with a LAW 80?'

Both men nodded enthusiastically. 'Sure thing, Billy,' said Des. Ken chipped in with, 'Perfect – that'll make their eyes water.' It would, too. The LAW 80 is a single-shot, rocket propelled anti-tank weapon with a discardable launcher tube. It packs a tremendous wallop and has the advantage of being man portable; it is not guided, however, so the firer has to get close enough to be sure of his aim.

'But there are also two vehicles that need to be covered,' Des added. 'They're military-type trucks, three-tonners with canvas backs. They're sitting on the other side of the road right in front of the target.'

'Anybody in them?' I asked.

'Don't know. We couldn't see from where we were. But there could be.'

Having registered this as yet another potential problem, I looked at my watch. It was already more than half an hour since I had sent Mugger back for the others and I still couldn't hear the vehicles. Where the hell were they?

Five minutes later I heard footsteps, then made out the dark shapes of men coming towards us. The three of us knelt by the bunker entrance and slipped the safety catches off our M16s. The adrenalin surged through my body like a shot from a hypodermic and all my senses went on full alert. I wasn't expecting the enemy to approach from this direction but you could never be sure – or too careful.

Then I heard Mugger's voice calling me in a loud whisper and lowered my weapon. In a few more strides he was standing in front of me with Pat beside him.

'Where are the vehicles?' I asked.

'We could see a big enemy bunker down near the target and thought it might be risky to bring the wagons any closer,' said Pat.

I could hardly believe it; indeed, for a moment I couldn't speak. Then, turning to look at him, I said in cold fury, 'I've told you before what I think of opinions. Just take as many guys as it needs and get back up there and bring those vehicles down here as I ordered. Every minute you waste puts the moon higher in the sky and turns more of a spotlight on the target area.' I paused, then added, 'And that means putting everybody's life at risk.'

I had my temper under control, but it was still perfectly clear to them all that I was furious. I believe my anger was justified, however. Some of these characters were acting so cautiously that they were putting all of us in danger, although they didn't realize it. Without the vehicles, our firepower was massively reduced, and the further away the Land Rovers were from the target the less effective the supporting fire they could give. At the same time I also had no doubt that some of the men were muttering to themselves that I had suicidal tendencies, that I was completely off my rocker and was going to get us all wiped out. Well, let them think it. This mission was going ahead as planned.

Eventually – after a further, wasted, twenty minutes – the Land Rovers arrived and I told all the guys to get their kit and gather round in a loose circle. I still only knew a few of them by name, so when it came to detailing them off for the various tasks ahead I had to rely on Pat to pick out most of the bodies I needed.

When they'd assembled I issued confirmatory orders. 'There are two vehicles parked across from the target,' I told them. If I'd never had their attention before, I had it in full measure now. 'I want four men to go forward and cover those, and another two to go to the same spot with a LAW 80 to take out the enemy bunker beyond the end of the berm on our left. I also want a Land Rover fitted with a Milan to be positioned just on the road over here' – I pointed to a spot thirty metres away to our right – 'to take out the main bunker on the right of the target.'

Because of the extra potential trouble spots identified by Des and Ken, I had already accepted that I would have to cut down on the strength of the main assault team. I tasked three members of my original team, plus Major Peter, to the specific areas I had just indicated – two to the left-hand bunker, two to the vehicles – and waited while Pat selected the other men who were needed for particular tasks.

'Four vehicles and those of you not selected by me or Pat will wait here as a reserve, ready to come forward if needed. Everyone else, apart from the Milan wagon and crew, will go forward with Pat in three of the wagons and set up a fire-support position at the end of the berm to the left of the road. From there you'll be able to give covering fire if and when it becomes necessary.'

I looked at the camouflaged faces of the men sitting and kneeling around me.

I only recognized a handful of them in daylight. At night, now they had cam cream on their faces and most were wearing steel helmets, I could scarcely tell one from another. I wondered again how many of my dirty not-quite-three-dozen would be present at our debriefing in a few hours' time. My plan wasn't perfect, but no plan ever could be totally foolproof. Worse, I had had to adapt it as our recce produced more and more evidence that the intel we'd first received was, to put it mildly, over-optimistic. Nevertheless, I believed that it was the best I could come up with given the situation and our resources. We were about to find out whether I was right. Meanwhile, it was time to wind up the briefing.

'Let's keep it quiet for as long as possible,' I told them. 'I don't want those bunkers being taken out unless it goes noisy – and preferably not until the first charges go off when we break through the outer wall. Then Pat and the rest of you can hit them with everything you've got and hope it either scares, confuses or occupies them enough so that we can get out without suffering too much damage.

'Right guys. Any questions? Okay. Let's go.'

And with that we moved out.

Chapter Twenty-One

I led my demolition team and six other men off to the left, to make use of whatever shadow cover was available close to the berm, and then headed north towards the road junction and the final jumping-off point for the target.

Pat and his three Land Rovers drove along the same route after us. The crew of the wagon carrying the Milan, which only had thirty metres to travel, had been told to move into position ten minutes after the rest of us had left.

The demolitionists were Mugger and Ken and a quiet Yorkshire corporal named Tom. A tall guy, very fit and strong, it was he who had driven the Gaz containing the bodies of the three dead Iraqis back to where I was flown in, apparently prepared to put up with the corpses in exchange for having a closed vehicle with a heater. As backup there was myself, Des and Captain Timothy, the young officer who had joined us from the infantry. Each of us carried one of the explosive charges that had been made up back in the LUP. I had the shaped charge for the fence and Des the charge for the wall, while Timothy had the charges we would use to blow the doors in the bunker. In addition, each of us was carrying a powerful high-explosive charge with which we would take out the switching gear.

When we reached our jumping-off point we were just two hundred metres from the relay station. From there all we could see of the building was the wall around it and, behind it, the steel antenna soaring into the night sky. The wall seemed to be of concrete, grey in colour apart from one section, a few metres wide, which appeared to be a different shade. From that distance, however, even with the moonlight, we couldn't make it out properly.

The six men who had moved forward with us – one of them with a LAW80 – had already broken away and crossed the road to come up on the two trucks. To the right and less than fifty metres beyond them was the large bunker, where I could easily make out the enemy coming and going. Even though it was late there seemed to be quite a lot of activity. About a hundred and fifty metres to our left the other bunker was now clearly visible. It too was brightly lit inside and had enemy personnel moving about. There were other, smaller buildings behind the left-hand bunker, and about a hundred metres beyond the target was the large military encampment that we had spotted during the recce.

'A few more than the thirty guys we expected,' breathed Des.

'Yeah, but by the time they realize what's going on we'll be back at our LUP,' I answered softly. 'So let's just brass it out and get it over with.' I looked at the other five, then nodded. Time to go.

As we stepped out in single file, slightly crouched but moving fairly quickly, I could see to our left, where the low growl of the Land Rovers had died away, that Pat had the wagons parked a few metres apart and facing the different directions from where trouble might be expected to come. We pressed on, slinking over the MSR and past the right-hand bunker.

Whether the Iraqis in the right-hand bunker actually saw us or not I don't know. But no one shouted or challenged us and in less than a minute we had reached the wall. Ken, whose job it was to blow this first obstacle, led the way, followed by Des, who was carrying the charges. Mugger, who would bring down the fence, was next, and then me with his charges. Behind me was Tom, who would blow the bunker's main door, and Captain Timothy carrying his charges.

Close to, we could see straight away what made one section a different shade from the rest of the wall. It was plastic sheeting. An already dodgy mission was growing stranger by the minute.

'Pull the stuff back and let's see what's behind it,' I hissed. At once Ken and Des peeled back one edge, then Des turned and said, 'The wall's already been blown. There's a bloody great hole here.'

'Well, let's get through it,' I said. We were crouched down by the wall, but with the moonlight we would be immediately visible to anyone who looked hard enough from the trucks, the bunkers, or even the smaller buildings to our left. It felt as though we were standing in the spotlights on stage in a packed theatre.

Within thirty seconds all six of us were through the gap and had pushed the plastic sheeting back in place. Inside, there was total chaos. The place had obviously suffered a direct hit from an Allied bomb or missile. In places the fence was twisted and flattened, and in others completely torn from its cement base. Of the main bunker there was almost nothing left. There were buckled steel girders and shattered concrete everywhere. Some of the wreckage was so precariously balanced that it looked likely to crash down at any moment.

I took a look around for an entrance to the three underground rooms, but the stairway and the rooms had been completely buried beneath the rubble. The whole site was extremely hazardous, and I realized that one or more of us could get badly injured simply walking in the ruins, especially since the moonlight on the wreckage left large areas in deep shadow. It was perfectly certain, too, that there wasn't any switching gear left for us to destroy. Curiously, I felt a sense of anti-climax. Still, there was one thing we could do.

'Des, you and Timothy dump all your explosives here and get back to the gap in the wall and wait for us there. Now we're here we'd better bring down the mast, if nothing else.' Since the mast was still up, it could still receive and transmit signals via the antennae and dishes on it – which meant the site could still get Scuds off towards Israel. Thinking quickly, I offloaded my own explosives and told Mugger, 'Let's blow the mast and get out of here.'

'These charges are not really suitable,' he replied mournfully. 'They're no good for cutting steel.'

This was too much. First we had intelligence that told us the place was defended, if at all, by about thirty Iraqis. Then Intel had failed to tell us that there were a military camp and fortified defensive positions around the relay station. Meanwhile, somebody had neglected to tell us, or RHQ, that the site had already received an extremely accurate air or missile raid. Finally, having successfully reached our target unseen with more than a hundred pounds of explosive charges, we found that those charges probably would not do the one job that still needed doing. Well, we were bloody well going to do something, I thought.

'Surely you can do something?' I asked Mugger. He considered for a while, and finally nodded. 'If we pack a charge and a third of the other explosives around each of three of the mast's four legs, then it will give us about thirty-five pounds per leg. With luck that will do the job.'

'Okay. Let's do it,' I said. 'It sounds much too damned quiet out there for it to last.' By now we had been almost in the centre of an enemy installation for ten or fifteen minutes. It seemed incredible that nobody had noticed us, but how much longer could we trust our luck to last? I had a strong suspicion that the answer was 'not much', but the demolitionists were already on the case. Mugger, Ken and Tom quickly divided the explosives into three piles, then each of them grabbed one pile and headed in a crouch for one of the steel legs of the mast.

I waited between two of the legs, aware that these three guys were playing with high explosives that could blow us all to atoms in a millisecond if anything went wrong. So while I hoped that they wouldn't take too long, I also didn't want them to be foolishly hasty.

Ken was the first to finish, then, thirty seconds later, Tom came over to join us.

'What's keeping Mugger?' I asked.

'He's going to pull the three switches,' Ken answered. By now we were scarcely bothering to lower our voices.

'Right,' I told them. 'You two go and join Des and Timothy and all of you get through the wall and wait there. We'll be right with you.'

A minute later Mugger appeared out of the darkness and gave me a big grin. 'Okay Billy,' he said. 'They're each on a two-minute delay, so let's head for the great outdoors.' He was, as usual, as cool as a cucumber and, like any artist, supremely happy in his work. I didn't need any extra prompting, and we lit out for the wall like greyhounds.

At which point our good fortune took a nosedive. We were through the tangled fence and close to the gap in the wall when all hell broke loose. There were several single shots followed by a burst of automatic fire, then the enormous whoosh of a Milan going in and, seconds later, a huge explosion as the missile struck home. Then everyone seemed to let rip together. Rounds were zipping overhead and we could hear them smacking into the other side of the wall.

There were bullets flying everywhere, riddling the sheeting covering the gap while, above, tracers created amazing patterned arches. We were safe enough on our side of the wall, but not for long. Behind us, no more than ten metres away, was over a hundred pounds of high-explosive getting ready to blow in less than ninety seconds.

'What do you reckon, Mugger?' I asked.

'We haven't got much fucking choice, have we?' he replied.

I grinned at him. 'No. I suppose not. So let's go.' And with that I ducked round the plastic sheet and into the open area on the other side. The other four were all lying by the wall outside.

'Line abreast and back to the jumping-off point,' I yelled. 'And let's move it. It's all going to blow in a few seconds.'

Surging forward, we spread out like the three-quarter line in a rugby game and belted towards the dark, looming mass of the north end of the berm. Though I swear that not even the finest line-up ever made it from one end of a rugby pitch to the other at the speed we travelled that night. Of course, we were all as fit as professional athletes, and given the amount of adrenalin fizzing around in our muscles we'd have been good for a few world records – if anyone could have spared the time to clock us.

We were halfway between the wall and the jumping-off point when the first explosive charge blew, followed seconds later by another boom and, almost immediately afterwards, by a third.

None of us stopped to watch the effects, however, for there were bullets whistling all around us. As I ran I looked to the left. The bunker there was gushing flames and smoke from its gun slits and entrance, which meant the Milan had done its job.

The bunker on the other side was still intact, and there seemed to be a lot of the enemy fire coming from that direction. But Pat and his team on the 110s had the heavy machine-guns in action, while some of the guys with him had brought their grenade launchers to bear and were peppering the bunker with high-velocity fragmenting metal. As a result, most of the enemy fire was wild, since they were reluctant to face the streams of 0.5-inch rounds and 40mm grenades.

We ran to within a few metres of the Land Rovers' position, and I yelled to the fire-support team that we were all through and evacuating the area. On we dashed. Suddenly we were at the north-south road and I could see dark shapes over to our right where the enemy trucks were parked. Our guys there were firing on groups of Iraqi troops who were taking cover at the sides of the ruined bunker and in a few small huts, or crouching behind low humps of sand and rock.

The enemy soldiers appeared to be using automatic rifles and light machine-guns, as well as standard magazine rifles – and there seemed to be a lot of them. My immediate impression, however, was that none of them was capable of shooting very straight. Not that it mattered. You could just as easily die from a lucky shot as from the perfect aim of a sniper.

Among the SAS men near the trucks I thought I could make out Major Peter in the group closest to us. I yelled, 'Cease fire and retire with us back to the vehicles,' meaning the four 110s we had left behind near the abandoned L-shaped bunker. We continued to run up the slight slope, parallel with the berm. When we reached them the wagons were all intact, including the one that had fired the Milan, which had rejoined the other three after taking out the bunker. Tracer and bullets were still flying everywhere, and back towards the target we could hear the roar of the Brownings, the lighter rattle of the GPMGs and the thump of the grenade launchers as Pat and his fire-support group continued to lay down a stream of heavy and accurate fire.

As I reached the vehicles and turned around I found Major Peter jogging the last few paces towards us. 'Some night,' he said. 'I wouldn't have missed it for the world.' But it was not until later, during our debriefing back at the LUP, that I learned what had turned our mission noisy, and Major Peter's part in it.

He and the three troopers who had been detailed to check out the enemy trucks with him were right alongside the vehicles as I and my team disappeared through the bunker wall. Crouched down, they waited with their weapons ready, occasionally scanning the scene through their Kite sights. Then, some ten minutes later the cab door of the leading truck had opened to reveal a bleary-eyed military driver who had almost certainly been asleep. Bleary or not, however, he spotted our guys and immediately made a grab for a rifle he had propped up on a seat next to him. It was the last thing he ever did. Reacting instantly, Major Peter levelled his M16 at the Iraqi's chest and fired several rounds – the single shots we had heard as Mugger and I headed for the gap in the wall, just before automatic fire tore the night apart. The driver was probably dead before his hand touched his own weapon. Seconds later the enemy troops in the right-hand bunker opened fire and our man on the Milan decided that the moment had come for him to take it out. It was then that the whole shebang went *very* noisy.

Apparently the shooting woke the driver of the second truck. He was more cautious than his colleague in the other vehicle, however, for he climbed down on the side away from our guys. He immediately spotted the trooper who was about to loose off the LAW 80 at the left-hand bunker and, with commendable courage, leapt on his back and started trying to strangle him. Luckily he was spotted by one of Major Peter's unit, who rushed forward through a curtain of bullets and clubbed the Iraqi on the back of the head with his rifle butt.

With its aluminium and plastic parts, the Colt M16 may be very light, but it is still solid enough to knock someone senseless if used in the right way. Our guys left the Iraqi where he fell, no doubt to crawl off later with a bad head. They could have shot him, but there was no point. He was unarmed and now out of the game, nor was he going to recover fast enough to cause us any further problem. It was the right decision. He was a brave man, and enough men were dying already that night.

There was one serious consequence of his action, though, for it meant that the LAW missile was never fired at the second bunker. By the time the operator had it set up again on his shoulder, my team and I were belting back across the area in front of him and the risk of hitting one of us by accident was too great. That and my yelling at them to retire caused him to give up on his task and fall back after us.

As Major Peter and the others joined us at the vehicles, I happened to glance up to the top of the berm, and saw about a dozen figures milling about up there. They seemed to be dressed in dark kit, rather than the normal olive drab of Iraqi soldiers. I yelled, 'Who are those guys on top of the berm?' and someone shouted back, 'It's okay, they're the Iraqi truck drivers from the parking area.' I assumed that the man who answered was one of those I had left with orders to guard the wagons and secure the area. I also assumed that they must have checked the top of the berm and dealt with anyone who might have been up there.

It was now that I made what was potentially the most serious mistake of my life. I believed what I heard and relaxed. Seconds later the figures on the berm disappeared and I thought that, frightened by our presence and all the firing, they had made themselves scarce. I should have sent a patrol up there to cover us and make sure there was no danger from that quarter. After all, why would a group of Iraqis stand on top of a sandbank looking down at an armed enemy if they didn't have to?

The answer was not long in coming. The watchers on the berm can't have had their weapons with them when we first saw them. They must have gone off to collect them, however, because a few minutes later we found ourselves taking a lot of incoming fire. In the space of a few seconds Mugger had two bullets through his clothing and I felt one whip by my head, just missing me. Some of the rounds were literally parting our hair, and one slammed into the Milan on my vehicle, wrecking the delicate firing mechanism. At first we couldn't even tell where the firing was coming from; then, finally, we traced it to the top of the berm where we had seen the figures earlier.

Once again luck was with us because the enemy firing down on us were obviously not Saddam's crack Republican Guard. All they were doing was spraying rounds indiscriminately in our direction, although if they had taken time to aim and concentrate their fire they could have wiped us all out. We weren't even under cover. None the less, once we realized where the danger lay we started to give it back in spades, with our M16s, medium and heavy machine-guns and grenade launchers pouring concentrated fire in their direction.

Yet despite returning a heavy and accurate fire towards the Iraqi troops on the berm, the general consensus among our guys seemed to be to get out of there – fast. So much so, in fact, that without waiting for orders, several of them started firing up the motors and heading the wagons towards the south. As one of the last to leave fishtailed away in a skidding start, its front wing struck me a violent blow on my thigh and belt kit and sent me flying through the air. As I went in one direction my rifle, which had been knocked from my hand, went in another.

Half winded, I staggered to my feet, and found the last of the four Land Rovers we'd left here revving up next to me. 'Jump on or we're fucking going without you,' a voice yelled. It wasn't much of an option, for bullets were ricocheting off the vehicle's sides and bonnet. Someone grabbed my arm, and I scrambled aboard as the wagon lit out, with enemy bullets still pinging off the sideworks. My M16 – with twenty gold sovereigns still hidden in the butt – was left behind. I often wonder whether whoever found the weapon also discovered the secret hoard of gold. It would go a long way nowadays, given the present state of the Iraqi economy.

As we bucked and bumped our way south the wild gunfire from the berm gradually died away, though I could still hear the sound of more distant firing. I hoped that most of it was coming from Pat and his fire-support group, and that they were already pulling back from their covering position. About a kilometre down the road our little convoy pulled over and stopped, and I jumped out of the Land Rover which had brought me that far. The sudden, almost panicky withdrawal had annoyed me, and as the men dismounted I called them together.

'I don't know what all that was about,' I told them, 'but I now want to get back to a situation where things happen because of orders, and not because it's what takes people's fancy.' I paused to let that sink in, wondering whether to pitch into them harder. They had pulled out without my order. Then again, they had performed brilliantly throughout the mission.

I decided, there and then, that that was all I was going to say about the sudden disorderly withdrawal. A few moments later and I would have given the order to pull out anyway. We had been taking a lot of incoming fire, and in the heat of the moment some of the lads decided to get out of there. More important than bollocking them for a momentary lapse was to find out if anyone was hurt or missing. My pride came second to that by a long way.

Miraculously, when I asked for casualties everyone shook his head. There were no wounded. No one had even a scratch, and no one was missing. My only concern now was for Pat and his men because we were unable to raise them on the radio. Ken volunteered to take a bike and go back to advise Pat to pull out, if he hadn't already done so. It was a good offer, but after a moment's consideration I turned him down.

'No. Stay where you are,' I told him. 'If anyone goes back we're likely to have a blue-on-blue incident. Pat knows we got out. He was in an excellent fire-support position. Let him pick the right moment to pull out while we wait here. Then he'll find his own way back to us.'

Ten minutes later we heard the growl of engines as the four Land Rovers emerged out of the darkness. All their crews were intact. As soon as they drew up alongside Pat's men jumped out and suddenly everybody seemed to be hugging and back-slapping everybody else. Even for the SAS, the end of a mission brings a tremendous release of tension, made up partly of relief and partly of pleasure at having performed well in a difficult and dangerous task. By some incredible miracle, and against far greater odds than we could have anticipated, we had managed to get in and out of the enemy stronghold with every member of the unit present and unwounded. In doing so we had undoubtedly killed and wounded numbers of Iraqi troops, as well as firing the demolition charges on the mast. We had also thoroughly alarmed and confused the enemy.

My only regret was that, looking to the north, I could still see the steel antenna pointing skywards, the moon glinting on its lattice of girders.

'All that explosive and effort and we couldn't bring the bloody thing down,' I said to Mugger.

'Don't give up yet,' he said. 'Blasting metal is a funny business. I suggest we check later today before we write the demolition off as a failure. The mast might easily go at any moment. Perhaps if we're lucky it'll be just as Saddam is paying them a courtesy call.'

If Mugger proved to be right, then it would mean a perfect mission: target destroyed and zero casualties. I could hardly wait for daylight and the opportunity to check whether his optimism was justified. Meanwhile we had to get away, so once the guys had quietened down a bit I ordered them to mount up and move out, Pat's vehicle taking the lead, as usual.

Just after first light we arrived back at our LUP where the Unimog was still sitting, untouched, beneath its cam net. We deactivated the booby traps around it, after which I told the guys – all except the first four who were down for sentry duty – to have a brew and some food and get their heads down for a few hours. Then, having made my way back to my vehicle, I was just about to get on the radio and report the results of our mission to HQ when Ken came running over.

'It's down!' he yelled. 'The mast is down!'

'How the hell do you figure that?' I asked.

'From here you can just see the top of it through the binoculars in the morning sun,' he said. (The low angle of the sun in the early morning makes it possible to see things at a distance that will not catch the light to the same degree when the sun is higher.) 'Well, the first time I looked it was still there. But when I looked a couple of minutes later it had gone. Which means it must have collapsed.'

This was excellent news – if it was true. We had to know.

'Look, Ken,' I said, 'if you're up to it, I'd like you and Ron to go back on bikes to just this side of the motorway – from where the tower should be plainly visible – and do a recce. Don't take any risks, but if you can get to a point from where you would be able to see the mast if it's still standing, you'd be doing us all a favour.'

'No problem,' he replied. 'I'm pretty damned certain we did the business back there – so I'd like to check for my own sake. It'll make skipping through all those bullets a damned sight more worthwhile.'

Although I hadn't known him before I took over Alpha One Zero, Ron, whom I had detailed to go with Ken, had proved to be an excellent member of the patrol. He was an expert motorcyclist, and had already saved us a lot of time and effort in our forays across the Iraqi desert. He later received a Mention in Despatches for his sterling work throughout our time in Iraq.

Once the pair of bikes had set out I whistled up ops in Al Jouf and gave them our news, adding that we believed the mast had been successfully brought down. The ops officer told me he would organize an A-10 – the fearsome, and fearsomely ugly, American tank-busting aircraft designated the Thunderbolt, but usually known by its nickname of 'Warthog' – to make a run over Victor Two and check it out.

My report on the mission had been brief and straightforward. It simply stated 'mission accomplished'. As in every action, the Regiment had, against all the odds, accomplished its all but impossible mission in spectacular style. But it could have ended very differently. I had felt uneasy about the operation right from the start, and even more so when we found the target had already been successfully bombed. There had been a lack of intelligence, and the information we did get had been inaccurate to the point of endangering our lives. We had been told there would be very few enemy defenders, and that had turned out to be wrong. We had not been told that the relay station had already been destroyed, even though Allied HQ must have known of the bombing. After getting off the radio I lit a cigarette and reflected on the whole business. Whatever the truth, we had done the business and got out with all our personnel and all our vehicles intact.

An hour later Ken and Ron were back, to report that the mast had indeed been toppled, and that the enemy were buzzing about like stirred-up flies, dashing up and down the new motorway in armoured cars and trucks, but giving no sign of pursuit in our direction. To crown it all, that afternoon Al Jouf ops reported that the pilot of the A-10 sent to overfly Victor Two had confirmed that the mast was down.

There were no herograms. I told the guys we would stay one more night, our fourth, in this same location, so that we could sort ourselves out a little and repack our gear – in other words, do a little house-cleaning. You'd be amazed at how filthy the interior of a Land Rover becomes after a few unwashed SAS members have lived in it for more than a handful of days. Having given them that news, I suddenly realized how tired I was. Time to turn in, I thought.

Just as I was about to crawl into my sleeping bag, however, Des came across.

'Ken did a great job today,' he began. I nodded. He seemed rather ill at ease, but after a moment continued, 'Perhaps when this is all over you can do something for him.' When I still said nothing, Des plunged gamely on. 'He was told just before coming out that he was being RTU-ed. That means moving away from Hereford back to the Paras, and his wife is packing the boxes at this moment.'

'What's he done?' I asked.

'Been done for drinking and driving for the third time.'

'You're right, he doesn't deserve to be chucked out after all he's done,' I said. 'I'll take it up with the CO as soon as we get back.

'Now, piss off and let me get some sleep. And don't even think about waking me, unless it's the end of the world.' And with that I tugged the top of my sleeping bag over my head, shutting out the daylight.

Chapter Twenty-Two

IN the event, we remained at the same LUP for a fifth night, moving out before sunset on 9 February, heading south. We had been tasked with a new mission: to locate an area that would accommodate all the SAS patrols operating behind enemy lines.

We knew that for the next two weeks or so there wasn't going to be enough moonlight for the Chinooks to fly in fresh supplies; that was why we had recce-ed the abandoned airstrip for a possible resupply flight by a C-130. The CO, however, had come up with a staggering alternative. In what was to prove to be one of the most audacious plans in the Regiment's history, he decided to send ten 4-ton trucks, with six Land Rovers acting as escorts, some one hundred and fifty kilometres into enemy territory to bring us our essential supplies of food, water, ammunition and fuel.

The convoy was scheduled to pull out of Al Jouf the next day, and to be on the Iraqi border, ready to steam in, by the 11th. We had until then to seek out a location, within the convoy's range, that could accommodate up to a hundred and fifty men and their vehicles, and to make it completely secure.

When I told the men of the plan, just before we moved out, they reacted with an enthusiastic chorus of approval. Following our recent activities, the prospect of a major get-together within the next few days was welcome news. My other announcement wiped away the smiles in an instant, however. Over the radio HQ had informed me that, while checking out an enemy communications site, three of our men from the other Alpha half-squadron had been separated from their unit, along with a Land Rover, during a fierce firefight in the early hours of that morning. One of the men was believed to have been badly, possibly fatally, wounded, but at this stage I had no names.

We were always left with a sick feeling whenever we learned that a member of the Regiment had been on the receiving end, but for the guys in my patrol, all of them members of A Squadron, there were close friends involved whom they had known for years. They would more than probably be men who had visited their homes, or joined them with their wives and children on family outings. The news also made us reflect on just how lucky all of us had been to get out with our skins intact the day before.

It took us two days to find a suitable resupply area, but eventually we located the perfect place in the Wadi Tubal, about fifty kilometres south of our former base. It was a wadi within the main wadi, about a hundred metres wide by five hundred long. The entrance, which was very narrow, zigzagged, making it impossible for anyone to see in without advancing almost into the wadi, while a steep bank across the far end sealed the place off as a kind of cul-de-sac. The sides were high and steep, and from the heights above the whole mini-wadi became invisible if you stepped back just a dozen paces from the edge. It was an excellent defensive position, with plenty of space inside for at least seventy vehicles.

At dawn on the 11th, when I called in to report the area secure, my own news was completely overshadowed by an update on the plight of our mates in Alpha Three Zero. I was told the three men had now been identified as Kevin, Jack and Barry. They had been involved in a firefight with Iraqi troops that had lasted for forty minutes, and in the course of which Barry, the squadron sergeant-major, had been badly wounded in the leg and groin. Their Land Rover had been wrecked, so the two other men had carried him, under continuous enemy fire, as far as they could, and had then managed to escape, still under fire. They were lucky to be alive, but it was very doubtful whether Barry had survived.

Everyone was shocked by this news, for Barry was an extremely popular member of A Squadron and of the Regiment. As a result we were all still rather subdued and not much inclined to start socializing when the first half of D Squadron – Delta One Zero – arrived late that evening. They had been spotted and guided into the rendezvous area half an hour before sunset by one of the two vehicle outrider patrols I had stationed beyond the wadi entrance.

Within 'our' wadi there were four or five fairly wide ravines that had been etched into the cliff faces by the action of flood water over the centuries. I had decided to allot one of these to each half-squadron, and one for the supply column's escort. The two Delta units would face one another across the wadi, and the other half of A Squadron could settle in to the ravine opposite the one in which we were located. The supply trucks themselves could line up in the centre of our little wadi, which would make the dishing out of fresh supplies much easier.

I left D Squadron to themselves that evening, but the following morning went over to where they had arranged their Land Rovers and

Unimog. I soon spotted the OC, Major Alan, an extremely competent officer who got on well with just about everybody and was highly respected by all the men. He was talking to base on the satcom as I approached, but on seeing me he beckoned me towards him. I heard him say, 'He's just walked up, so I'll put him on to you,' then he handed me the radiophone. It was the ops officer at Al Jouf with fresh orders for us.

I was being told to pull my entire patrol out that afternoon, and drive 130 kilometres to the north-west to relieve the other half of D Squadron – Delta Three Zero – who were running short of water and rations. We were not to meet up with them, but were simply to take over their task of keeping watch on one of the MSRs, while they made their way to Wadi Tubal for resupply.

'Well, what makes you think we're any better off?' I found myself saying down the satellite link. 'We have virtually no rations and we're down to our last few litres of water. As for fuel, we don't have enough to get us there and back. The convoy is due in this evening, so if we wait here just a few more hours for our supplies we can replace Delta Three Zero and stay up there pretty well indefinitely.

'If we do it your way, we'll need relieving ourselves in a couple of days – or less. And even that depends on our scrounging water and rations from Major Alan's unit, which, if they're anything like us, I'm not even sure they've got.'

'You have your orders, and that's the way it's got to be,' came back the deadpan reply. 'You're to get under way as soon as possible.'

I couldn't understand HQ's reasoning. It didn't make any sense. Our last resupply had happened at the same time as Delta Three Zero's, yet someone up the line had calculated that our reserves would miraculously hold out for several days longer than those of our mates in the Delta patrol. There was no escaping our orders, however. Even so, I was quietly seething by the time I'd signed off and given the handset back to Major Alan.

Thank God, D Squadron's sergeant-major was an old friend. A no-nonsense professional who didn't suffer fools gladly, he was also a straight-up guy who hated bullshit as much as I did. When I told him what was going on he called his group together and ordered them to dig out all their spare rations and water and hand them over to me. 'Just leave yourselves the bare minimum,' he told them. 'These guys are going to need it a damned sight more where they're going to than you do here.'

There was a bit of good-natured grumbling, but in twenty minutes D Squadron had piled together enough food and water to last us an extra couple of days. We also got their spare grenades, rifle rounds and machine-gun belts, as well as a few high-explosive charges and other fizz-bangs. After the attack on Victor Two we were dangerously low on ammunition and explosives, and there was no way of knowing whether or not we would find ourselves involved in another major firefight where we were going. It could always happen to us at any moment, so we were doubly grateful for the extra ammo.

At times, though, it was easy enough to forget that we were a 150 kilometres behind enemy lines and about to go much deeper in. Nevertheless, it was important that we did not relax our guard for a single moment. Looking at the number of contacts each patrol had experienced so far, the odds against us running into further trouble were not great.

When I had all the replacement kit I was able to scrounge from the boys in Delta piled before me, I called in our eight 110s and their crews, and the Unimog, and told my guys to dig out all their remaining grub and water and add it to the pile. Then I divided everything equally between each vehicle. Incredibly, while supervising the division of the kit I discovered that one of my crews had concealed a whole jerry can of water in the back of their Land Rover.

Coming on top of the ops officer's bloody-mindedness, this hoarding of water by some of my own men was the last straw. I gave them the mother of all bollockings, during which I called each of them every kind of selfish bastard imaginable. 'With friends like you we don't need Saddam's lot against us,' I concluded, before dividing the extra water between the other vehicles.

We finally pulled out just after 1500 hours, and bombed along towards the target area as fast as the terrain would allow. Astonishingly, Major Alan told me later, as our dust settled on the north-west horizon, the dust cloud raised by the incoming resupply convoy, nicknamed the 'Wadi-Bottom Wanderers' by HQ, was spotted to the south. With great daring they had made the whole trip in daylight, led by the same Major Bill who had nursed Alpha One Zero over the berm and into Iraq, before I joined the patrol.

Our journey was almost completely uneventful. For the first couple of hours we travelled in bright sunlight, and were able to make fast progress over the gravel plain. But we slowed after sunset. The complete absence of moonlight meant that we were back to relying on the night sights and thermal imager. To make matters worse, we were also driving into a thin sleet which the wind hurled at us almost horizontally. In open vehicles without even a windscreen, we were soon chilled to the bone.

The only significant episode in that drive was a curious, if not a sinister, one. After some hours we came upon a deserted farmhouse. Lying scattered everywhere around it were the remains of a large number of goats' carcasses. The animal skeletons lay among various bits and pieces of shattered wreckage surrounding the farm, which might have come from an aircraft or missile. There were also what appeared to be large fragments from numerous heavy shells in among the other debris. When someone suggested that the place might have been a test site for chemical-warfare weapons a few of the guys began to look a bit nervous, and started to search out their gas masks and NBC suits. I told them not to bother. If any of the toxic gas had still been hanging about, we would all have been on our backs, either dying or dead. Looking back now, I believe that what we had actually stumbled across was just an old artillery and missile range. From the look of it, I doubt whether it had been used in years.

We reached the main supply route from Amman to Baghdad just after 2100 hours, and I established an LUP about a kilometre south of MSR3, although well to the west of where we had last seen the road at Victor 2. There were a lot of tall mounds of what appeared to be sandstone scattered about the site, which on closer examination turned out to be anthills. They provided excellent cover.

While the rest of the patrol set up the usual protective ring of vehicles, and sentries were posted, I took my Land Rover forward and established an OP overlooking the highway. From there we were able to observe the traffic – a surprising amount of it making its way along the MSR. Most of the movement was from the west to the east – supplies coming in from Jordan, Saddam's only ally. There was every kind of truck imaginable, from cattle wagons to huge articulated lorries.

Shortly before dawn we drove back to the LUP, and I allowed the men, apart from the sentries, a few hours' sleep before moving the whole patrol further along the highway to the north-west. The weather had cleared, and as the afternoon was one of bright sunshine we had to drive slowly to keep down the amount of dust we threw up, which could have acted as a giant indicator to the enemy, pinpointing us exactly. Again I set up a base about a kilometre short of the highway, then established night and day OPs closer in. The movement of traffic was very much as it had been the day before, which meant that we saw nothing to excite comment, much less a mobile Scud convoy. Why on earth we had been sent all that way, at that juncture, to relieve Delta Three Zero in such a mundane and routine assignment I will never know. Somehow we managed to yawn our way through the day, doing what we could to relieve the boredom. Mercifully, that evening we received orders to pull out and return to Wadi Tubal. Had HQ delayed even another twenty-four hours we would have been in fairly serious trouble. Our water was exhausted and so were our rations, and by the time our convoy snaked its way through the zigzag entrance into the mini-wadi I had picked out for our resupply zone, our protesting stomachs were making almost as much noise as our wagons' engines.

The sentries who waved us through were from the supply-convoy escort unit, which was made up of guys from B Squadron and some members of HQ Squadron, who had been flown out from Britain as support backup. This meant that apart from the dead and wounded and those missing in action, virtually the whole SAS fighting force in the Gulf was present at the one location – probably the largest ever concentration of the Regiment's active units in one place at the same time. I almost hoped the Iraqis might find us. They would have received a very nasty surprise when they realized what they were up against.

Yet if we couldn't go down in regimental records as having fought a great battle in Wadi Tubal, we could at least make our mark in some other way – in addition, that is, to the already remarkable, if not crazy, feat of bringing supplies in overland into enemy territory. The presence of so many of the Regiment's fighting men, and of the supply convoy and its escort, in a wadi in Iraq set me thinking.

I decided to hold a Sergeants' Mess meeting. In our home barracks these are normally held every month, and as Regimental Sergeant-Major I was automatically Chairman of the Mess Committee. However, as I had been RSM only since the first week in December, and as we had been tied up, first with preparations to move to the Gulf, and then with our actual deployment subsequently, I had found no time to call my first mess meeting.

I calculated that there were at least thirty sergeants among the men now in the wadi, and that was more than enough. My first action, therefore, after we'd parked the Land Rover, was to go in search of the Regimental Quartermaster Sergeant, Gary, who, besides being in charge of logistics, was the President of the Mess Committee. I found him, inevitably, by one of the 4-tonners, engrossed in something connected with his beloved stores. We shook hands formally, and I told him, 'Gary, we're going to have a mess meeting.'

His eyes widened. 'Have you gone barking mad?' he asked.

'No, I'm absolutely serious. The meeting will be at noon today, on the side of that hill over there,' and I pointed to where a shale-covered area of the wadi side sloped less steeply up to the cliff-like brim above.

At 1200 hours that day, 16 February 1991, thirty-five members of the Sergeants' Mess, including myself as Chairman and Gary as President, met on the rocky slope. The other sergeants and warrant officers sat in a line two deep, and Gary and I stood facing them to conduct our business. Apart from the setting, and the fact that every man had his rifle with him, it ran much like a mess meeting back at Stirling Lines. After the usual votes of thanks we came to the main proposal, which was to spend up to £20,000 on new leather furniture for the mess over the next two years. It was then agreed that the next mess dinner would take place in April, and that there would be a Christmas function which members would attend in mess dress, but without medals, and with no guests present. There were various minor decisions about mess facilities agreed and noted, and minutes were kept of the whole meeting, scribbled in an exercise book to be taken back to Hereford and typed up properly.

To begin with, some of the guys had been brassed off. When they assembled on the slope they believed that they had been called to some kind of war briefing, during which they would be given details of a major offensive involving A and D Squadrons. So when I announced a regular Sergeants' Mess meeting they had difficulty taking it in. I could see that some of them thought the idea was mad. They could probably hardly wait to get back to their mates and start laughing their heads off. But I hope that, eventually, they all understood the purpose behind what I had done. In the midst of Britain's biggest military involvement in the Middle East since the Second World War, one hundred and fifty kilometres behind enemy lines – right in Saddam's own back yard – the SAS were making sure that life went on as normal. In effect, we were proving that no tinpot dictator could disrupt us to the point at which our normal routines might have to be abandoned. Or, to put it another way, we were saying 'Up yours!' with a vengeance.

I also believe that holding the meeting showed that the Regiment still had style. So too did Generals de la Billière and Schwarzkopf. 'Stormin' Norman', as he had been nicknamed by the media, declared that we had shown more panache than any troops he had ever heard of, and said he would be proud to be allowed to sign the minutes of our mess meeting. As for DLB, he said that he was honoured to have served with guys who could exhibit such unique style in the middle of a war, and he too asked to sign the minutes. In the end – and in addition to myself and Gary, as was usual – our CO, the Deputy Director of Special Forces, Lieutenant-General Sir Peter de la Billière and General H. Norman Schwarzkopf, US Army, all signed the minutes. It is also a matter of record that every proposal agreed at the meeting was carried out after our return to Hereford.

Nevertheless, the mess meeting, although important for morale, was very much a side issue at the time. Our main purpose in the Wadi Tubal was to take on supplies. The three other half-squadrons – Alpha Three Zero, Delta One Zero and Delta Three Zero – had already taken their pick so we, who had actually prepared this site for the convoy, got to go last. Sod's Law in action once again.

The 4-ton trucks were lined up along the centre of the wadi and we drove our Land Rovers past, picking up a different commodity from each truck in turn – water, fuel, ammunition, clothes, rations and fresh food. As far as the latter was concerned, there were still a few chickens and steaks left, but our very dear comrades had obviously feasted well during the past three days, and the choicest delicacies were long gone. Still, at least there was some fresh meat for the stewpot as well as fresh vegetables and fruit, instead of the tinned and packaged rations we had been existing on for the past few weeks. Our Regimental Quartermaster had also brought along a few non-issue supplies, including cartons of cigarettes and packets of rolling tobacco, courtesy of MoD. For the brief time it took for him to hand them out he was by far the most popular man in camp.

Because our 110s and the Unimog were being almost entirely restocked, resupply also meant completely emptying out the Land Rovers and giving them a good scrape and brush down inside. It's astonishing just how much gunk accumulates in a vehicle over a fortnight or so when three or four men are calling it home.

Later that evening, over a fresh, tailor-made cigarette, I caught up with Major Bill and with the guys of D Squadron and the other half of A Squadron. The news was mixed. King Hussein of Jordan had committed his country on Saddam's side at the beginning of that week, but the Iraqis were still coming off worst in Kuwait and in their own country from the incessant Allied bombing. Nearer to home, it seemed that ours was the only fighting patrol not to have suffered casualties, although the Regiment appeared to have inflicted far greater damage in return.

One D Squadron unit had caught a complete Scud convoy on site, and laser-defined it for a speedily summoned-up flight of strike aircraft. The American pilots had scored heavily with a series of direct hits, which had fragmented the Scud and effectively turned its liquid fuel into napalm, vaporizing the attendant troops, technicians and all the vehicles.

It had not all been one-sided, however. Another section of D Squadron had been ambushed and, in the ensuing firefight, had suffered a number of casualties; they had left the enemy in far worse condition, though, with many Iraqi soldiers killed and wounded. Yet among all the reports of the various patrols' engagements, it was the heroism of Barry, the A Squadron sergeant-major, which impressed me the most, especially now we were able to get the full story from the rest of his comrades in Alpha Three Zero.

He had been in a Land Rover, one of a two-vehicle recce patrol, with two NCOs, Kevin and Jack, when they found that they had strayed in too close to an Iraqi military communications station and were inside the enemy's defensive ring. The Iraqis had let them drive past and had then opened up from behind them with everything they had. One of the 110s had managed to get clear, but Barry's wagon, reversing at high speed with two machine-guns in play, had run up and over a small berm and plunged into a ditch on the far side.

The vehicle had ended up with its front wheels in the air, and Barry was flung out of his front seat. When the other two freed themselves from the wreckage and got to him, they found him bleeding badly from a number of gunshot wounds to the thigh and lower legs and already sliding in and out of consciousness. They also thought that some of the bones of his hips had been shattered by the hits he had taken.

Taking it in turns, the two NCOs had then half-carried, half-dragged Barry to the cover of a small mound, which sounded like an anthill similar to the ones we had seen two days earlier. While one moved Barry, the other had kept the Iraqis at a distance with single-shot fire, the two unwounded men exchanging places every fifty metres or so. Their situation had seemed hopeless, although, like the true SAS men they were, they had not given up hope. As they prepared to make their final stand a couple of hundred metres from the crashed wagon the enemy had gradually begun to close in on them. With their spare ammunition in the crashed 110, they only had what they were carrying on them, and they had realized that it was only a matter of time before they would have been badly wounded or even killed, or else forced to surrender.

Although barely conscious, Barry had been aware enough to realize that they were in a pretty dire position, and had therefore ordered them to get the hell out of there while he tried to hold off the enemy. He had added that him alone against a few dozen Iraqis was reasonably fair odds. Jack told me later that he had offered to 'top' Barry – put a bullet in his head to save him from possible Iraqi torture – before they made their escape, but the sergeant-major had preferred to take his chances.

Thanks to Barry, the two of them had managed to escape the enemy-occupied zone and, using their TACBEs, had made contact with an Allied aircraft. Its pilot had helped guide them to a rendezvous with the rest of their half-squadron.

As I listened to their story that evening in the wadi, I felt a tremendous admiration for these two guys, who had risked their lives trying to pull their sergeant-major out. I felt, too, an overwhelming awe and respect for Barry, whose offer to hold off the enemy while Kevin and Jack got away had called for remarkable courage. These feelings were tinged with sadness, for it seemed almost certain that Barry must have been killed in that last stand, or else have died of his wounds. I also could not help wondering if I had that kind of courage myself, and hoped that I would never be called upon to find out.

On Sunday, 17 February, we said our goodbyes and went our separate ways, the convoy and its escort back towards Saudi Arabia, and the four half-squadrons to their designated operational areas. To my regret, one of my unit was leaving with the convoy.

Major Peter, who had flown in with our resupply chopper on the 4th, had probably gained more 'on-the-ground' experience than anyone had bargained for when he was sent in. He had been in the forefront of the Regiment's biggest mission of the Gulf War so far, and had shot his first enemy in a face-to-face encounter. It was never intended that he should stay with Alpha One Zero for more than ten days; it just happened to be his luck that he should have arrived at a pretty hectic time.

Now he was due back in the UK to attend a staff course the following week, something that had been arranged months before, as these things are. If he didn't show up it would set back his whole career. But that was the British Army, playing it by the book, as usual. Before he pulled out, he came over to my vehicle to say goodbye. We shook hands.

'You know I don't want to leave,' he said. 'These have been the most important days in the army for me so far. I could never have known what it's really like without doing it myself. I can't honestly tell you I didn't have doubts about getting out, because I did. But you got the job done and got us out of there in one piece. Thanks to you, I've got stories I can tell along with the best of them.'

When Peter left, technically Pat reverted to being my 2IC. In reality, however, when I wanted to confide in or consult anyone – which was, I have to say, rarely – I turned to Des. I knew I could count on him for any support if and when I needed it. It was not an officially recognized relationship, and in truth I felt no great need for a 2IC at all. I knew exactly what I wanted to do.

Alpha One Zero was now tasked to head in the opposite direction from where we had first operated, north-west, to an area near the Jordanian border nicknamed the 'Iron Triangle'. (We had been on its eastern flank when we had taken over Delta Three Zero's task on the MSR, before returning to Wadi Tubal.) It was a tract of country covering some two hundred and fifty square kilometres of inhospitable desert wilderness, mainly hills and wadis, bordered by three main roads which formed a rough triangle. Within the vast wadi system inside the triangle there were thought to be possible Scud-launcher locations.

Our route took us across fairly flat terrain, and in broad daylight we made such good speed that we were approaching our target area less than six hours after leaving Wadi Tubal. I decided to have the patrol lie up just short of the new motorway, marked on our maps as 'under construction', and send in a recce team. This motorway, being built to replace MSR3 as the main Amman-to-Baghdad highway, was the same road we had negotiated on our way to blow up the Scud microwave guidance system at Victor Two, some one hundred and fifty kilometres to the north-east. There we had filled in the central culvert with sandbags. Here, if the map was accurate, I planned to make a much more stylish crossing.

Up to this point, Serious had not been given a single task that would have allowed him to demonstrate his skills or his leadership qualities. To give him a chance to show how good he was, I selected him to see us over the new motorway and into our target area. When I called him over to my vehicle, however, he immediately put on his suspicious face. He was not used to being summoned by the RSM, and probably thought I had caught him out in some misdemeanour and was about to give him a bollocking.

'Yes, Billy?' he asked.

I let him sweat it out for a few moments, then unfolded my map on the bonnet of the Land Rover. On it I indicated to him where the new motorway should cross in front of us, about three kilometres to the west of our LUP. As I've said, our maps – air charts for pilots, in fact – were not that good and lacked accurate detail, but there seemed to be some kind of a junction system there, with what appeared from the map to be a bridge. Crossing bridges and using roads is usually taboo in the Regiment – they are often guarded, and anyway you are very exposed on them – but sometimes you have to break the rules. To me, this looked like one of those times.

'I want you to go ahead and take a look at this place,' I told him. 'Because I'm putting you in charge of getting us all safely across the motorway. A bridge could be the easiest way of doing it.'

'And an easy place to get caught,' he said, reasonably enough. 'If they've built roads around this triangle it must be because there's something important in there. And that means there are going to be troops on these roads ready to go in where they're needed. A bridge is where they're most likely to be hanging around.'

It may be a flaw in my character, but I have never been very good at listening to people telling me what I already know. Now my irritation began to show.

'Look, Serious,' I said. 'Before you start thinking again that I'm going to get you all killed, just go and have a look at the bridge. If you can't work out a way to get us over by that route then start looking for an alternative. But at least look at the simple way first before you start telling me that we have to drive under roads or along culverts, and all the rest of that complicated crap.'

He had the sense to keep quiet, so I told him to pick out a second vehicle to go with him and report back before midnight.

Serious was back within the time limit I had set, and with good news. The bridge and the new motorway running under it were still not operational and as a result were not lit at night. More to the point, the whole area was deserted. 'It's an ideal place to cross,' he enthused, completely forgetting that using the bridge had originally been my idea and that he had opposed it. Still, he'd made a good job of the recce.

'Well done,' I told him. 'We'll pull out in thirty minutes. This is one manoeuvre, I think, which we're better off conducting in the dark – even if Saddam's lads do seem to be playing away at the moment. Just pretend we're your lost sheep and shepherd us all across.'

It took less than an hour to cover the ground between our temporary LUP and the bridge, and once there I left it to Serious to organize our crossing. The big, six-lane dual carriageway passing under the bridge was completely finished, with even the lampposts in place along the central reservation. There was nothing out of place, and not a scrap of rubbish or spoil anywhere. The only thing missing was traffic, making the overall effect rather eerie, a feeling heightened by the strangeness of coming across what might have been an ordinary British motorway deep in enemy territory and thousands of miles from home. The bridge itself, probably constructed by British engineers, was a typical motorway overpass built on giant concrete pillars. There the similarity with roads at home ended, however, for the roadway over the bridge was paved for only a hundred metres or so on either side, and then petered out into desert.

'I wonder if they'll put in a road here that actually goes somewhere, or will it just remain a convenience for the shepherds to get their sheep and goats across the motorway?' I said to Mugger.

'More money than sense, if you ask me,' he answered, after a moment's thought. 'They could have run a prefab concrete tunnel underneath for a fraction of the price. But perhaps they were thinking of us when they built it.' I saw his teeth flash in a grin. He was obviously thinking of my remark to Serious, since he'd been hovering near by when I'd briefed the latter.

It was odd, too, that Allied pilots hadn't spotted the bridge and attacked it. The road must be very close to being finished, and with Jordan now firmly committed on Saddam's side, it could be brought into play at any moment as a much more efficient way of bringing supplies into Iraq – now suffering severely from embargoes imposed after the invasion of Kuwait – than the old supply route. A couple of well-aimed bombs on the bridge would well and truly block the motorway beneath. I made a note to pass this on to Intel – after we had got out of the Iron Triangle, of course. No sense in knocking out such a convenient escape route until we were well clear of the area.

When we reached the short paved run-up to the bridge, Serious, in the lead wagon, signalled us to halt. Then he sent two motorcyclists and four men on foot across the bridge to make certain it was still secure and that we had free exit at the other end. When they confirmed that all was well, he waved us on to go ahead in convoy. It was a real pleasure not to have the usual rattles and bone-jarring bumps of standard desert travel, even for a few hundred metres, but it was a luxury that lasted only a couple of minutes. Then the metalled road petered out and we were back to our normal clattering progress.

Once across, I told Mugger to pull up alongside the lead 110 and called across to Serious, 'Well done. Now take us in about five clicks and we'll lie up until daylight. Clearing this wadi system's going to be no job for vampires. It's one for the sunshine boys.'

It had been apparent to me since we'd first been tasked with the mission, and after studying the air chart of the area, that the only way to clear the system of mobile, or even fixed, Scud launchers was by patrolling it in daylight. The vastness of the wadis – some of which, though shallow, were immensely wide, and most of which meandered through low hill country and then, further west, ran into an open plain or plateau – meant that we could never cover enough ground by night, and might easily overlook some vital site in such broken country.

In order to cover the area I'd designated for each recce I adopted a leap-frog technique. From each starting point four Land Rovers would advance along one side of the wadi for a kilometre, and then halt. The other four, with the Unimog, would then advance two kilometres on the other side before halting, when it would be the turn of the first group to go forward another two kilometres, and so on. In the narrower wadis we advanced as usual in single file. It was tedious, repetitive work, but it had to be done. Nor was I much worried about being discovered by the enemy. We had no indication from Intel of substantial bodies of Iraqi troops in the area, and we would have warning of any approaching by the dust kicked up by their vehicles. I was also confident that, if we did meet with a body of the enemy which we could not drive off, then we would be able to escape relatively easily in the broken terrain, if necessary scattering to meet up again later at one of the prearranged RVs we selected each morning.

That afternoon we were plodding along an old riverbed, almost too shallow to be recognized as one, heading on to the plain to the north-west with the sun high over a distant mountain range ahead of us, when the leading vehicle – Pat's – stopped. Through the binoculars I had already spotted a place some fifteen or twenty kilometres ahead, which had masts or aerials sprouting from it and which might turn out to be a missile site. I jumped out, glad in some ways to be able to stretch my legs, and walked forward to Pat's wagon.

'What's the problem?' I asked.

'Enemy location,' came the reply.

'Where?'

Pat pointed towards the distant site. 'Over there.'

'You mean that thing in the distance? I saw that ages ago. Just keep going. That isn't a problem.'

This seemed to be too much for his driver, Yorky, who suddenly started babbling, 'You're going to get us all killed! That's the *enemy* over there. You're going to get us killed!' I was already irritated enough by the sudden, purposeless halt. Seeing him gibbering away like that snapped my temper.

'Shut it, you,' I ordered, and then motioned everybody out of their vehicles. As the crews of the lead Land Rovers started to comply, I sent back word with the duty motorcyclist for everyone to come forward.

I waited until all of them had gathered around me in a loose semi-circle. Then, fixing them with a glare as the last of them shuffled into place, I pitched in: 'I am sick to death of people questioning my decisions. Especially you' – and I pointed at Yorky. 'We are here to do a job, and we are at war. The task is to clear this wadi system. We are not going to do it slowly because that would take weeks. But we are going to do it, and it will be done my way.' I paused, before adding, 'Are there any questions?'

I looked around at the strange collection of curiously dressed scarecrows with their beards and shemaghs and rifles. Not one of them made a murmur.

'All right. Get in your vehicles and let's get the job done.'

Perhaps it was wrong of me to bawl out the entire patrol for the behaviour of one individual, especially as the men had proved themselves, in action and out of it, to be as tough, enduring, self-reliant and brave as the SAS demanded. Nevertheless, Alpha One Zero had made a very bad start to its time in Iraq, and I was determined, as much for the men's sake as for mine or the Regiment's, to wipe out the memory of that hesitant beginning. I meant us to become – and to be seen as – the best fighting patrol the SAS had.

This was only the second time I had had close dealings with Yorky, and it was the last. He had proved himself an extremely reluctant participant in the recce before Victor Two, when I had to send him back while the rest of us carried on. After the incident in the Iron Triangle I had no further truck with the man. Even such short acquaintance left a very bad taste in the mouth, however – though not as bad as the taste left by the fictions in his book.

Clearing the Iron Triangle took us less than three days, and we were therefore ordered further south to clear a similar wadi system near 'Ar Rutbah, an Iraqi town on the MSR that ran past Victor Two eastwards to Baghdad, and which lay just south of the new motorway. To reach our new area of operations we would head east of the LUP we had used for the last three nights, then swing south to cross the motorway at the same bridge before travelling on to establish a new LUP. From there we would be able to recce the wadi system to the west of us, as far as 'Ar Rutbah to the north-west.

I again put Serious in charge of crossing the motorway, reminding him that if we had been seen going in, the bridge would be the ideal place at which to set an ambush as we made our way out of the Triangle. His recce seemed to take for ever, but when we eventually recrossed the bridge I was certain there wasn't so much as a single desert rat within five kilometres that Serious hadn't taken note of.

Once we had safely crossed the motorway I notified Intel about the possible missile site we had spotted at the far end of the Iron Triangle, leaving it to Coalition HQ as to whether the Allied air forces should pay the place a visit. I also threw in my opinion that the bridge we had just crossed was another worthy candidate for the attention of our strike aircraft. My suggestions were, I was told, duly noted.

It was now two full weeks since our attack on the microwave station and I found myself almost wishing for some action. So did most of the men. It was hard to believe that scooting about hundreds of kilometres behind enemy lines could be quite so bloody yawn-making. The boredom was increased by the fact that our new area of operation was almost completely flat, with barely discernible wadis and few other features, natural or man-made. Patrolling for hour after hour in the vehicles, maintaining a constant lookout for enemy locations or movements, took its toll on all of us, and the absence of any excitement simply made the task duller. After our first day, however, we came across a man-made berm, and I therefore decided to test a pet theory I had been carrying around in my head for weeks. Halting the column, I asked the guys to break out their spades, indicated the sandbank rising above us, and set them to work. They probably thought I was mad, choosing to cut through the berm – which was about four metres high – at that point, when we could so easily have followed it to its end and returned back along the other side, to take up the next leg of our clearance pattern. None the less, it made a change from checking wadis out, and they set to with a will.

It took only thirty minutes to dig a gap wide enough and low enough to get the vehicles through. My theory was proved: this was the same patrol that had spent five days trying – and failing – to get over a similar berm.

Over the radio that night, 23 February, I received new orders for the patrol. We were to head south for the Saudi Arabian border and return to Al Jouf for what the army calls 'rest and recuperation'. When I passed on the news it brought smiles to the faces of everyone, not so much because we were going back to a safe zone, but because the journey would relieve the boredom of the past week. Had we been involved in a full-blown firefight with the enemy during that week, then I think we would all have been a good deal more reluctant to pull out.

From reports on the BBC World Service we knew that the Coalition's main land offensive had been launched against the Iraqi forces in Kuwait that day. Then, later that night, more up-to-date bulletins seemed to indicate that the war might be over much sooner than had been forecast by Allied HQ or the media. Indeed, some commentators were talking about the war ending in hours or, at worst, no more than days. It was difficult for us, sitting around a radio set at our LUP a hundred miles inside Iraq, to accept that the war could possibly be over before we reached Saudi Arabia.

Our spirits were high, however, and I dug out my rum bottle – still more than half full – and invited the sergeants to join me at my Land Rover to celebrate the war's imminent end. Harry, my radio operator, tried to sneak into the circle and grab a turn at the bottle, but I told him to fuck off. This was a Sergeants' Mess do – closed to outsiders.

The following morning, as we were about to pull out for the border, I took my crew's Union jack, which had been spread out as usual on the ground near my wagon, and tied it to the radio aerial behind the driver. The crews of the other vehicles followed suit, and as we neared the border we must have appeared, to anyone who saw us, like some ancient band of crusaders emerging from the desert with colours flying. There the resemblance would have ended, however, because in all other respects we looked like the most evil band of cutthroats from the filthiest souk in Arabia. Almost all of us were sporting ragged beards and wearing a strange mixture of military and bedouin gear, with shemaghs loosely wrapped around our faces. We were mainly filthy, and every one of us stank to high heaven. Nor can our piratical appearance have been helped by the fact that we were extremely heavily armed.

All of which explained why the Regiment had sent a special reception committee from Al Jouf, under the command of Major Bill, to see that we got back into Saudi Arabia safely. The last thing any of us needed now was a blue-on-blue incident between zealous border guards and our well-tested patrol. (It would turn out later that our caution was justified, for a very high proportion of the casualties among Coalition forces during the Gulf War were due not to enemy action, but – to use a really contradictory euphemism beloved of the media – to 'friendly fire'.) We came out at the old fort where Alpha One Zero had made its original, if delayed, crossing, and were treated to some pretty strange looks from the garrison of local troops. Had our guys from Al Jouf not been there to vouch for us, the Saudis might well have opened fire, believing us to be enemy brigands. With good reason, too, for in no way did we look like representatives of the elite of the British Army.

If there was something faintly unreal about our arrival back in Allied territory, reality struck within minutes of our crossing the border, and in the most mundane of ways. After thousands of kilometres of crunching our way over some of the most inhospitable terrain in the Middle East without a single puncture, the Unimog picked one up as it turned on to our first tarmac road in Saudi Arabia. So it was that we, the heroes of Desert Storm – well, in our eyes, at least – were reduced to changing a wheel at the roadside.

I took that opportunity to say my goodbyes. Having rounded the guys up for a last chat, I thanked them all and told them how well I thought they had performed. 'I want you to head back to Al Jouf under your own steam,' I concluded.

'Where are you going, then?' chirped up one soul.

'I'm off to 'Ar Ar,' I said, and with that I headed for Major Bill's vehicle.

Bill and I pulled out without further ado, heading for 'Ar Ar, with a hot bath and a cold beer high on my list of priorities. But when I arrived at the headquarters building on the airbase, which was jointly run by US and British forces, it was time for afternoon tea, an apparently immovable ritual in the life of the place. My beer was going to have to wait, and so was the bath.

I was unshaven, smelly and more than a little dishevelled when I walked into headquarters. Luckily I managed to find some guys I knew from the base's ops and planning office, and had just settled down with a decent brew and a cigarette when an American officer loomed over me. Looking down a nose straighter and longer than my cigarette, he told me, 'There's no smoking in here.'

'Why not?'

'Because it's a fire hazard.'

I had to laugh. 'You want to get out there,' I said, nodding towards the desert outside. 'Now that's what you call a fire hazard.' His face took on the tight-arsed look assumed by officers the world over when they think their dignity or authority is under threat. Since he plainly hadn't the remotest idea what I was talking about, however, I simply walked away. I wouldn't put my cigarette out, though.

Outside, I was buttonholed by a member of Delta Force, the US Special Forces equivalent of the SAS and effectively our sister group in America. Word of my arrival back from a fighting patrol in Iraq must have got around, for he asked me if I would mind giving his boys a briefing, as they were due to go into enemy territory the following night. They were heading for an area south of 'Ar Rutbah, tasked with taking over where we had left off the previous day. I went along to their tent and he called his guys around and I began answering questions. They wanted to know about enemy activity and locations, time and distance in relation to travel, navigation, concealment, resupply – in fact, the whole shooting match. When the questions eventually dried up I told them, 'The best way to do it is to go over in the morning and travel through the day.'

There was a shocked silence, during which they looked at me as though I were a Martian. What I had said went against everything they had been taught and had practised. 'You can make great speed,' I continued, determined to get the point over to them. 'You can bomb up the plain just like on a motorway doing about fifty, and you only need to slow down when you're approaching the target area.'

Soon after that they thanked me very much and ushered me out of their tent. I'm sure they put me down as just another crazy Brit who'd spent too much time in the sun, although they were too polite to say so. I found out later that they had ignored my advice and gone over the following night, as planned. They never saw any action because, as everyone now knows, the war was over by the next day.

I drove back to Al Jouf on the following day. My first action was to seek out the CO and ask for a private word with him. Once in his office, he was full of praise for our patrol's success, but I cut him off.

'I want to talk to you about Ken's RTU,' I said.

'What RTU?'

'I'm told it's because of a drinking-and-driving offence,' I explained. 'He's a great lad and he performed brilliantly behind enemy lines. Nobody could have been more positive or enthusiastic. He's a damned good soldier and, irresponsible driving aside, a role model for anyone else joining the Regiment. I don't think we can afford to lose him. He'll be an asset to the Paras if he goes back, but it will be our loss.'

The CO checked with Hereford and found that Des had been right. Ken was due to be returned to his original unit as soon as we got back from Saudi Arabia. Determined not to lose a good man, the CO spoke personally to Ken, and ended by telling him, 'You can write a letter to your wife now, telling her to start unpacking. You're not going anywhere.'

After that, things got back to normal very quickly.

There was a final, sombre accounting to be made, however. When the war ended we learned that three members of Bravo Two Zero were dead, Sergeant Philips and Corporal Lane from exposure and Trooper Consiglio from enemy fire, and of the remaining five members of the patrol all but one had been captured. In addition, a fourth member of the Regiment, Trooper Denbury, had been killed with Alpha Three Zero just six days before the war had ended, shot dead during a series of running firefight skirmishes with the enemy well inside Iraq.

Yet despite our sadness over losing four of our comrades, there was universal jubilation when it was announced that, almost unbelievably, Sergeant-Major Barry was alive. It turned out that he had been found, barely alive, by the enemy at the place where Kevin and Jack had left him, and had been transferred to a hospital in Baghdad. There, by some miracle, he was operated on by one of Iraq's top orthopaedic surgeons, who had done most of his training in Manchester and who spoke perfect English. The surgeon had told Barry that he was glad to be able to repay, in some small way, all the good things that had happened to him while he was in England. We learned that Barry would make a perfect recovery, and that he was to be flown out of Iraq by the Red Cross within days.

By the time I had typed up my report and produced a proper map of Alpha One Zero's desert wanderings, it was time to decamp back to Victor, in the by now far sunnier and warmer Emirates. From there we began to trickle back on the C-130s to Lyneham, and thence to Hereford. I arrived back at Stirling Lines on Gold Cup day, and the first thing I did was go to the bank and draw some money, which I put on a horse.

It lost. I knew I was home.

Chapter Twenty-Three

W E came home from the Gulf in late February and early March 1991, and at once began to pick up the threads of normal regimental life – or normal for the SAS, anyway. There was a good deal of media speculation at the time about the Regiment's role during the war against Iraq, most of it wildly off-target. The truth about what we had actually done would not begin to filter out until after the publication of General de la Billière's *Storm Command* in 1992 and, particularly *Bravo Two Zero*, 'Andy McNab's' own account of his doomed patrol, which came out in 1993 and completely rejuvenated both press and public interest in the SAS. It is an interest that amounts at times almost to mania.

I went back to being RSM, rather than the commander of half a Sabre Squadron, and everyone took up the threads of their lives and careers pretty much where they'd left off the previous December. The only truly out-of-the-ordinary events were the debriefings of all those SAS members who had been on patrol or in action during the Gulf War, which were held in front of the whole Regiment and recorded on video.

The principle – that everyone would benefit from hearing of the experiences of those who had been at the sharp end, and from discussions of mistakes as well as triumphs – was a sound one, and much was learned from those sessions that has subsequently served the Regiment well in other conflicts. The one jarring note, though, is that what was said then often differs wildly from what has been offered to the public in some of the 'SAS-in-the-Gulf' books published subsequently. I will come to this later, but will add the comment that readers should take some of the stories peddled to them in these books not with a pinch of salt, but with a shovelful.

Since 1991 also marked the fiftieth anniversary of the founding of the Regiment by David Stirling in the Western Desert during the Second World War, we also had to work on the arrangements for the various celebrations planned to mark the event. Apart from a formal dinner in the Guildhall in London at which the Prince of Wales spoke, it was also decided to hold a dinner in the Officers' Mess at Stirling Lines. The aim was to raise funds for the Regimental Association, and selected guests were invited to buy a ticket or tickets, priced at £250 each. There were ten people to a table, and each was presided over by a member of the SAS who, besides acting as host, was there to talk about the Regiment and its history. Perhaps unsurprisingly, the guest speaker was Margaret Thatcher, deposed at the end of 1990 as Prime Minister and leader of the Conservative Party, but still one of the most ardent advocates and supporters of the SAS.

After the dinner Mrs Thatcher stayed the night at the commanding officer's house as the guest of the CO and his wife, returning to the camp the following morning. Shortly after her arrival, two Puma helicopters touched down on the parade ground. One of the aircraft had brought General Norman Schwarzkopf, and in the other were General (as he now was) Sir Peter and Lady de la Billière. After the usual greetings, they were taken to a comfortably furnished anteroom on the first floor of the Officers' Mess, where Mrs Thatcher was waiting for them. They met for about an hour, and then the Iron Lady left for London, sweeping out of Stirling Lines with her usual efficient bustle. With the formalities – and politics – out of the way, DLB, being on his home ground, took General Schwarzkopf for a live demonstration at the building we call the 'Killing House'.

For a supposedly clandestine organization, an awful lot is known about the SAS, and the Killing House – or 'Close-Quarter Battle House', to give it its proper title – is nowadays probably the Regiment's least well-kept secret. Set in an area of Stirling Lines well away from prying eyes, the building was specially constructed in the 1970s to enable the SAS to practise anti-terrorist techniques, and particularly where we might be called on to deal with incidents involving skyjacking, kidnapping, hostage-release or assassination. It is a labyrinth of small rooms, passages, doorways and obstacles, the walls covered with thick rubber to prevent ricochets. The place is also equipped with life-sized targets – some of which can be made suddenly to appear or move by the instructors using remote control – representing not only terrorists or other enemies, but also innocent hostages or bystanders. Only live ammunition is used, in order to make the simulated situations as realistic as possible. The main room, in which people playing the part of hostages are placed, is equipped with a kitchen table and some hard chairs, as well as 'terrorist' or 'hostage' targets, and these too can be made to change position by the instructors. The whole place reeks of cordite, adding to its rather sinister atmosphere. Nevertheless, it is a very effective training area, and there are many people alive today – some of whom we never talk about – who owe their lives to skills that were developed and honed in the Killing House at Hereford.

It should really have some of those Royal Warrant coats of arms over the door, since it must certainly qualify for a 'By Appointment to . . .' tag, given all the royalty who have been there for demonstrations of our effectiveness. Mind you, if they had had any doubts when they went in, I'm certain that they didn't when they came out. It would be a very strange kind of person indeed who failed to be impressed by seeing the Regiment in action in the Killing House.

After the demonstration, 'Stormin' Norman' was brought back, with DLB, to the Officers' Mess for a buffet lunch with officers and selected NCOs from the Regiment who had taken part in the Gulf campaign. He talked to men at random, before presenting a ceremonial Bowie knife to the head of Britain's Special Forces. With his usual mixture of charm and candour he kept his speech low key, simply saying, 'One of our finest soldiers was Jim Bowie. It is fitting that you should have the knife he invented.' The assembled members of the Regiment understood, and appreciated, the message.

With the presentation out of the way, General Schwarzkopf came over to chat with me, and in particular to ask about the Sergeants' Mess meeting we had held behind enemy lines in the desert, and for which he had signed the minutes. We had got someone to take an official photograph of the meeting, and after our return to Hereford I commissioned David Rowlands, a well-known military artist, on behalf of the Sergeants' Mess, to paint a picture from the photograph. I had then got a printing firm to produce a limited edition of 150 high-quality prints from the finished painting, each of which was numbered. Now, in the Officers' Mess, I asked General Schwarzkopf if he would sign the prints, which would then be sold to members of the Regiment or used for presentation purposes. He was sympathetic, but explained that until he retired from the United States Army on 28 August he was forbidden, under American military law, to sign or endorse any product. He added, however, that if I were to get the prints to him after he had officially retired, then he would be willing to sign them.

The plan was that each of the limited-edition prints would have five signatures: the artist's, General de la Billière's, General Schwarzkopf's, the CO's, and mine. August came and DLB and the CO signed the prints, David Rowlands signed them, and I signed them. Then I took all 150 of them to Tampa, Florida, where General Schwarzkopf was based. He proved as good as his word, signing every one of the prints even though there were many other calls on his time. We sold them for £45 each, which made the whole venture self-funding, for the money we raised paid for the painting, the prints and for my flights to and from the United States. Thereafter, the original hung proudly on the wall of the Sergeants' Mess at Stirling Lines in Hereford.

That year brought other extraordinary events, and other VIPs to Hereford, among them the Queen Mother, who paid a formal visit to the Regiment that summer. As the RSM, I was placed next to her at lunch. It will come as no surprise to anyone that I found her charming, interested, and delightfully easy to talk to, and with the additional gift of making everyone feel perfectly at ease in her presence.

In the following year, by a happy combination of circumstances, a different kind of celebrity came to Hereford. Like many boys in this country, I had grown up hoping to play for Manchester United. I never did, of course; equally, though, I never imagined that one day I would host the team's visit to Stirling Lines. As a fan of Manchester United, when the telephone in my office in Hereford rang one morning in 1992, I immediately recognized the Scots burr of United's brilliant and now legendary manager, Alex Ferguson. To me who, as a small boy, had stood on the terraces at Old Trafford with my pockets jingling with change filched from my father, it was like talking to God. I almost stood to attention.

One of our guys, known as 'The Cat' because of his lack of goal-keeping agility, had run the regimental football team and after leaving the army worked at Old Trafford. Some days before I received Alex Ferguson's call, The Cat had told me that he'd spoken with the Manchester United manager, and wondered whether some of the United players could visit the camp at Hereford. I had a word with the CO and he agreed.

When Alex Ferguson telephoned, I said I'd work out an itinerary for the visit, post it to him and see if he liked it. Clearly he did, for a date was agreed. One Monday, therefore, the players and their manager arrived, and I met them outside Regimental Headquarters. It would take a whole chapter to describe everything that happened that day, but one incident will remain with me for ever. After I had briefed the players on the Regiment's history and they had asked all the questions they wanted, wc had a pie-and-chips lunch in the cookhouse. Then the real fun began.

I took them all to the Killing House for a demonstration of some of our specialities. As has been said, a part of our training routine in that building involves rescuing hostages being held by terrorists. So, to make the demonstration more realistic, we sat Alex Ferguson and two of his best-known and most valuable young players at the wooden table in the main room, then told them that they were the hostages and that they were not to move whatever happened. The rest of us stood in a corner of the room behind waist-high white plastic tape to watch the demonstration.

Moments later, our guys burst in yelling, 'Get your heads on the table!' Down went their three heads. Live rounds flew all around Alex Ferguson and his multimillion-pound football stars as the SAS team took out the life-size wooden target 'terrorists' standing behind and flanking the 'hostages'. Although they were in skilled hands, and the firing was over in less than a minute, it must have been a terrifying experience for the United guys.

We left them with their heads down on the table for several minutes. They'd been told not to move, and they didn't. The rest of the players were laughing because they realized that the shooting had finished and that our guys had disappeared. But still the three sat with their heads down on that six-foot table because nobody had yet told them to sit up. With the possibility of live ammunition being fired, they were not about to take any chances. Eventually we put them out of their misery and brought them out, and the day progressed from there, including live firing on the range, aerobatics in one of the Regiment's Agusta 109 helicopters, a drinking session in a local pub that soon had every boy in the neighbourhood turning up as word of United's presence spread like wildfire, and a buffet dinner in the Sergeants' Mess that ended, for some of us, at four o'clock the following morning. As they are still playing today I won't mention the names of the players who stayed up, because Sir Alex (as he now is) would probably fine them . . .

I still treasure the letter of thanks he sent me some days after the visit. When the team left in their coach after breakfast the following morning – their manager had had to leave before dinner the previous night, though he had left a tidy sum behind to buy drinks for all – they all said what a terrific time they had had. It really had been a good day, for us as well as for the United players. As for me, born and bred a Salfordian and a Manchester United fan, to have had Alex Ferguson ring me personally was one of the highlights of my army career.

About the rest of that career there is not a great deal left to tell. In 1992 I was commissioned in the rank of captain, and went to Germany on detachment for six months as second-in-command of a Challenger tank squadron in the Queen's Dragoon Guards. The squadron commander was a great guy called Duncan Bullivant, with the true cavalry officer's apparently devil-may-care attitude, but a shrewd brain and a soldier's gift for handling his squadron. We got on extremely well, and I was sorry when my tour expired. I then spent two years as a quartermaster with 21 SAS, based in London, and finally two years with 23 SAS in Birmingham, as training major. I left the army in November 1997 as a major.

It had been a long haul from an apprentice-joiner's job in the damp north-west.

Afterword

THE Special Air Service has always taken care of its dead, and the Regiment's dead of the Gulf War were no exception. Back at Stirling Lines in Hereford on the first Monday morning after our return from the desert, the commanding officer walked into my office and said: 'Funerals. Friday. At St Martin's, here in Hereford. The arrangements are down to you.'

Four of our men had died in the war with Iraq, while five had been seriously wounded and several captured. The prisoners of war were repatriated through the Red Cross after the fighting had ended, and the Iraqis also handed over the bodies of our dead. Because some time had passed since their deaths, each was returned to the UK in a lead-lined coffin.

The member of Alpha Three Zero who was killed was a guy called David 'Shug' Denbury, who had died in a firefight with the enemy just a few days before the war's end. His family wanted him buried privately in Wales. Since we always respected the wishes of the family in such cases, that left three of our men to be buried by the Regiment. All of them had been members of the ill-fated Bravo Two Zero patrol. Their names were Sergeant Vince Philips, Corporal Steve 'Legs' Lane and Trooper Bob Consiglio.

The CO continued, 'For a number of reasons, I want all three funerals to be held at the same time. It will be quite difficult to carry out, partly because, as I understand it, some of the men's relatives find their deaths hard to accept. Then there is the press coverage to consider. The media will know, from the families, exactly where and when the funerals are to be held, and while we can exclude them from the ceremony, we can't prevent them from hanging around outside the church. I don't have to remind you that we don't need photos of our guys on every front page and on the television news.' He turned to go, then paused and added – almost literally – a parting shot, 'Oh – and I also want a firing party at the graveside.' And with that he walked out.

The SAS had never before had a firing party at a funeral. A part of the reason was that they attracted too much attention; another was that though we bury our dead with honour, we tend to do so quietly. Now, however, there was no need to worry about drawing attention to the fact that several members of the Regiment had died on active service. Thanks to the press coverage, the whole world and his wife knew.

I had never before been ordered to arrange a single military funeral, let alone three at the same time, and I urgently needed information. So after the CO had left I went to the battered metal four-drawer filing cabinet in the corner of my office and pulled out the drawer marked 'A-K'. I felt an enormous sense of relief as I lifted out a cardboard file marked 'Funerals'.

My relief was short-lived. When I opened the file, there was nothing inside. Not so much as a single sheet of paper. There is something peculiar to military bureaucracy that allows people to keep clearly labelled but otherwise empty files around, presumably in order to raise false hopes in unsuspecting warrant officers. One of the great things about the army, however, is that (to use a catch phrase from a famous television advertisement of a few years ago) even if you don't know how to do something, you probably know a man who does.

Clinging to that belief, I rang the Academy Sergeant-Major at Sandhurst, who is the most senior regimental sergeant-major in the British Army. When he answered, I told him who I was and that we were burying three of our guys with full military honours in four days' time, with a firing party. 'To be perfectly honest,' I admitted, 'I don't have a clue. Can you please help?' He was not a man of many words, but he took my phone number and promised to get back to me.

Within thirty minutes I received another phone call, this time from the RSM at the Guards training depot at Pirbright, near Aldershot in Surrey. He gave his name and asked me what the problem was.

'I've got to hold funerals for three of our men who were killed in the Gulf, two to be buried and one to be cremated. The service for all of them is taking place in the same church at the same time. We are also having a firing party – and I don't have the first idea how to set about organizing any of this.'

He considered what I'd told him for no more than a moment, and then said, 'I'll have two guys down to you in Hereford inside three hours.' I thanked him, replaced the receiver, and set about detailing the men necessary to provide pall-bearers and a firing party. Since the funerals were for three men of B Squadron, it was obvious that it was from that squadron that the ceremonial parties would be drawn; besides, the men would have insisted that it should be they who attended their friends' last journey.

That afternoon I was sitting at my desk, studying form in the racing pages of the *Daily Mirror*, when there was a knock on the door. On my shouted 'Come in!' two immaculately turned-out Guards drill sergeants stamped in and came to attention, banging and crashing their boots on the floor.

When they burst in, they almost frightened me to death. I swear that their boots had a shine you could shave in, and you could have used the creases in their perfectly fitting uniforms as razors. They were huge men, and they glowered at everything and everyone from under their slashed-peak caps.

The RSM at Pirbright had been as good as his word, and had sent his best ceremonial drill instructors to make sure that we didn't have any mistakes at the funerals. I asked my visitors their names, then stuck out my hand and told them that I was Billy Ratcliffe, RSM of 22 SAS, and that upstairs, waiting in the briefing room above my office, were the men from B Squadron I'd lined up for pall-bearing and firing-party duties.

'They are under your jurisdiction and command,' I continued, 'until such time as you come to tell me that everything is OK and that rehearsals have gone well.

'I'll take you upstairs now and introduce you, and then I'll leave you. Tomorrow I will arrange for the undertakers to be at St Martin's Church here in Hereford, where the funerals will be held, with a sample coffin of the right weight so that you can practise. Meanwhile the gymnasium is yours to rehearse the firing party and the pull bearers.'

As we ran up the stairs, I told the two giants, 'You can do what you like with these men.' It seemed to me – though I couldn't be certain – that they might have smiled. Guards training instructors can do anything with anyone.

We marched into the briefing room and mounted the small stage at one end of it. At once some smartarse shouted 'Hello, lovely boy!' a camp phrase from the television sitcom *It Ain't Half Hot, Mum*. This time the two drill instructors really did smile, though it was undoubtedly the smile on the face of the tiger. I thought, Just you wait, sunshine. You won't be jeering at these guys for very long.

B Squadron didn't know what had hit them. It took the two Guards NCOs about three days to knock them into shape and get everything organized to their satisfaction – and that was a very exacting standard indeed. They handled their task brilliantly, and by the time they were pronounced ready, B Squadron had nothing but respect for their temporary drill instructors. The men of the SAS are military professionals and, to a considerable extent, perfectionists, and they know – and admire – professionalism and perfectionism in others.

We arrived at St Martin's Church on Friday morning to find the press and television crews camped all around. I could understand their interest, but I didn't want the relatives of the dead men to be upset even further by all this media intrusion. The journalists and cameramen, as well as a good number of interested spectators, were kept away from the church and graveyard by a cordon of policemen from the local force, and it was the police who now came up with a bright idea. An inspector commandeered a huge articulated truck that was driving up the road where St Martin's is situated. He persuaded the driver to position his vehicle in front of the church, effectively blocking the view of the photographers and television crews so that they could not get sight of the coffins leaving the main door after the service and being carried around to the graveyard at the rear.

As the funeral service ended, the ceremonial party, led by the padre, made their slow way out of the church's main door. With solemn dignity – and in perfect step – the immaculately uniformed pall-bearers carried the coffins on their shoulders at the slow march, escorted by the firing party with their M16s. Behind each bearer party followed the family of the dead man, headed by a senior member of the Regiment. I walked immediately behind the third coffin, that of Sergeant Vince Philips. Behind me came his widow and their two young daughters. The children were sobbing. It was heartbreaking to hear them saying brokenly, over and over again, 'I want my Daddy . . . I want my Daddy.'

How do you explain a father's death to his children? How can you help them? I wanted to pick them up and comfort them, but I couldn't. Neither could I let it be seen how enormously moved I was by the sobs of those little girls, and the tears of the families who had lost their men.

At the SAS plot in the graveyard behind the old church of mellowed sandstone, the procession halted beside the open graves. The padre spoke the closing words of the burial service and two of the coffins were lowered into the earth. The firing party discharged its volleys, each one a single, seamless crack of gunfire. And when the final, mournful bugle note of the Last Post had sounded, we buried our dead and said our own private goodbyes to mates some of us had known for years.

Then we went to the 'Palud-R-Inn Club', which was our ironic nickname for the NAAFI at the camp, for what turned into a monumental wake. It would be a considerable understatement to say that a lot of strong drink was taken aboard by the SAS on that Friday afternoon. Time heals grief. But alcohol sometimes helps time go a bit faster. Everyone said that it was what the dead men would have wanted. Perhaps they were right, though I couldn't escape the feeling that what they would most have wanted was to have been there.

As everyone knows, several former SAS soldiers have written pseud-onymous accounts of their service with the Regiment, and in particular books about their exploits during the Gulf War. No member of the Regiment can, or will, tell the whole truth about his service, if only for operational reasons, but some of these Gulf War books are so highly fictional in places that they have almost no value at all. As far as I'm concerned the truth is sensational enough without anyone having to embellish it with fictionalized incidents, or heroics involving desperate firefights with hordes of enemies, or wild exploits with mythical 'fighting knives'. These fantasists may have hidden their real identities from the public by writing under pseudonyms, but the guys in the Regiment know exactly who they are and talk of them either with contempt or ridicule, or both.

Since a number of these accounts affect me directly, I feel that I have some right to comment on a few of the wilder inaccuracies, exaggerations or distortions they contain, some of which amount to actual untruths. Two books, in particular, caught the public imagination, 'Andy McNab's' *Bravo Two Zero*, and 'Chris Ryan's' *The One That Got Away*, published in 1993 and 1995 respectively. The books sold in enormous quantities, and both authors have gone on to make successful new careers for themselves as writers of both non-fiction and novels. I have no quarrel with their success; what I do question, however, is the public perception of the SAS, and of individuals in the Regiment, that has resulted from these and similar books.

'Ryan' was the only surviving member of the eight-man Bravo Two Zero patrol not to be captured by the Iraqis. When he was debriefed in front of the Regiment after the war, we all marvelled at his skill, courage and endurance in surviving seven nights and eight days alone while walking a staggering 186 miles to the Syrian border and, ultimately, safety. In his official debriefing, however, which was recorded on video, 'Ryan' made no mention of encountering any enemy troops during his epic trek to freedom. Yet in his book there are several accounts of contacts, and even a description of an incident when he was forced to kill an Iraqi sentry with a knife. If these incidents happened, then I personally find it difficult to believe that they could have slipped his mind during the debriefing.

In my opinion, his survival story was remarkable enough to warrant a book in its own right. It saddens me, however, that he – or his publishers or other advisers – may have felt it necessary to add material to underline the heroic nature of his escape. It is clear from a comparison of the videoed debriefing with the text of the book that many of the embellishments in the latter are, at best, exaggerations, and the fact that ITV believed it enough to commission and screen a film version is, to my mind, an added insult to the men who died on that mission.

'McNab', the commander of Bravo Two Zero, endured weeks of privation and torture at Iraqi hands and, with his three fellow captives from the patrol, bore up under it as only an SAS soldier could. As has been said, we had learned while still in the Gulf that the surviving members of Bravo Two Zero had either been captured or, in 'Ryan's' case, had walked to safety. When the war ended the four captives were handed over to the Red Cross and eventually returned to Hereford where, like everyone else who had gone into action, they all underwent debriefing. In front of the Regiment, each gave his personal account of what had happened in the desert and, later, in a succession of Iraqi gaols. Having been present at the official debriefings of the five survivors of the patrol, and having several times seen the videos made at the time, I was somewhat taken aback by many of 'McNab's' anecdotes as he recounted them in *Bravo Two Zero*. What I found most surprising was that, in the book, he made no mention at all of the separate meetings he and his men had with the CO and myself, meetings during which we tried our best to persuade him to take a vehicle or, failing that, to cut down on the amount of kit he and the other seven members of the patrol would be carrying. Considering what were, I'm convinced, the results of not following our advice, I find it odd – I will put it no higher than that – that he didn't feel the meetings worth mentioning. After all, the failure of that mission ultimately cost the lives of three men, and led to four others being captured and tortured. That's a casualty rate of nearly 90 per cent. Moreover, the sole member of the patrol to get away was in no shape, after his epic walk, to take any further part in the campaign.

During the debriefings at Stirling Lines, there was mention of the patrol being involved in several firefight skirmishes with Iraqi infantry, and of returning fire as they fought their way out. There was no suggestion at the time, however, that they had accounted for hordes of the enemy. But in *Bravo Two Zero*, 'McNab' writes about having been involved in extremely heavy and dramatic contacts with Iraqi armoured vehicles and substantial contingents of infantry, actions far larger and more colourful than anything mentioned in the Hereford debrief.

He also claims that intelligence sources later established that his patrol had killed or wounded 250 Iraqis in the few days before their capture or death, a figure taken up and repeated as fact in at least one book about the Regiment published subsequently. I find this difficult to believe, however, as the claim runs counter to the largely proven military theory that in most circumstances it takes a battalion of 500 men to take out a company of 100 enemy. Normally, therefore, it would require 1,250 men to take out 250 enemy – yet 'McNab's' 'intelligence sources' claim his patrol accounted for that number with just 8. In fact, Bravo Two Zero's kill rate goes against all the teachings of the Royal College of Defence Studies and other military experts. Coupled with the fact that no mention was made at the official debriefing of this number of Iraqi troops being accounted for, I consider it unlikely that 250 of the enemy were killed and wounded by Bravo Two Zero.

What was much more serious, to my mind, was Bravo Two Zero's disregard of 'McNab's' own written orders, filed with Operations before the patrol's departure for Iraq. These orders are always written, and are presented to the ops officer prior to deployment to outline a commander's intentions during various eventualities in the field. 'McNab' wrote very clearly that in the event of serious compromise, and of his patrol having to resort to an escape attempt, they would head south towards Saudi Arabia.

To their south were friendly forces in the form of the two half D Squadron and two half A Squadron patrols – a total of about a hundred and thirty men and more than thirty vehicles, carrying formidable firepower and equipped with powerful communications. Yet instead of complying with his own written orders, 'McNab' and his men headed towards the north-west and Syria, even though they knew that a major obstacle lay in their path – the River Euphrates. It does not take an Einstein to work out that more people, settlements, industry, farms, roads and military installations will be found along a major river. To head for one in hostile territory is a recipe for disaster.

Had it only been their own lives that they were risking it would not have been so bad. But they were indirectly putting at risk the lives of all those who might be involved in attempts to rescue the missing patrol. Such missions were indeed organized by the CO once it was clear that Bravo Two Zero was in trouble, and involved both our own and American personnel. On two consecutive nights RAF and US helicopters searched for many hours in the desert area where Bravo Two Zero had been dropped and to the south – along their designated escape route. They were not to know that the reason they could find no trace of the patrol was because its members were by then miles away to the north-west.

In the end three of 'McNab's' patrol never made it back, two of its members dying of exposure and one being killed in action. He named all three of them in *Bravo Two Zero*, as did 'Ryan' in *The One That Got Away*, even though, true to its tradition of silence, the Regiment had not released the names other than to the families. I have to say that I find it insensitive, to say the very least, that both men should hide behind aliases to write their stories, but have the poor taste to identify their dead colleagues by their real names while almost everyone else in their narratives has a pseudonym.

Both Serious ('Cameron Spence') and Yorky ('Peter "Yorky" Crossland') also used aliases to write their own far-fetched versions of events on patrol with Alpha One Zero during the Gulf campaign, and both also revealed the real names of the dead SAS men. Since none of them are still serving, what possible good reason could these four men have for concealing their true identities?

Unlike the books by 'McNab' and 'Ryan', Serious 'Spence's' *Sabre Squadron* (1997) and Yorky's *Victor Two* (1996) are both about the Alpha One Zero patrol that I was sent into Iraq to take over. Not unnaturally, I feature in both books, generally in a pretty unflattering light. When I arrived to take command of the patrol I knew, of course, that some of its members were going to resent deeply my way of doing things. But I was equally certain that no one was going to come out and say so. Yet in both books – which are, it must be said, among the more fanciful personal memoirs of service with the SAS in the Gulf War – the authors describe how they would approach me for what seem to have been cosy little chats, often offering advice or telling me where I was going wrong. There are detailed accounts of the arguments they had with me and even mention of almost coming to blows when I failed to act out their wonderful plans. I may as well state here, categorically, that these accounts are as fictional as their authors' aliases – besides, it is a simple fact of military life that no one argues with the RSM. Neither book mentions me by my real name, but by pseudonyms that are, if anything, even more ridiculous than those the authors have given themselves.

Well, I can live with that, but the air of self-justification that hangs over both books also conceals the fact that much of what they contain is – to put it politely – extremely inaccurate. Memory can and does play tricks, of course, and never more so than among men who have been in stressful and often dangerous situations; even so, Yorky and Serious can't *both* have been the first Allied soldiers to have fired a shot in anger in the land war, as both claim in wildly differing accounts of the ambush of the Gaz and the Iraqi officers in it. In addition, the Iraqis were shot before they reached the Land Rovers under their cam nets, although *Sabre Squadron*, in particular, has one of the enemy officers actually peering under the net before being blown away by the author himself.

Various other miraculous things happened on that patrol, or so Serious would have his readers believe. Among much else, he claims to have played a major role himself in the blowing of the fibre-optic cables. He obviously didn't feel that the fact that, at the time, he was more than 50 kilometres away, searching for a landing ground with Pat, should be allowed to interfere with his narrative. I have to say, too, that both Serious and Yorky's accounts of our patrol become even more outrageous as their stories develop, but to go into every incorrect fact, every piece of make-believe or every exercise in wishful thinking would fill an entire chapter.

I will add a footnote, however, to our attack on the Victor Two communications station by mentioning the highly colourful versions presented by Serious and Yorky. The former, alias 'Cameron Spence', writes that we knew *before* the attack that the bunker and fences were bomb damaged; that the situation went noisy *before* the demolition team reached the target; that four charges were laid to bring down the mast (in fact, it was three); and that he was personally involved in firefights against hundreds of Iraqis.

Yorky claims that it was he who started the firefight by firing the first rounds which killed the truck driver, who was actually taken out by Major Peter – as Pat's driver, Yorky was in fact with the fire-support group and nowhere near the trucks (although, in a neat twist, his book describes how annoyed he felt when Peter 'claimed' the first kill; mind you, 'Spence' also has Peter stepping to the rear of the wagon and emptying a whole magazine into the back. This didn't happen, either).

He too claims to have been involved in a hectic firefight with hordes of Iraqis, and writes of watching the mast fall just seconds after the explosions, rather than several hours later. As to his behaviour during the CTR just before our attack on Victor Two, he justifies this by claiming that we were in the midst of large numbers of the enemy, and that he was acting properly while I was behaving like an irresponsible idiot bent on getting everyone killed.

I remain mystified as to why both authors felt they needed to embellish their stories, when the actual events were every bit as dramatic. I also confess to being irritated by the portrayals of me as a kind of dangerous fool, heedless of the advice of (apparently) much better soldiers around me, although I can't say it bothers me too much, and I am content to let readers decide for themselves. What is most saddening, however, is that so many SAS books, all written under pseudonyms, have been published which contain deliberate lies, distortions and fantasies. Saddest of all, perhaps, is the fact that in reality some of these would-be supermen were far from actually being the heroes they proclaim themselves to have been in their *Boy's Own*-style autobiographies.

If there is to be any purpose to history, it has to be written as accurately as people can recall it – otherwise its lessons, good or bad, will be lost. It is for this reason that the Regiment held the debriefings of those of its members who had fought in the Gulf, to get at the truth and thereby learn what had gone right, and what wrong. To obscure that truth by trying to exact revenge for real or imagined slights, or by awarding oneself a greater and more heroic part in events, is not only to mislead – and thus defraud – the readership, it is to debase history itself. And I can see no reason, even for the sake of writing a bestseller, why the proud history of the Special Air Service Regiment should be dragged down to the level of cheap war fiction.

To me, as to so many others who served in it, the SAS remains the finest fighting regiment in the world. To have been accepted into it was the proudest moment of my life, and to have served in it is an honour and a privilege accorded to very, very few. I know that I have been enormously fortunate, as I also know that, whatever the actions of a handful, I shall never lose my respect for the men of the sand-coloured beret.

Glossary

110 custom-built long-wheelbase (100 inch/279cm) 4×4 Land Rover deployed on active service by SAS mobile patrols. Sometimes also known as 'pinkies', short for 'Pink Panthers', a name given to the Regiment's Land Rovers when they were painted in a pink desert camouflage

2IC second-in-command

A-10 designed and built in the USA, the Fairchild A/OA-A10A twin-jet, single-seat close-support aircraft, officially designated the Thunderbolt II, more than proved itself in the ground-attack role during the Gulf campaign, destroying literally hundreds of Iraqi tanks as well as other targets. Formidably armed and armoured, its odd looks have ensured that it is more usually known by the nickname 'Warthog'. USAF A-10s flew numerous missions during the Gulf campaign in support of SAS patrols in Iraq, or acting on information provided by those patrols

AAM *see* **AIM**

adoo Arabic for enemy: Marxist-backed rebels of the People's Front for the Liberation of the Occupied Arabian Gulf (PFLOAG), operating in Oman, principally Dhofar, to overthrow the Sultan and his government. The adoo were mainly based in, and were supplied and supported by, Oman's neighbour, the People's Democratic Republic of Yemen

Aermacchi MB-339 Italian-designed and built single-jet, single-seat light ground-attack aircraft, based on the Aermacchi MB326 twin-seat trainer, and deployed by the Argentinian Air Force and the air arm of the Argentinian Navy during the Falklands campaign

AIM air-intercept missile (or air-to-air missile – AAM)

AK-47 Soviet-designed, magazine-fed 7.62mm automatic assault rifle, produced in many variants; built under licence in other communist states, notably China, the former East Germany, Hungary, Poland, and the former Yugoslavia, it is one of the most numerous shoulder weapons in the world. Also known as the Kalashnikov Model 1947, the 'AK' stands for *Avtomat Kalashnikov* (Russian: Kalashnikov automatic) after its designer, Mikhail Timofeyevich Kalashnikov (1919–)

AP armour-piercing

ASM air-to-surface missile

badged to be accepted into the SAS, the point at which newly joined members, having passed **Selection** (q.v.), receive their sand-coloured berets with the famous 'winged dagger' badge

bait Dhofari house or native hut (Arabic)

basha shelter for sleeping; hence 'to basha' meaning to get some sleep

belt kit soldier's webbing and attachments, holding much of his personal equipment, ammunition, water bottle etc.

bergen soldier's rucksack

berm man-made sandbank or dune, usually from 6 to 16 feet high, often with a ditch on the side facing enemy or unfriendly territory. The berm along the Iraqi/Saudi-Arabian border extended in places for many miles

blue-on-blue an incident in which friendly forces mistakenly fire upon each other; a casualty resulting from such an incident. Also known by the euphemism 'friendly fire'

Boss slang for anyone in command, whether of a patrol, a troop, or a squadron or larger unit

Browning M2 US-designed, Second World War-vintage 0.5-inch heavy machine-gun, mounted on some SAS 110s (q.v.) in the Gulf campaign. An air-cooled, belt-fed weapon with a rate of fire of 450-575 rounds per minute, it is capable of penetrating over 40mm of armour at ranges of more than 800 metres. Also known as the '50-cal', the weapon first saw service with the Regiment in the Western Desert in 1942

Browning High Power 9mm semi-automatic pistol built by the Belgian arms company FN. With a 14-round magazine and considerable stopping power, it has long been the SAS's handgun of choice

burmoil 45-gallon steel drum used to transport fuel; often reused for water

burnous native goatskin coat; also known to the SAS in the Gulf War as a 'bedou' or 'Al Jouf coat'

C-130 Hercules long-serving 4-turboprop transport aircraft of great ruggedness, reliability and adaptability, and capable of short takeoffs and landings from grass, scrub, desert and other surfaces besides tarmac. Designed and built by Lockheed in the USA, and in service with, among many others, one of the RAF's Special Forces squadrons (No. 47 Squadron)

C-5 Galaxy giant American-designed and built transport aircraft of the USAF, built by Lockheed. Powered by four jets, the Galaxy is capable of carrying, among other payloads, six Apache strike helicopters or three light tanks, as well as large numbers of troops, at jet speeds

casevac military abbreviation for casualty evacuation

chaff clouds of metal-foil fragments fired from a discharger by a ship or aircraft, or other potential target, to confuse the radar of an enemy aircraft, ground station, missile etc.

CH-47 *see* **Chinook**

Chinese parliament discussion among a group of soldiers, regardless of rank, to agree a course of action

Chinook giant twin-turboshaft, twin-rotor transport helicopter, widely in service with the USAF and RAF, and used by RAF Special Forces flights; designed and built by Boeing in the USA, its official designation is CH-47; its RAF designation was originally HC1, with the uprated aircraft designated HC2 and dedicated Special Forces aircraft HC3

CINCFLEET Commander-in-Chief, Fleet. During the Falklands War this was Admiral Sir John Fieldhouse, and the term was used to apply either to him or to CINCFLEET HQ at Northwood, on the north-western outskirts of London

click slang for kilometre

cross-deck to move personnel and/or stores from one ship to another by helicopter

CO commanding officer

CSM company sergeant-major

CTR close-target reconnaissance; the final reconnaissance carried out just before an operation or assault is launched

Delta Force US First Special Forces Operations Detachment Delta – formed in the 1970s, Delta Force is the US armed services' equivalent of the SAS, and the two units maintain close contacts

DPM disruptive-pattern material: cloth printed with camouflage shades and patterns and made up into uniforms etc.

DS directing staff; those permanent members of a training establishment or course responsible for the programme and for those attending it

DZ drop zone: the designated area for a parachute landing

EW electronic warfare; early warning

F-15E Strike Eagle fighter-bomber variant of the F-15 Eagle twin-jet, single-seat fighter. Designed and built in the USA by McDonnell Douglas, the F-15E version first flew in 1986, and saw much service in the Gulf campaign. A front-line aircraft of the USAF, it is also in service with the Israeli and Saudi Arabian air forces

F-16 Fighting Falcon fast and versatile single-jet, single-seat multi-role fighter aircraft designed by General Dynamics in the USA in the early 1970s, but now built by Lockheed after its takeover of the former.

Extremely agile in combat, the F-16 has excellent visibility from the cockpit, and is equipped with advanced avionics; like the F-15, it was widely deployed during the Gulf campaign

FAC forward air control or controller: soldier or soldiers equipped with radio to guide supporting aircraft on to their target

FAV fast attack vehicle

firqat Arabic name (literally, 'company') for an irregular unit formed, mainly from **SEP**s (q.v.), to combat the ***adoo*** (q.v.), the Marxist-backed insurrectionists of the **PFLOAG** (q.v.) operating in Oman, and especially Dhofar

flash bang also known as a stun grenade; an SAS invention, on detonation these devices emit a blinding flash of magnesium coupled with a loud report, temporarily stunning and disorienting opponents, but without causing shrapnel or blast damage

forward mounting base a unit's main base during an operation, from which it will move forward to the **FOB** (q.v.); for the SAS in the Gulf War the forward mounting base was at Victor in the **UAE** (q.v.)

FOB forward operating base; for the SAS in the Gulf War, this was at Al Jouf in north-western Saudi Arabia

FOP forward observation point

friendly fire *see* **blue-on-blue**

Gazelle a Franco-German design, the Eurocopter SA341 Gazelle is a single-turboshaft, single-rotor light helicopter used mainly for army/air cooperation, reconnaissance and light support duties

geysh Arabic word meaning 'army', used in Oman of the regular troops of the Sultan of Oman's Armed Forces. A high proportion of the geysh were Baluchis, and effectively mercenaries in the Sultan's employ

glasshouse British Army gaol

GPMG general-purpose machine-gun: the British version of the Belgian-designed and built FN MAG, the 'gimpy' (as it is affectionately nicknamed) is a 7.62mm belt-fed, air-cooled medium machine-gun designated L7 in the British Army, and with a cyclic rate of fire of 750-1,000 rounds per minute; rugged and reliable, it has been in service for many years

GPS global positioning system; a hand-held electronic device that receives information from a number of orbiting satellites, so allowing its operator to pinpoint his position to within a few yards at any time of day and in any conditions. An invaluable navigational aid, the SAS used the Magellan GPS during the Gulf campaign

green maggot sleeping bag

HALO high altitude, low opening: SAS-developed technique for inserting patrols by parachute, involving freefall from above 25,000 feet to about 4,000 feet at night and 3,000 in daylight

Harrier *see* **Sea Harrier**

headshed SAS colloquialism for any person or body in authority; thus a 'headsheds' meeting' for a large mobile patrol might be a meeting of all officers and **SNCO**s (q.v.), while the 'headshed' at Stirling Lines would be the CO and senior **RHQ** (q.v.) officers and NCOs. The word derives from the Malayan campaign of the 1950s, and has its origins in the watersheds so frequently encountered in the Regiment's operations against the communist insurgents there

Hercules *see* **C-130**

hexamine solid fuel in the form of small rectangular blocks, used in soldiers' portable stoves

Huey single-turboshaft, single-rotor general-purpose helicopter designed and built in the US by Bell, and designated UH-1 (originally HU-1 hence its nickname; its actual manufacturer's designation is Iroquois). Widely used in different variants in Vietnam as a transport, casevac helicopter and gunship, the Huey was built in greater numbers and served with more air forces than any military aircraft since the Second World War, and is still in use throughout the world in a number of roles, including anti-submarine and command-post versions. As a transport, it can carry up to 10 troops

Hunter a single-seat, single-jet fast interceptor that first entered RAF service in 1954, the Hawker (now British Aerospace) Hunter saw service with the Sultan of Oman's Air Force, and was also sold to many other countries. The aircraft's all round excellence and multi-role capability are borne out by the fact that it is still in service with a number of countries in Europe, South America and the Far East

I Corps Intelligence Corps; there is an I Corps unit permanently attached to 22 SAS

Intel, intel an Intelligence unit or members of that unit; intelligence in general as transmitted to troops in the field

jebali inhabitant of the jebel area of Dhofar

jebel also *djebel*: Arabic for hill or mountain; specifically, the mountain area of Dhofar in which the *adoo* (q.v.) principally operated

JSIW Joint Services Intelligence Wing

Katyusha Soviet-designed and built unguided short-range rocket, often fired from multiple launchers

Kite sight British-designed and built lightweight weapon-aiming system, capable of being fitted to most combat rifles and light anti-tank weapons; permits the firer to aim even in total darkness.

Klepper collapsible 2-man canoe used by SAS Boat Troops and the **SBS** (q.v.)

LAW light anti-tank weapon

LAW66 shoulder-fired 66mm **LAW** (q.v.), carried by the SAS in the Falklands campaign

LAW80 shoulder-fired 80mm **LAW** (q.v.), carried by the SAS in the Gulf War

locstat to record and save the actual coordinates of a fixed feature, position or target

loop line nylon cord, some 30 feet long, with loops at each end, and carried by SAS patrols; immensely strong, they can be quickly joined to make longer lines, and can even be used to tow vehicles

LPD landing platform, dock

LSL landing ship, logistic

LUP lying-up place

Lynx twin-turboshaft, single-rotor multi-role helicopter built by Westland in the UK, in service with both the British Army and the Royal Navy (which have their own variants, designated AH and HAS respectively), as well as the RAF. Capabilities include search-and-rescue, light support and as a troop transport, in which role it can carry up to 9 troops

M16 the American-designed and built Colt M16 (earlier designations were Colt AR-22 or Armalite) entered service with the US armed services in the late 1950s and, like the **AK-47** (q.v.), is now one of the most widely used assault rifles in the world. A fully automatic weapon of 5.56mm calibre and built largely of aluminium and plastic, it is tough, reliable and light. It was first used by the SAS in the Borneo campaign of 1963-6, and increasingly adopted by the Regiment in the ensuing twenty years; it is now the standard-issue rifle of the SAS, which prefers it to the British-designed and built 5.56mm **SA80** (q.v.) assault rifle with which the rest of the British Army is equipped. SAS soldiers often use M16s fitted with the M203 40mm grenade launcher fitted beneath the barrel

M203 *see* **M16**

M79 single-shot 40mm grenade launcher, used by the SAS on **Operation Storm** (q.v.) in Oman

Mentor antiquated single-piston-engined, twin-seat trainer that entered service with the USAF in 1948, the US-designed and built Beech T34A Mentor saw service in the Vietnam War as a spotter/reconnaissance aircraft. During the Falklands campaign, four Mentors of the Argentinian Air Force were destroyed on the ground at Pebble Island by the SAS

MID Mention in Despatches

Milan wire-guided anti-tank missile system deployed by some SAS mobile patrols during the Gulf campaign. At 35 kilos in weight the system is too heavy to be carried by foot patrols, but mounted on the rollbar of a 110 (q.v.), proved devastatingly effective against both mobile targets and fixed defences; its sighting aid, **MIRA** (q.v.), also proved invaluable. The 6.65kg missile has a range of 2,000 metres and can penetrate armour up to 106cm in thickness. Milan first demonstrated its worth in action during the Falklands campaign of 1982

Minimi Belgian-designed and built 5.56mm air-cooled light machine-gun used by some SAS patrols in the Gulf campaign. With a cyclic rate of fire of 750 1,000 rounds per minute and capable of being fed either by belt or a box magazine, the Minimi can also take the standard **M16** (q.v.) magazine; at 6.8kg it is light enough to be carried by foot patrols

MIRA Milan infrared attachment, a sighting device fitted to the **Milan** (q.v.) missile system. Primarily a night sight, MIRA can be detached from the missile housing and used as a hand-held sighting/detection aid, in which role it proved itself with SAS mobile patrols during the Gulf campaign

Mk19 US-designed and built fully automatic 40-mm grenade launcher, mounted on some SAS 110s (q.v.) in the Gulf campaign. Belt fed and air cooled, the Mk19 (also called M19) has a rate of fire of up to 375 rounds per minute, and an effective range of 1,600 metres; the variety of grenades it can handle includes high-explosive, smoke and armour-piercing

MoD Ministry of Defence

MP5 9mm, magazine-fed submachine-gun designed and built by the German concern Heckler & Koch, and available in a number of variants. The various weapons in the MP5 series have been the SAS's preferred submachine-guns for many years

MSR main supply route: major roads traversing Iraq, principally those from Jordan to Baghdad; some are metalled

MTO motor transport officer

NAAFI Navy, Army and Air Force Institutes; the organization which, for many years, has provided the British armed forces with shops, canteens, and other services

Naps tablets issued during the Gulf War to Coalition troops, to counteract the effect of possible enemy **NBC** (q.v.) measures

NBC nuclear, biological and chemical, as in 'NBC warfare'; generally used of the protective NBC suits and headgear issued to all servicemen during the Gulf campaign, and of NBC precautionary measures, such as injections and tablets

OC officer commanding

O-group orders group; a formal briefing given by a commander before an operation to subordinate commanders, who are tasked with passing the relevant information on to their own subordinates

OP observation post

Operation Storm codename for SAS involvement in Britain's then secret war against Marxist-backed insurgents (see *adoo* [q.v.]) in the Sultanate of Oman, 1970-6

Patriot MIM-104 Patriot, US-built **SAM** (q.v.) specifically designed to destroy incoming enemy **SSM**s (q.v.). During the Gulf War, Patriot was used against Iraqi **Scud** (q.v.) missiles to considerable effect both in Saudi Arabia and in Israel

PE plastic explosive

PFLOAG Popular Front for the Liberation of the Occupied Arabian Gulf; *see adoo*

PNGs passive night-vision goggles

pot soldiers' slang for a steel helmet

prime time SAS nickname for free time which, if there were no operations, training or courses, members of the Regiment were permitted to spend as they wished, provided they remained within reach of **RHQ** (q.v.)

PTI physical training instructor

Pucara an Argentinian-designed and built twin turboprop close-support/counter-insurgency/reconnaissance aircraft, the FMA IA-58 Pucara was deployed by the Argentinian Air Force during the Falklands campaign; the SAS destroyed six Pucaras on the ground at Pebble Island, and shot down another with a **Stinger** (q.v.) missile

Puma twin turboshaft, single-rotor tactical transport helicopter, designed and built as an Anglo-French venture between Westland and Sud-Aviation (later Aerospatiale), and designated HC1 in RAF service, which it entered in 1971. Capabilities include deployment for **casevac** (q.v.), as a troop transport (up to 16 fully equipped troops), as a medium-lift transport, and as a helicopter gunship

PX Post Exchange: US armed forces equivalent of the British **NAAFI** (q.v.)

R&R rest and recuperation

REME Corps of Royal Electrical and Mechanical Engineers

RFA Royal Fleet Auxiliary

RHQ Regimental Headquarters

RQMS regimental quartermaster sergeant

RSM Regimental Sergeant-Major

RTU-ed returned to unit; the fate most dreaded by candidates for or members of the SAS. It usually takes effect immediately, and sees the soldier in question sent back to the regiment or corps from which he has come; however, no official stigma attaches to being RTU-ed

RUC Royal Ulster Constabulary

RV rendezvous

SA80 British-designed and built 5.56mm magazine-fed fully automatic assault rifle: currently the standard-issue rifle of the British Army (but not the SAS, which favours the lighter and more reliable US-built **M16** [q.v.])

SAM surface-to-air missile

SARBE *see* **TACBE**

satcoms satellite communications; satellite-link telephone

satlink *see* **satcoms**

SBS Special Boat Service (formerly Squadron), Royal Marines; in some respects the SAS's sister service although, as its name suggests, geared more towards maritime operations

Scud antiquated Soviet-designed and built intermediate-range **SSM** (q.v.), deployed by Iraq during the Gulf War against targets in Israel and Saudi Arabia. Although inaccurate, Scud can carry conventional, biological, chemical or nuclear warheads, and can be fired from mobile, as well as fixed, launch sites, which are difficult to locate by aerial reconnaissance; furthermore, Iraqi engineers had considerably extended its range and marginally improved its crude guidance system, making it still a weapon to be feared

Sea Harrier shipborne version of the British Aerospace (formerly Hawker) Harrier in service with the RAF, the Fleet Air Arm's Sea Harriers downed 22 Argentinian aircraft during the Falklands campaign for the loss of just 6 of their own (2 of which were lost in accidents, and the remainder to ground fire or **SAMs** [q.v.]). The world's only vertical take-off and landing combat aircraft, the Harrier is also in service with the US Marine Corps, in which form it is built in the USA by McDonnell Douglas as the AV-8

Sea King twin turboshaft, single-rotor naval search-and-rescue and anti-submarine helicopter designed by Sikorsky in the USA as the SH-3, and built by Westland in the UK. Used in a variety of roles, it is now designated the H-3. Operating with the Task Force, Sea Kings provided valuable service during the Falklands campaign, although one aircraft, carrying 3 crew and 27 men, crashed into the sea with the loss of 22 lives, the majority of them SAS

Selection the process undergone by all servicemen seeking to join the SAS. Run by the Regiment's Training Wing at Hereford, it is a mentally and physically gruelling combination of training and endurance tests, divided into phases and run over many weeks. At the end of it, a successful candidate will be **badged** (q.v.), although it will be another two years before he is either accepted or rejected as a full-time member of the Regiment. The two **TA** (q.v.) regiments, 21 and 23 SAS, have their own Selection training programme

SEP surrendered enemy personnel; term used during the campaign in Oman (*see* **Operation Storm** [q.v.]) for *adoo* (q.v.) who gave themselves up to the authorities, many of whom would then join a *firqat* (q.v.)

shaped charge a powerful explosive demolition charge, the 'shaping' directing the blast in such a way as to cause maximum destruction to the object to be breached or destroyed

shemagh Arab headdress cloth; also called a *keffiyeh*

sitrep situation report

Skyvan a twin-piston-engined light transport aircraft designed and built by Short Brothers of Belfast between 1963 and 1986; many are still in service as short-haul cargo or passenger transports. Capable of carrying 19 passengers, the SC7 Skyvan saw service with the Sultan of Oman's Air Force during the campaign in Dhofar, two of these aircraft being damaged irreparably in accidents in 1974; during the Falklands campaign of 1982 a Skyvan of the Argentinian Navy was wrecked in an accident at Port Stanley, and another destroyed on the ground by the SAS at Pebble Island

SLR self-loading rifle; 7.62mm semi-automatic magazine-fed rifle designed by the Belgian FN arms concern. The standard-issue rifle of the British Army, by which it was designated L1A1, until the introduction of the **SA80** (q.v.) in the 1980s, the British version was hampered by the fact that it could fire only single shots, and by its length and weight; the almost identical FNs used by the Argentinians in the Falklands were fully automatic

SNCO/JNCO senior/junior non-commissioned officer

SOE Special Operations Executive; British clandestine organization formed during the Second World War to insert agents into German-occupied Europe and maintain them in place

SOPs standing operational procedures; instructions issued as guidelines in the British Army, for instance by directing staff (*see* **DS**) or regimental headquarters (**RHQ**), and designed to cover widely differing circumstances a soldier or soldiers might encounter

souk Arab market

Spargan Soviet-designed and built 12.7mm belt-fed, air-cooled heavy machine-gun, usually tripod mounted

SP team Special Projects team: the Regiment's counter-terrorist team, formed by each of the four squadrons in rotation, serving in the role for six months at a time, and based in the UK

spy glass a compact, hand-held night-vision device that operates by thermal imagery

SSM surface-to-surface missile; squadron sergeant-major

Stinger US-designed and built, shoulder-launched SAM; utilizing a passive infrared homing system and equipped with an IFF (identification friend or foe) device, Stinger is a 'fire-and-forget' weapon, meaning that once the missile has locked on to a target the operator does not have to guide it. Introduced in the US in 1981, it was used with success by the SAS in the Falklands (*see* **Pucara**), and was carried by SAS patrols in the Gulf War

stun grenade *see* **flash bang**

Swift scope a telescopic single-lens monocular – a powerful optical instrument used for observation at long ranges

TA Territorial Army. The SAS has two TA regiments, 21 and 23 SAS

tab SAS and Para slang for march, equivalent to the Royal Marine Commandos' 'yomp'

TACBE tactical beacon; a light and compact surface-to-air rescue beacon, weighing only some 250 grams, which is used to make direct contact with aircraft flying overhead if other means of communication have failed. Its principal disadvantage is that its signals are easily detected by enemy direction-finding equipment. Also known as SARBE (search and rescue beacon)

time pencil chemical timing device used to detonate explosive charges

Trimpack electronic satellite-navigation device, used by SAS patrols in the Gulf campaign

UAE United Arab Emirates: an independent group of seven emirates on the Persian Gulf, including Abu Dhabi and Dubai

Unimog Mercedes-Benz 4x4 light truck, used as a support vehicle by SAS mobile patrols

VC10 airliner originally designed by Vickers in the mid-1950s for BOAC

(British Overseas Airways Corporation – later, with other companies, British Airways). Although a fast and comfortable aircraft, it did not succeed commercially, but remains in service with the RAF as a fast transport and as a tanker for in-flight refuelling.

wadi Arabic for valley or dried-up watercourse

Wasp single-turboshaft, single-rotor five-seat general-purpose shipborne helicopter. Designed and built in Britain by Westland, the Wasp was deployed on board Royal Navy warships during the Falklands campaign; a missile from HMS *Endurance*'s Wasp severely damaged the Argentinian submarine *Santa Fe* off South Georgia. Navy Wasps were given the designation HAS1

Wessex twin-turbine, single-rotor light-support helicopter, designed and built in Britain by Westland and designated HC2 in RAF service, which it entered well over 30 years ago. The Wessex proved invaluable during the Falklands campaign, and the aircraft also saw service with US forces during the Vietnam War, as well as with other British services and with other armed forces around the world. Capabilities include deployment as a troop transport (up to 16 fully equipped troops), as a search-and-rescue helicopter, and as a trainer; Wessex were also used for VIP/royal transport duties with the RAF's Queen's Flight. There are still two RAF squadrons operating the aircraft

whiteout extreme blizzard conditions

wilco SAS term for someone who is positive, willing, cooperative